Diversities of Innovation

Innovation is often understood exclusively in terms of the economy, but it is definitely a result of human labour and ingenuity, and of the relationships among individuals and social groups. Some societies and governmental structures are clearly more successful than others: they act in divergent ways, fostering innovation and employment, and they utilize varied opportunities from different fields of research, from new products and from their educational systems.

Thus, innovation varies fundamentally between countries, and public policies – in matters such as energy technology, environmental technologies, facing climate change, and advancing conditions of life – can be determined according to different societies' needs.

This volume brings together a range of world experts to compare countries and continents and help develop a fuller picture of innovations and their social basis. It will be of interest to researchers in regional studies and economics, as well as labour unions, practitioners, and policy makers.

Ulrich Hilpert is Professor and Chair of Comparative Government in the Faculty of Social and Behavioural Sciences at Friedrich Schiller University, Jena, Germany.

Regions and Cities

Series Editor-in-Chief
Joan Fitzgerald, *Northeastern University, USA*

Editors
Ron Martin, *University of Cambridge, UK*
Maryann Feldman, *University of North Carolina, USA*
Gernot Grabher, *HafenCity University Hamburg, Germany*
Kieran P. Donaghy, *Cornell University, USA*

In today's globalised, knowledge-driven, and networked world, regions and cities have assumed heightened significance as the interconnected nodes of economic, social and cultural production, and as sites of new modes of economic and territorial governance and policy experimentation. This book series brings together incisive and critically engaged international and interdisciplinary research on this resurgence of regions and cities, and should be of interest to geographers, economists, sociologists, political scientists, and cultural scholars, as well as to policy makers involved in regional and urban development.

For more information on the Regional Studies Association visit www.regionalstudies.org

There is a **30% discount** available to RSA members on books in the **Regions and Cities** series, and other subjects related to Taylor and Francis books and e-books including Routledge titles. To order just e-mail Emilia Falcone, Emilia.Falcone@tandf.co.uk, or phone on +44 (0)20 3377 3369 and declare your RSA membership. You can also visit the series page at www.routledge.com/Regions-and-Cities/book-series/RSA and use the discount code: **RSA0901**

133. The Entrepreneurial Discovery Process and Regional Development
New Knowledge Emergence, Conversion and Exploitation
Edited by Åge Mariussen, Seija Virkkala, Håkon Finne and Tone Merethe Aasen

134. Strategic Approaches to Regional Development
Smart Experimentation in Less-Favoured Regions
Edited by Iryna Kristensen, Alexandre Dubois and Jukka Teräs

135. Diversities of Innovation
Edited by Ulrich Hilpert

136. The Theory, Practice and Potential of Regional Development
The Case of Canada
Edited by Kelly Vodden, David J.A. Douglas, Sean Markey, Sarah Minnes and Bill Reimer

For more information about this series, please visit:
www.routledge.com/Regions-and-Cities/book-series/RSA

Diversities of Innovation

Edited by Ulrich Hilpert

Routledge
Taylor & Francis Group

LONDON AND NEW YORK

First published 2019
by Routledge
2 Park Square, Milton Park, Abingdon, Oxon OX14 4RN

and by Routledge
605 Third Avenue, New York, NY 10017

First issued in paperback 2020

Routledge is an imprint of the Taylor & Francis Group, an informa business

British Library Cataloguing-in-Publication Data
A catalogue record for this book is available from the British Library

Library of Congress Cataloging-in-Publication Data
A catalog record has been requested for this book

ISBN 13: 978-0-367-73106-9 (pbk)
ISBN 13: 978-1-138-18907-2 (hbk)

Typeset in Bembo
by Integra Software Services Pvt. Ltd.

Contents

Figures

Tables

Contributors

Mariza Almeida has a PhD in Industrial Engineering. She is currently Adjunct Professor of the Industrial Engineering Course at the Federal University of the State of Rio de Janeiro, Rio de Janeiro, Brazil, working on the following research topics: triple helix of university-industry-government; incubators and science parks, innovation, and entrepreneurship.

Sharmistha Bagchi-Sen is Professor in the Department of Geography at the State University of New York (SUNY) at Buffalo. Her research interests are in innovation and industry studies. Her recent book (co-authored) is *Shrinking Cities: Understanding Decline and Shrinkage in the United States* (Routledge).

Paul M.A. Baker is the Senior Director of Research and Strategic Innovation at the Center for Advanced Communications Policy (CACP) at Georgia Institute of Technology. His research focuses on postsecondary skills training, innovation networks, workforce development, and accessibility of information technologies by people with disabilities.

Alberto Bramanti is Associate Professor of Applied Economics at Università Bocconi, Milan. He is Fellow of the Green Center (Bocconi University), focusing on territorial economics (both regional and urban), and Fellow of the Regional Studies Association, UK.

Xiangdong Chen is Professor of International Technology Transfer and Innovation Studies at The School of Economics and Management, Beihang University.

Sunyang Chung is a Professor of Technology Management and Policy, Department of Technology Management, School of Business, Konkuk University, Seoul, Korea. His main research areas are technology management, S&T policy, regional innovation strategies, innovation theory, and sustainable development.

Willie Donnelly is President of the Waterford Institute of Technology (WIT). He is founder of the Telecommunications Software and Systems Group (TSSG) which performs research into mobile services, the internet of things, and communications management. Since 2004, he has been collaborating on the development, implementation, and actuation of a sustainable and flexible regional open innovation system engaging the quadruple helix of regional actors to meet societal needs in any given region.

Matej Drev is an Applied Economist whose research focuses on the economics of technological innovation and international economics.

Elena Gimenez Fernandez, Universidad Complutense of Madrid, and Visiting Professor at University Rey Juan Carlos, Madrid.

Bill O'Gorman is Director for Research at the Centre of Enterprise Development and Regional Economy (CEDRE), School of Business, Waterford Institute of Technology. He has also manged several European-funded projects related to developing Regional Innovation Systems. Since 2004, he has been collaborating on the development, implementation, and actuation of a sustainable and flexible regional open innovation system engaging the quadruple helix of regional actors to meet societal needs in any given region.

Desmond Hickie is an Emeritus Professor at the University of Chester. He was Founding Dean of the Chester Business School and of the Faculty of Business, Management, and Law at the University of Chester. He has researched and written about the aerospace industry for over 30 years, including projects funded by the European Union, the Economic and Social Research Council, the European TUC, and the Friedrich Ebert Stiftung. He has developed and delivered innovative postgraduate leadership and management development programmes for a number of international businesses and UK public authorities, including BMW, Landrover, Ford, and the Littlewoods Group.

Ulrich Hilpert is Professor of Comparative Government at the University of Jena. His main areas of research are comparative studies in technology, innovation, regional development, global networking, and skilled and university-trained labour. He is Fellow of the Academy of Social Sciences (FAcSS), was chairman of the IPSA Research Council of Science and Politics and the ECPR Standing of Politics and Technology. He has been visiting professor at a dozen universities in Europe and the US and consultant to the EU and a number of national and regional governments, labour unions, and business organisations.

Valerie Hunstock is Doctor of Philosophy, University of International Business and Economics (UIBE), Beijing, China.

Neil Jones is a Senior Affiliate Professor of Strategy at INSEAD. He studies the competitive implications of technological change in addition to teaching MBA students and designing executive education programmes.

Ruixi Li is Doctor of Management Science, Lecturer at China University of Labor Relations.

Connie L. McNeely, PhD, is Professor of Public Policy in the Schar School of Policy and Government, and Co-Director of the Center for Science, Technology, and Innovation Policy, at George Mason University.

Xin Niu is Doctor of Management Science, Division Chief, China Reform Holdings Corporation Ltd.

Alain-Marc Rieu is Professor Emeritus, Department of Philosophy and Senior Research Fellow, *Trans-Science project*, IETT, a the University Lyon-Jean Moulin. He is also Guest Professor, Collaborative Design Center, Osaka University.

Francesco D. Sandulli is Information Society Chair at Universidad Complutense of Madrid and has served as Innovation Vice-Chancellor at the University Camilo Jose Cela at Madrid. His research on the impact of digital transformation on skills as well as on open innovation and entrepreneurial strategies has been published in leading journals. He has been Visiting Scholar at Haas School of Business at University of California, Berkeley, and worked as strategy consultant in innovative projects at large multinational corporations.

Walter Scherrer is professor of economics at the Department of Economics and Social Science, University of Salzburg, and academic director of the postgraduate programme Global Executive MBA at the University of Salzburg Business School. His publications include contributions to international journals and edited books on innovation economics and the role of public-private partnerships in innovation. He has lectured on innovation policy at Fudan University/Shanghai, University of Bologna, and University of Ljubljana.

Florian Schloderer is a lecturer at INSEAD based at the Middle East Campus and works for the INSEAD Randomized Controlled Trials Lab. His research focuses on social categorization and networks in the context of new industry emergence and organizational change. Prior to joining INSEAD, he worked for his family's business and received a doctoral degree from the Department of Economic and Organizational Studies at the Bundeswehr University, Munich.

Torsten Schunder is a doctoral student in the Department of Geography, State University of New York (SUNY) at Buffalo. His research interests are in energy poverty and fuel transition, including cooking fuel transitions. He is also interested in innovation patterns in renewable energy.

Michael Vassiliadis serves as the Chairman to the Industrial Union for Mining, Chemical and Energy Workers (IG BCE), and president of the IndustriALL Europe, the federation of all industrial unions in Europe. He also serves as a Member and Vice-Chairman on the Supervisory Boards of several multinational companies in the chemical, mining, and energy sector including BASF, Henkel, RAG, and STEAG.

Preface

There is a rich body of research and publications concerning different aspects of innovation. The views are different because the researchers' questions are different and academic disciplines have divergent interests. In addition, there has been a fundamental change because of globalisation and newly industrialised countries. Industries require different competences, potentials for innovation, markets, and demands, readinesses for technology transfer, skilled labour forces, networking, and levels of industrial development. The research on regions, human capital, countries, or industries helps to deepen our knowledge about innovation. Simultaneously with this growing variation, there is a search for best practice and governments employ similar policies and often aim at similar short lists of technologies. Nevertheless, the effects and the successes of public policies are very different – and the contexts in which they were developed and implemented were also highly divergent. Consequently, the processes of innovation and situations differ greatly.

This book aims at both a better understanding of the diversities of innovation and a discussion of the different contributions to innovation. It is important to understand that innovation is more than just a matter of entrepreneurs and academics. The socio-economic effects of innovation relate to the manufacturing of products and labour, which means these relate to appropriately skilled labour. This clearly characterises the kind of industrial development and opportunities which exist in different situations. Such differences are based on a match of industries, skills, public policies, research structures, societal structures providing for the labour, and access to markets. Although such situations are highly varied and indicate the diversities of such processes and have the potential to make it look ineffective, nevertheless there are opportunities for a better understanding. There are relationships between the different elements of innovation forming specificities and altogether forming precise situations, thus contributing to a rich diversity – but also referring to its origins and relationship.

There were two international workshops held at the University of Oxford and in Berlin with participants from academia, labour unions, and enterprises. The resultant highly constructive exchanges – of research, experiences and ideas – have found their way into this book. They reflect the shared view that individual academic disciplines, or particular views from practitioners, are helpful to learn more about the process. To understand innovation better there is a need to combine such competences, which help to identify opportunities among the rich diversities of innovation. Matching the situation to the set of opportunities is clearly important, and in order to provide for socio-economic development, the role of the labour force of a region, country, or metropolis is critical. Consequently, the discussions paid particular attention to the constitution of individual situations and how contexts match the situations. This discussion is reflected in the structure of this book and will be continued during the workshops to come and help to provide for a deeper understanding of innovation and expand the comparative understanding of such processes.

This book can be read and used in the way it is laid out and may help the reader to think freely about new understandings which reach out across different countries, regions, and situations. But it may also be of interest for those who work on some of the individual subjects. The comparative view may contribute some additional perspectives and will link up with other variables, contexts, or processes of development. Innovation is obviously a highly complex process, which generates a lot of diversities that can be identified empirically. Although the full complexity may not always be within the scope of the analysis, it always helps to relate to existing situations rather than examining pre-defined indicators. The investigation of empirical situations helps a lot to understand the innovation process in general – and it is important to understand innovation as a process with different periods and contributions over time.

The creative and highly international context, of a discussion between academia, labour unions and practitioners, was generously supported by the *Hans-Böckler-Foundation, Düsseldorf, Germany*. The interest of the foundation in the comparative view of such processes made it possible to have this exchange of ideas over several years and is to be continued during the coming years. We all thank the foundation for their strong engagement. As an editor, I am also grateful to the patience of the authors while discussing and adjusting the chapters to make this edited book as coherent as an edited book can be. I look forward to the continuation of these activities and we happily welcome the new, additional contributors who have already joined our deliberations and those who, no doubt, will join us in future. We have explored a lot of open questions, which require a continued exchange of expertise between academia, labour unions, practitioners, and policy makers.

Ulrich Hilpert

Berlin and Jena

Part I

Introduction

1 About socio-economic development, technology and government policies

Diversities of innovation

Ulrich Hilpert

Changing situations and newly emerging problems create a constantly rising demand for new technologies and innovation based on existing opportunities. Environmental problems, increasing climate change, transportation technologies and treatment of diseases call for advanced solutions, whilst urbanisation, social change, communications and the exchange of information create specific situations, which require the provision of technological products and services. There are many examples of new demands for technologies or technological solutions of existing and emerging problems (Hilpert 2016a). While exploring innovation and new technologies there are many dimensions, which are important and influence such processes. There is the relationship between public research and new technologies, human capital and education, regional situations and Islands of Innovation, existing opportunities and long waves of socio-economic exploitation. Many such constellations have been researched to provide a deeper understanding of their processes and to facilitate appropriate policies of different levels of government. The research is based on studies of different countries and regions with different governmental systems (federal vs. centralised) following different political ideologies (neo-liberal vs. social-democratic), based on different technologies requiring various contributions from academic research (biotechnology vs. environmental technologies). These concern different industries inhibiting the potential of innovation or the manufacture of new products (mechanical engineering vs. the application of new materials) and the fundamental change of existing products because of the supply with new parts (automotive industries applying electro-engines vs. 3D-printers manufacturing products). There is a rich diversity of situations referring to a similarly rich diversity of industries, research capabilities, human capital and industrial structures.

Thus, innovation and new technologies also converge with changes in products, manufacturing and organisation. While the first industrial revolution exploited the opportunities of steam engines by organising manufacturing accordingly, the current fourth industrial revolution exploits the opportunities of artificial intelligence and electronics, which have a fundamental impact on changing organisation globally. Consequently, what was innovative will not continue to be so, because becoming mature is a permanent process associated with new technologies and innovation. The global dislocation of mature manufacturing and industrialisation to less-developed countries is a consequence of competition among industrialised countries and from newly industrialising countries referring to different levels of production costs and regulations. Thus, what is not appropriately innovative in leading western countries may match the situation in less advanced countries and may help to build an industrial basis at different locations in other situations. While it lacks its innovative contribution in leading countries, it has an innovative impact in other, less industrialised countries. The context is decisive when evaluating a development and a technology to induce innovation. Countries or locations based on a lower level of industrialisation can take innovative advantage of technology from the second or third industrial revolution, while in the most advanced situations Industry 4.0 is the challenge they have to face and to cope with. The technology applied needs to be new and have an innovative impact in the context where it is newly introduced.

While innovation is widely related to new technologies it is important to keep in mind that such new opportunities cannot be applied similarly in all situations. Different industries demand different technologies. As chemical and pharmaceutical industries benefit particularly from biotechnologies, robotics contributes to mechanical engineering and plant construction or carbon fibre may contribute to advance automobile industries. Even a similar technology referring to the same government programme may indicate divergent innovative development because of the situation, in which they are applied (Bagchi-Sen and Kedron 2016). In addition, new opportunities based on 3D-printers or gearless electric engines for cars may change the design and the way they are manufactured. The diversities of industries and technologies as well as the opportunities to introduce new products or to advance existing products indicate that specific innovations clearly demand particular conditions. Industrial structures help to identify such diversities easily because new technologies might be applicable in such industries and their products. If this is not the case new technological opportunities will emerge but have no impact on industries for which they are not suited. Accordingly, other technologies may suit better but may not be applicable in other industries elsewhere. While this appears to be clear and obvious, this has far reaching effects on participation in innovation and on the strategies underpinning innovation policies: technology is not innovative *per se*, its socio-economic opportunities depend on the suitability of the reference industries in which it is used (i.e. those industries in which an innovation may be applied to develop new products or processes) (Abel and Deitz 2009).

During different periods of industrialisation countries, regions and locations have developed particular industrial structures and manufacturing competences. Such specificities are to be identified easily and are well known. Silicon Valley and the San Francisco Bay Area are the home of outstanding microelectronics and computing industries, Seattle is an important base of Boeing and Microsoft. The Boston Area participates strongly in almost all new technologies. In East Asia electronics industries manufacture products, which are developed elsewhere and are distributed across the world, or have become the basis for new global players as in Japan or Korea. German mechanical engineering is well known, French pharmaceutical industries are globally present and the Airbus Industry clearly indicates the locations which possess the tradition and competence to contribute to a product based on highly complex engineering. Many other examples can be added. It shows that these situations are highly diverse and the technologies demanded vary according to industries and locations. Traditions are continued through new technological opportunities and competences have constantly been enhanced to advance both the industry and the product. While this is taking place, the different processes draw upon diversities of technologies, which match particular opportunities at particular locations, which are the home of particular collections of industrial competences. The implicit selection processes taking place among technologies are a clear consequence of these divergent contexts. Technologies can contribute to socio-economic development only where they find appropriate contexts, which are usually characterised by existing reference industries.

The more complex such processes become, the more innovation is related to competences and traditions. Earlier periods of industrialisation (e.g. based on the steam engine) were highly innovative but they demanded fewer or only minor preconditions to be met. A transfer of such manufacturing industries to less advanced countries or locations was, of course, more easily achieved than would be the case for those industries, which require a complex manufacturing base. The labour force was usually unskilled or semiskilled, the manufacturing was widely organised along the assembly line and enterprises were structured in a rather hierarchical way. Consequently, countries and regions vary according to the innovative opportunities of these industries and complexity of their products. Regions or countries are ready to maintain their positions, when there are opportunities for socio-economic development based on innovation providing for advanced products or the advancement of manufacturing. There are clearly different opportunities, which may not be available in all situations. Future development depends on the matching of both situations and existing technologies of innovative opportunities.

Since different technologies emerge simultaneously divergent paths of innovation exist according to their applicability to reference industries. New challenges emerge due to the complexity of products and manufacturing, which can enjoy the advantage of new technologies only if the available labour is appropriately skilled and educated. Consequently, the socio-economic realisation of leading-edge innovation is related with human capital and an appropriate labour force. In addition, the existing labour force needs to meet the demands of the technologies to be applied. Thus, innovation needs industrial structures and a highly skilled labour force to exploit opportunities, which emerge from research and development. Such highly advanced processes can be created only when the appropriate situation exists. This makes innovation a highly selective process, which privileges particular opportunities among the rich diversity of technologies to be applied. Given the highly varied situations formed by industries, the labour force and research infrastructures in different regions and countries, as a consequence innovation processes vary a lot and focus on different elements – even though the technological fields or the industries concerned are rather similar. Within this context, skills and education provide the enabling basis for socio-economic effects to be realised.[1] This necessitates more than just a discussion of human capital. It refers to systems of skilling and education, which have emerged over time in relationship with industrial competences. Skills and education are related with societal dynamics and social change creating particular situations. When it comes to innovation, industrial societies are more than just a description of a societal context or social structure, these might become a critical basis of constant socio-economic development.

Such processes of innovation are highly complex and they depend on a variety of dimensions including the question – which type of industrial revolution is most appropriate. In particular the appropriateness of a certain level of innovation indicates that there is more than just an arrangement of criteria required. It needs to suit a situation, which has emerged during prior industrial development. Consequently, particular contexts are prepared to take advantage of specific innovative opportunities (Hilpert 2016a); there are windows of opportunities, which are available for some regions or locations but not for others. The more demanding leading-edge innovation requires outstanding research, a highly skilled and educated labour force, modern industries and enterprises ready to collaborate and to transform ideas into socio-economic development, and hence the smaller is the number of locations, which can participate in such processes. Labour markets become highly important concerning human capital which is attracted, and the number of creative personnel, which are available. This convergence of quantity regarding the size of the labour market and concerning the quality of knowledge workers privileges certain arrangements, which can be met only in a small number of locations. Only a small number of locations perform in a way that is attractive to innovative labour or creative knowledge workers, so clearly those regions which can provide a large labour market for such personnel have a strong advantage. Size allows for more job opportunities or careers within a region or a location for spouses or partners of individuals in question to finding a job (Power and Lundmark 2004). Because of the size requirement metropolises provide the most appropriate situations for participation in such processes of leading-edge innovation (Franco and Filson 2000; Berry and Glaeser 2005; Coulombe and Tremblay 2009). Thus, most of the Islands of Innovation, which are in a position to concentrate such processes in a small geographic area, are located in metropolises (Lawton Smith and Waters 2005; Abel and Deitz 2009). There the context is formed to participate in such processes.

The context becomes very important for the participation of a location or region in such development and is critical for the level of innovation which can be applied (Hilpert 2016c). While participation during earlier periods of industrial development did widely include unskilled or semiskilled labour (e.g. textile industries, the manufacturing of electronics, consumer goods, mass production in general) more advanced products did demand advanced skills and higher education. Such early industrialisation was widely separated from research and development, and manufacturing to a far extent was based on repetitive duties. The contribution of unskilled and semiskilled labour on such levels of industrialisation is quite high and privileges locations and countries, which can provide competent, cheap labour. Still today such situations exist (e.g. textile industries in Bangladesh) and attract industries to locate plants, which suit such situations and manufacture marketable goods although these industries are too mature to continue at other places or where these flourished before. This process is also to be seen among former developing countries, which became Newly Industrialised Countries (e.g. due to differences in production costs a dislocation of manufacturing from China to Vietnam has already taken place) was to be identified and it indicates different levels of industrial development. What is mature in one country can have an innovative effect in situations of other countries, where the context of development, regulation or production costs is different or less developed. Labour costs or regulations (e.g. concerning working conditions and environmental conditions) play an important role. To arrange such contexts for less advanced industrialisation is much less complex. It can be achieved comparatively easily through effective government agencies. When the demand for unskilled labour matches the situations in such countries, they can arrange the context for such manufacturing and establish a situation, which is considered to provide them with modernisation or innovation in socio-economic development.

Improvement of skills and education helps newly industrialised countries participate in more advanced industries and may create situations of sustainable innovation (e.g. Korea, Singapore and metropolises in China and India; Tsui-Auch, Chia and Liu 2016).[2] Thus, government policies are important to form the context for both less advanced processes of industrialisation and more modern processes of innovation. While the profits of capital invested can also be generated on the basis of less advanced industries, governments may have a particular interest in gaining more advanced processes of, innovation as they provide opportunities for higher values added through modern industries and for higher standards of living through higher incomes based on modern products. Standards of living are not merely to be measured on the basis of incomes but also concerning the advanced services supplied. Even smaller incomes can build large demands and markets, which are ready to allow for innovative and improved processes if the number of customers or clients is sufficiently large. Thinking about innovation could also indicate that a situation is formed, which allows for advanced supply (e.g. health service for poorer people). The context for such innovation is arranged with regard to investment, but even more important is a context with regard to a skilled and educated labour force and research capabilities, which meets the requirements of new industries, advanced technologies, modern manufacturing or innovative services.

While aiming at such processes to achieve higher levels of innovation some lessons from Western countries were suitable to learn from. The agglomeration of such capabilities privileges places where creative personnel can be attracted. In Western countries there is a high convergence of Islands of Innovation and metropolises, because such agglomerations of research institutes, spin-off enterprises from public research, education of innovative labour and participation in collaborative networks generate a strong dynamism towards synergies (Laudel 2005; Favell, Feldblum and Smith 2006; Hilpert 2016c). Such innovative metropolitan situations build innovative labour markets and attract a brain drain towards such metropolises (Power and Lundmark 2004; Berry and Glaeser 2005; Abel and Deitz 2009; Coulombe and Tremblay 2009).[3] The availability of highly divergent competences provides the potential for collaborative networking as a basis for advanced new products. Similarly, newly industrialised countries aim at building such agglomerations, which increasingly emerge as knots in innovative networks formed through collaborative research (Chung 2016).[4] Government policies are important both to form such contexts with increasing levels of innovation and to realise such aims towards advanced socio-economic development. But such policies can perform effectively only when they match the situations, which change over time. Windows of opportunities open and close, and the regional or national context provides for development only when a match with innovative opportunities at a particular point in time can be realised.[5] Such windows can open and close for leading-edge innovation and technology, but they can also relate to a translocation of manufacturing mature industries to less-developed countries where it acts as an innovation within this particular context. In addition, such processes which do not refer to the leading-edge processes can be combined with modern communication technologies or modern materials and make it less a matter of dislocation but more a relocation within a changed global context. Shared global markets still exist, and provide a dynamically changing context.

When it comes to the current fourth industrial revolution and digitisation, there are changes and windows of opportunities, which will affect most leading countries as well as the less-developed countries. In leading Western countries jobs with routine work will widely disappear, but only a few will be transferred to low-wage countries. Instead these jobs may be replaced through new equipment, robots or machines. Due to the change in production costs based on new technologies and the continuing high quality of products some manufacturing may even return from low-wage economies to traditional industrial centres characterised by high wages. Also some new opportunities may emerge on the basis of internal development based on emerging markets outside of Western countries. Consequently, innovation and new technologies change many situations and demand particular contexts. The increasing complexity of innovation requires a deeper understanding of how to create a context, and to provide for participation in beneficial socio-economic changes. Different societies, industrial structures and human capital are decisive, when building the basis for particular innovative opportunities. There are rich diversities of innovation, which demand a deeper and systematic understanding of how to participate and which processes of innovation may be suitable.

Emerging divergent phenomena – different identifications of innovation

When exploring innovative products and processes of development, it becomes immediately obvious that countries vary in their areas of particular competence and that any individual country may vary in its specialisms and competences over time. The introduction of steam engines in England became the basis of mass production and of Manchester Capitalism. A reorganisation of manufacturing was introduced and the conflictual relationship between capital and labour was introduced (Marx 1962 [1890], 1963 [1893], 1964 [1894]; Smith 2008 [1776]). This initial industrialisation was characterised by simple products, the introduction of assembly lines and the split of manual work into simple individual production steps. Consequently, there were two levels of products to be considered: (1) the mass products employing the new machines and equipment and (2) the producers of capital goods such as machines and plant. Those who developed, designed and manufactured the new machines and plant enabled a massive increase in productivity. This period, which today can be identified as Industry 1.0, illustrates the innovation based on a technological competence and the capability of engineers to apply such opportunities to the economy and to meet the demands of the customers.

The relationship between application and development continues and it builds a particular competence among producers of capital goods. Design improved, reflecting customer demand and the utilisation of new technological opportunities, materials and scientific findings. It is this relationship between enterprises, supplying capital goods, mechanical engineering equipment, minerals and shipping, with their customers which allowed the building of a body of such competences. The demand for these products allowed the improvement of capital goods and for the increasing knowledge employed in design and manufacturing. The strength of such products provided the basis for exports to other countries with similar situations and demands. Dealing successfully with situations in their home countries helped to build a leading competence and a continuing export of goods, which were considered to be innovative for their time and situation when these were introduced during the early stages of industrialisation. A close relationship between markets and producers emerged as a basis for innovative products and indicated demand for particular kinds of products and their use by customers.

Consequently, a country or region may continue to have a leading competence in knowledge intensive capital goods as long as the markets' demand such products and suppliers can supply the markets (Piore and Sabel 1984; Sabel et al. 1991).[6] The attractive economic opportunities for such products raise the interest of other potential capital goods suppliers to meet these markets (Chung 2016, Tsui-Auch, Chia and Liu 2016). Consequently, different situations of countries or regions provided the basis for divergent competences in innovative products (Hickie 2006; Hilpert 2006). In addition, because of the maturation of products and the dislocation of manufacturing to other countries' competences, which formerly were appropriate to markets and customers' demands leading industrialised countries may have lost those markets, or they adapted to the changing demands of their customers by providing improved and innovative products. The continuing modernisation of industrial manufacturing towards current digitisation and Industry 4.0 consequently changed the markets requiring particular competences to provide the products demanded. Continuing industrial change and modernisation increases both the demand for investment in modern equipment and the level of capital goods products alongside the increasing complexity of manufactured goods (O'Sullivan and Mitchell 2013; Dolphin 2015). A changing international division of labour based on newly industrialised countries and increasing international trade contribute to the continuously expanding markets for higher value added products. Consequently, industrial development in different countries derives from divergent opportunities concerning the manufacturing of consumer products and capabilities in the design of capital goods and complex products.

Such industries became highly attractive because these took particular advantage from processes of industrialisation elsewhere. To meet such constantly emerging and increasingly demanding opportunities, divergent competences were required. Such products were based on divergent competences, which were contributed by different partners or departments when they collaborate to meet market needs. The competences developed along with industrialisation and the increasing competition among manufacturing industries in areas of mass production created a continuing demand for better, more efficient and precise capital goods. Thus, when new technological opportunities were applied a relationship emerged between manufacturing in low-cost countries and the creation of appropriate industrial plants. Exporting such plants and equipment, traditionally by leading industrialised countries in Europe and the US, consequently allowed them to take advantage of industrialisation elsewhere. High value-added and increasing socio-economic growth created a strong attraction to such industries also towards these newly industrialised countries to follow opportunities of innovative development (Chung 2016; Liu 2016). Similar to European latecomers in industrialisation (e.g. Germany) more recently countries such as Japan, Korea or Singapore have changed from being importers of advanced products and capital goods, to become countries which can also enter such markets based on their own attractive products.

Such modern capital goods helped to keep locations in such a situation to provide for their markets although labour costs may have increased (Dhéret et al. 2014). On the other hand, countries with low-labour costs and little regulation may continue to supply markets needing less advanced capital goods.[7] The demand for innovative tools and equipment may be highly divergent depending on the situation of a country. The more advanced the products are, and the higher the levels of their precision, the higher the demands concerning both human capital and leading-edge capital goods. Consequently the expectations regarding capital goods vary with the opportunities of existing labour. This strong relationship induces a competition among capital goods suppliers according to the demands and the levels of complexity required by consumers. Less innovative products need to be manufactured by less-skilled or unskilled workers and need different and simpler capital goods, which can also be supplied by newly industrialised countries. The improving competences located outside of the traditional industrial centres provides the basis for emerging centres in newly industrialised countries oriented in less advanced capital goods, which meet particular market demands. Consequently, there is a horizontal competition among technologically advanced countries and hierarchically with new centres of expertise gaining competences, which were not available to them before, and which help to upgrade their industrial development.

Such processes introduce new processes of accumulation of both capital and knowledge to be invested and applied in research, education and in the modernisation of industries. Nevertheless, there is a divergence of demands to be met by manufacturers of more simple capital goods, which help to develop new competences in such countries. Although these may not be state of the art, they may contribute to more mature manufacturing of less technology intensive products. Consequently, reflecting opportunities in the markets such competences are highly divergent among countries, because of divergent supplies of capital goods to these markets and the established research structures and traditions, which have emerged. Although in different markets similar areas might have been investigated, these were not identical, and because they may foster further product development they provide a basis for collaboration on new capital goods and high-value products (Hickie 2006). New technologies did help to modernise existing products and to make such opportunities available for new areas of application. The implementation of microelectronics in the 1980s helped to improve mechanical engineering and to develop more specialised machines (e.g. concerning parts for electronics or automobile industries contributing to supply chains). New materials allowed for the improvement of engines and energy plants, and more recently the improvement of batteries has allowed for innovation in automobile industries.

Competences from different origins were merged when new or fundamentally re-designed products entered the markets. Californian electronics industries and the findings of Silicon Valley facilitated the improvement of mechanical engineering in Germany and Switzerland. While it was research intensive to develop new products, such as personal computers and smart phones, it was less complex to manufacture them, and thus this could be located in countries with low-labour costs and weak regulations. Thus, highly regarded Apple products are manufactured in China. Other countries also gained from the transfer of knowledge and manufacturing capacities.

Korea became a major manufacturer in electronics products, and also Taiwan has become a home of well-designed personal computers and mechanical engineering. It is important to see how competences in research and design on the one hand, and management and manufacturing on the other hand, can create a particular synergy which is in the end embodied in new or fundamentally improved products. The diversity of areas and strategies of innovation matches opportunities in markets and manufacturing to meet consumers' demands (Hilpert 2016a).[8] Market niches, highly specialised markets or an optimum combination of technology with particular situations of manufacturing create both opportunities and diversities of socio-economic development based on processes of innovation, which suit the particular situation.

Such innovative opportunities are not equally available throughout a country. Individual regions, locations or metropolises develop their own profile based on industrial structures, available labour and research capabilities matched with public policy programmes. While they jointly may demonstrate the economic performance and strength of a country individually they are not identical but often highly divergent. There were continuously changing situations when new technologies were applied during periods of industrial development and transportation. Consequently, countries can inhibit highly divergent opportunities. The number of individual industrial regions or conurbations, which exist within a country, indicates divergent opportunities when new technologies are ready to be exploited. This affects a particular industrial sector that may be addressed but also concerning the application of technologies across different sectors based upon the competences, which are developed during collaboration of the different industries, which co-exist at the same location. The mix of industries may become fundamentally important when new technological opportunities emerge indicating that there are cross-industry opportunities.

Consequently, opportunities of innovation vary significantly, no matter whether these are based on new techno-scientific findings, new technologies to be applied or on the capability to organise and manage changing socio-economic situations. Existing structures, established research profiles and socio-cultural traditions create particularly different situations. Opportunities in microelectronics changed mechanical engineering and measurement instruments; biotechnology changed medical instruments and pharmaceuticals; and new materials changed automobiles and transportation. The number of innovative opportunities could be pursued widely and adding to the point that innovative processes are highly specific and follow highly divergent tendencies. Such innovative processes are particularly selective and include regions, which suit the opportunities in question (Hilpert 2006). The extent to which they can benefit from these processes depends on how strongly they match the conditions required for the exploitation of new techno-industrial opportunities, which meet market opportunities or are the basis for new customers and demands.

While industrial sectors need to be ready to exploit such technological opportunities, contrastingly, new technologies frequently can be applied in divergent situations and in a number of industries and products. Such technologies link to divergent situations and allow multiple opportunities for producers of technologies to meet the demands of a rich number of customers, who rely on new technologies to make their products more innovative and continue to perform strongly in their markets. Such producers of new technologies, which are applied to a final product, are less dependent on markets for particular products but they need to keep their technologies innovative and applicable in many different industries (Sabel et al. 1991).[9] The situation associated with the new producer of the electric automobile Tesla and other brands of electric cars presents impressive examples. When designed and manufactured, more than 60 per cent of the parts for Tesla cars, come from German suppliers, predominantly from Bosch (private conversation with the author). While Tesla must directly compete with the electric car market, the suppliers can provide parts for all the brands and can take advantage of their competence for other products and markets. Thus, developing and providing new technological opportunities allows for a change in design and innovation in automobiles. In combination with the existing level of innovation, which is already achieved in the final product, manufacturing, market supply and management processes of innovation indicate a strong diversity concerning the quality of the final product, the individual markets and the socio-economic effects of such processes. Consequently, there is a rich diversity of innovation emerging, based on a situation that already exists.

When taking such situations into account it becomes obvious that industrial structures are important, but there is no need to focus on innovative processes *per se* (Breschi and Lissoni 2009). Competences and technological opportunities at other places can be as important as a complement to the industrial structures in regions far away from where they were generated. Thus, opportunities are created across different locations, technologies and sectors. The availability of such opportunities to be combined despite geographical distances increases the potential of innovative initiatives and processes (Hilpert 2016a). Diversity becomes richer, as more potential industries are emerging, most opportunities for new technologies are developed to suit such industries. Consequently, the globally growing number of locations of particular industries and competences allows for a constantly increase in the number of innovative situations.

The more specific such technologies became and the more these were applied across industrial sectors, the more divergent were the situations built upon the capabilities of clearly identifiable geographic areas (Bellini and Pasquinelli 2016). Such innovative situations emerge from opportunities induced because of individual combinations of industrial competences with new technologies, which are rarely replicated elsewhere. In addition, as the relationship between distant contributors to innovative processes is generally increasing, transportation becomes crucial for both collaboration on research and design and also for shipping parts and products. Thus, processes of innovation emerge in highly divergent situations following different opportunities and rationalities, but they are identifiable as a relationship between existing industrial competences and the opportunities of new technologies in particular situations which are arranged by companies and researchers, or which relate to particular public policies.

Dynamisms of divergent opportunities – constellations of innovation and contextualisation

Although structures indicate existing competences and opportunities of innovation the process itself and the diversities documented clearly demand particular activities which change situations and allow for innovative findings and new products. The more advanced products and industries are, the more vital is the demand for academic and technological research. Thus a constant demand for various areas of public and private research is emerging and even increasing. Collaboration in public research across countries and continents builds bodies of knowledge and competence which in turn are related to particular regions or metropolises within countries. Due to the fact that strong competences are available only at a limited number of locations, consequently, newly launched government programmes on new areas of research are realised predominantly at established Islands of Innovation. Those locations can be clearly identified geographically and provide by far most new findings and opportunities.

Metropolitan situations have shown their strength in becoming hubs of such processes and they converge strongly with the collaborative system of Islands of Innovation. Innovative situations in metropolitan locations meet large labour markets for knowledge workers, which allow for people to change jobs and for opportunities for spouses to find employment (Power and Lundmark 2004; Coulombe and Tremblay 2009). In addition, the locations of leading-edge research attract academics, researchers and knowledge workers to take jobs in such stimulating environments (Mahroum 1999; Laudel 2005; Hilpert and Lawton Smith 2013; Trippl 2013). It is most interesting that the attraction of such locations continues over long periods of time and they are frequently recreated in different technologies at different points in time (Hickie 2006). Islands of Innovation have continued their leading position over three decades and despite the fact that dramatically increased funding opportunities in the leading countries allows for other locations to participate in such research areas (Hilpert 2016d) and to attract knowledge workers to take jobs in such newly emerging locations (Hilpert and Lawton Smith 2013). Simultaneously, new industrial countries have been successful in building centres of excellence in particular areas of academic research, which became recognised globally as partners in collaborative research (Mahroum 2000b). Thus, Seoul in Korea, Shanghai, Beijing and Hong Kong in China, Bangalore in India, and Singapore in Asia have emerged as Islands of Innovation concerning academic research, while at Rio de Janeiro or Sao Paulo in Brazil such opportunities are identifiable (Chung 2016; Hilpert 2016d).

Existing Islands of Innovation and newly emerging innovative locations outside of the traditional centres in western countries benefit from complementary dynamism. Vital processes in outstanding Islands of Innovation help to continue modern industries or to modernise existing industries, while simultaneously additional competences from new industrial countries contribute to the global body of knowledge and allow for additional collaborations and more research findings to be applied. Although leading-edge research continues to be dominated by Europe and the US, there are newly established contributors when the opportunities for innovation are increased.[10] Consequently, high-tech industries or industries based on high-tech products can also emerge at different places to the established innovatory processes, which have already become well known over the last few decades. As new competitors emerge using additional competences there are also new collaborators available to participate in a rich diversity of innovation, and which can also contribute based on divergent cultures of research.

Participation in innovative development is fundamentally based on the capabilities which exist at individual locations. In science-based innovation participation in such collaborative networks is based on the building facilities of leading-edge research. Attractive opportunities in research and a thought-provoking environment help to bring innovative academics, researchers and knowledge workers to a particular location (Mahroum 2000a; Marginson 2006; Lawton Smith and Waters 2013; Hilpert 2013a). Due to new findings in research and well-regarded publications such locations are noticed because of their capabilities and become highly acceptable partners in research projects and locations for an exchange of scholars and personnel. Such vital situations can be arranged widely through government policies, which support research and education in particular areas. Although it may take some time to become recognised globally, some countries manage both to contribute to and participate in such networks almost within a single decade.

Spin-off enterprises from university research and university education, which also meet the regional demand for skills and competences, provide the basis for the future economic exploitation of research and academic knowledge. Since such enterprises also hold patents or are appropriate partners in R&D, simultaneously, they are active in the transfer of knowledge and technology to individual larger firms or entire industries. While the number of highly innovative research institutions and enterprises at a location allows for a greater number of fruitful collaborations, in addition, this situation also helps to develop innovative processes within a country and region (Simonen and McCann 2008; Breschi and Lissoni 2009). Consequently, such situations are characterised by a concentration on particular technologies and areas of research, which are favoured by the countries in question (Abel and Deitz 2009).

While building research centres can be achieved within a foreseeable period it is much more time consuming and difficult to establish an industrial competence to manufacture highly complex technological products based on an industrial history. Engineering helps to continuously improve products and the organisation of manufacturing. While the product itself might not be new (e.g. aircraft, automobiles, mechanical engineering, transportation, telephones, optical and medical instruments) the application of new technologies had a fundamental impact by changing the product (Hickie 2016). Such constant improvements rarely demand immediate redesign of products or a reorganisation of manufacturing. Skills of blue-collar workers continue to be important and modernisation through the additional competences of workers help to take advantage of existing tacit knowledge in relationship with new technological opportunities.[11] Products and economic exploitation consequently demand such competences to allow for innovation.

New opportunities need to merge with the capabilities of existing industries to induce technology-based innovation. The skills of blue-collar workers, thus, become of critical importance for the economic realisation of innovation. Workers' tacit knowledge is important to apply such opportunities, because it widely contributes to modernisation that has socio-economic effects. Taking these factors into account industrial competences, a skilled workforce and the capability of particular products is a basis which turns opportunities into techno-industrial innovation of socio-economic significance. Such situations relate to particular development and competences in various areas, which cannot be built or transferred to another country or region easily. Consequently, processes of technology-based innovation, which require complex constellations of knowledge and skills, are closely related to particular contexts at those locations. It is clearly the relationship with the existing context which facilitates innovative impact when meeting new or changing markets.

New technologies need to relate to industries that are ready and prepared to apply and to take advantage of such opportunities. The improvement of final products will strengthen their market position and the modernisation of plants will make manufacturing more efficient and profitable. Such reference industries are characterised by highly individual circumstances forming divergent contexts because of both the innovative development and existing industrial structure at a location, as well as how the country is positioned in the global division of labour. Consequently, there are situations of research and technology-based innovation, which emerge from competences of existing industries and exploit opportunities in particular markets (Hickie 2006). Socio-economic and political contexts are important for innovation and they are decisive concerning participation in particular area of research. The context of a location or region needs to suit the opportunities of new technological opportunities under the conditions of both a global division of labour and global networks of collaboration.[12]

In countries and regions with highly innovative industries and enterprises appropriate situations can be supported or even organised by government policies which address highly skilled labour of all kinds and leading-edge research. The continuous upgrade of the labour force and constant support in particular areas of research helps to keep regions innovative. Thus, because of the constantly increased application of research and technologies to manufacturing there is a growing number of blue-collar labour who are university-trained engineers. Government policies addressed to both education and techno-scientific research help to provide a basis for highly innovative products, which

exhibit high values added. The extraordinary qualities of a product and opportunities for its application immediately create a market, which is formed by those
who expect an advantage from exploiting such leading-edge technologies. The
context of such innovation is formed by the situation of consumers creating
a demand for such technological products which can be provided in regional or
local situations ready to realise innovative developments, which are aimed at
matching such demands. Strategic policies can help to build such innovative
situations because they support the labour force required to apply technological
opportunities during the manufacturing of high value-added products.

Markets and competition can create situations of continuing innovation in
manufacturing technologies and of the more effective management of globalising
industries. Digitisation and processes, which are associated with Industry 4.0 can
provide opportunities for the relocation of manufacturing.[13] While low-labour
costs were a basis for the dislocation of many areas of simple mass production to
Newly Industrialising Countries, currently, there are tendencies for an even
more complex system of global division of labour. In some longer established
industrial areas a return of manufacturing is expected and, simultaneously, in less
innovative countries processes of industrialisation require a changing relationship
between low-cost manufacturing and the application of new technologies. There
might be situations where the introductions from early periods such as Industry
3.0, or even 2.0, can help to provide some innovation. Such a situation needs to
be complemented by organisation and management, which takes advantage
of new technologies, namely information and communication technologies.
Consequently, current situations do not provide early opportunities of early processes in less-developed countries to catch up with leading Western countries in
particular industries. The current situation, which allows for an introduction of
technologies from earlier periods of industrialisation, demands complementary
technological and managerial advances to cope with a continuously changing
and challenging globalisation.[14]

Again, contextualisation is decisive for innovation.[15] While a certain technology might be out-dated in leading innovative countries they can have an innovative impact in other situations where they are matched with low production costs
and cheap labour. But, modern technologies create a new relationship between
markets and consumers in a global division of labour. In particular information
and communication technologies introduce wide-ranging changes. Digitisation
characterises such changes in globalisation and, simultaneously, allows for a new
definition of tailored contributions, when the gig-economy helps to exploit
cheap university trained labour in less-developed countries. When jobs can be
'Taylorised' into pieces and result of their work can be transferred via internet,
consequently, then orders will go to locations and countries where this can be
achieved at low costs. Thus, new technologies associated with digitisation and
Industry 4.0 can be found in different situations, which refer to changes based
on diversities of innovation.[16] When particular arrangements of industries,
techno-scientific research, skills, markets and costs meet new technologies there
are different opportunities creating rich diversities of innovation.

Such processes frequently address existing markets with new, better and additional products but the formation of new markets creating a demand can also help to induce innovative solutions. While existing markets widely exclude people with small incomes from participation, in contrast, the formation of sufficient markets based on large numbers of people can create economically interesting opportunities. The different instruments and opportunities of government policies can help to create situations ready to apply improvements to services and make available technologies which were absent before.[17] Again, the relationship between existing socio-economic situations and innovation to improve these situations is important. The different situations when Western highly industrialised countries are compared to Newly Industrialised Countries (NICs), or even less-developed countries, provides a large area for improvement based on technologies, equipment or processes, which are outdated or inappropriate in more technologically advanced countries but can induce an innovative push and contribute to strengthen socio-economic development in other countries or regions. The context is important to understand what is considered to be an innovative process in a given context. Divergent socio-economic contexts clearly indicate divergent processes of innovation.

While these situations and processes are very different and often lagging far behind when looked at from leading-edge countries with advanced technological opportunities, nevertheless, these can be complemented by modern and current technological opportunities. Such combinations of less advanced equipment with appropriate new technologies make these innovative processes particularly individualised. It is not just to catch up through different phases of industrialisation and development, as currently leading countries did before, but it involves building their own markets and opportunities by benefitting from new technologies when applying those in situations where they match less advanced situations. Such contexts can be arranged through organisations which aim at collaboration and through government policies that take advantage of existing opportunities concerning diversities of innovation.[18] Organising markets, of course, is not just about introducing new technologies. This demands an idea or policies, which recognise the opportunities that exist in the situations they are facing. Such contexts do emerge in vital markets, but the character of the demand can also change to create more socio-economically advantageous markets.

Capable management and appropriate organisation play crucial roles in inducing innovation. The more complex such processes become the more obvious is the importance of non-technological contributions for effective implementation. The organisation of even a low-income population can provide a context that allows for better medical services, which is a significant improvement, although they may not yet be as state-of-the-art as in leading western countries. Organisation and management is clearly important for providing a context which allows for innovation. Similarly, although it is a very different situation, the highly complex organisation of aircraft industries with all their suppliers and application of new technologies and materials provides an example that refers to the demand for particular structures in management and how these allow for the formation of the context required for innovation.[19] They need to take the opportunities to transform the context and to induce new and innovative situations. Thus, almost any kind of demand can provide opportunities for innovation and modernisation once these are organised to form a situation that creates new markets for products and services. New technologies help to manage this by building linkages across countries and continents, which create divergent processes of innovation according to the context they encounter (Hickie and Hilpert 2016).

Consequently, innovation varies due to its character in relation to both the kind and level of technology. Innovation does not exclusively follow from leading-edge technology and findings. It can also be generated by the application of existing technologies in different situations. Even such technologies, which may be outdated in leading western locations and countries can help to advance other situations. Nevertheless, the combination with some recent technologies (e.g. communication and information technologies or biotechnologies) indicates particular new processes for development. Although this may help some of developing countries or regions to identify their potential of innovation, it clearly indicates that such processes are highly embedded into the global processes. While leading-edge research and technologies build networks of innovation based on collaboration in research as well as in economic exploitation, even the processes, which can be identified in such less-developed situations demand complementarity in globally available technologies.[20] Although there are particular opportunities for national or regional policies it is obvious that the national or regional identification of innovative opportunities always includes the global environment of both available technologies and markets. Such phenomena emerge from constellations of individual situations and how these are embedded into a global environment.

Societies matter for socio-economic development

Industrial structures and innovative processes require particular competences and skills in the labour force. The better the skills and the more those match the requirements of modern industries and advanced products, the better are the opportunities for innovation.[21] Complex products with high value added, in general, need matching labour of high competence. It is important to understand the relationship between such labour and opportunities for innovation. While there are additional opportunities from applying new technologies, new materials or finding new areas of application, there are also regional situations characterised by a particular mix of industries, enterprises and labour force. Consequently, innovation is not just based on research, enterprises and industrial structures but simultaneously requires social structures, which are characterised by skilled labour. A mismatch of skills clearly limits the opportunities for beneficial economic effects based on manufacturing, whereas a rich variety of skills and competent enterprises increases the opportunities for applications, which allow for a transfer of innovative competences across industries as a basis of new solutions, improvements and new products.[22]

It is a match of industrial structures, products and the skills of the labour force, which helps to identify innovative opportunities. While most advanced industries, and the continuous upgrading of skills and the rising percentage of highly skilled personnel within the labour force, help to apply most complex technologies and advanced manufacturing processes; it is also clear that less advanced industries cannot take advantage of higher skills to a similar extent. Migration of such labour can be identified. This is well known among knowledge workers, researchers and academics. Countries such as India and Italy are constant exporters of university-educated labour and those holding a PhD (Khadira 2001; Murano-Foadi and Foadi 2003; Ackers 2005; Laudel 2005; Marginson 2006). There is a frequent and constant exchange of personnel following the locations of Islands of Innovation and building a network among the regional innovative labour markets which widely converge with networks of collaboration concerning techno-scientific research and the economic exploitation of new technologies. (Hilpert and Lawton Smith 2013; Trippl 2013). Consequently, particular innovative regional or metropolitan societies are characterised by rather specific social structures, which require highly skilled people and a significantly higher proportion of population from abroad.[23]

Societies need to match the demand for both skilled blue-collar labour and university-educated labour in innovative industries.[24] Nevertheless, new technologies can also match the needs of particular locations, which are characterised by the needs of mass production industries. This may refer to textile and clothing industries as well as to the manufacturing of electronics products such as laptops or mobile phones. Low transaction costs and cheap unskilled labour continue to the advantage of China and the countries in South East Asia. Even rather custom-made production can be achieved despite geographic distances. Suits, shoes, shirts or rather simple metal products can be ordered to precise measurements and in particular via the internet, transmitting the precise information. Modern transportation systems help to reduce delivery periods and to provide markets close to the time of order. Three-dimensional measurements, transfer of the design and individual demands concerning material, outfit or variations can be transferred electronically and fabricated according to the customers' demands. Costs and prices for such products are reduced and, consequently, help to expand such markets. Similarly, costs of advanced electronic products (e.g. personal computers or smart phones) can be kept under control and meet the demands of markets rather spontaneously. Such transfer of information for manufacturing products can be conducted electronically. This helps to organise flexible manufacturing, In addition, the transportation of an individual product can be followed or steered according to changes in demand.

Similarly, in agricultural production, newly developed and highly fertile seeds can be applied without fundamental changes in the crop or harvest. While small farmers may not change their habits and local forms of agriculture may continue, they can take advantage of newly bred crops, which of course creates a market for such seeds in future. Also in industrially organised agriculture the work practices do not change a lot, but new seeds and new farming equipment are developed and applied. Even printing books and journals can be separated. While printing journals and books demanded typesetters, today print follows from computer-based work and does not require such competence at the location of the work. The final work and the typesetting are entirely different contributions and are realised in different places. There is no need to be capable reading or setting type when print can be realised on the basis of electronically transferred proofs.

Thus, when these new technologies are introduced, they need not to be complemented by social classes that have gained high-level skills and advanced education. Basically, the work that needs to be done has not changed a lot. Sewing high-end clothing, manufacturing expensive shoes, assembling smart phones or growing crops continues and demands little new or additional knowledge. Whereas management of such business and the organisation of work and manufacturing has widely changed because of new information systems, the electronic transmission of design or fast intercontinental transportation. Workers in factories or in the fields face rather marginal improvements of their skills. Whereas those who run and maintain the equipment or manage the processing of an order and contact with distant customers have to improve their work capabilities with regard to technologies, language and appropriate process organisation. Nevertheless, there is a rather limited social change towards higher skills and a well-educated population. Such organisation of economy and manufacturing, or growing crops, can merge with new technologies and contributes to a continuation of globalisation, which favours advanced industrialised countries as developers and providers of such technologies and products. Although the transfer of manufacturing competences through plants and assembly lines, for example the automobile, steel or chemical industries (e.g. in Mexico, Brazil, India) did help to establish such industries. On the other hand, it it did not help much to build a strong infrastructure in research and development or design. Industrialisation continues to be widely oriented towards simple products and thus has little impact on building innovative societies, which require higher skills and education.

Nevertheless, reverse engineering helped to introduce an aircraft industry in Brazil based on smaller airplanes. When copyright, licensing and patenting was ignored in China or India this has helped to develop industrial competences, as have well-known processes of foreign investments, which were made by enterprises from leading western countries. Within former Third World countries, locations emerged based on industries and labour and ready to develop markets on the basis of their own products and on their own competences in research, design and manufacturing. Personnel could become highly skilled and well educated and today form societal situations which continuously help to provide the labour demanded by the modern manufacturing of products, which relate to modern industries and higher value added.

Consequently, advanced industries can be established in such countries and the supply of jobs helps to keep skilled and university educated labour at these locations. Taking advantage of certain market opportunities was related to social change, which is characterised by the growing share of people with skills and the level of education required.

While this indicates that there is already development, which relates to particular opportunities provided by the diversity of innovation, it again demonstrates the importance of an appropriate workforce and the jobs created. Thus, India has managed to establish a particularly well-recognised development in Bangalore which started with the electronics industry and software. It became one of the centres of computer games in the world. In addition it is well known for its competence in biotechnology. Similarly, metropolises like Singapore, Shanghai, Beijing, Hong Kong, Seoul, Rio de Janeiro or Sao Paulo became recognised centres in biotechnology attracting gifted researchers, knowledge workers and academics to take jobs (Hilpert 2013a, 2016d). But, simultaneously, India is an example of a country, which constantly is an exporter of talent and university educated labour force. (Mahroum 2000b; Khadira 2001; Marginson 2006). The leading universities of the country produce graduates with a high international reputation.

Such individuals frequently aim to take attractive job opportunities abroad (predominantly in North America or Europe). Also well-educated engineers or researchers of East Asian origin leave their countries and frequently start enterprises (e.g. in Silicon Valley) or are highly recognised employees of innovative firms (Mahroum 1999; Saxenian 2002; Ackers 2005). Thus they contribute to innovative societal situations abroad and continue to do so because of a lack of jobs in their countries of origin or because they enjoy the different social culture they now live in.[25] Consequently, the match of innovative jobs with appropriately skilled and educated personnel helps to build a regional society, which is characterised by the agglomeration of such individuals, while in their home countries their contribution towards an innovative society is missed (Ackers 2005; Farwick 2009). Simultaneously, in the regional or metropolitan contexts where they migrate to, there is a clear tendency towards both an internationalisation of such locations and a population from different national and cultural backgrounds (Saxenian 2002; Ackers 2005; Regets 2007).

Within individual countries trans-regional migration of highly skilled blue-collar workers was already well known (Ackers 2005). After 1990, in Europe such highly skilled blue-collar labour became increasingly mobile because they were free to move to other countries such as Britain or Germany. Labour markets attract innovative personnel and help to supply the workforce, which is required for modern economic processes. Hiring such additional personnel is limited to the number of jobs to be filled and so will not necessarily balance the available jobs with the available labour force in regions and countries with an oversupply of skilled personnel.[26] Although this allows for a flow of skilled personnel a mismatch in the exporting regions or countries will continue due to the lack of appropriate jobs. Thus, skilled labour may exist in the exporting regions or countries but it needs to match industrial opportunities to support innovative processes. While innovation demands skilled labour to generate socio-economic effects, the labour needs to match opportunities of techno-industrial innovation.

Existing mismatches have serious effects on societies, because, existing skills cannot be exploited for innovation and higher value-added production. When labour markets for such employment are not available employers demand either additional education and further training or else jobs requiring less-skilled labour are filled with overqualified and experienced personnel (OECD 2017). A realisation of innovation and the generation of socio-economic effects needs a match of skills in the areas of modernisation. A labour force, which is formally well skilled but does not meet the areas of competences, which are required by modern and innovative industries, will not help such processes nor will make such places and attractive to locate advanced manufacturing. Focussing on university-trained labour, or on areas which are not currently demanded by such enterprises, will have neither a positive impact on socio-economic development nor on employment similar to that in leading countries or regions. The simultaneity of both innovative industries and innovative societies provides the basis for innovative processes because there is a match of industrial competences and a skilled labour force.

This highlights that it is not simply that skilled labour has to be available, but also that these skilled workers need to be suited to the innovative processes in their labour market. Given there is no match with the current opportunities there will be neither a strong enabling of existing industries and enterprises, nor will there be an attraction to locate particular areas of development and manufacturing to such places. While in well-matched situations, skills help to constantly modernise industrial structures,[27] this can hardly be noticed or expected where this match is missing. Thus, one can identify processes, which are the opposite to those based on established innovative societies. A continuing mismatch will reduce opportunities of innovation and induce a tendency to increasing societal polarisation. There is little innovation, less higher value added and only few can participate in this socio-economic development. Societies, which do not exhibit an innovative potential based on appropriate skills and education are at risk of falling behind and to have a growing population of skilled but inappropriately employed labour force.

While skills and education in innovative societies help individuals to participate in socio-economic development they cannot experience such a positive tendency in less innovative societies. Thus, the lack of attraction towards innovative industries to locate new plants and departments of research and development at such places introduces an attraction for particularly well-skilled and educated personnel to migrate to other places (Mahroum 2000a; Laudel 2005; Favell, Feldblum and Smith 2006; Marginson 2006). Consequently, locations, which are characterised by these situations, have strong disadvantages concerning opportunities for innovation because there is a lack of appropriate industrial structures and a problem with supplying the labour force which matches the demand for skills as a basis of innovation. This is a difficult situation, because skilled labour will not find jobs nor frequently stay in the region because of the existing labour markets. On the other hand, new job opportunities are hard to provide since enterprises will not open new plants nor will start-ups emerge in large numbers due to the lack of an appropriate labour force. Nevertheless, suitable social structures and societal situations can be arranged during processes of development.[28] Over a period of generations a matching can be effective, when combining industrial develop- ment based on advanced industries and higher values added with government policies, which support the constant development of a skilled labour force. This helps to establish a societal situation, which is characterised by well- educated individuals ready to fill jobs in innovative industries.

The availability of such labour is important to allow for both products with higher value added and complex technologies. When taking into consideration that innovative processes are clearly characterised by regionally divergent processes of innovation this also indicates that regional societies and innovative industrial regions need to create matches for such development. In particular, Islands of Innovation, which are frequently based in metropolises are also both participating in, and contributing to, continental and global networks. Competences and products are exchanged as well as innovative labour moving among the regionalised innovative labour markets and integrating into both the innovative industries' labour forces and the metro- politan societies. Among these Islands of Innovation rather similar structures of both innovative industries and innovative societies have emerged and mutually contribute to innovative processes, which are widely globally and continentally embedded (Hilpert 2013a; Hickie and Hilpert 2016). A constant process of collaborative innovation within such networks of both R&D and economic exploitation has helped to further develop structures which are beneficial for all who participate in such exchanges. Established educational systems and universities, which are ready to provide graduates with the com- petences required enjoy support from public policies from different levels of government (Bercovitz and Feldman 2006).

While these are existing structures to be continued according to opportun- ities for innovation countries, regions and metropolises which aim at innovative processes, they will have to manage social change in a way that supplies the existing and emerging demand for a skilled and well-educated labour force. Societies which cannot build the skilled labour required will face problems in innovative development and consequently during future socio-economic devel- opment, providing attractive jobs and sustainable industrial structures. Those countries will generate an outward migration of highly skilled labour, which does not match the labour markets formed by the demand of enterprises and research institutions based in the sending region or country. Regional or metropolitan societies, which are characterised by a mismatch of skills will not have a positive impact on prosperity but may face frustration from those employed in jobs below their skills and competences. Thus, similar to divergent industries, technologies and traditions in academic research and cultures the societal situations of locations vary a lot and indicate additional diversities, which are important at a basic level and have to be taken into consideration when understanding or inducing processes of innovation which suit the existing situation.

Diversified innovation

There are many different situations and constellations, which influence the individual processes of innovation. The relationship and driving forces for such development differ according to existing situations and emerging opportunities. Thus, innovation can be identified both as a process and by its result. This means, that products, services or the organisation of innovative manufacturing play a role and indicate that industrial structures and enterprises matter. Different products, specialisation or divergent application of new technological opportunities indicate the diversities of such processes, which need to be understood to have a better idea of innovation in general. Consequently, specific competences provide a basis for innovation, which relate to the exchange of[29] knowledge and the synergy of collaborations for new products. Clusters indicate such differences (Lawton Smith and Waters 2005; Simonen and McCann 2008), but even more interesting than a regional concentration of particular enterprises are the innovative opportunities, which include particular technologies, competences, research and skills for marketable products. While these inhibit particular opportunities and address new areas of industrial development certain new technologies they may not respond to other technologies or opportunities. Geography is an indicator for (Bercovitz and Feldman 2006) innovative processes, which exist in some situations or are not available in other constellations. It relates to on-going processes and indicates which enterprises and competences are included or related by collaboration in spite of geographic distance.[30]

Industrial sectors and competences, traditions in technologies and academic research or markets, which are supplied, are important to identify how diverse the geography of innovation is and where regions or metropolises can participate. It helps to visualise the diversity, but the process itself requires a workforce that is ready to manufacture innovative products or to offer innovative services. Highly skilled blue-collar labour, experienced knowledge workers and engineers, or gifted academics are not located in a geographically even distribution, although the general structures as indicated before may be similar. The uneven distribution of a workforce and differences among regional societies in the orientation towards skills and education indicate additional diversities concerning socio-economic development based on the exploitation of innovation and technologies. Although regions and their structures may tend to be similar due to such societal differences and the existing labour force there are significant differences in coping with technological change and innovative processes (Hilpert 1992). Regional or metropolitan societies of highly skilled and well-educated workers provide a fundamental basis for such modern socio-economic processes. Shared attitudes of workers and entrepreneurs towards new technologies, and continuing change based on innovation associated with permanent adjustment and the modernisation of competences, allow firms and regions to take advantage of such changes much more spontaneously than orientations towards keeping and protecting established situations and structures.

Such a situation, which provides for the structure required and the labour force to realise the socio-economic development is embedded in a particular context. The process can have its positive effects only if both collaborators for academic research and for industrial R&D are available. Leading-edge research reaches out into new areas. While established areas of research have already formed their centres of excellence and provide for university-educated labour, new areas are based on a rather small scientific community, which has just emerged and is still limited by the number of institutions and individuals involved. Consequently, the lack of an academic labour force of a particular region or metropolis is balanced by the most efficient exploitation of those knowledge workers, researchers or academics who are ready for collaboration. International networks are formed to collaborate on such new research questions (Criscuolo 2005) followed by new findings, which are generated within such networks. Since these initiatives provide the basis for spin-off enterprises and start-up firms there are also economic partners emerging for collaboration on marketable products (Simonen and McCann 2008; Breschi and Lissoni 2009; Hilpert 2013b). Thus the context is widely influenced by the relationship with an international situation of collaboration and competence on the one hand, and marketable products on the other hand.

Thus, even technologies, equipment or skills, which are not state of the art, can induce innovative processes, when compared with the previous situation. The context and situation in the light of production costs can form constellations of resources, which are considered as an innovative improvement when compared with a previous situation. Similarly, services can be regarded as innovative in a particular context although they may not be state-of-the-art.[31] The arrangement of a context by forming markets even on a national basis can help to generate innovative improvements and can contribute to solutions of problems or standards of living. Although innovation is frequently understood in relation to state-of-the-art technology, products or services, using less advanced technologies can also have favourable socio-economic outcomes, provided they are addressed to the satisfaction of current market needs. The embeddedness of such situations and their relationship with markets helps to create innovative initiatives, although such technologies, organisations or markets in leading-edge contexts are outdated and may refer back to quite old industrial history. The implementation of technologies and the organisation of manufacturing, which are not at the state of Industry 4.0, are perfect examples to understand why these may be innovative in other situations.

Processes of development are understood in the light of these situations and existing opportunities. Since technologies or typical periods of industrial development can be identified along long waves they can be at different levels of innovation although they refer to similar technologies (e.g. cars, machines, electronics). Innovation and change are rather closely related. Although the context is important for what is considered to be of innovative impact, clearly, there can also be an application which is more at the fore-front of innovation or which refers to maturation of a technology. Positions of countries, regions or metropolises differ by industries, technologies and over time during periods of socio-economic development. The relationship between the level of innovation and both the situation and the context characterised by a particular point in time is important to develop a deeper understanding of processes of innovation. This helps to identify the emer-gence of opportunities, the continuation in a different context and the change of opportunities in processes of development and change.

In taking this into consideration there is a clear relationship with societal structures characterised by increasing social classes with high-level skills and education as a basis for innovation. This indicates the positioning of countries and industries during such developments of long waves[32] and the relationship with the time to change social structures according to the demand for a higher-skilled labour force for advanced jobs. Innovative soci-eties are characterised by permanent change towards skills and university education by gross numbers, share of the labour force, social classes and gender. While there is discussion about the demand for human capital by innovative industries it needs to be understood that to realise innovative processes such a labour force needs to be developed prior to the demand for it. Again, time and processes of development are to be understood in the light of innovative processes, which follow to, and from, such structures and opportunities.

Consequently, innovation is characterised by its diversity of sources, situations, contexts and processes over time. In addition there are differences concerning industries, research findings, available skills and social cultures, which influence how such processes are realised and become empirically identifiable. This also refers to the rich diversity of processes and opportun-ities for innovation allowing countries, regions or metropolises to position themselves according to their potentials and contexts. When understanding innovation as a process it allows for learning about the interrelationship among its different elements and how these contribute at a particular point in time, while understanding the context and driving forces. Government policies support different activities (e.g. scientific research, industrial change, skills and education, markets and trade) focussing on particular industries, technologies or skills. A closer look into the diversities of innovation will help to both understand why these cases are so highly specific and, simultaneously, to get a better idea of the general innovation process and how it is inhibited by the empirical diversities.

Notes

1 See the contribution by Michael Vassiliadis. See also the problem of lacking skills and the difference between basic education and skills acquired through training on the job in the contribution by Paul M.A. Baker, Matej Drev and Mariza Almeida. Although a basic education is fundamental to develop a skilled labour force, the system of gaining skills is important for the innovative processes to be realised or to participate in.

2 For the relationship between industrial development, societal change and education see also the contribution by Sunyang Chung to this book.

3 Concerning the role of metropolitan situations and the clustering or concentration of competences and innovative industries see the contribution by Alberto Bramanti.

4 For a better understanding of the role of metropolises and the collaboration among such agglomerations see also the contribution by Xiangdong Chen, Ruixi Li, Xin Niu and Valerie Hunstock to this book

5 See the contribution by Walter Scherrer on long waves of economic development, when thinking about where a particular country or industry is positioned during processes of innovation and maturing of industry.

6 See the chapter by Alberto Bramanti on the contribution of innovation to existing industrial structures and their future development.

7 See the contributions by Michael Vassiliadis and the one by Paul M.A. Baker, Matej Drev and Mariza Almeida on the role of innovative and skilled labour for modern industries.

8 See the contribution by Desmond Hickie, Neil Jones and Florian Schloderer on the importance matching both innovative opportunities and market opportunities.

9 See the chapter by Alberto Bramanti on how such innovative opportunities can contribute to existing industries and potential products.

10 See the contribution by Marc-Alain Rieu referring to the increasing demand for collaboration because of the intensive competition on new technologies and new products applying new technological opportunities. Consequently, academic research and economic exploitation is becoming more and more transnational continental or global.

11 Concerning the strong contribution of highly skilled labour and blue-collar workers for socio-economic effects of innovation see the chapter by Michael Vassiliadis.

12 Concerning the relevance of context for research and innovative ideas see also the contribution by Alain-Mar Rieu.

13 See also the references of Alberto Bramanti in his chapter concerning opportunities of Industry 4.0.

14 Regarding the demand for constant modernisation and implementation of new technologies, materials or management techniques see the chapter by Desmond Hickie, Neil Jones and Florian Schloderer.

15 Concerning the importance of context for innovation and the diversity of such situations see the chapters by William O'Gorman and Willie Donnelly also by Torsten Schunder and Sharmistha Bagchi-Sen.

16 concerning government policies on innovation and some expectations on Industry 4.0 see Alberto Bramanti's chapter.

17 Se the chapter by Torsten Schunder and Sharmistha Bagchi-Sen concerning the organisation for better health services and the availability of modern instruments.

18 See the contribution by Alian-Marc Rieu concerning the importance of diversity as a requirement of creative investigation.

19 Concerning the importance of management to realise innovation see the Chapter by Desmond Hickie, Neil Jones and Florian Schloderer with regard to the specific challenges of aircraft industry. In addition, organising a proper context and

managing a particular situation which may not immediately be understood as fundamental to innovation see the chapter by Torsten Schunder and Sharmistha Bagchi-Sen.

20 For the demand for collaboration see also the contribution by Alain-Marc Rieu.
21 See the chapter by Michael Vassiliadis for the contribution of innovative labour for advanced socio-economic development.
22 See the chapter by Connie L. McNeely on the important contribution of diverse social and professional backgrounds to finding new opportunities of innovation, application and economic exploitation.
23 Concerning the relationship between industrial structures and the societal situation which provides for the skilled labour required see the chapter by Alberto Branmanti.
24 See the contribution by Francesco D. Sandulli and Elena Gimenez Fernandez on the problems of mismatching skills and demands on the labour markets, when there is an oversupply of skilled labour.
25 Concerning the role of both a culturally diverse labour force and situation in enterprises see the contribution of Connie L. McNeely.
26 See the chapter by Francesco Sandulli and ... concerning the importance of skilled labour and the problem of a mismatch between industrial structure and labour markets.
27 See the chapter of Michael Vassiliadis on the importance of a skilled labour force regarding innovative processes and constant industrial modernisation.
28 Concerning the role of highly skilled labour for societal change and the role of processes of innovation for industrial change see also the contribution by Sunyang Chung to this book.
29 Concerning the risk of similar research strategies and standardisation of research and development of new producers see the chapter by Alian-Marc Rieu
30 Concerning the decreasing need for geographic proximity and the increasing collaboration despite geographic distance see also the chapters by Xiangdong Chen, Ruixi Li, Xin Niu and Valerie Hunstock and by Alain-Marc Rieu.
31 For the innovative effect of contributions which may not be state of the art see the chapter by Torsten Schunder and Sharmistha Bagchi-Sen on the origination of a new context to improve the situation, which will be considered as innovative by those who can enjoy the new and better medical services.
32 For the development of the the long waves see the contribution by Walter Scherrer to this book.

References

Abel, J. and Deitz, R. 2009: Do colleges and universities increase their regions human capital? Federal Reserve Bank of New York: Staff Reports No. 401.

Ackers, L. 2005: Moving people and knowledge: scientific mobility in the European Union. In: *International Migration*, 43 (5), 99–131.

Bagchi-Sen, S. and Kedron, P. 2016: Governance of biofuel production in the United States. In: Hilpert, U. (Ed.): *Handbook of Politics and Technology*, Routledge Ltd., London and New York, 299–309.

Bellini, N. and Pasquinelli, C. 2016: Branding the innovation place: managing the soft infrastructure of innovation. In: Hilpert, U. (Ed.): *Handbook of Politics and Technology*, Routledge Ltd., London and New York, 79–90.

Bercovitz, J. and Feldman, M. 2006: Entrepreneurial universities and technology transfer: a conceptual framework for understanding knowledge-based economic development. In: *Journal of Technology Transfer*, 31, 175–188.

Berry, C. and Glaeser, E. 2005: The divergence of human capital levels across cities. In: Harvard University, Taubman Center Research, Working Papers, WP05-03, Cambridge, MA.

Breschi, S. and Lissoni, F. 2009: Mobility of skilled workers and co-invention networks: an autonomy of localized knowledge flows. In: *Journal of Economic Geography*, 9, 439–468.

Chung, S. 2016: Korean government and science technology development. In: Hilpert, U. (Ed.): *Handbook of Politics and Technology*, Routledge Ltd., London and New York, 222–235.

Coulombe, S. and Tremblay, J.-F. 2009: Migration and skills disparities across Canadian provinces. In: *Regional Studies*, 43 (1), 5–18.

Criscuolo, P. 2005: On the road again: research mobility inside the R&D network. In: *Research Policy*, 34, 1350–1365.

Dhéret, C., Morosi, M., Frontini, A., Hedberg, A. and Pardo, R. 2014: Towards a new industrial policy for Europe. In: ECP Issue Paper No 78, November.

Dolphin, T. 2015: *Technology, Globalisation and the Future of Work in Europe*. Essays on Employment in a Digitised Economy. IPPR, London.

Farwick, A. 2009: Internal migration, challenges and perspectives for the research infrastructure. In: Working Paper 97, Berlin: German Council for Social and Economic Data (RatSWD).

Favell, A., Feldblum, M. and Smith, M.P. 2006: Mobility, migration and technology workers: an introduction. In: *Knowledge Technology and Policy*, 29 (3), 3–6.

Franco, A.M. and Filson, D. 2000: Knowledge diffusion through employee mobility. In: Federal Reserve Bank of Minneapolis: Research Department Report 272, Minneapolis: Federal Reserve Bank of Minneapolis.

Hickie, D. 2006: Knowledge and competitiveness in the Aerospace industry: the cases of Toulouse, Seattle and North-West England. In: *European Planning Studies* (EPS), 14 (5), 697–716.

Hickie, D. 2016: Competition in international automotive and aircraft technologies. In: Hilpert, U. (Ed.): *Handbook of Politics and Technology*, Routledge Ltd., London and New York, 310–322.

Hickie, D. and Hilpert, U. 2016: Transatlantic comparison of continental innovation models: a differentiation of regionalised processes of innovation in Europe and the US. In: Hilpert, U. (Ed.): *Handbook of Politics and Technology*, Routledge Ltd., London and New York, 37–49.

Hilpert, U. 1991: *Regional Innovation and Decentralization. High tech industry and government policy*. Routledge Ltd., London and New York, 320.

Hilpert, U. 1992: *Archipelago Europe – Islands of Innovation*. Synthesis Report. Brussels: Commission of the European Communities, XII/411/92, 290.

Hilpert, U. 2006: Knowledge in the region: development based on tradition, culture and change. In: *European Planning Studies*, 14 (5), 581–599.

Hilpert, U. 2013a: Networking innovative regional labour markets. Towards spatial concentration and mutual exchange of competence, knowledge and synergy. In: Hilpert, U. and Lawton Smith, H. (Eds.): *Networking Regionalised Innovative Labour Markets*, 3–31. Routledge Ltd., London and New York.

Hilpert, U. 2013b: Labour for regional innovation. The role of researchers for development and patterns of recruitment. In: Hilpert, U. and Lawton Smith, H. (Eds.): *Networking Regionalised Innovative Labour Markets*, 35–57. Routledge Ltd., London and New York.

Hilpert, U. 2016a: *Handbook of Politics and Technology.* Routledge Ltd., London and New York, xxiii + 491.

Hilpert, U. 2016b: Changing opportunities in global and regional contexts: the relationship between politics and technology. In: Hilpert, U. (Ed.): *Handbook of Politics and Technology,* Routledge Ltd., London and New York, 1–34. intro.

Hilpert, U. 2016c: The culture-technology nexus: innovation, policy and successful metropolis. In: Hilpert, U. (Ed.): *Handbook of Politics and Technology,* Routledge Ltd., London and New York, 149–161.

Hilpert, U. 2016d: Metropolitan locations in international high-tech networks: collaboration and exchange of innovative labour as a basis for advanced socio-economic development. In: Hilpert, U. (Ed.): *Handbook of Politics and Technology,* Routledge Ltd., London and New York, 281–298.

Hilpert, U. and Lawton Smith, H. 2013: *Networking Regionalised Innovative Labour Markets.* Routledge Ltd., London and New York, 204.

Khadira, B. 2001: Shifting paradigms of globalization: the twenty-first century transition toward generics in skilled migration from India. In: *International Migration,* 39 (5), 45–71.

Laudel, G. 2005: Migrant currents among scientific elite. In: *Minerva,* 43, 377–395.

Lawton Smith, H. and Waters, R. 2005: Rates of turnover high-technology agglomerations: knowledge transfer in Oxfordshire and Cambridgeshire. In: *Area,* 37 (2), 189–198.

Lawton Smith, H. and Waters, R. 2013: High-technology local economies: geographical mbility of the highly sklled. In: Hilpert, U. and Lawton Smith, H. (Eds.): *Networking Regionalised Innovative Labour Markets,* Routledge Ltd., London and New York, 96–116.

Liu, X. 2016: China's path towards becoming a major world player in science and technology. In: Hilpert, U. (Ed.): *Handbook of Politics and Technology,* Routledge Ltd., London and New York, 380–395.

Mahroum, S. 1999: Global magnets: science and technology disciplines and departments in the United Kingdom. In: *Minerva,* 37, 379–390.

Mahroum, S. 2000a: Scientists and global spaces. In: *Technology and Society,* 22, 513–523.

Mahroum, S. 2000b: Scientific mobility: an agent of scientific expansion and institutional empowerment. In: *Science Communication,* 21, 367–378.

Marginson, S. 2006: Dynamics of national and global competition in higher education. In: *Higher Education,* 52, 1–39.

Marx, K. 1962 (1890): *Das Kapital. Kritik der politischen Ökonomie. Der Produktionsprozeß des Kapitals.* Vol. I, Marx Engels Werke, Bd. 23, Dietz Verlag, Berlin, 955.

Marx, K. 1963 (1893): *Das Kapital. Kritik der politischen Ökonomie. Der Zirkulationsprozeß des Kapitals.* Vol. II, Marx Engels Werke, Bd. 24, Dietz Verlag, Berlin, 559.

Marx, K. 1964 (1894): *Das Kapital. Kritik der politischen Ökonomie. Der Gesamtprozeß der kapitalistischen Produktion.* Vol. III, Marx Engels Werke, Bd. 25, Dietz Verlag, Berlin, 1007.

Murano-Foadi, S. and Foadi, J. 2003: Italian scientific migration: from brain exchange to brain drain. Paper presented on the Symposium on Science Policy, Mobility and Brain Drain in the EU and Candidate Countries at the Centre for Studies of Law and Policy in Europe. University of Leeds, July 27-28, 2003.

O'Sullivan, E., Mitchell N. 2013: International approaches to understanding the future of manufacturing. In: Future of Manufacturing Project: Evidence Paper, No 26. Government Office for Science, London.

OECD. 2017: *OECD Employment Outlook 2017*. OECD Publishing, Paris, 216.

Piore, M.J. and Sabel, C.F. 1984: *The Second Industrial Divide: Possibilities for Prosperity*. Basic Books, New York, NY, ix and 355.

Power, D. and Lundmark, M. 2004: Working through knowledge pools: market dynamics, the transference of knowledge and ideas and industrial clusters. In: *Urban Studies*, 41 (5/6), 1025–1044.

Regets, M. 2007: Research issues in the international migration of highly skilled workers. A perspective with data from the United States. In: Working Paper, SRS 07-203. Arlington, VA: Division of Science Resources Statistics, National Science Foundation.

Sabel, C.F., Herrigel, G., Kazis, R. and Deeg, R. 1991: Regional prosperities compared: Massachusetts and Baden-Württemberg. In: Hilpert, U. (Ed.): *1991. Regional Innovation and Decentralization: High tech industry and government policy*, Routledge Ltd., London and New York, 177–195.

Saxenian, A. 2002: Silicon valleys new immigrant high-growth entrepreneurs. In: *Economic Quarterly*, 16 (1), 20–31.

Simonen, J. and McCann, P. 2008: Firm innovation: the influence of R&D cooperation and the geography of human capital inputs. In: *Journal of Urban Economics*, 64 (1), 146–154.

Smith, A. 2008 (1776): *An Inquiry into the Nature and Causes of the Wealth of Nations*, ed. by K. Sunderland. Oxford Paperbacks, Oxford, UK, 688.

Trippl, M. 2013: Star scientists, islands of innovation and internationally networked labour markets. In: Hilpert, U. and Lawton Smith, H. (Eds.): *Networking Regionalised Innovative Labour Markets*, Routledge Ltd., London and New York, 58–77.

Tsui-Auch, L.S., Chia, S.I. and Liu, A. 2016: Putting Singapore on the global innovation map: the shifting role of the state in the rapidly changing environment. In: Hilpert, U. (Ed.): *Handbook of Politics and Technology*, Routledge Ltd., London and New York, 191–206.

Part II

General perspectives on divergent innovation

2 Skilled labour and continuing education

The role of the social partners for divergent opportunities of innovation

Michael Vassiliadis

Introduction

In the late 1990s and early years of the turn of the century, Germany was often dubbed the "sick man of Europe" (e.g. Economist 2004). However, contrary to most other European countries and the United States, Germany did not see a serious increase in unemployment as a result of the financial and economic crisis in 2008 and 2009, despite a sharp decline in GDP. Yet just a short time later, in 2011, Germany reached an all-time high in exports with 1,738 billion US dollars. Despite the "Rise of the Others" (Zakaria 2009), the German economy stood its ground in the face of international competition. Nowadays, Germany is often referred to as an "economic superstar" (cf. Dustmann et al. 2014).

The deregulation of the Labour Market in the middle of the last decade resulted in unemployment and social security benefits being combined, cuts in unemployment benefits as well as the activating of measures under the banner of "challenge and support" and is now considered to be an economic blueprint for other countries affected by The Crisis. The so-called "Hartz-reforms" increased the pressure on certain employee groups and were in part responsible for the lowering of wage levels.

Both evaluations – of Germany as "economic superstar" and of the effects of the Hartz-reforms – seem highly exaggerated given international economic power shifts and the current challenges that Germany faces. In this presentation, I set out to argue that Germany's economic success cannot alone, nor primarily be explained by the so-called Hartz-reforms to labour market.

Much more important were the intact industrial structures and value chains, the high level of education of the employees, a varied research landscape and the specific characteristics of the German system of industrial relations. Although the collective bargaining law and the works constitutional law represent the legal framework of this system, its core and basis are, however, thousands and thousands of agreements and contracts between the three main actors: employers' associations, trade unions and works councils. In the last two decades, these three groups have searched for – and partly found – innovative solutions for new challenges in the face of German reunification and growing international competition.

Consequently, I will first describe the global shifts in the world economy and the solid performance of the German industry in the last two decades by means of selected indicators.

Secondly, I will briefly outline the "German Business Model (GBM)".

Thirdly, I will subsequently describe the strengths of the innovation system based on the link between vocational and academic qualifications.

Well-trained and continually updated employee skills and qualifications form – together with a varied research landscape – the precondition for an innovative industry location. Employees are not only a cost factor, but also a driving force for innovations. For the GBM, globalisation not only brings the opportunity or risk of relocating, but also a strengthening of the GBM's roots. This fact is not only recognized by the employers' side, but also by employees, employee representatives on supervisory boards and the trade union movement at large, all of whom are strongly supportive of innovation. Fourthly and finally, I would like to illustrate this development with some company examples.

Industrial production and global power shifts

In a current survey, IW, the Institute of the German Economy, points out that worldwide economic power has been concentrated in a group of 50 countries (G50) (IW 2015). In 1995, these 50 countries accounted for approximately 94 percent of worldwide GDP. Standing at 91 percent in 2012, this percentage has only slightly dropped.

The G50-countries can be divided into established and emerging countries. According to IW's count, the 26 established industrial countries constitute the OECD-countries minus Central and Eastern Europe and Turkey.

Based on this distinction, the following picture emerges:

- In 1995, the 26 traditional industrial countries still held a percentage of 81.4 percent of worldwide economic power. In 2012, the percentage was only 63.5 percent. This represented a drop by almost 20 percentage points.
- The emerging industrial nations, which according to IW include mainly China and Central and Eastern Europe, have particularly grown. Their percentage of the economic "cake" rose from 1.8 percent to 27.8 percent between 1995 and 2012.

Thus, we have seen an important power shift in the last two decades. Here, the established industrial countries have lost significant ground in the industrial value chain and worldwide trade:

- Between 1995 and 2012 the percentage of the industrial value chain held by the established industrial G50 countries fell from 83.8 percent to 58.7 percent.

- Moreover, world trade was lost: the emerging countries improved their worldwide percentage from 14.3 percent to 25.1 percent.

In short, after the end of the East-West conflict at the beginning of the 1990s, the established industrial countries faced new competition from Central and Eastern Europe as well as in the emerging nations. China has been the main driving force in this process. IW states: "Of all the gains in percentage in the gross value added in the processing industry, China accounts for more than half. With exports, the Chinese contribution is at around 60 percent" (IW 2015, p. 11).

Even without China's exceptional development, the global power shift would probably have occurred, but to a much lesser degree.

The percentage lost by the established countries is, however, only one side of the global power shift. On the other side, the companies in the established industrial countries have gained new markets in the emerging markets. The share of imports for the emerging countries has risen from 13 percent in 2004 to 25 percent in 2012. Companies in the established countries have benefitted from this additional demand, at least in absolute terms.

The established industrial countries have seen absolute growth in recent decades.

Although they have lost percentage-wise in relative terms, they have benefited from the growth in the emerging economies and the opening-up of new markets. IW estimates this gain at around 347 billion US dollars (without taking into account the textile and leather industry).

Germany's gain amounts to a total of 140 billion US dollars, even though the country has been hit by a relative loss in the worldwide industrial value chain, where Germany's share fell from 9.2 percent to 6.3 percent between 1995 and 2012. However, IW states that:

> through the strong growth effects in the emerging nations, German industry was able to hold its own. Between 1995 and 2012, the industrial value added in Germany grew by 37 percent, whereas it fell by seven percent in Japan over the corresponding period. In France it fell by just 3 percent and increased by 9 percent in Great Britain.
>
> (IW 2015, p. 12).

Therefore, the question is: how can we explain the enormous growth of 37 percent in Germany? IW points to the "GBM".

The German business model (GBM)

Germany traditionally has a strong and broad-based industry sector with many small and medium-sized enterprises – the so-called "Mittelstand". The 5.6 million people working in these industries generate almost one quarter of the gross value added. No other industrial nation within the OECD achieves such a high and stable percentage of economic performance from equivalent sectors.

Sound economic supplier networks and clusters contribute to the fact that German industry was, and is, able to maintain a technological and economic edge and to be successful globally due to a strong technological and innovation orientation.

Worldwide, German companies play a leading role in many key sectors of industry, such as the car industry, mechanical engineering and plant engineering, in aviation, electrical power generation as well as in the chemical and pharmaceutical industries and their supplier industries. Their innovative power is high due to intensive cooperation with the sciences.

We often overlook the fact that Germany also has a strong position in Information and Communication Technology/ICT. This economic sector, however, is less end-consumer oriented than in American IT companies. German IT companies are more focussed towards other businesses. With approximately one million employees, the ICT sector occupies 5th place worldwide, according to a monitoring report by the Federal Economic Ministry. This sector contributes more to the value chain than mechanical engineering and slightly less than the car industry (BMWi Monitoringbericht, 2014).

The oft-stated impression that Germany produces only in the medium or high-technological area is also only partly correct. It is true that we have seen a trend in the last two decades that "simple workplaces" or "simple production processes" have more and more frequently been relocated to other countries.

The production of chemical precursors, however, has been retained in more than 800 German-based chemical companies. This sector or cluster is both primary and special, providing synergies to numerous other industrial value chains such as the plastics industry, mechanical engineering and the car industry. Germany is one of the few countries worldwide that have a strong primary chemicals industry as well as a large speciality chemistry industry (VCI 2013; Voß 2013).

The products in the traditional ceramics industry also contribute to the fact that Germany's value chain percentage of the iPhone is higher than China's (OECD 2013). In addition, there are still some so-called "simple" production processes and workplaces in Germany, although their number is decreasing.

On this broad economic base, exports towards the emerging nations has developed more favourably in Germany than in the remaining established countries.

"Germany could only hold its export share towards the target countries in (South) East Asia, while the German percentage of all imports into the other emerging nations decreased" (IW 2015, p. 13). Due to the abovementioned growth effect in the emerging nations, Germany has still been able to increase its exports into these countries in absolute terms.

Gaining export share in several emerging countries was only achieved by South Korea; which is considered an established industrial country, according to the IW. Other traditional industrial countries, such as Japan, France and Great Britain partly experienced strong downturns in their corresponding market positions (IW 2015, p. 13).

When considering Germany's strength, the experience and process of German reunification is a factor which must not be underestimated. The collective pay structure came under considerable pressure in 1990, when a large number of skilled workers from the former GDR joined the country, which started a process of adaptation.

One has to say in advance that remuneration, working time and other components of collective agreements are negotiated autonomously between the trade unions and the employers' associations at the regional and industry sector levels. Government intervention has only recently been allowed with the adoption of the minimum wage.

Works councils are heavily involved in the collective bargaining process. Thus, all actors can directly contribute to the co-operative process based on their unique and current perspectives and views on distribution options and challenges. An important result of this process it the fact that collective agreements in Germany are much more consensual and perceived as less confrontational than in other countries. The principle of autonomous collective bargaining is the essential mainstay of social partnership.

When the costs of reunification increased dramatically, and the national and federal budgets became more precarious [and government options for intervention became more limited with increased competition from Central and Eastern European countries resulting in increased unemployment], a strategic change occurred in Germany. To save endangered jobs, it was mainly the industrial unions who opened up the collective agreements in the early to mid-90s via so-called "opening" or "hardship" clauses (cf. Bispinck et al. 2010). Companies with economic or financial difficulties could then fall below the traditional level set by collective regulations for a limited period of time, if the works council and the respective trade union could reach agreement on such a course of action.

It is true that these "hardship clauses" resulted in growing inequality in income growth. It strengthened, however, the international competitiveness of many companies and innumerable Germany-based jobs were saved. As diverse collective agreements often involved restructuring and innovative concepts on the employers' side, the influence of the employee representatives on the economic development of the company, and the innovation process itself, grew.

Many employees and works councillors take the question of product and process innovation very seriously. Innovations enable companies to emerge stronger from the crisis and to participate early in the economic recovery through new marketable products. Product innovations, service innovations, organisational and technical process innovations are important components of long-term corporate success.

For IG BCE, the Industrial Mining, Chemistry and Energy Union, innovations represent the key to our country remaining at the forefront in an era of globalisation and realisation of sustainable development. We need innovation on a broad level – in research and development, technology and production methods and in the organisation of work. Innovations have to respect the economic, social and ecological balance. Therefore, IG BCE measures innovations by the extent to which they contribute to social, economic and ecological progress. This means, in particular, safeguarding and creating resource-saving workplaces.

The flexible collective options described above represented an essential reason why Germany was able to cope better with the financial and economic crisis than other countries. On the one hand, there were established procedures between employers, trade unions and works councils to deal with the Crisis. On the other hand, the government created the conditions for securing qualified workplaces in the short-to-medium term by broadening the regulations for structural short-time working to 24 months and with the introduction of a Keynesian-like programme which boosted the purchasing of cars by means of a scrapping bonus.

The solutions that companies introduced were generally accepted by the workforce, as they involved a time limit. The industrial relations system proved solid.

Strengthening innovation systems by combining vocational and academic qualifications

The German production and innovation model in the industrial sector is grounded in a particular combination of highly qualified graduates (mostly in natural sciences and engineering) from higher education institutions with highly trained skilled workers from the dual vocational system. This serves to avoid the constraints and imbalance of reliance on purely academic knowledge, which is often seen in other countries' business models. Instead, there is a fusion of diverse and high quality levels of skill and understanding.

This fusion combines vocational skills with process-oriented competency to application-oriented analytical skills and abstract theoretical–analytical knowledge. An essential part of the success of the German model stems from the close proximity between research and development and production, which goes hand in hand with a "spatial neighbourhood" of qualified skilled employees: from skilled workers of diverse disciplines, technical lab assistants and development engineers to chemists. High quality innovations result from, amongst other things, a common professional language spoken by differently qualified employees exchanging experiences and ideas through mutual and regular interchange.

A mix of skilled workers and higher education graduates shows the strongest innovation effects where knowledge exchange between different kinds of qualifications is supported by complementary human resources and organisational measures such as teamwork, job rotation and empowerment. The involvement of companies in the dual-vocational training system has an innovation-promoting effect. This training is designed and delivered by third-party training partners who are required to stay at the forefront of technological change and innovation. By doing so, it ensures that skilled employees are constantly invested in, gaining the most up-to-date qualifications and skills-sets.

I would like to focus in the following section on the third-largest sector of industry in Germany, the chemical industry. In this sector, special options have been developed. In the last three decades, a pragmatic model of social partnership has developed, which can serve as a role model.

On the basis of their constitutionally anchored mandate, the central task of the collective bargaining parties in the chemical industry is to regulate working and economic conditions. Through continually building and intensifying mutual trust, the Industrial Mining, Chemical and Energy Union and the Federal Employers' Association [BAVC] have developed, over a thirty-year period, a special form of cooperation; evolving from parties in conflict to those in cooperation and finally into social partners. They safeguard their respective interests and constantly have in mind their joint responsibility for the sustainable design of the chemical industry in particular, and society as a whole.

Social partnership as practiced today in the chemical industry is the most efficient and beneficial form of interaction between collective bargaining parties for the well-being of its membership. It expresses itself especially in updated centralised collective agreements, non-payscale social partner agreements, the joint institutions of the social partners as well through active participation from all stakeholders in the chemical sector's Social Dialogue.

Under the umbrella of Chemie[3] (Chemistry to the power of three) the Chemical Industry Association (VCI), the IG BCE and the Federal Employers' Association in the chemical industry strongly encourage sustainable development. A comprehensive understanding of sustainability is applied. The Chemie[3] initiative takes into account firstly, economic success as the basis for prosperity; secondly, the protection of man and the environment through environmentally friendly products and process solutions, high safety standards, product responsibility, intelligent efficiency and raw material strategies as well as, thirdly, via social responsibility.

A trademark of the chemical industry is the clear commitment to the dual vocational training as a core element of a sustainable HR policy. This commitment towards training also finds its expression in the collective bargaining policy of the social partners in the chemical sector. A collective agreement called **"A future through training"**, was concluded in 2003. It has been renewed several times and was re-developed in 2014 to become the collective agreement entitled **"A future through training and career start"**.

Some key data on training in the chemical sector are:

- over 28,000 trainees and dual students;
- about 1,000 companies providing training throughout Germany; and
- more than 50 different training occupations and numerous dual-study programmes – the spectrum ranges from natural sciences and technical and commercial occupations to training offers in the hospitality industry, IT and the Media.

The system of dual vocational training in companies and vocational schools represents the supporting pillar for skilled employees' assurance in Germany. Every year, the dual vocational training system creates career prospects for hundreds of thousands of young people and contributes successfully in times of demographic change to guaranteeing competitiveness and sustainability of home-based industry. It has gained widespread recognition internationally.

The chemical–pharmaceutical industry, with its 1,900 companies employing about 550,000 staff, relies on a well-functioning, dual vocational training system in order to secure qualified young employees. Currently, around 28,000 young people are being trained in 50 different occupations, more than two-thirds of these in natural science and technical training programmes. From the chemical social partners' point of view, the success and the high quality of the dual vocational training system in Germany is based to a large extent on the performance of, and cooperation with, the companies providing training and vocational schools. Practical skills are linked with theoretical knowledge, so that the employee can understand his/her task more comprehensively and can be flexibly employed.

Now more than ever, companies depend on qualified personnel. In the competition for suitable trainees, they face more and more challenges resulting from demographic change. Demographic change does not stop at the factory gate. More often than not, training places remain unoccupied and we hear more and more complaints about a lack of skilled employees. Companies not only need competent chemists, they also need smart lab technicians and motivated skilled employees of other disciplines. Only with a broad basis of qualified skilled employees and academics can the companies in the chemical industry remain successful and competitive in the long run.

The urgent problems of the future can only be tackled with a comprehensive strategy for the assurance of skilled employees. The offers in this field range from support for youths with learning difficulties via a continuous quality improvement programme in schools and higher education for the design of modern occupational training programmes that take into account the specific needs of young people. In addition, it is necessary to strengthen vocational training and further training in the companies and to considerably improve the finances, personnel and equipment of schools that are partners of the companies.

The chemical sector was the first to develop comprehensive answers to demographic challenges with its **collective demography agreement** concluded on 16 April 2008. The chemical sector formula for demographic change provides companies and their staff with a perfectly tailored tool. It contains four elements: demographic analysis, measures for a healthy and age/ageing-appropriate design of work processes, measures for qualification throughout one's working life and measures for (private) retirement provisions as well as the use of different instruments for a flexible transition between vocational training, working life and retirement phases. In practice, the agreement offers five tools that account for: long-term working time, part-time working for older workers, working incapacity supplementary insurance, partial pensions and collectively agreed pensions.

With the **collective agreement on qualifications**, which came into effect on 1 January 2004, employers and employees in the chemical industry are backing decisively the principle of life-long learning and corporate competitiveness.

The Optional Collective Agreement enables the corporate partners to agree on a well-planned and systematic qualification in the company. It provides a framework for designing company-specific qualifications and implementing them in voluntary plant agreements. To maintain and further develop the innovation power in this sector, the social partners bolster the collective agreement regulations for training and qualification with other initiatives and measures.

Despite all efforts, the German education system is undergoing substantial changes which also affect the abovementioned advantages of the German innovation system. The ratio of those in occupational training and higher education has dramatically shifted in recent years. Whereas 92 percent of young people started work with some form of vocational training in the middle of the 1960s and only 8 percent started with an academic qualification, there was for the first time in German history almost equal numbers of beginners in higher education (50.1 percent) as in the dual vocational training system (49.9 percent). On the other hand, there are fewer skilled workers who move up to become engineers through further training, which was often the case in the 1990s.

In order to maintain a broad basis of well-qualified skilled employees of different disciplines, and a good mix with academic graduates which is important for the Germany innovation system, a range of different measures and possible solutions present themselves:

1   First of all, it is important to invest in the continued preservation and further development of the attractiveness of the dual vocational training system. This must be guaranteed through the high quality of the training and its ongoing adaptation to the new challenges of the knowledge society.

2   Additionally, the strengths of the vocational training need to be better communicated to the outside world – especially towards foreign managers and other decision-makers, who do not know the dual vocational training system exists. To this end, the respective institutions of the vocational training system (social partners, Federal Institute for Education, companies, vocational schools and the national and federal governments) need to make improvements.

3   All institutions of the vocational training system are required to create sufficient entry opportunities for youths with weak school performance – either by offering traditional training places or – if necessary – through supporting measures for the transition into training.

4   For talented and ambitious young people who have completed their vocational training, there should be clear career perspectives by means of personal development options and increased transfer opportunities to the system of higher education.

Ultimately, only those enterprises who win the battle for the "best brains" will be successful. In a declaratory way, already today nearly every company publication refers to their workforce as their most important resource: The importance of having the right interaction between management and employees is increasingly emphasized. Many companies have introduced new concepts that "look after" the employees. These concepts grant employees more self-responsibility. Companies need and want a comprehensive commitment from their employees. Many companies have started to implement the organisational changes that are necessary in this respect.

Given these challenges, companies must have an interest in establishing a new equilibrium between the undeniable need for flexibility and a modern, rebalanced social security for the employees. Only then will companies be attractive for the new talent that they wish to recruit.

Skilled employees and academic personnel that are well-qualified, flexibly deployed and adaptable to challenges and change form the basis of the German innovation model.

The driving force of corporate co-determination

As mentioned above, the German system of co-determination and collective bargaining offers many possibilities for employees and works councillors to make a strong commitment to innovation. Besides the inventiveness of German companies and the efficient public research, it is above all the employees who contribute to Germany's economic success. An essential precondition for maintaining Germany's technological performance capability has been, and will remain, motivated and highly qualified employees.

According to a survey by Horváth & Partner (2009), employees are the most important driving force for innovation in companies. Accordingly, employees are the most important source of new ideas – even more so than managers, customers and business partners.

However, works councillors and employees only have the rights to information regarding innovation and investment planning – except in the case of the abovementioned agreements on restructuring concepts. They can only contribute to innovation proposals for securing jobs on the basis of Article 92a of the Works Constitution Act.

The co-determination rights of the employees' representatives on the Supervisory Boards are more comprehensive. "Transactions requiring approval" refers to decisions relating to the area under discussion, but also to strategic determinations. On the Supervisory Boards, innovations are included and this leads to the fact that the influence of employees' representatives on the innovation strategy of the companies can in certain cases be considerable.

In practice, however, works councillors also have – despite their limited rights – a variety of possibilities to co-design innovation policy in their companies. This role can be illustrated with the example of the energy and resource efficiency.

IG BCE is convinced that the change from a carbon and resource intensive path to climate-driven and socially acceptable economic growth has to be promoted. Energy and material efficiency are not only urgently needed from an ecological and climate-oriented point of view, but also from an economic and social perspective. The corresponding developments guarantee advantages in competition, market share and added value as well as increased income.

The federal government's energy policy envisages a 20 percent efficiency improvement by 2020 compared to 1990. The national sustainability strategy aims to double the raw material productivity over the same period. IG BCE believes that companies will only achieve such improvements in resource efficiency by a joint effort with employees and employees' representatives, as works councillors and employees are the experts in the workplace. They have comprehensive knowledge on how materials, water, energy and land use can be minimised. Often they have innovative ideas for new products, services and processes.

An operating company in a chemical industrial park can serve as an example. Between 2008 and 2012, this company (Currenta) tried to increase its energy efficiency by 20 percent within the framework of the "climate protection programme A++".

In this process, the sub-project "smart energy savers" was initiated in which employees were asked to come up with ideas for efficiency increases. In the end, 360 innovation proposals were submitted, addressing improvements in the most varied of areas. Upon the implementation of many of these proposals, an energy saving of 30 GWh/a (Giga Watt hours per year) or a reduction of CO_2-emission by 15,000 t was achieved. This volume corresponds to the emissions of about 10,000 private households in Germany. The employees' proposals resulted in about one tenth of the total energy efficiency increase in the company. To reach the corporate objective for energy saving, investment in the technology and modernisation of the waste air incineration plant, as well as in the common water treatment plant, were made and operational methods were optimised.

Another interesting example is the invention made by an employee who is also a works council member, who managed to produce new tyres from the buffings of old tyre treads by utilising a unique recycling technique. By doing so, the recycling percentage per tyre was almost doubled and rubber and fillers were saved to a large extent. Recently, the production process was tendered worldwide and Hannover, Germany won the contract for efficiency and cost reasons. Around 100 new jobs are being created as a result.

These cases reveal that one of the future tasks for trade unions will be to offer even more possibilities for works councillors to make an impact on the processes of corporate energy and resource efficiency. Employees and employees' representatives have to be actively involved in the corresponding restructuring processes. Only if the employees are able to accompany the restructuring of their workplaces in an active and qualified way, can sustainable corporate targets be achieved saves and creates jobs that fulfil the criteria of "Good Work".

Innovative development processes can only be put into practice in conjunction with, and not contrary to, the employees' active engagement. The works councillors and IG BCE have been making use of the advantages of a participation-oriented and project-oriented way of working to make sure that innovation processes meet with the required acceptance. In this way, the solutions become company related and also take into account the interests of the employees. Works councillors accomplish an essential task in cooperation with the union shop stewards for successfully changing processes in innovative companies. These results have been impressively confirmed in several recent surveys on employees' representation in innovation processes (cf. Kriegesmann and Kley 2012; Schwarz-Kocher et al. 2011).

Conclusions

Traditionally, Germany has a strong industrial base comprising a vital and diversified sector of medium-sized companies. The essential ingredient has been intact economic networks throughout the value chain. Continually updated forms of cooperation contribute to the fact that the German economy was, and still is, able to create temporary technological and economic advances and to remain ahead of the international competition through a strong orientation towards technology and innovation.

To secure the competitive edge over the international competition, innovation strength is required. Through major innovation investment and the broad involvement of employees, tailor-made solutions for customers are developed which often facilitate new and more efficient product lines. This technological and innovative edge represents a decisive advantage in competitive global markets. Only with better products and more efficient processes can the cost disadvantage of the German business model be achieved. The introduction and implementation of innovations is not an easy task. In open economies, other countries are quickly catching up on such technological advances.

The basis for the innovation processes is considerable investment in the education sector, in state-funded primary and applied research as well as corporate research and development. This triggers new technologies and their application to existing production and products. Current fields of innovation are biotechnology in medical engineering and measuring devices, microelectronics and mechanical engineering, new materials in car manufacturing as well as energy technology for the turnaround in energy policy. The orientation of the product strategy towards megatrends and sustainability creates competitive advantages.

The development of new technologies and the production of technology-intensive, high-tech products requires employees with high and constantly updated qualifications and skills. This forms – together with a diverse research landscape – the precondition for an innovative industrial base. Employees are not only a cost factor, but also a driving force for innovation.

The percentage of employees with an academic degree is constantly rising in Germany. The importance of research and development is growing and the transfer of scientific findings into industrial use and application is increasing. A country can only remain in pole position in science and technology if employees maintain and continually renew and improve their high levels of competency. The (international) exchange between researchers and engineers becomes an important precondition for participating in worldwide research networks and thus engendering this competitive edge. Continual first-rate education in universities is a fundamental prerequisite here.

The comparison between Europe and the USA points towards the importance of top-quality and high value-added industrial production. The competence for these developments lies in long traditions of innovation and in the constant ability of employees to work with these new products or components in the production process. Without a corresponding continuous investment in skilled employees' competences, such processes of technological-industrial innovation are impossible to achieve. "Blue-collar labour" thus becomes an essential component of success and helps to establish modern industrial structures.

Political and collective regulations form the basis for modern industrial systems. The importance of qualified employees at all levels of corporate organisations – independent of university degrees or vocational training – places educational policy and continuous training at the centre of modern industrial systems. Political policy which is translated into law that allows for further training as well as free access to scientific and technical education and training without tuition fees represents an important precondition for these innovation processes.

Complementary to the legal provisions, the trade unions in Germany have in recent years negotiated collective regulations for designing further training and the acquisition of additional skills and thus have laid the foundation for continuous corporate innovation processes. Building on basic knowledge from school education or qualifications for skilled employees, experience is linked with new skills and allows for a constant increase in productive quality and efficiency. Trade union strategies for the layout of collective agreements become important elements of innovation processes and for the use of new technologies.

Innovations are a result of research and development and its practical application in the production process. Current in-company empirical research has revealed that co-determination in Germany tends to have a positive impact on innovation processes. However, differences exist across industrial sectors depending on product types, company size and customer requirements. Regulation at the corporate level is needed, which a pragmatic social partnership can achieve. Collective agreements in the chemical industry are regarded as industry-leading in terms of flexibility, innovation and modernity.

Globalisation not only involves the risk of relocation, but also prospects for strengthening the homeland's industrial base. A growing world population makes for additional demands on energy, raw materials, food, clean water, drugs, communications and mobility. To satisfy these needs, innovations are increasingly necessary.

This fact is not only recognized by enterprises. Employees, employees' representatives and trade unions in Germany are increasingly promoting sustainable innovations. An orientation towards capital yield alone will not be enough to live up to the megatrends of the future. Only through a political and collectively agreed development of human resources is it possible to have a successful industrial society, which paves the way for common prosperity.

References

Bispinck, R., Dribbusch, H. and Schulten, T. 2010: *German Collective Bargaining in a European Perspective: Continuous Erosion or Re-Stabilisation of Multi-Employer Agreements?* WSI Discussion Paper, No. 171, Düsseldorf.

BMWi. 2014: *Monitoringbericht*, Bundesministerium für Wirtschaft und Energie, Monitoring-Report. Digitale Wirtschaft 2014, Innovationstreiber IKT, Berlin, December.

Dustmann, Ch., Fitzenberger, B., Schönberg, U. and Spitz-Oener, A. 2014: From Sick Man of Europe to Economic Superstar: Germany's Resurgent Economy. In: *Journal of Economic Perspective*, Vol. 28, Number 1, Winter 2014, 167–188.

Economist. 2004: *Germany on the Mend*, November 17. www.economist.com/node/3352024.

Horváth & Partner. 2009: Innovationsstudie, *Das verschwendete Innovationspotenzial – geniale Ideen im Unternehmen finden und nutzen.* Stuttgart, 9–16.

IW. 2015: Institut der deutschen Wirtschaft Köln Consult GmbH, *Globale Kräfteverschiebung. Kräfteverschiebung in der Weltwirtschaft – Wo steht die deutsche Industrie in der Globalisierung?* Studie im Auftrag des BDI, Köln.

Kriegesmann, B. and Kley, T. 2012. *Mitbestimmung als Innovationstreiber. Bestandsaufnahme, Konzepte und Handlungsperspektiven für Betriebsräte.* Berlin: edition sigma.

OECD. 2013: Interconnected Economies. Benefiting from global value Chains. Paris: OECD. https://www.oecd.org/sti/ind/interconnected-economies-GVCs-synthesis.pdf.

Schwarz-Kocher, M., Kirner, E., Dispan, J., Jäger, A., Richter, U., Seibold, B. and Weißfloch, U. 2011. *Interessenvertretungen im Innovationsprozess. Der Einfluss von Mitbestimmung und Beschäftigtenbeteiligung auf betriebliche Innovationen.* Berlin: edition sigma.

VCI. 2013: *Die deutsche chemische Industrie 2030.* VCI-Prognos-Studie, Frankfurt, January, 2013.

Voß, W. 2013: *Ressourceneffizienz als Herausforderung für Teilsegmente der Basischemie in Deutschland.* Ein Projekt im Auftrag der Hans-Böckler-Stiftung, Bremen, September, 2013.

Zakaria, F. 2009: *The Post-American World.* New York, 2008 (Deutsche Ausgabe: Der Aufstieg der Anderen: das postamerikanische Zeitalter, Munich: Siedler).

3 Surfing the *long wave*

Changing patterns of innovation in a long-term perspective

Walter Scherrer

The outset

The concept of *long waves* in the economy goes back to Kondratieff (1926/1935) and Van Gelderen (1913/1996) who suggested a link between "technological revolutions" and long-term economic development. Five technological revolutions have emerged since the coming of the industrial society in the late 18th century[1]; incremental innovations, cross-fertilization of industries, and imitation have led to a swarming of innovations and triggered a *surge of development*.[2,3] In such a concept, hence, innovation plays a key role for explaining long-term economic development.

In this chapter we analyze if, and how, the concept of long waves of economic development contributes to explaining the diversity of innovation and innovation policies which can be observed in the economy. Some features of innovation patterns might develop differently across waves and therefore are specific for an individual wave, while other elements might be repetitive in each wave more or less independent from the technologies which trigger and characterizes the wave. Therefore, from a long wave perspective the diversity of innovation can be analyzed along two avenues: first, the nature of innovation may vary *between* waves, and second, there may exist patterns which make the innovation process vary in distinct phases of the long wave *within* each wave.

Wave-specific innovation patterns

Studying the historic specifics of innovation, Sundbo (1995) identified three paradigms which are typical for describing the nature of the innovation process in three long waves. In the upswing of the third long wave innovation activity between the 1880s and early 1890s[4], was seen to be dominated by individual entrepreneurs who founded new companies that produced new goods for newly developed markets. This *"entrepreneurial paradigm"* resembles the early Schumpeterian mode of innovation ("Schumpeter Mark I") in which the entrepreneurial act is at the core of the innovation process.

During the fourth long wave (which started in the late 1930s) innovation was considered to be predominantly driven by large industrial firms. As introducing new products to the well-established markets in developed economies had become more difficult, firms focused on technical product development. Innovation activities were no longer primarily conducted by individual entrepreneurs but by highly esteemed engineers organized in the research and development departments of big companies. Within this *"technology-economic innovation paradigm"* (which closely resembles "Schumpeter Mark II"), technological possibilities, well identifiable trajectories of change, intra-firm interaction among multiple types of employees, and institutionalized routines determine innovation activity.

In the current fifth long wave according to Sundbo a *"strategic innovation paradigm"* was formed in the 1980s and 1990s in which innovation is less technology driven but more market driven. Market saturation in many developed economies, and the inability to meet the diversified demand of consumers in a technological framework which was largely based on mass production, made firms focus increasingly on markets. The innovation process thus has become determined by firms' strategies, and therefore it is the whole firm (and not only the R&D department) which contributes to the innovation process. Market analyses and strategic partnerships with other firms have become important, and the firm's interface with the market is crucial. While Sundbo (1995, 1998) focuses on strategy development at the firm level, the argument is coherent with the rising significance of the innovation system approaches which have emerged in the 1990s (Freeman 1987; Lundvall 1992; Nelson 1993), and which add to understanding innovation activity in the fifth long wave.

While those two innovation paradigms which have emerged in preceding waves (the entrepreneurial paradigm and the technology-economic paradigm) were typical for these waves, these paradigms have not been completely abandoned after waves faded out. In recent times they have played a strong role, particularly in building the information and communication industries which have triggered the fifth wave: On the one hand many fields of innovation at least initially have been dominated by deliberately entrepreneurial firms (e.g. Apple, Microsoft, Facebook), on the other hand the technology-economic-paradigmatic research and development activities of big corporations which have already long existed and which cooperate with universities in basic research have been important in the mobile phone industry (e.g. Nokia, Samsung). The strategic innovation paradigm therefore seems to be particularly relevant for explaining the diffusion of ICT to other industries during the fifth wave.

The paradigms of the earlier waves have also been developed further in later waves: E.g., the entrepreneurial paradigm has been extended towards "intrapreneurship": entrepreneurship may not only involve founding new firms but can be organized in a way that it can be accomplished also within existing firms. The technology-economic innovation paradigm has been extended to include firm-external expertise and customers into the innovation process and thus contains elements of systemic approaches.

The nature of the innovation process also differs between waves because of the different inherent characteristics of the new technologies which trigger the waves, and which require *different knowledge bases* which may give rise to diversities of innovation. Industries are dominated either by analytical, synthetic, or symbolic knowledge bases, although most industries also contain elements of non-dominating knowledge bases (Asheim *et al.* 2007). An analytical knowledge base refers to innovation activities in which scientific knowledge is highly important, in which cooperation between firms and research organisations is focused on basic research, and knowledge is highly codified. A synthetic knowledge base is characterized by innovation through applying and newly combining existing knowledge, by industry-university cooperation in applied engineering, and by tacit (i.e. non-codified) knowledge being particularly important. In industries in which a symbolic knowledge base is dominant, innovation is the result of creating meaning, aesthetic qualities and desire, and creating economic value by attaching certain attributes (symbols) to products and services.

Up to the fourth long wave, industries with a synthetic knowledge base were among the major triggers of the long wave dynamics: mechanical engineering (e.g. steam power, textile machinery, electrical engineering in waves number one to three) and manufacturing of advanced equipment for extractive industries (e.g. oil in the fourth wave, coal in prior ones) are typical industries in which synthetic knowledge bases dominate. The dominant synthetic knowledge bases required skills strongly based on concrete know-how, craft, and practical abilities; innovation policy therefore focused on providing or supporting professional schools and on-the-job-training.

The current fifth long wave which is driven by modern ICT is the first one in which analytical knowledge bases have dominated and in which symbolic knowledge bases (e.g. new media industries) are important, too. The dominant role of analytical knowledge bases and the prominent role of codified knowledge, along with the widespread use of ICT which diminished the importance of distance as an obstacle to communication and information exchange, have facilitated know-how exchange over long geographical distances. Therefore, compared to preceding long waves, for any country it has becomes easier in the fifth long wave to potentially benefit from the economic opportunities of new technology.

Obviously, the dissemination and availability of ICT infrastructure has also been important for enabling firms outside the ICT sector to use these technologies for its business and to develop synergies with their particular competences. Firms have extended systematic research and development efforts, and governments have developed and refined distinct technology and innovation policies. The mostly analytical knowledge base of the ICT industries has made policy focus more on basic research and formal education in order to support innovation activity. Strong positive externalities derive from building up and continuously upgrading ICT infrastructure, and not surprisingly this has become a major government task, at least in peripheral areas where market forces do not warrant the supply of such infrastructure. Beyond than merely providing a new infrastructure for business the triggering industries of the fifth wave (ICT) provide powerful means of information collection and processing which are used as a tool of innovation not in most other industries. While this potentially has accelerated the development and dissemination of new technologies and thereby provides another basis for diversities of innovation it is not yet clear if this will also speed up the long wave-dynamics. This will depend on the characteristics and perceived risks of future new technologies and the divergent opportunities which have an effect on the kind of application, on the willingness of society to adapt to technology-driven change, and on the way politics will respond.

Summing up, diversity of innovation has increased significantly in the current fifth long wave. This renders implications for innovation policy: with time passing by, the co-existence of competing innovation paradigms has enriched the toolbox of economic agents for shaping the innovation process. For innovation policy this poses a challenge because it is not clear which paradigm to follow and where to input its scarce resources.

Changing patterns of innovation during the phases of a long wave

A long wave starts with the emergence of a new *"techno-economic paradigm"* (TEP; Perez 1983, 2002)[5] which is more than just an innovation paradigm in Sundbo's sense but instead is a comprehensive paradigm which influences economic development as a whole. The diffusion of a TEP and the technologies which trigger a long wave may have complex ramifications as it depends on the actual and expected trajectory of their performance potential (Scherrer 2016). Frequently the new technology improves established technology, which makes firms tend to further develop the existing technological framework instead of investing in a new TEP with uncertain consequences. Policy makers might find it also attractive to stick to the existing development path based on the prevalent technological framework, at least in the short term, because there is less potentially conflict-ridden institutional change needed compared to introducing a wholly new TEP. Lock-in effects can aggravate this tendency, and long gestation periods of new technologies and their dependence upon the availability of complementary inputs may influence its diffusion (Rosenberg and Frischtak 1983, p. 147ff). The search for regularities of the innovation process along the phases of the wave therefore has to be seen against these complex timing issues.

Regularities of the innovation process exist although countries or regions are affected differently by the emergence of a new TEP and *national or regional policies may respond differently* to it (Scherrer 2016). Kondratieff (1926/1935) claimed that long waves occur almost simultaneously worldwide, Hirooka (2003) considers long waves as a technology leadership phenomenon with the possibility for lagging countries to catch up, and Goldstein (1988) holds that synchronization occurs among countries in similar stages of development.

Radical innovations are not ubiquitious but emerge concentrated only in a few places; such "islands of innovation" can persist over a period of at least 30 years (Hilpert 2003). At the same time, the emergence of a new TEP creates new opportunities particularly for newly industrializing countries and increases the potential for national public policies to support catching-up processes. The ICT-TEP provides a good example for innovation-based catching up being a viable strategy as the economic performance of some (mostly Asian) nations has shown.

The opportunities of national and regional economic agents and policy makers for establishing successful catching-up processes based on innovation are influenced by the impact of the new technologies on the dissemination of knowledge. Already in preceding waves, new communication and transportation technologies (e.g. telegraph, telephone, airplane) have facilitated and accelerated the dissemination of knowledge thereby allowing for diversities of innovation across countries. With the "new" information and communication technologies which have spread out during the current wave, joint research and innovation effort across countries has been further facilitated as they easily allow for: building international cooperation networks, co-publication, and co-patenting. For those countries and regions which are able to actively participate in such networks, in general, a more synchronized innovation activity is to be expected. This again allows for catching-up processes of countries to take place which did not succeed in benefitting from preceding long waves. However, institutional change at the international level seems to reduce the scope for individual state intervention in the recent wave (Castellacchi 2005, p. 32f) suggesting a mismatch between the techno-economic sub-system and the socio-institutional sub-system of society and indicating that divergent opportunities and divergent advantages of diversities of innovation exist.

The long wave-perspective on innovation suggests that the innovation process during a wave will take *a turn from financial market-driven innovation to demand for goods-driven innovation*. Firms will exploit existing technologies as long as they are sufficiently profitable and only when the productivity potential of technologies has diminished will they turn to radically new ways of doing business. This is the time when waves build up and are ready to be surfed! The interplay between "real economy" entrepreneurs and financial investors in the irruption and frenzy phases of the wave drives the innovation process and explains why major innovations occur in clusters although radical inventions are expected to be randomly distributed over time (Mensch 1979). In the later phases of the wave, incremental innovations and cost saving process innovations drive most of the scaling-up investment (Perez 2010) as production volume and productivity become crucial for market expansion. The change of the wave's driving force from a focus on the supply side (the development of new technologies fuelled by financial markets) to the demand side of the economy has major implications for economic policy that reach far beyond mere innovation policy with its focus on technology, research and development.

There is also some *phase-specific variation of the role of knowledge bases*. Historical evidence shows that, in principal, those industries which trigger a long wave (Freeman and Louçã 2001) basically can be dominated of any possible type of knowledge base: analytic, synthetic, or symbolic. The knowledge base within these industries coins the TEP at least in the early phases of a wave and the pattern of regional participation. Although in the later phases of a wave, when the new TEP spreads out, the (by then) already established technology will reach more and more sectors which are characterized by other knowledge bases than the ones in the triggering industries. Further, symbolic knowledge bases tend to become more prominent in later phases of a wave because processes, products, and services based on the established technologies will become commonplace, and hence value added can be increased by attaching symbolic value to goods and services (e.g. through branding).

The long wave-perspective further suggests that the innovation process during a wave will take *a turn from science-based[6] to technology-based innovation* (Hilpert 1991). This turn can be envisaged with a product-life cycle metaphor according to which a TEP undergoes – like products – a life cycle during the phases of a long wave as the wording of some phases ("irruption", "synergy", "maturity" phase) already suggests. Particularly in the early phases of the wave, the innovation is more science-based but as new technologies are increasingly applied in traditional products and industries technology-based innovation becomes more important in later phases (Scherrer 2016). This entails that the technical risks and uncertainties of the innovation process will be predominant in the early phases of the long wave and market risks will become relatively more important in the later phases. Diversities of innovation also emanate from the different opportunities of industries to participate in the absorption of newly emerging technologies. The shift from science-based to technology-based innovation during the dissemination of a TEP is of a general nature and seems to be particularly relevant in the fifth long wave which has been triggered by industries largely characterized by analytical knowledge bases.

Input factors and combinations of input factors which are required for efficient production on the basis of the new TEP vary along the phases of the wave thus impacting the preferential locations of production during the wave. In principal, such changes can emerge from regional differences in taxation, regulation, environmental conditions, labour cost, and other typical determinants of firms' choice of a business location. Concerning the change of business locations these factors tend to be strongest in the later phases of the long wave. The relative weight of *basic* research in the core fields of the prevailing TEP decreases during the wave compared to that of *applied* research. This facilitates the formation of new "islands of innovation" (Hilpert 2003) as geographical expressions of diversities of innovation. Strong investment in skill development will foster research capacities in the further development of those technologies which trigger the wave outside the already well-established islands of innovation. In the current long wave, the build-up of the mobile phone industry in South Korea is a good example.

The long wave-perspective on innovation also suggests some *variation in the degree of "openness" of innovation* during the wave. Systemic approaches to innovation consider innovation as "open" if the process of innovation does not take place within the boundaries of an individual firm but involves many other agents like customers, suppliers, research institutes, and universities. If knowledge is widely distributed across many different sources and if it is concentrated in sectors in which it is difficult to build up in-house capacities, then open innovation approaches are particularly important for expanding firms' capabilities and markets (Chesbrough and Crowther 2006). The degree of openness of innovation – which is also dependent on socio-cultural con-stellations – and its possible variation during a wave is important also from an innovation policy perspective as it has implications for the design of systems of innovation. In particular, a high degree of openness of innovation should let policy makers put more emphasis on systemic instruments of innovation policy in order to strengthen links between innovation agents.

In a long-wave perspective the irruption phase of a new TEP is charac-terized by fundamental breakthroughs in the wave-triggering technologies and industries which are at the core of the TEP. Openness often relates to links between those industries, universities and other research organizations, and government as a facilitator of innovation. The role of, and response from, lead users (the "avant-garde") and very demanding customers is important during this phase of a new TEP. In the frenzy phase, knowledge from different industries and sectors needs to be integrated as technological revolutions result from combining knowledge from different sectors and combining different technologies in a way which allows new possibilities to emerge. Openness matters for defining and finding markets, for improving and further developing new products, and, more generally, for popularizing new technologies and the related TEP. This *industry-crossing aspect* again is a source of diversities of innovation and will become even more important in the later phases of a long wave when the new technology and its related TEP are rolled out over (most of) the economy. Conducting joint applied research by firms and research organizations, and integrating business cus-tomers from different industries and private customers into the innovation process, is then supportive for firms' innovation effort to become effective.

This pattern of varying openness of innovation along the phases of a long wave fits well into the recent ICT-based long wave. Diversity of innovation arises through the application of new knowledge in different contexts, in different products and services, in different markets, and in different socio-cultural constellations. Whether this pattern matches up with preceding waves is doubtful though because the concept of innovation openness is constituent for systemic approaches to innovation and to the "strategic innovation paradigm" (Sundbo 1995) which had only just emerged in the 1990s. So while on the one hand the variation of openness of innovation along the phases of a long wave could be considered *specific* for the ICT-TEP, it is also likely that the "strategic innovation paradigm" will survive the fifth long wave (just like the innovation paradigms of preceding long waves have survived) and therefore will play an important role in future long waves.

Finally, the process of *adaptation is an important source of diversity of innovation* during the phases of a long wave. The shift from science-based to technology-based innovation during the wave mentioned above goes hand in hand with the roll-out of the new technology and the related TEP and adaptation of economic agents and institutions to the new TEP (Hilpert 1991). The new technology does not emerge simultaneously in all countries, the speed and intensity of the diffusion of a new TEP is not the same in all regions, and the speed and intensity of adaptation to it will not be the same, either. The new technology is rolled out from core industries and sectors in which the new TEP emerged to other sectors of the economy which intensively use the new technologies and incorporate them into their products and processes. Particularly in the later phases of the wave the search for new applications within existing technologies are sought for. Adaptation cannot be successful if new technology is merely implemented on existing organizational structures as the productivity paradox that "one can see computers everywhere but in the productivity statistics" (Solow 1987) recalls.

Taking up the business opportunities which emerge from the roll-out of a new TEP requires adapting existing processes, services, and products, but it also means creating new ones which are only loosely connected to the new technology. Adaptation does not primarily refer to the diffusion of technology as such, but to the diffusion of the techno-economic paradigm to sectors and industries which are neither among the triggering industries nor among those industries which took up the new technology in its processes or goods and services they produce. Adaptation refers to industries which are indirectly affected in their production processes and production possibilities: it requires economic agents to change their way of doing business and adapting to the new TEP thus giving way to an enormous diversity of innovation outcomes.

At the firm level, adaptation to a new TEP means transferring the best practice organizational model of a new TEP into an industry that is neither among the ones which trigger the wave nor among the intensive users of the new technology. Two examples may illustrate this: in the fourth wave tourism industries in many countries experienced strong growth in the 1960s and 1970s – *inter alia* – by adapting to the extension of paid vacation in many industrialized (European) countries. The resulting boom in (mass-) tourism was made possible because of strong productivity increases in the manufacturing industries which were the lead appliers of the then prevailing TEP. In the fifth long wave the application of the organization principles of the ICT-TEP has changed industries like retailing or the airline industry profoundly. In the beverages industry the adaptation of these principles enabled a single company to even create a global market for a new product ("energy drinks"). From a policy perspective, these examples show that adaptation processes have often been accomplished with little or no specific policy support and even without unintended side-effects of policy measures.

Adaptation becomes relevant as soon as the major properties of the new TEP and implications for those industries which are not among the triggers of the long wave can be conceived. Adaptation therefore will become an issue for the most innovative firms during the frenzy phase and will be a topic in all industries in the later phases of the wave. As the properties and implications of the new TEP can be conceived more clearly the longer the TEP has been unfolding early adopters can create a competitive advantage. At the same time, they face the risk of misperceiving the properties of the new TEP and the risks involved with adapting their business model to the TEP's expected implications on their industry.

The discussion of adaptation shows that it is not necessary to be among the leaders in the core industries of a new TEP in order to reap the benefits from it, but it is sufficient to adapt properly to its requirements and the possibilities it offers. During the roll-out of the new TEP in the later phases of the wave, in principal, all countries have a chance to benefit from it as all countries and regions tend to be affected by the new TEP at least indirectly. Therefore, the process of adaptation to a new TEP is critical for a nation's ability to influence its long-term economic welfare. Depending on the adequacy of policies and economic agents' behaviour within a long wave, successful adaptation therefore is crucial for the nations to catch up during a long wave, while less and less successful adaptation efforts may entail that some countries fall back (at least relatively).

Long waves and changing patterns of innovation policy

While the concept of an innovation policy has emerged only since the mid-1970s to late 1980s (Boekholt 2010, p. 355) government policies had affected innovation activity long before without using the label "innovation policy". Policy fields include infrastructure (railways, roads) and education policy but also micro-economic policies (e.g. industrial and competition policy, labour market policy, taxes, and transfer payments) and macro-economic policies (e.g. foreign trade policy, monetary, and fiscal policies). The impact of such policies on a nation's innovation activity can be either a direct one (e.g. subsidizing innovation activities) or an indirect one (e.g. skill formation subsidized by government), it can be an intended impact or an unintended side-effect of a policy (e.g. interest rate variation motivated by accommodating macro-economic fluctuations has an impact on investment, risk-taking, and thus ultimately, on innovation). These examples show that, in principal, policy measures from all fields of government policy have ramifications which ultimately have implications on a country's innovative capacity and the scope and intensity of innovation activity in that country. The multitude of innovation-related policy fields, of instruments, and of impact channels of course entails much diversity in the innovation processes and outcomes.

While it is important to recognize that all policy can be considered innovation policy in a wider sense, such a view would render the concept "innovation policy" less meaningful. The conceptualization of the innovation process and its improved understanding has made it possible to refine government policies for innovation and make it more focused. The following long wave-based view of four topics of innovation policy diversity shows that institutional and regulatory decisions have a strong impact on the diffusion and scope of use of a new technology and its related TEP, and on the degree to which a society can benefit from the TEP during the phases of a long wave. A strict distinction between *phase*-of-wave-specific innovation policy issues and wave-specific innovation policy issues may not always be possible.

From a long wave perspective, *the challenges for innovation policy are subject to change during the phases of a wave.* Chronologically, the series of challenges begins with the fundamental risk that a nation misses out on taking up the technological developments which are the key elements of a new paradigm (Scherrer 2016). Such risk can be mitigated if private and public agents are permanently involved in research in many disciplines in order to maintain economic agents' and policy makers' awareness and capability to pick up those new technologies which turn out to be drivers of a new TEP. This requires building competences not only in the private sector, but also in the public sector to enable government to implement technology policies appropriately and to allow for a long time horizon of public policy (Drechsler 2009). Different degrees of public sector openness and responsiveness to technological developments across countries and regions, different political systems, and different processes of policy-making therefore are likely to create different innovation paths. The risk of "missing" a TEP and thereby the lack of access to diversities of innovation is undoubtedly a phase-of-wave-specific issue which materializes for innovation leader countries already from the irruption phase (or even before). For innovation follower countries such a risk is particularly relevant from the frenzy phase onwards when the build-up of infrastructure and investments in the new technology are to be addressed although its direct profitability may not (yet) be warranted.

In the turning point phase it becomes apparent that the institutions of the previous TEP no longer provide an environment in which all the possibilities of the new TEP can be utilized. Competences which accommodate the new TEP need to be developed from the frenzy phase of the wave onwards. Investment in skills and engagement of firms in organisational change and market-oriented innovation (which again is influenced by skills of economic agents[7]) become key challenges from the frenzy phase onwards to the later phases of the development wave. Policy makers may respond differently to that challenge, and cultural and other environmental conditions will have an impact on the potential success of such policies, thereby both creating diversity of innovation policies and innovation outcomes and taking advantage of diversities of innovation.

Modes of innovation policy-making may vary with regard to the degree of "state closeness" over a long wave's lifetime and thus create diversity of innovation policies. Entrepreneurs try to find out the most profitable business opportunities created by the new technology through trial and error; deregulation of the economy and financial innovations – both typically occurring in the frenzy period of long waves – support this process. In the early phases of a wave deregulation or – in the case of newly emerging technologies – non-regulation is considered conducive to innovation and economic growth because regulations potentially place obstacles on experiments with new technologies (Scherrer 2016). Regulatory barriers to innovation are torn down as (de-) regulation should improve incentives to innovate and reward successful entrepreneurs with huge profits. This means that individual interests govern regulation and pro-business governments tend to dominate politics (Perez 2002) particularly in the irruption and frenzy phases.

Drechsler (2009, p. 95ff) suggests that

> the regard in which the state and its power are held, the attitude towards the state and its power … is indeed a matter of the period, not the paradigm. In the first phases of a development wave, there is 'state distance'.

In the turning point and synergy phases a re-regulation is required as the potential of the TEP related with the current wave and the institutional requirements for exploiting this potential are perceived more clearly now by the many firms and large parts of the population. This means that in a process of creative destruction of institutions the rules of the game have to be accommodated to the requirements of the new TEP adequately and related government intervention is required to take place which implies that the regime of regulation turns to more "state closeness". In particular, a re-coupling of the real economy and the financial economy is required by

> eliminating the excessive financial layering and increased regulation of the financial system through more rigorous government control in a way that does not prevent the full deployment of the new technology led by production capital reaping the full economic and social potential of the now prevailing paradigm.
>
> (Kregel 2009, p. 203).

Promoting skills and launching public programs in support of firms' organisational change and market oriented innovation would then be part of a macroeconomic strategywhich aims at stimulating the economy and facilitating the exploitation of the productivity potential in the synergy and maturity phase of a TEP. Such a macroeconomic policy is geared towards the demand side and is particularly important in the turning point and synergy phases when monetary policy tends to be less effective. Economic policy therefore might shift emphasis from the supply side in the early phases of the wave (when innovation is driven by capital markets) to demand policies in later phases (when innovation is increasingly driven by the demand for goods and services based on the new TEP) (Scherrer 2016).

Possible differences in strategy design and implementation again make diversities of innovation occur very likely.

As adapting to a new TEP is crucial for a country to benefit from a long wave *enhancing the economy's and the whole society's adaptability* is a task of public policy. The uptake of new technologies and the related TEP by individual firms and whole innovation systems in those fields which are not triggering the long wave dynamic is to be fostered. This process means collecting and processing information in order to find out the new TEP's implications for firms' operations which involve much more than just imitating the behavior of other firms which have already implemented the new TEP in their operations. Public policies to enhance these firms' adaptability to technological and organizational change in the different phases of the long wave are therefore regularly part of innovation policies.

Three modes of active government intervention in order to develop the absorptive capacity of firms with regard to the take-up of new technologies are relevant (Bessant and Rush 2009) and are likely to vary and thereby becoming a source of diversity of innovation policies during the phases of a wave. Particularly in the early phases of a long wave, adaptation-enhancing policies aim at raising the level of firms' awareness by different ways of letting the target population know ("broadcast mode"). In later stages agents can be used to engage with the adopter to help frame and explore the promising practice ("agent-assisted mode"). Finally, approaches can be used that encourage learning from and with others ("peer-assisted mode"). The agent-assisted and the peer-assisted modes are more relevant in later phases of the wave because a sufficient number of "agents" and "peers" have to be formed before. All three modes of developing firms' absortive capacitys may (or may not) be combined with financial incentives for firms. In any case diversity of innovation policy is created both by the three different basic modes of government support of adaptability and many different opportunities to implement these modes in practice.

Finally, *education and skill formation policies* matter for the development of innovation capabilities and add to the diversity of innovation policies and innovation performance of countries. In the earlier phases of a wave the supply of skills in the core technologies is important. These skills will develop mostly among the young generation which can start developing skills from without being "burdened" by skills which once were useful and important in the waning TEP; they approach the new technologies from a game perspective and not from a learning task perspective.

The further the TEP progresses the roll-out of the new technology should be complemented by disseminating the skills and competencies which are necessary for producing goods and services and implementing new organizational models in the changed environment. In principal, all skill levels are affected, and life-long learning is boosted because also adults have to become "literate" with the requirements of the new TEP. Skill requirements of many low-skilled workers tend to be affected by the new TEP's productivity-enhancing property in the course of its roll-out into all sectors of the economy already in the early phases but increasingly from the synergy phase of the wave onwards. Skill development of workers and – particularly in the current long wave – delegating responsibility to workers become important elements of innovation strategies at latest in the synergy phase of the wave in which innovation turns from science based to being technology based. The resulting tendency of job-enrichment implies that both functional and social skills requirements undergo a change and need to be developed.

From the frenzy phase onwards investment in skills therefore is a challenge both for public policy makers and firms. In later phases of the wave this task could be gradually facilitated when goods and services based on the new TEP will have become more user-friendly due to refinement of products and processes, and when social acceptance of the new technologies and the related TEP has become manifest in society. Given the wide variety of skills required for innovation, in countries with an already robust educational attainment (which is the case in most OECD countries), the policy focus for skills development for innovation should be on creating an environment that enables individuals to choose and acquire appropriate skills and that supports the optimal use of these skills at work.

Long waves and the public–private sector interface

The emergence and diffusion of a new TEP has an impact on the design of the public-private sector interface in the innovation realm. The discussion of innovation "openness" and the previous section on innovation policy have shown that this interface is of crucial importance for the innovation process. Again, irrespective if certain measures of designing this interface are labelled "*innovation* policy" or not: policy impact on innovation matters. This may be illustrated by examples of policies at the public private sector interface which provide historical evidence for each long wave. In the 19th century concessions and public-private partnerships were used to mobilize private capital for building large parts of the railway infrastructure. In the late 19th century the founding of technical colleges and universities in order to build up the relevant skills of the workforce was initiated and supported by industrialists and enabled some European countries (e.g. Germany) to become leaders in the long wave driven by mechanical engineering and electricity. Since the early 20th century government procurement of (mostly military) aircraft was used as a specific industrial policy in order to foster innovation and exploit economies of scale (also) in the civilian aircraft production. More recently, the creation of the ARPA-net as a major forerunner of the internet which began in the late 1960s is a good example of a product developed at the public-private interface. These examples suggest that there are important and manifold interdependences and complementarities in the innovation process between the private and the public sectors, and that this might be reflected in a diversity of configurations of the public-private interface.

Therefore, a "good ride" on a wave requires co-ordinating public and private sectors well. *Systemic innovation theories* – which explicitly focus on interfaces between agents in the innovation process – claim that neither the private sector alone nor the public sector alone matter for the success of innovation policy but it is the innovation system. Securing the presence and quality of necessary elements of an innovation system and securing the connectivity among agents of an innovation system – each with regard to knowledge-related activities and entrepreneurial activities – are typical targets of innovation policy which are rooted in a systemic approach (Wieczorek and Hekkert 2012).

From a long wave-perspective the public-private interface in the innovation realm may be affected on the one hand by wave specific features and on the other hand the interface is likely to undergo some change during the phases of a wave. The critical interfaces for interaction among agents in innovation systems are likely to depend on the knowledge base of those industries and technologies which trigger a long wave. Generally, "we should expect that the mechanisms that give rise to diversity and selection will differ as the techno-economic context changes" (Lundvall 2013, p. 44). By implication, interfaces between the public and the private sector may vary across waves thus giving rise to diversity of the innovation process over time.

In all phases of a wave the design of systems of innovation is important for a country's ability to adapt to the requirements of a new TEP and its capability to benefit from it. Not all aspects of innovation policy which address the public-private sector interface may vary in the same intensity along the phases of a long wave or may vary at all. E.g. fundamental research – which is a traditional target of government policies and justified by mainstream economic theory on grounds of positive externalities – is relevant in all phases of a long wave: major breakthroughs in science do not occur regularly but it is the clustering of major innovations in time that triggers the rise of a long wave of economic development. Therefore the existence of a public-private sector interface in fundamental research need not undergo much change during the dissemination of a TEP. *Diversity of design of this interface* between countries is therefore not a phase of wave-specific but a country specific phenomenon determined by differences in institutions, ideologies, government policies and other country specific factors. Diversities of policies aimed at innovation therefore are rooted in different political structures, divergent opportunities, the availability of resources (budget, personnel), different governmental systems (federal vs. centralised), and responsibilities being allocated to different parts and levels of government (federal vs. centralised, particular ministries).

The focus of other elements of the innovation systems is likely to shift during the phases of the long wave. In general, the setup of innovation systems is likely to (or from a normative point of view: should) accommodate the specific properties and challenges of the innovation process which typically unfold during the dissemination of a TEP. E.g. with the shift from science-based to technology-based innovation the public-private interfaces in innovation systems will increase its focus on participation of economic agents from outside of those industries which trigger the TEP. Different policy approaches between countries towards innovation systems will further foster the differentiation of regional and national patterns of innovation-relevant public-private sector interfaces and of ways how regions and countries adapt to a TEP.

Public-private partnership (PPP) is a specific configuration of the public-private sector interface. PPPs cover all kinds of arrangements of cooperation and involve partners in order to map out a strategy and a framework for accomplishing a common goal defined by public and private agents (Grimsey and Lewis 2005, p. 6). Sharing risk between public and private partners is constituent to PPP. As the amount of risk attached to innovation activities varies during the wave, PPP can be utilized as a means of optimizing the risk allocation between the public and the private sector. This will be, again, a source of innovation policy diversity and consequently of innovation diversity.

PPP is of interest in the innovation realm for two reasons: PPP on the one hand is a policy instrument which enables or facilitates the dissemination of a new TEP by building up relevant infrastructures based on cooperation between the public and private sectors. PPP here is understood as a contractual relationship between government and private partners according to which

> the private partners deliver the service in such a manner that the service delivery objectives of the government are aligned with the profit objectives of the private partners and where the effectiveness of the alignment depends on a sufficient transfer of risk to the private partners.
>
> (OECD 2008, p. 17).

Within the long wave framework this type of PPP is most relevant in the frenzy phase and to a lesser degree in the later phases when most of the infrastructure for the new TEP is built up or expanded. Political, institutional and organizational support for PPP differs significantly between countries (Verhoest *et al.* 2015) and thereby re-enforces diversity of innovation policies.

On the other hand PPP is a distinct form of cooperation between the public and the private sector explicitly aiming at innovation activities. PPP then is either a mode of fostering the generation and exploitation of innovation activities by providing the organizational frame for "producing" innovations, or a mode of policy delivery in the field of innovation often with a focus on technology transfer which comprises innovation strategy development, innovation program and project implementation (Kristensen *et al.* 2016). PPP in general are able to contribute to the presence of relevant structural elements in an innovation system with regard to both knowledge-related and entrepreneurial activities. The diversity of PPP arrangements allows for considerable variety of innovation systems' characteristics across regions and industries, and therefore the properties and qualities of an innovation system's elements and of the connectivity among agents of such an innovation system vary across goals, sectors and regions (Scherrer and Kristensen 2016).

Public procurement for innovation is also a specific configuration of the public-private sector interface in innovation policy. It has existed at least implicitly both as a concept and as an empirical phenomenon already for centuries and it is characterized by diverse approaches used across countries (Lember *et al.* 2014). The prominent role of government procurement strategies and public expenditure for innovation is highlighted by Mazzucato (2011) showing that – at least in the US – strong government influence on innovation exists in all phases of the long wave. According to the type of innovation embedded in the resulting product it is useful to distinguish three types of public procurement for innovation in order to disclose the potential for diversity of innovation along the phases of a long wave (Edquist and Zabala-Iturriagagoitia 2012): *Developmental* public procurement for innovation is particularly relevant in the early phases of a long wave (irruption and frenzy phase). The goal of such a procurement process is to create radically new products or systems; in many countries there has been a long tradition of this type of public procurement in the arms and space industries. *Pre-commercial* procurement is also more relevant in the early phases of a wave than in the later ones; here government purchases via direct public R&D investments ("contract research") expected results. Finally, *adaptive* public procurement for innovation is relevant in later phases of the long wave in order to support the diffusion of a new TEP in the synergy and even maturity phase of a long wave. Here the innovation which is achieved with the product procured is incremental in nature; it is new only to the place of procurement and adapted to specific national or local conditions.

Finally, the *public sector* itself adapts to the new TEP in order to better utilize its potential for providing policies and services efficiently. Government services largely are an input for private production and consumption they have an impact on economic development and competitiveness of the private sector. Depending on the respective government's abilities to recognize the potential of adapting to the new TEP and to respond to the related challenges innovation in the public sector[8] differs across regions and countries. Most importantly, the impact of a new TEP on the production methods of the public sector affects also the interface between private and public agents. If government is among the lead appliers of a new TEP or a laggard depends on the properties of and specific political interest in technologies. In those cases and government functions in which the public sector is closely intertwined with the industries which are potential triggers of the long wave dynamics (e.g. arms, aircraft and space industries) government is a lead user of the technology and likely also a lead-applier of the related TEP. If new technologies like in the recent long wave tend to affect firms' production methods first then the public sector might lag behind the private sector: e-government followed e-business. The application of technologies and organizational principles which are attached to a new TEP undergoes a similar life cycle in both the public and the private sector.

Summing up, from a long wave-perspective innovation policies and the public-private sector interface are affected threefold. First, some aspects of such policies are not likely to be affected along the phases of a long wave (e.g. public-private cooperation in fundamental research). Second, some aspects of such policies are subject to change according to the changing challenges in the phases of the diffusion of a TEP (e.g. the role of public procurement). And third, the configuration of the public-private sector interface in innovation systems includes both phase-of-wave-specific and wave-specific elements.

Conclusion and outlook

Although the long wave model states that in the process of long-term innovation dynamics there regularly is a wide range of possible innovation outcomes stemming from different regulatory regimes and from the potential impact of policy-making on finding the – more or less – appropriate set of institutions to accommodate the prevailing TEP (Scherrer 2016). Attitudes towards innovation and chosen modes of innovation policy do actually matter and create diversity of innovation. Such diversity of innovation and of innovation policies can be observed both with regard to different long waves and with regard to different phases within a long wave.

From a very long-term point of view we finally might speculate if it is possible for a country or region which successfully surfed one wave to extend this momentum and have a "good ride" on the following wave. There are at least three channels of extending that momentum to the next wave and to facilitate "hopping from wave to wave". Successfully preparing for a next wave to come can mean, first, that an economy with a large stock of physical capital has a good basis for successfully surfing the next wave because of its endowment with capital. This channel provides a chance for economically lagging countries because they can successfully catch up in one wave without being among the technology leaders of the respective TEP via adaptation. Successful adaptation will allow these countries to accumulate capital and increase productivity which facilitates the acquisition of those resources which are required for successfully surfing the next wave.

Successfully preparing for a next wave can also mean that, second, skills have been acquired during the current wave. The stock of human capital matters particularly, because if a country's population in one long wave experienced that education and skill formation do pay off, this should be conducive to establishing a general attitude in favour of acquiring skills which are required for successfully surfing the next new long wave, too. Therefore (re-) investing resources into research and development and skill formation yield long-term benefits with a positive impact which is felt beyond the wave in which these policies were established.

Successfully preparing for a next wave may also mean that, third, if a society has been capable of adjusting its institutional structure successfully to the requirements of the current TEP this might be supportive for meeting the challenges of the next TEP. While the capability to adjust suggests a certain amount of societal flexibility and its willingness to meet challenges this is probably the weakest channel because it does not automatically mean that a society which succeeded in adjusting to the requirements of the current wave will automatically succeed in adjusting to the requirements of the next wave. "Winners" of the old TEP might be strong enough to markedly decelerate structural change, and lock-in into existing structures might be an obstacle to realize the potential of the new wave.

Notes

1 The first wave was triggered by innovations in steam power and the textile industry and started in the 1790s in Britain, the second wave by the steam railway (1840s), the third by steel and heavy engineering (1880s), the fourth by applying the principles of mass production (late 1930s), and the fifth wave by modern information and communication technologies (late 1980s). For an overview see Scherrer (2016), for detailed descriptions of waves see Freeman and Louçã (2001).
2 Although the notion "surge of development" tends to be more adequate the wording "long wave" which is commonly used in the literature will also be used in this chapter.
3 The key factors or key inputs which drive a long wave are characterized by rapidly falling relative cost, an almost unlimited availability of supply over long periods, and a clear potential for use or incorporation in many products and processes throughout the whole economic system. As improvement innovations are subject to the law of diminishing returns and profits are competed-away the innovating impulse will dissipate over time.
4 Sundbo does not refer to the first and second long waves.
5 A TEP is based on new sets of interrelated technologies and organisational principles that allow a step change in potential productivity in practically all economic activities ("irruption phase"). Entrepreneurs' and investors' search for opportunities created by the new technology involves a huge amount of speculation which entails the build-up of a financial bubble ("frenzy phase"). The bubble's burst signals the "turning point" of the long wave. As social and institutional change is lagging behind technological change, only those societies which adapt its regulatory and institutional framework best to the requirements of the new TEP can exploit its economic potential fully ("synergy phase"). Finally, in the "maturity phase" markets become increasingly saturated and the potential for improvements within this TEP get exhausted. Consequently, both real-economy entrepreneurs and financial investors start searching for opportunities outside the prevailing paradigm thereby giving way to a new long wave.
6 "Science" is considered not only to be an activity performed within research-oriented organizations like universities or R&D departments of firms but also – which is particularly relevant in the early long waves – by individuals who search for technological novelties (e.g. by experimenting).
7 Because of its importance a distinct section is devoted below to education and skill formation policies.
8 It has to be borne in mind that the concept of "public sector innovation" is somewhat blurred as it lacks the test of acceptance in a competitive market which is the clear criterion of success for innovation in the private sector.

References

Asheim, B., Coenen, I., Moodysson, J. and Vang, J. 2007: Constructing knowledge-based regional advantage: implications for regional innovation policy. In: *International Journal of Entrepreneurship and Innovation Management* 7 (2–5), 140–155.

Bessant, J. and Rush, H. 2009: Developing Innovation Capability: Meeting the Policy challenge. In: Drechsler, W.J.M., Kattel, R. and Reinert, E.S. (Eds.): *Techno-Economic Paradigms: Essays in Honour of Carlota Perez*. London: Anthem Press, 19–38.

Boekholt, P. 2010: The Evolution of Innovation Paradigms and their Influence on Research, Technological Development and Innovation Policy Instruments. In: Smits, R.E., Kuhlmann, St. and Shapira, P. (Eds.): *The Theory and Practice of Innovation Policy. An International Research Handbook*. Cheltenham: Edward Elgar, 333–362.

Castellacchi, F. 2005: Innovation, diffusion and catching up in the fifth long wave. In: *Futures* 38 (7), 841–863.

Chesbrough, H. and Crowther, A.K. 2006: Beyond high tech: early adopters of open innovation in other industries. In: *R&D Management* 36 (3), 229–236.

Drechsler, W.J.M. 2009: Governance in and of Techno-Economic Paradigm Shifts: Considerations for and from the Nanotechnology Surge. In: Drechsler, W.J.M., Kattel, R. and Reinert, E.S. (Eds.): *Techno-Economic Paradigms: Essays in Honour of Carlota Perez*. London: Anthem Press, 95–104.

Edquist, C. and Zabala-Iturriagagoitia, J.M. 2012: Public Procurement for Innovation as mission-oriented innovation policy. In: *Research Policy* 41, 1757–1769.

Freeman, C. 1987: *Technology Policy and Economic Performance: Lessons from Japan*. London: Pinter.

Freeman, C. and Louçã, F. 2001: *As Time Goes By. From the Industrial Revolutions to the Information Revolution*. Oxford: Oxford University Press.

Goldstein, J.S. 1988: *Long Cycles: Prosperity and War in the Modern Age*. New Haven and London: Yale University Press.

Grimsey, D. and Lewis, M. (Eds.). 2005: *The Economics of Public Private Partnerships*, International Library of Critical Writings in Economics, Volume 183. Cheltenham: Edward Elgar.

Hilpert, U. 1991: *Neue Weltmärkte und der Staat: staatliche Politik, technischer Fortschritt und internationale Arbeitsteilung*. Opladen: Westdeutscher Verlag.

Hilpert, U. (Ed.). 2003: *Regionalisation of Globalised Innovation. Locations for Advanced Industrial Development and Disparities in Participation*. London: Routledge.

Hirooka, M. 2003: Nonlinear dynamism of innovations and business cycles. In: *Journal of Evolutionary Economics* 13 (5), 549–576.

Kondratieff, N.D. 1926/1935: Die langen Wellen der Konjunktur. In: *Archiv für Sozialwissenschaft und Sozialpolitik* 56 (3), 573–609; English: The long waves in economic life. In: *The Review of Economic Statistics* XVII (6), 1935.

Kregel, J. 2009: Financial Experimentation, Technological Paradigm Revolutions and Financial Crisis. In: Drechsler, W.J.M., Kattel, R. and Reinert, E.S. (Eds.): *Techno-Economic Paradigms: Essays in Honour of Carlota Perez*. London: Anthem Press, 203–220.

Kristensen, I., McQuaid, R.W. and Scherrer, W. 2016: Public Private Partnership as an Instrument of Innovation Policy. In: Hilpert, U. (Ed.): *Routledge Handbook of Politics and Technology*. Oxford: Routledge, 249–261.

Lember, V., Kattel, R. and Kalvet, T. (Eds.). 2014: *Public Procurement, Innovation and Policy. International Perspectives*. Berlin: Springer.

Lundvall, B.Å. 1992: *National Systems of Innovation. Towards a Theory of Innovation and Interactive Learning*. London: Pinter.

Lundvall, B.Å. 2013: Innovation Studies: A Personal Interpretation of 'The State of the Art'. In: Fagerberg, J., Martin, B.A. and Andersen, E.S. (Eds.): *Innovation Studies. Evolution and Future Challenges*. Oxford: Oxford University Press, 21–70.

Mazzucato, M. 2011: *The Entrepreneurial State*. London: Demos.

Mensch, G. 1979: *Stalemate in Technology*. Cambridge, MA: Ballinger.

Nelson, R.R. (Ed.). 1993: *National Innovation Systems. A Comparative Study*. Oxford: Oxford University Press.

OECD. 2008: *Public-Private Partnerships*. Paris: Organisation for Economic Cooperation and Development.

Perez, C. 1983: Structural change and the assimilation of new technologies in the economic and social system. In: *Futures* 15, 357–375.

Perez, C. 2002: *Technological Revolutions and Financial Capital. The Dynamics of Bubbles and Golden Ages*. Cheltenham: Edward Elgar.

Perez, C. 2010: Technological revolutions and techno-economic paradigms. In: *Cambridge Journal of Economics* 34 (1), 185–202.

Rosenberg, N. and Frischtak, C.R. 1983: Long waves and economic growth: A critical appraisal. In: *American Economic Review* 73 (2), 146–151.

Scherrer, W. 2016: Technology and Socio-economic Development in the Long Run: A "Long Wave"-Perspective. In: Hilpert, U. (Ed.): *Routledge Handbook of Politics and Technology*. Oxford: Routledge, 50–64.

Scherrer, W. and Kristensen, I. 2016: Public Private Partnerships as a Systemic Instrument of Regional Innovation Policy. Evidence from Sweden. In: *International Public Administration Review* 14 (1), 37-54.

Solow, R.M. 1987: We'd better watch out. *New York Times Book Review*, July 12, 36.

Sundbo, J. 1995: Three paradigms in innovation theory. In: *Science and Public Policy* 22 (6), 399–410.

Sundbo, J. 1998: *The theory of innovation. Entrepreneurs, technology and strategy*. Cheltenham: Edward Elgar.

Van Gelderen, J. [J. Fedder, pseudo]. 1913/1996: Springvloed Baschouwingen over industrielle Outwikkalieng en prijsbeweging. In: *De Nieuwe Tijd* 184 (5/6); English: Springtide. Reflections on Industrial Development and Price Movements. In: Freeman, Ch. (Ed.): *Long Wave Theory*. Cheltenham: Edward Elgar, 1–56.

Verhoest, K., Petersen, O.H., Scherrer, W. and Soecipto, R.M. 2015: How do governments support the development of Public Private Partnerships? Measuring and comparing governmental PPP support across 20 European countries. In: *Transport Reviews* 35 (2), 118–139.

Wieczorek, A. and Hekkert, M. 2012: Systemic instruments for systemic innovation problems: A framework for policy makers and innovation scholars. In: *Science and Public Policy* 39, 74–87.

4 Building research diversity

Alain-Marc Rieu

Beyond the innovation mantra

The *OECD Science, Technology and Industry Scoreboard 2017* proves once again that the solution of last resort to overcome the on-going systemic crisis is to be found in "frontier technology" as the source of industrial innovation. Industrial innovation is supposed to save mature industries, to create new ones, new companies and jobs, which will be paying taxes, which will finance public services, social policies and, in the end, research and innovation policies. The magic circle or virtuous spiral looks, unfortunately, like a steam engine trying to fight its own entropy. What is supposed to happen between this deep source of innovation and the river of growth and welfare remains hidden in a black box. Innovation is our present mantra, used by governments and companies as a magic wand to solve all problems. But magic wands and their gurus explain little. Innovation is foremost a question of practices developed through institutional arrangements associating companies, universities and government. Good practices are not to be found in each of these institutions but in their connections and interactions. These interactions cannot be reduced to any method, which could be copied or taught and then applied. They remain largely informal. So they prove difficult to study in detail and then difficult or impossible to replicate, adapt and adopt. Why some methods and practices are inefficient proves equally difficult to study and explain.

Paradoxically, in such concrete cases, concepts and theories prove extremely useful. They provide a framework in which a goal can be adequately formulated and they also open a space for experimentation. In summary, conceptual innovation matters. These concepts are not drawn from nowhere. They carry experience. They are constructed through various conceptual experiments and case studies. Amongst the most powerful and influential conceptual innovations produced in the last thirty years were the National Innovation System model (OECD 1997) of the late 1980s and the Triple Helix model (Etzkowitz and Leydesdorff 1998) of the late 1990s. These two models are closely related, each solving some paradoxes raised by the other. During the present systemic crisis, intensified by growing environmental constraints, intensified debates and research on innovation, new versions of these two models were formulated.[1] This new research proves the continued heuristic value and its evolutionary potential of these models.

These new circumstances question the established reference point and standard found in Silicon Valley. However successful it might have been, it is neither "a global model, nor a unique anomaly".[2] It certainly was an inspiration but constructing Silicon Valley into a model to imitate proved a vain exercise and a costly enterprise. Silicon Valley studies led to a more precise understanding of the singular conditions of its emergence and reinvention through time. But the evolution of Silicon Valley since 2000, the burst of the Internet bubble, research trends in the San Francisco Bay area on its future beyond ICT,[3] doubts also about US long-term competitiveness, create new interests and further research on these models.

In summary, growing environmental constraints and the on-going systemic crisis[4] have transformed the conditions for research and innovation in all industrial nations. These two models had, and still have, a growing influence at the regional, national and local level. Their interpretations and implementations differ according to contexts. The context matters and makes the difference. Today, in this post-Fukushima context (Rieu 2013), these models need to be redefined by comparing some of their versions. Furthermore, the report by Leydesdorff and Etzkowitz (2003) on the 2002 Triple Helix conference in Copenhagen, "Can the 'public' be considered as a fourth helix in University-Industry-Government relations?", opened the way for new research on the helix, which is proving particularly relevant. This paper shall further explore this opening and reconfigure the Helix model according to the present context.

The risk of growing standardization

It is not enough. The real problem is the present systemic crisis. This crisis is often considered to be proof that advanced industrial societies have entered a "secular stagnation" (Summers 2013) or at least a "long-term recession" (Gordon 2010). They cannot expect in the future to repeat the growth rate, which had transformed them since the 19th century, because this high growth was generated by the aggregation of a series of technological discovery. In other words, mature societies should renounce the hope of restoring their historical virtuous spiral or to invent a new one.[5] The virtuous spiral could only happen once. The reason for the present recession is the high improbability that a new technological wave would generate another, new, long period of growth in industrial societies. The reason is that these countries have reached such a high level of development that a technology, however disruptive, cannot generate a further level of growth so high that it would radically transform the economy, the institutional system and even the culture. Digital technology is certainly a disruptive innovation with deep economic and social consequences, but it did not generate a disruptive growth level.

Theory matters. The notion of "systemic crisis" opens a different perspective. The problem is to question established conceptions of innovation and to focus not on technology but on the institutional environment in which innovation emerges and takes shape within a social system. This is what Science and Technology Studies have been explaining since the 1980s and this is what the twin models are doing. But the present situation requires questioning models, which developed in a different context. Paradoxically, the strong influence of the Triple Helix model leads to a better understanding of its limitations and presuppositions. Explicitly or not, it still inspires research policies and institutional reforms around the world. But its adoption and adaptation have transformed this conceptual construct into an international norm. In the present context, its role as a norm requires opening debates and research because several counter-productive effects are identified or anticipated. For instance, comparing recent research and innovation policies in the European Union and Japan shows which consequences can be observed or predicted with a high degree of probability.

The first problem is an increased standardization of research. For research and other upstream activities, for universities as well as national and regional research policies, competition has greatly intensified since the 1980s. This competition has been explained and justified by different theories, mainly by Michael Porter's theory of comparative and competitive advantage. But the institutional arrangement at the core of this theory is an Innovation System (national, regional or local) and the operative core of this *system* is a Triple Helix dispositive. Over time this competition requires an alignment of the competitors, which generates a growing standardization of research and innovation activities. Researchers in advanced industrial societies tend to work in the same fields and on the same themes in institutional environments (organizations, hierarchies, even building design), which have become very similar. The short-term and long-term consequence of this situation is a growing standardization. Competition reinforces this pattern of evolution.

Science might be universal and technology generic, we might observe the emergence of various types of "knowledge economy", in the US and Japan as well as in each Western European nation and at the EU level. Similar attempts in China since 2006, and in Russia or Brazil obviously require deep institutional reforms (including political) to be really successful.[6] These various types of knowledge economies already compete with each other or intend to compete in the future (Rieu 2008). This intensified competition is reinforcing standardization further. Each nation intends to *catch up* to narrow the gap with the leader. The leader has to invest resources in order to preserve or reinforce its leadership as the model showing the road to follow. Even if nations competing in science and technology have set historical precedents since the 17th and 19th centuries in Europe, since the birth of modern science,[7] these are new challenges. Nations do not compete anymore on the basis of their historical differences, of divergent national interests, but to overcome them. Nowadays, at the level of research activities, competition does not oppose nations to each other but makes them converge. Apparently, this convergence reinforces the dominance of the nation, which pretends to be ahead, to be the norm to imitate and reproduce, obviously the United States and within the US, Silicon Valley. But since at least the 1990s, various American think tanks and government agencies have explained how US competitiveness is eroding and why the government should continue to invest more in research and education. The Unites States needs to remain the standard by which others are measured in order to sustain their technological hegemony and industrial leadership. Clearly the level of investment to maintain this hegemony is to the detriment of more fruitful and diversified fields of research.

These problems express the mutation of the conception, organization and role of all knowledge activities in advanced industrial societies since the 1980s, the new "regime of knowledge" in which our societies develop and compete. All major research institutions now have the same priorities and objectives. They do not imitate each other but they have entered a mimetic competition, which nobody controls and reinforces its convergent trajectory. The benefits are real: research standardization facilitates the worldwide cooperation of researchers, laboratories and research programs. This convergence even reinforces quality standards and hierarchies, the search for "excellence". But this standardization creates two problems: underneath global and even "open" cooperation, it intensifies competition between laboratories as well as between nations and regions not according to their capacity to generate new research and progress, but to transform this new knowledge into innovations, new industries, new products and services. This situation has obvious positive consequences but the reforms, which can be observed, tend to replicate the model and therefore intensify the mimetic competition – further intensifying standardization. From the point of view of the two main challenges, i.e. intensified environmental constraints and a systemic economic crisis, results are below expectations. Established conceptions of innovation and research policies do not fully respond to the present conjuncture. It might be a cause, among others, of the so-called "long-term recession".

This situation also has an impact on the other end of the innovation process, on research and research institutions. Because of this cooperation and standardization, where progress really happens in the world is *apparently* becoming secondary. Few laboratories are making a difference between the progress they really make and the progress they participate in. Laboratories and researchers have the feeling of belonging to a general progress in science and technology. Apparently, researchers develop the same project in different contexts, the climate seems to be the only thing that differs. Graduate and post-graduates circulate between projects looking very similar. This is, of course, an illusion: these similarities hide not only the hierarchy between universities based on the budgets, equipment and selection of researchers, but it hides the institutional contexts in which these laboratories and universities are embedded, their relations to industry, government, society and their respective strategies. The institutional context makes the difference. The full extent of this problem is not taken into account, not even identified, neither by governments and civil societies, nor by social scientists who tend to underestimate research and innovation issues. This evolution is obviously reinforced by the need to respond to the present economic and social conjuncture.

Research itself and research institutions are following a potentially dangerous path. This is the second problem: self-reinforcing standardization reduces research and innovation diversity. The reduction of this diversity has a negative impact on research and innovation potentials and therefore on long-term progress. The present growth of research activities intensifies this negative impact at the very moment when advanced industrial societies expect to find the path to their future in scientific progress and technological innovation. In the short term, this standardization does not sterilize research because, as said before, it facilitates the circulation of knowledge and researchers. But reducing research diversity generates a path dependency, which in the long term will tend to sterilize research. These processes are largely invisible and ignored. In summary, it is odd to defend biodiversity and at the same time be blind to the necessity of sustaining and even increasing research diversity.

Innovation in the neoliberal paradigm

The standardization of research and the reduction of its evolutionary potentials need to be put in a broader perspective. As mentioned before, the convergence of research fields and research organizations brings obvious benefits: it concentrates and aggregates human capital and financial resources. It rationalizes knowledge production and distribution for economic growth and social progress. This convergence is also the result of scientific methodologies and large-scale communication of data and research outcomes as well as the result of the increased exchange and circulation of researchers. These positive elements cannot be ignored when humanity is facing increased challenges, deceases, unequal access to food, education and information, energy shortages, industrial pollution and climate change, not to mention security issues. But these positive elements need today to be reinterpreted in a different perspective.

Since the 1980s, this convergence has not only intensified but has also mutated. The first energy and natural resources crisis in 1970s was the initial sign of the emergence of an environmental constraint and the first proof that it would deeply transform our economies, societies and the relations between nations, cultures and territories. Beyond politics and ideology, the neoliberal paradigm and its various practices have been a response since the 1970s to this crisis (Rieu 2012). This explains why paradoxically neoliberal solutions are still implemented today in order to solve problems generated by these very solutions. In this context, a new "regime of knowledge" has emerged and was identified. But its presuppositions and long-term consequences are not yet fully analyzed and evaluated.

The convergence of research fields, of research and innovation models and institutions, is certainly driven by the need to produce new knowledge. But this need is also driven by an intensified competition between economies and societies. The US, Japan and Western European nations have been sharing the same diagnosis of the present world conjuncture and they have, one after the other, implemented a similar response to the globalization process. In the 1990s, it became clear that the long-term future of each advanced industrial societies was to be found in their capacity to generate new knowledge and to translate innovation into new companies and new products, which would create the virtuous circle of growth, jobs, State revenues for financing welfare policies, infrastructures and, of course, research and innovation policies.[8]

In this context, the competition in science and technology between all OECD nations intensified. This new wave of industrial and political competition stimulated all activities related to the production and transfer of knowledge. The main actors of this change were not only managers or politicians; they were scientists, researchers, engineers, even post-doctoral students, and also specialists of recent disciplines like science studies and management of technology. Research policies found a new meaning and a new urgency. Until then, these actors were deeply embedded in social and political systems. Now their interests and values – the logic of their activities – became more openly asserted. Many reforms of research institutions, universities and "national systems of innovation" have been developed since the 1980s. This evolution has its ideology: the formation and management of a "knowledge economy", often taken for a "knowledge society".[9] This project has different versions: the EU Lisbon strategy, the EU seven Framework programs for Science and Technology and the new *Horizon* policy as well as Japan's successive Basic plans. Other versions are the various debates, reports and policies in the US concerning competitiveness and innovation.[10] From this new perspective, Silicon Valley remains a model, but this model is definitely not an overall solution.

The increased standardization resulting from a shared diagnosis and similar responses has reinforced the hegemony of the nation at the source of this process and most advanced in it. As mentioned before, the challenge for the US of sustaining this hegemony dates as far back as the late 1980s.[11] When the level of convergence generates standardization of research fields, institutions and policies, beyond quantitative indexes of scientific progress, leadership becomes sheer hegemony. This hegemony generates negative effects and become unsustainable. Today all industrial nations, including China and India, tend to train their scientists and engineers, organize their research institutions and even their territory according to a model developed in the US. Their basic goal is not to produce new knowledge but to *catch up*, to compete with the United States and reduce the US hegemony or leadership by modernizing their industrial base and creating new industries. This could be accepted by mature and new industrial nations as long as it generated positive effects for all players. But in the face of growing environmental constraints, because of the present systemic crisis, this evolutionary path is counter-productive. In the past, competition through collaboration intensified knowledge creation and innovation. Increasing standardization now reduces research diversity and, in the end, science and technology's productivity.

The concentration of research and training institutions, of expertise, of financial institutions and legal firms required for sustaining or establishing "innovation ecosystems" creates deserts of competence, unequal employment and training opportunities. Not only in China and India but also in the USA or Great Britain. The Triple Helix model developed in this context and it intensifies the counter-productive effects of this evolution. It explains why it needs to be criticized and overcome. It achieved two contradictory tasks. In the context opened in 1980s by the *Bayh-Dole Act*, it first explained how economic growth required a new institutional arrangement in order to strengthen innovation. Universities were decoupled from public policies and slowly recoupled with business creation and growth. In return, they found new financing resources for research and innovation in this new academic deal. They could grow but they also acquired new responsibilities. Secondly, the Triple Helix model explained how to reach and manage leveraging between government, industry and universities. It provided easy access to enter the black box of innovation. As mentioned in the introduction, nothing is so easy and invoking Silicon Valley as a mantra is not a solution. The Triple Helix belongs to the neoliberal movement, which has revolutionized the world since the 1980s. But it was also regulating the neoliberal revolution by explaining that economic development was based on innovation and that innovation processes were based on collaboration and interaction between university, industry and government. It is part of the problem, not the solution. Its limitations, presuppositions and failures show a path beyond the neoliberal moment.

A fourth helix for building research diversity

Reversing the trend toward standardization has as its goal the aim of assuring research long-term productivity in the hope of responding to present challenges. The goal is to organize and sustain research diversity. In 2007, Andy Sterling (2007) built a conceptual framework for studying and managing diversity: "Diversity concepts employed across the full range of sciences (…), display some combination of just three basic properties: (…) 'variety', 'balance' and 'disparity'". The variety of research traditions depends on their historical, social, cultural and even economic contexts. But today saving this variety does not mean securing or protecting an imagined historical scientific or technical identity (disparity). It means producing new knowledge and innovating in a world of intensified and mimetic competition. It means stepping out of this competition by developing alternative or simply a variety of perspectives. There is nothing heroic about this. Restoring or creating diversity depends, first of all, on the capacity of academic and research communities to conceive and explicitly debate their own objectives, methods and values with the goal of reaching a "balance" between variety and disparity. Institutional innovation and academic autonomy are key issues in this process. The problem is not to isolate or protect research universities from their economic contexts and social duties. On the contrary, the problem is to give research communities an increased capacity to negotiate their priorities and responsibilities with firms and government.

A Helix model responds to this situation. The problem is: which one? It shows that the "research university" is not *submitted* to its interactions between firms and government. But it has to assert and play its full role. Institutional innovation does not mean that an "entrepreneurial university" should be organized and managed like a firm. It simply requires stressing the logic of research and innovation, of teaching and training, the various time frames of these activities and their specific institutional requirements. Diversity is a requirement for progress in science and technology as important as standardization. Standardization is a communication requirement while diversity is a requirement for productive and creative investigation. There is no contradiction between the two, but any confusion is negative because it hides the institutional requirements for innovation processes. The individual and collective risk to differ, to develop new fields and hypotheses is a basic duty and responsibility in order to assure long-term research productivity.

Finally, this implies a different conception of competition. To compete within the same model and for the same objectives is quite different than competing on different grounds and for alternative but also complementary objectives. New modes of collaboration and positive competition can be imagined. Competition is a negative, partial or biased type of collaboration in search of one's own *advantage* at the expense not only of the other(s) but at the expense of a mutual benefit. Collaborative competition is a key issue. Positive competition does not or should not reduce diversity – but on the contrary – reinforce diversity, intensify global progress and common knowledge. The Helix model is reaching a point where long-term and collective progress should become a goal for all knowledge-based societies.

Therefore, the only way to respond to standardization and negative competition is to build and intensify diversity. This requires exploring the Helix concept and model differently. The most fruitful idea was the introduction of a *fourth helix*. During the 2002 Triple Helix conference in Copenhagen, the idea was raised to introduce "society" as a fourth helix. Adding this new helix was at first the institutional recognition achieved by Science and Technology Studies and their growing role in policy design. The report on the conference written by Leydesdorff and Etzkowitz (2003), the two originators of the theory, discussed this idea and this discussion opened a new range of debate and research on the Helix theory. But their conclusion was that this idea was redundant because "society is everywhere in the Triple Helix". The problem was, and still is, to establish what "society" really means, or stands for, in a reformed Helix model and theory. In fact, a fourth helix has always been in the middle of the triangle made up of government, universities and firms. But it still is a black box inside a black box.

To give a name and content to this virtual fourth helix has become an urgent question of research and debate. First of all, the fourth helix should not be reduced to "culture", to national traditions because of the historical State control over research activities. To clarify what "society" really means in this context, various answers and experiments exist and they all need to be debated: connecting to civil society, solving social problems, answering social needs, reducing inequities and inequalities, facilitating and taking the point of view of everyday life, bottom up, developing public infrastructure and services, developing skills, creating jobs and employment, establishing a clean and safe environment as well as sustainable social and economic development. Recently the *EU Horizon 2020 research, technology and innovation program* redefined its foresight methodology and added two new conceptions of this virtual fourth helix. They need to be mentioned because these two *officialised* fields in Human and Social Sciences will be generously funded by Brussels and will draw many answers. The second is a new urgency: "Secure societies-protecting freedom and security of Europe and its citizens". The first one "Europe in a changing world. Inclusive, innovative and reflexive societies" is another conception of a fourth helix.[12] The collective report *The future of Europe* states that "the European commission is preparing the funding of grand societal challenges (Burgelman *et al.* 2015)".

The introduction of a fourth helix transforms the model in many ways beyond the purpose of this paper. The fourth helix has clearly the role of regulating interactions between the three poles of activity and power: universities; government and the State administration; firms, industries and their related services. Industrial property law and technology transfer offices in universities are partly playing this role. Finally, a fourth helix is playing a basic political role outside established political institutions. It regulates the evolution of the whole social system. It reconfigures the relations between politics and technology, research and economics, civil society and research, politics and economics. This mutation was indeed quite predictable, seems irreversible and cannot be opposed by the state apparatus or the business communities: when science and technology concern all aspects of life in society, the way we are educated, work, commute, communicate and even reproduce, a mutation is sooner or later going to take place. All these aspects of life in society first become the target of science and technology policies but they also become the source and inspiration of all these policies. The best experiment was the "social turn" of Japan's 3rd and 4th Basic plans for science and technology, even if the first one was disrupted by the 2008 crisis and the second one by the 2011 Fukushima catastrophe.[13]

This is not enough. The fourth helix needs to receive a practical meaning in order to play its role in relation to universities, government and the economy. It needs to be structured and organized in order "to make sense". In the EU and Japan, making sense is considered an urgent need to prove to "society", to individuals and groups, that research and innovation policies bring *visible* solutions into the daily life of people, that the benefits are worth the costs of these policies. It is a search for legitimacy. Various solutions are implemented: on-line surveys in the EU, citizen debates, studies on social needs and social problems, etc. These solutions are difficult to evaluate but obviously further research is needed. To refer to "society" is to indicate the opening of a new or different "public space". Such a public space cannot be reduced to "citizen debates". It is not possible to invoke "society" without referring to the role of human and social sciences. The need to study these issues and problems is a major concern for all these disciplines. The need to disseminate their findings is crucial for society. It is also crucial to reform the formation of scientists and engineers, at all levels, so that they perceive their work not only "from inside out" as they always did, but also "from outside in", from the point of view of society. This social turn of science and technology policy is slowly reorienting research toward different local goals and situated priorities. The energy transition intensifies all these problems and solutions. We also realize that we don't really know anymore what *society* stands for. But we know at least that this social turn is a turn toward growing diversity.

Irreversibility, risk and democracy

In 1994, long before the present systemic crisis but during one of its precursors, at the early stage of the globalization process, at a moment when Germany was absorbed by its reunification and unification of two incompatible institutional systems, when Japan's power structure was measuring the full depth of its own crisis, Ulrich Hilpert (1994) was explaining and exploring the paradoxes of the state apparatus, of government and public policies, in their new role and status. It was a decisive moment when different types of policies and theories, highly influential, were designed.[14] The role of the State was transformed by the neoliberal decoupling of the State, the economy and society as the source of the globalization process. But the task of the state remained essential for establishing the conditions for economic growth and innovation processes. This task had become far more complicated: in this new configuration, political decisions and public policies too often led to unintended and even counter-productive consequences. But the jungle of economic interests was also leading to untended and counter-productive consequences. These unforeseen consequences were obvious at the national level: growing unemployment due to delocalization in low-wage regions, increased inequalities between classes and territories. At the international level, not only mature economies had to face the rapid growth of export economies in East Asia (mainly China) competing with their own industries, but this unequal growth led to an increased marginalization of whole regions in the Middle East and Africa. Whole populations felt and were excluded: they would later re-enter history with a vengeance.

In 1994, Ulrich Hilpert and his co-researchers were trying to establish a diagnosis and to find a solution. Their purpose was to overcome these paradoxes and solve these problems by designing new types of regulations and institutional arrangements. The discrepancy between the specific time frames (duration) of political action, firm management and innovation processes, the dynamics of their interactions reshaping contemporary industrial societies in a sort of endless spiral, required a new model. This spiral eventually became a helix. The *National innovation system* concept and the *Helix* theory were born in such books and took shape in this context.

Today, Japan is often considered in Europe and North American to be a dragon of the past century. The fact is that Japan was the first nation to find itself – since the end of the 1980s – in the situation, in which other mature industrial societies have found themselves since 2008. The BRICs might have reached this point before having been able to fully take off. The present Chinese administration is trying to escape from a situation it probably considers to be inevitable. So Japan was in the advance and is still a forerunner. I can only provide small hints of Japan's trial and error responses to its long-term crisis. But I explained in some detail the need to escape from the neoliberal mimetic trap by questioning established models and concepts (however recent) of innovation. In summary, social innovation is just as relevant as technological innovation. The urgent problem is a reconstruction of what is commonly called "society". I don't pretend to have any real solutions. I just explained why it is a call for diversity situated at the core of social and economic systems in a different type of research and innovation policy.

This is not playing with words but a serious problem: the intellectual competence and the level of investment required for designing and implementing a relevant research and innovation policy are so high that the resulting orientation is, or nearly is, irreversible. The cost and consequences of epistemic mistakes are so huge that they remain largely invisible. Collective time and funds spent on these policies are not available anymore for exploring other solutions. A trajectory path is created and will last. The best (or worse) example is the case of France with its nuclear policy: French society is in a trap and is unable to escape from it. The costs to escape from the trap and develop an alternative are too high.

The society, which designs such a large-scale policy, is therefore taking an extreme risk. The only solution to manage such a risk is to share it amongst the largest amount of people possible. This political and social technique is called democracy. To involve the largest amount of people is also to reduce this risk as much as possible: it is a call for individual and collective intelligence. For those concerned, it requires a high level of competence, experience and/or responsibility. The only solution to manage this situation is to organize such a policy as an experiment in advanced democracy. Citizen debates have become commonplace, but still with mixed results. They are just a forerunner of major political reforms adapted to growing environmental constraints, to comprehensive research and innovation policies and to the transformation of social and economic systems. Understood from the point of view of society, such science and technology policies require new political philosophy and institutions.

Notes

1 For a recent reformulation of the *National Innovation System* model, see Mariana Mazzucato (2013). The book studies how the state has made, and can still make, a difference while being "entrepreneurial" and "creative".
2 It was the title of the Triple Helix conference, Stanford, July 2011.
3 Information and Communication Technology.
4 When some explain that the crisis is over, it is necessary to indicate that the crisis is systemic because it was first financial in the mid-2007. It became economic and social in 2008, then global and monetary, increasing international tensions and generating regional wars. When the crisis engulfed new industrial nations and energy producers, it generated an increased wave of mass migrations further deconstructing the world order.
5 In a neo-Marxist approach, Wolfgang Streeck (2014), in *Buying time. The delayed crisis of democratic capitalism*, refuses any sort of prophecy, fate or destiny. He explains the successive policies, which generated and justified at the same the fear of a long-term recession. But innovation is not taken into account. In this paper, I also refuse the prophecy of a long-term recession but try to find a response by extending the concept of innovation.
6 See my comments (Rieu 2006) in the debate "Inventer une *société de la connaissance*. Le Japon en comparaison". Ten years later my position is the same concerning China.
7 See Roger Hahn (1971). The book studies the mimetic rivalry between the Royal Society (1663) and the Paris Academy of science (1666) as well the European-wide consequences of this rivalry on the development of "modern science".
8 Concerning Japan, see Rieu (1996).
9 On the need to draw a distinction between "knowledge economy" and "knowledge society", see Rieu (2005).
10 See for instance the reports published by the Information Technology and Innovation Foundation (www.itif.org) or the role of innovation in President Obama's 2011 State of the Union speech. He officially converted to the innovation mantra in order to restore or reinvent the golden circle.
11 The Washington, DC Council on competitiveness was founded in 1986. See www.compete.org. Its reports tell the story of American anxiety of losing the basis of its post-war economic and military hegemony.
12 It will be popular: news from Brussels have explained that this field will be very "open". A strong risk today is not to see "security" becoming one of the "grand societal challenge". The risk is to see "security" becoming a fifth helix, in competition with "society", establishing direct relations with government, industry and universities. Establishing a fourth helix is to assert that "society" is the regulation between the state apparatus, industry and university, that "security" falls within this regulation.
13 Both plans were unfortunately stalled, the 3rd one when the 2008 crisis engulfed Japan, the 4th plan was expected to be launched in April 2011 but the 11 March 2011 catastrophe in Fukushima radically transformed the conditions of its implementation.
14 My paper (Rieu 1996) written for the Japan's National Institute of Research Advancement is a typical example of this conjuncture.

References

Burgelman, J.-C. Chloupkova, J. and Wobbe, W. 2015: Foresight in support of European research and innovation policies: The European Commission is preparing the funding of great society challenges. In: M. Pausch (Ed.): *The future of Europe*. Springerlink.com.

Etzkowitz, H. and Leydesdorff, L. 1998: The triple helix as a model for innovation studies. In: *Science & Public Policy* 25 (3), 195–203.

Gordon, R. 2010: *Revisiting U.S. productivity growth over the past century with a view of the future*. Working Paper 15834, Cambridge, MA: National Bureau of Economic Research. www.nber.org/papers/w15834.

Hahn, R. 1971: *Anatomy of scientific institution: Paris Academy of Science, 1666-1803*. Berkeley, CA: University of California Press.

Hilpert, U. (Ed.) 1994: *Zwischen Scylla Und Charybdis? Zum Problem Staatlicher Politik Und Nicht-Intendierter Konsequenzen*. Wiesbaden: Westdeutscher Verlag.

Leydesdorff, L. and Etzkowitz, H. 2003: Can 'the public' be considered as a fourth helix in university-industry-government relations? Report on the Fourth Triple Helix Conference, 2002. In: *Science and Public Policy* 30 (1), 55–61.

Mazzucato, M. 2013: *The entrepreneurial state: debunking public vs. private sector myths*. London: Anthem.

OECD. 1997: *National innovation systems*. Paris: OCDE Publications. https://www.oecd.org/science/inno/2101733.pdf

Rieu, A.-M. 1996: *Japan as a techno-scientific society: the new role of research & development*. TokyoNational Institute for Research Advancement Review. Autumn, 3–6. www.nira.or.jp/past/publ/review/96autumn/rieu.html.

Rieu, A.-M. 2005: *What is knowledge society?* STS Nexus, San Jose: Santa Clara University, Center for Science, Technology and Society. http://halshs.archives-ouvertes.fr/halshs-00552293/fr/.

Rieu, A.-M. 2006. Inventer une *société de la connaissance*. Le Japon en comparaison. www.diploweb.com/forum/japon07052.htm.

Rieu, A.-M. 2008: Géostratégie de la recherche et de l'innovation. In: *Hermès*, CNRS Editions 50, 67–73. http://halshs.archives-ouvertes.fr/halshs-00360140/fr/.

Rieu, A.-M. 2012: Beyond neo-liberalism: research policies and society. The case of Japan. In: *The Copenhagen Journal of Asian Studies* 29 (2), 58–78.

Rieu, A.-M. 2013: Thinking after Fukushima (2). Epistemic shift in human and social science. In: *Asia Europe Journal* 11 (1), 65–78.

Sterling, A. 2007: *A general framework for analyzing diversity in science, technology and society*. SPRU online paper 156. www.sussex.ac.uk/spru/. Accessed 9 February.

Streeck, W. 2014: *Buying time. The delayed crisis of democratic capitalism*. London: Verso.

Summers, L. 2013: www.youtube.com/watch?v=KYpVzBbQIX0. Accessed 8 November.

Part III
Labour and innovation

5 Diversity as innovation and opportunity

Transformative affect in S&T workforce participation

Connie L. McNeely

The innovation zeitgeist is all encompassing, with scientific and technological breakthroughs transforming societies at all levels of interaction. Moreover, linked to economic progress, infrastructure expansion, and cultural engagement, advances in science and technology (S&T) mark centres of creativity and productivity, affecting national markets and workforce determinants in today's global innovation-driven economy. New technologies and innovations have led to new organizational and cultural environments, new workforce demands, and new opportunities for knowledge workers (Hilpert 2016; NAS 2015). Indeed, across academia, industry, and government, S&T enhancements and capacities have influenced and are influenced by concomitant workforce concerns and interests. Accordingly, maximizing opportunities for S&T education and employment, as the basis for innovative and productive contribution, has become a policy and organizational priority in countries around the world.

Related policy discussions in recent years have been framed principally in terms of workforce needs and economic utility, national development, and international competitiveness. The basic argument on which related debates turn is that an agile and qualified S&T workforce must be developed to create the innovation needed for growth and prosperity. Accordingly, central to efforts for economic growth and progress, countries must maximize the development and utilization of all of their human resources and talent. To that end, a more inclusionary approach to participation in S&T is required, such that enhancing opportunities for S&T education, training, and careers for individuals and groups across society has become a prominent topic in related planning and policy dialogues. However, it is clear that, bound in fundamental ways to education, epistemic and professional networks, and other such societally defined and determined features and circumstances, S&T employment — despite economic utility — relies not just on base supply and demand, but, more fundamentally, on socio-cultural processes and institutional and structural dynamics and relations (McNeely and Schintler 2016; Pearson *et al.* 2015).

This situation raises a fundamental question for consideration: Who can take advantage of the workforce opportunities presented by S&T? Addressing this question ultimately concerns relevant workforce participation and contribution to the S&T enterprise, and involves exploring the changing parameters of S&T

workforce participation reflected in demographic profiles and access. More to the point, to gain insight into related processes and effects, these issues are engaged here relative to institutional and societal relations associated with innovation and organizational and cultural dynamics and structures. The theoretical and conceptual case is delineated, with empirical references, for examining the dynamic processes attending participation and representation. The primary analytical consideration is the effect of the underrepresentation of selected socially identified and categorized individuals and groups — most notably minorities and women — in the S&T workforce not only in terms of narrowly conceived productivity, but more broadly affected societal well-being and projections. Underrepresentation means that the productive capabilities of these groups are not being engaged relative to their share of the population and, thus, that contributions and opportunities for advancements are being denied both to them and to society more generally. Underrepresentation points also to questions of sustainability, inequality, and social justice as paramount for understanding challenges and prospects for future engagement and progress, and for recognizing variations across disciplines and countries. The bottom line is that disparities in representation remain a general condition such that the advancement, access, and productive contributions of minorities and women have become critical points of contention in policies concerning national progress and innovation.

Innovation relies on knowledge-based capital and skills for effecting performance and related activities. That is, the availability of knowledge and skills is critical to meeting the challenges of growth and progress, defined through performance and productivity, which, in turn, are defined according to workforce activities and parameters. In this regard, a crucial task for this analysis is to move beyond current discussions of human capital that principally focus on outcomes only, doing little to engage or challenge the underlying dynamics and determinant structures, as well as ignoring possibilities and opportunities for change. More specifically, institutional forces and contextual relations are examined here relative to the potential to enhance as well as to increase the participation and, thus, potential contribution of underrepresented groups in S&T arenas. After a brief discussion of background issues regarding the contingent nature of related processes, a review of basic theoretical concerns is provided as a foundation for understanding and informing the analytical delineation that follows. Then, to shed light on determinant institutional and cultural structures, dynamics, and relations, relevant constructs and processes are examined in terms of changing labour needs relative to innovation and productive capacities across levels and units of analysis. An underlying comparative perspective is maintained in order to shed light on overarching institutional and cultural structures and dynamics, and related processes and interactions are considered in terms of labour needs relative to innovation and productive capacities across different levels and units of analysis. Emphasis is placed on developing a systemic understanding of diversity and meaning in S&T innovation against a backdrop of structural bias and hierarchically delineated workforce relationships.

Thus, a social lens is employed here to view and better understand innovation as an embedded social process. Looking to theoretical and empirical analyses of S&T workforce diversity, a 'science of broadening participation' perspective is engaged to develop an understanding and systematic approach for analyzing indicators and interactions in representation. While focus here is on minorities and women, diversity is framed more generally relative to a variety of demographic factors such as race, gender, ethnicity, age, disability, class, etc. It is a contextually understood and determined condition, and the structural and institutional bases on which related processes are grounded result from defined interaction and decision-making that reinforce, reproduce, and maintain disparities (cf. DiTomaso *et al.* 2007), ultimately denying and subverting potential sources of productive participation and contribution. Put simply (yet not so simply), diversity matters. Building an inclusive and productive S&T workforce is central to developing the innovative capacity needed for growth and prosperity. As such, diversity demands attention to the participation and incorporation of minorities, women, and a range of underrepresented groups, transcending and defying existing systems of privilege and stratification. This is the challenge of diversity.

The contingent S&T terrain

In an atmosphere of constant demands for new technologies and innovation in public and private arenas, jobs based on S&T knowledge and related skills are increasingly the sine qua non for productivity and mobility. While variations are found in and across countries and regions, technological changes generally have transformed skill and job requirements, thereby affecting supply and demand for related talent, education, and training. Especially in 'developed' countries, demand has been growing in sectors in which specialized technological skills increasingly are favored across sectors, causing disruptions in low- and middle-skilled positions. That is, technological changes have favored the high-skilled worker (Lund *et al.* 2012). More specifically, these changes 'create a need — and therein a significant opportunity — for many actors to respond to these challenges. The individuals, companies, and countries that can truly understand these changes and act on them will be the ones that are most able to prosper' (NAS 2015, p. 13). Arguably, this 'Fourth Industrial Revolution' or 'Industry 4.0' (Schwab 2016), based on transformative technology and innovation diffusion and improving resource allocation, 'has the potential to not only sustain and accelerate productivity growth, but also to make that growth more inclusive', by allowing more workers 'to reap the benefits of the knowledge economy' (OECD 2015, p. 18).

Such arguments also have indicated that technological changes offer an opportunity to right past inequities and disparities in workforce characteristics and structuration. However, whether or not they actually represent 'a significant opportunity' in this regard depends on a number of societal conditions such that

... some groups — particularly women, racial minorities, and people from low-income families — remain significantly less able than others to take advantage of value creation opportunities, whether because of unequal educational opportunities, the lingering effects of historical inequity, or discrimination. This inequity negatively impacts the nation's prosperity, not only because fewer people can become the innovators that create economic growth and jobs, but also because teams of people that have more women and people with diverse characteristics have been shown to be more innovative.

(NAS 2015, p. 106)

Accordingly, a country's competitiveness depends on whether and how it educates and engages all of its potential talent (cf. WEF 2013, p. 31).[1]

Education and employment divergences

While a direct causal link between productivity and levels of employment may not be specifically posited (Miller and Atkinson 2013), the politics of employment and the cultural role of employment as an indicator of sustainability and resilience are critical considerations for participatory value claims. As such, the role of educational attainment and human capital development takes center stage, influenced by technology enhancements and capacities. Human capital typically is defined as knowledge, skill, and other attributes relevant to working capabilities, and, in more focused terms, as the outcome of an individual's investment in education and work experience for future benefit (Gardiner 2000). Therefore, education, as the principal training ground for the skilled workforce, features prominently at various levels of analysis in determinant processes. The more that individuals acquire the skills required to adapt to technological change, the more easily resources can lead to productive uses (Carey *et al.* 2012, p. 26).

However, while most developed countries have seen increases in related educational attainment, some, such as the United States (U.S.), have eroding levels, especially as related to selected groups. For instance, projections indicate that 45 percent of U.S. jobs by 2018 will require at least an associate degree, but only 26 percent of Black and Latino Americans (and 14 percent of Latino immigrants) display that level of education (Cárdenas and Treuhaft 2013). Although, when allowed access and opportunity, minorities and women perform at increasingly high levels in S&T fields (EC 2000; UNESCO 2007), issues related to an increasing mismatch of skill supply and demand stand out as especially important for influencing inequality in a more general sense, considering people in terms of resource misallocation and waste. Practically speaking, their potential is not matched by appropriate education, and they are effectively barred from contributing to innovation and productivity. In a situation in which 'lifelong learning will become increasingly necessary to combat slowing growth and rising inequality'

(OECD 2015), minorities and women are in the position of always playing catch-up in education and the workforce. The process by which disadvantage begets further disadvantage — especially that related to educational attainment and societal relations — depicts the broader institutionalized and systemic nature of discrimination and underrepresentation, thereby inhibiting the development and supply of creative human capital.

Regarding employment, a generally accepted point is that the number of jobs requiring S&T capabilities is growing. Such is the case across education levels, with particular emphasis on training for skilled blue-collar workers. The information technology and communications (ITC) field offers a vivid illustration in this regard. ITC is ubiquitous, with related goods and services representing important drivers of productivity growth and economic performance across all sectors (EC 2013). ITC accounts for a substantial part of gross domestic product and employment in the European Union (EU) countries and around the world. However, there is some concern about the supply of workers with the skills necessary for fulfilling the needs of employers. ITC employment historically has been and remains predominantly 'mainstream' male, but ITC digital expansion has raised crucial questions about *those who use it* and *those who work with it*, especially in light of labor market and socio-structural dynamics. Demands for specialist skills evolve very quickly in ITC and, due to increased applications across economic sectors, demand and competition for workers with relevant technical skills are increasingly apparent (EC 2012a). As such, the rapid and dramatic changes in ITC have been framed in terms of both challenges and opportunities potentially impacting individuals and groups usually identified as underrepresented in the broader S&T workforce, raising issues of divergent demands. In recognition of such issues, the ITC workforce must be examined relative to demographic factors such as race, ethnicity, migration status, and nationality, in addition to gender and other markers of diversity that are reflected in labor market relations and processes. Investigating diversity outcomes in terms of education, hiring, and career pattern differentials requires addressing labor market conditions that can affect ITC workforce participation and representation.

The larger point is that minorities and women continue to face longstanding systemic barriers to S&T participation and advancement. Generally speaking, gender and racial disparities in S&T occupations persist despite advancement in educational attainment (ILO 2012; OECD 2012; Pearson *et al.* 2015). The institutionalized and systemic nature of discrimination and bias makes it an especially intractable situation. Evidence of ascription-based selection and representation patterns points to key ways in which discrimination and bias continue to determine workforce outcomes, directly and indirectly, such that minorities and women remain the least integrated into the S&T workforce. For example, women and minorities together represent less than 30 percent of S&T professionals, and that proportion has declined since 1990, reflecting a clear 'failure in the pipeline' (New America 2015). Fundamentally, this situation refers to a limitation and deficit in researcher development and innovation. It represents a bottleneck in which processes of research and innovation take little advantage of this workforce resource.

Women's potential in S&T fields, even with relevant educational qualifications, remains generally untapped in the labour market itself. Although women in developed countries obtain more than half of all university degrees, their share of qualifications in S&T is only 30 percent (ILO 2016). Countries like the U.S. and Germany, for instance, despite increasing degree attainment, also have high career drop-out rates for women in S&T occupations, such as engineers, due in large part to 'unfriendly' organizational cultures (Trübswetter et al. 2016). Even in fields in which women have reached or even exceeded parity in educational attainment (e.g., the biological sciences), the playing field is not at all level; minorities and women are typically disadvantaged in any case. Workforce underrepresentation is still the norm and stereotypes of (white European descent) males as dominant and superior persist (Smyth and Nosek 2015). Frankly, in light of institutionalized sexism, such attitudes and images are not surprising, indicating the need to interrogate underlying socio-structural, cultural, and institutional dynamics as fundamental barriers to innovative potential and realization.

Also, the *socio-spatial aspects* of such issues are highly apparent, especially given the global innovation system in which questions of *networked labour markets* become even more salient in the face of determinant social, economic, and political forces. As shown in earlier research (e.g., Hilpert 2012, 2016), metropolitan areas with high S&T employment tend to have overall stronger economies and there is a tendency for highly skilled S&T workers to be concentrated in a limited number of locations, for example, selected English speaking countries (e.g., U.S., United Kingdom, Canada, and Australia), Germany, France, and the Nordic countries. These countries operate as central nodes in the innovation-driven knowledge economy. These concentrations themselves operate to attract additional S&T workers from other less central locations, making for a somewhat spiral process of attraction and reproduction for individual decisions and societal tendencies in the globally networked labour market.

As a result of Industry 4.0 technological changes, new markets and jobs are being created, and new ways of working are becoming more widespread. As discussed above, estimates indicate that, by the end of the decade, 77 percent of jobs will require some kind of S&T related skills. However, divergent pathways in education and labour market trends lead to divergent outcomes in workforce representation, resulting from complex horizontal and vertical relations within which some individuals or groups are more represented and have more influence and control over the creation and flow of knowledge and opportunity. These structural relations reflect dynamics that, in the face of widely ranging contextual factors, lead to disparities and restrictions in the access and participation of certain segments of the population, directly and indirectly, intentionally and unintentionally.

Contextualized supply and demand divergences

National and organizational differences in views and pressures for diversity are useful for understanding labour divergences. Globalization and the capacity of individual countries to deploy S&T resources have implications for participation and status in the related workforce. National labour market needs and opportunities for minorities and women as knowledge workers, especially in light of societal hierarchies and relationships, are core issues in this scenario. In a desire to meet perceived S&T labour demands, many developed countries have expanded migration quotas for highly skilled workers, with accompanying incentives and special allowances in terms of financial, legal, and social rights and privileges (Kapur and McHale 2005; Hart 2010; Teitelbaum 2014). Basic research and knowledge exchange, along with investment linkages might turn on educational investment and high-skill migration. However, workers are not unlimited resources and continued (and growing) dependence on 'imports' arguably reflects a lack of investment in the future. Moreover, labour market needs can change in response to S&T innovations and potential. As such, overriding reliance on external sources to fill those needs may not be prudent, especially in the long term (McNeely and Schintler 2016).

Also, these kinds of approaches to filling labour needs effectively bypass minorities and women. Their potential remains untapped and the societal situation continues as divergent and unmatched employment and innovative opportunities. Discrimination and bias actually subverts market logic and, again, translates into wasted resources. The complex interplay of how race and gender are defined, along with how they are influenced by educational access and by employer practices and workforce requirements, is enacted within labor market and organizational settings. Along with professional networks and social capital, relative educational attainment and occupational mobility are enhanced by inclusive opportunity structures (McNeely and Camacho 2010), which can facilitate broader participation across social groups and S&T employment sectors and contribute to innovative productivity.

Workforce diversity is a relational concept referring to the composition of organizational or work units in terms of demographic or cultural characteristics held to be salient and symbolically meaningful in relationships among group members (DiTomaso *et al.* 2007). Related disparities in participation and representation illustrate the mutability of identity and exclusion-inclusion processes. More to the point, terms such as 'minorities' and 'women' are not neutral categories; they are 'saturated with inequalities'. Moreover, related complexity is reflected in intersectional configurations defined by and turning on axes of inequality. These configurations also connote agency, grounded in ways of thinking about how inequalities based on race, ethnicity, and gender (along with nation, sexuality, wealth, etc.) interact in systemic processes (cf. Bhavnani and Talcott 2014).

A foundational point is the ascriptive basis on which these issues are enacted and their outcomes determined. The concern here is the complex and systemic processes by which ascriptive characteristics underlie and determine power and status delineations and outcomes. Whereas notions of development and mobility cross organizational and social contexts, their enactment often relies on ascriptive perceptions, the logic of which frames S&T workforce disparities relative to a combination of issues (cf. DiTomaso et al. 2007): who is hired, who is given positions of responsibility and decision-making authority, who gets access to organizational resources and opportunities, and who is rewarded for their contributions, and on what basis. Note that such issues are more than normative; they denote systemic benefits or contradictions, as the case may be, for participation and innovative contribution.

Diversity as and for innovation

Competition for talent in today's innovation-driven economy demands the development, recruitment, and retention of a diverse and agile workforce (cf. Forbes 2011). Accordingly, one of the most persuasive arguments for diversity and for innovation is based on evidence showing that the most successful organizations have made steady progress in implementing diversity and equality policies (EU 2005; Herring 2009; Hunt *et al.* 2015), and relevant data are supported by case studies highlighting that diversity can lead to higher productivity and real organizational gains (Forbes 2011; Insights 2013). Research in various countries has revealed the 'business case' for diversity, with evidence indicating higher levels of success, productivity, and benefits to organizations based on diversity and inclusion across leadership structures and team collaborations (Herring 2009; Hunt *et al.* 2015). Additionally, the business case for diversity also rests on benefits from resolving labour shortages and the recruitment and retention of high quality workers (EU 2005), without ascriptive bias and exclusions, especially since a diverse workforce operates to attract top talent, whatever the source and identity (Hunt *et al.* 2015).

As a case in point, looking to the bottom line, U.S. companies with the highest levels of racial diversity have been found to earn nearly 15 times more sales revenue on average than those with the lowest levels of diversity (Herring 2009). Even more revealing has been research in various countries showing that 'companies in the top quartile for racial and ethnic diversity are 35 percent more likely to have financial returns above their respective national industry means' (Hunt *et al.* 2015). Accordingly, one can argue that, while skills and education are fundamentally important, diversity allows for more creative opportunities and innovation. That is, the synergy resulting from the combination of education, skills, and diversity leads to higher values added overall.

Furthermore, the business case for diversity is reflected in findings showing that companies with leadership characterized by a greater share of women and of racial and ethnic minorities are better able to win top talent and are able to improve and show better performance in their decision-making, employee satisfaction, and customer orientation. In fact, evidence indicates a linear relationship between racial and ethnic diversity and increased financial returns. Arguably, in this sense, highly skilled and educated minorities and women are indicators of innovative opportunities for socio-economic development and organizational success.

Thus, for example, in the United Kingdom, greater gender diversity on senior-executive teams corresponds directly with higher performance outputs; for every 10 percent gender increase, earnings show growth of 3.5 percent. In the U.S., for every 10 percent increase in racial and ethnic diversity on senior-executive teams, earnings rise at a rate of at least 0.8 percent before interest and taxes. Moreover, across various developed countries, companies have shown a 15 percent greater likelihood for financial gains above industry medians when in the top quartile of gender diversity, and an even greater 35 percent more likelihood when in the top quartile for racial and ethnic diversity (Hunt *et al.* 2015).

Diversity is a resource in this sense; socio-cultural diversity, reflected in an educated and highly skilled workforce, is a resource for innovation and productivity. That is, *diversity provides a competitive advantage* for organizations and countries that can attract and retain relevant talent (Hunt *et al.* 2015). Related innovations refer to building inclusive S&T communities across levels and units of analysis, aiming 1) to establish equality and equity, 2) to enhance creativity and excellence, 3) to stimulate S&T productivity and development, and 4) to make the conduct of S&T more responsive to market demands and to society (cf. Bonder 2015; Schiebinger and Schraudner 2011). Moreover, positive associations of educational attainment and workforce participation with individual, organizational, and country level productivity are consistent with theoretical and empirical evidence that empowering minorities and women means a more efficient use of a country's human capital endowment, and that reducing inequality reflects enhanced productivity and economic growth. Indeed, a direct impact can be posited: *Disparities and inequities in S&T education and employment are counter-innovative.*

Ascriptive dynamics as counter-innovative

The institutional and cultural processes by which positions, wages, and mobility are negotiated (explicitly or implicitly) point to discriminatory constructions. These processes advantage certain groups over others, irrespective of real or potential capabilities. In employment, discrimination occurs when, for example, minorities 'are accorded inferior treatment in the labour market or workplace relative to the white majority, even when comparably qualified in terms of education, experience, or other relevant criteria'. Thus, opportunities and advancement are not based on capabilities. On the one hand, the effect is to deprive people of opportunities that they deserve through devaluations and outcomes based on ascriptive status and characteristics (cf. Wrench 2014). On the other hand, the effect is also to deprive society of the contributions that they could make.

Note too that such arguments can apply to the 'other side of the coin', demanding attention to communities of practice, as indicated by, for example, membership in key organizations, such as professional bodies and trade-based unions. Underrepresentation in such organizations translates into a lack of collective representation for selected groups and individuals. Of course, this question of representation is somewhat circular in effect, and speaks to broader implications of participation and observed disparities. In effect, under-representation means that minorities and women are not participating; they are not included in critical leadership structures or value-added relations which, in turn, means that they are inhibited from making positive contributions. This situation arguably inhibits productivity and contradicts productive processes as noted above in the discussion of the business case for diversity.

This understanding looks to two critical aspects of relational dynamics to articulate a comprehensive and comparative treatment of S&T participation (cf. Pearson *et al.* 2015): 1) the social organization of S&T, and 2) hierarchical societal relations. Together, the social organization of S&T and larger hier-archical societal relations constitute foundational issues by which to under-stand S&T participation. They point to institutional and systemic challenges to building an inclusive and innovative S&T workforce, noting the broader socio-political, economic, and cultural environment as a major determinant of relational outcomes.

The social organization of S&T must be understood relative to global, regional, and national contexts and to organizational cultures and environ-ments. Indeed, S&T mobility and stratification generally reflect variation in representation and inclusion in comparative terms, noting again that labour demands are embedded in social processes, which ultimately can determine innovation. This point highlights fundamental changes that have been wrought in the locus of S&T work and related epistemic communities. These issues speak to both variation and isomorphism in the manner in which S&T is organized at different levels of analysis, whether cross-nationally or cross-organizationally. Thus, for example, blue collar workers in Germany and in Japan often are credited with innovative improvements, thereby highlighting questions about organizational cultures, hierarchies, and communication and management structures that can affect innovation processes and outcomes.

Along the same lines, attention to societal relations emphasizes how race and gender impact the structural and cultural interactions and dynamics of S&T work and participation and, more to the point, how horizontal and vertical dimensions of representation impact access and career prospects in related fields. Furthermore, focus on outcomes and supply-side factors in the workforce fails to address questions of power and bias that are fundamental to determinant processes leading to observed disparities, as encompassed in S&T social organization and societal hierarchical relations. The issue is not merely a question of representation, but of equity. Structural outcomes are largely determined relative to power and status, with power making possible access to opportunities and resources (DiTomaso *et al.* 2007), and those who are currently underrepresented in the high-skilled workforce remain at issue. Despite apparent gains in some fields, minorities and women continue to encounter barriers to access, participation, and power. It is still the case that, in most fields and in most contexts, certain individuals and groups are consistently underrepresented in effective decision-making and leadership positions, even in fields in which they reflect high levels of degree attainment and S&T acumen. That is, 'the larger structure of marginalization persists' (Frehill *et al.* 2015, p. 2).

Whether direct or indirect, intentional or unintentional, ascriptive bias and discrimination often outweigh competency, skill, and potential, especially in communities of practice in which decisions are dominated by (privileged) elites. *These seemingly irrational processes constitute the institutionalized reproduction of inequality across time and place.* However, they are only irrational if the fact that markets operate within and as part of the broader social context is ignored; they are completely rational in a context in which ascriptively determined discriminatory systems predominate, ignoring or stifling additional sources of creativity and innovative contributions, and operating to maintain disparities in advantage and power. They point to implicit contradictions in market rhetoric and practice and are counter-innovative.

Contributive value creation

To understand such issues, an approach is needed that will 'reconcile the efficiency of markets with the values of social community that markets themselves require in order to survive and thrive' (Ruggie 2003, p. 231). In this sense, looking beyond industries and firms, civil society organizations (labor unions, professional associations, advocacy groups, etc.) can offer legitimacy as well as ideas and insights on related processes determining S&T workforce parameters (Hart 2010), and can be considered for developing cooperative mechanisms for ameliorating related problems and for providing value and benefit across levels and units of analysis. Albeit within the current system, modern unions attempt to create pathways and opportunities for worker mobility and influence, as do other organizations supporting social transformation and rights for different groups. Their activities can be framed profitably as expanding contributions to innovation derived from broadening participation.

In fact, evidence shows that diversity is a better indicator of success than conventional indicators such as company size, employee age, or number of employees (Herring 2009). The relative performance across organizations in the same sector and same country points to diversity as a competitive differentiator that shifts market share towards more diverse companies (Hunt *et al.* 2015). Indeed, racial and ethnic diversity is associated with increased sales revenue, more customers, greater market share, and greater relative profits; gender diversity is associated with increased sales revenue, more customers, and greater relative profits. Such findings support a *value-in-diversity perspective* positing that a diverse workforce, relative to a non-diverse one, is beneficial for business (Herring 2009). Arguably, S&T underrepresentation translates into a significant loss of human resources for development and progress, and lack of workforce diversity ultimately stifles productivity and innovation (Butler *et al.* 2009; Hewlett *et al.* 2013; Hunt *et al.* 2015; Page 2007; PICPA 2015).

Invoking policy and process

Projections positing shortfalls in the supply of S&T personnel have prompted governments to consider questions of enhancing participation in related fields. However, given typical biases and exclusionary practices affecting conditions for developing the S&T workforce, supply side approaches have been insufficient. Wider institutional policies are needed, such as recruitment into pivotal positions and to important committees so that minorities and women can develop contacts, access inside information about organizational politics, and gain visibility (cf. Etzkowitz *et al.* 2010, p. 87). That is, participation is an element of the broader process for enhancing productivity; change to more inclusive participation would be a value-added contribution and innovation.

Understanding institutional and cultural challenges and constraints and how they operate to sustain — to reproduce and maintain — discriminatory processes is required to determine possible solutions and pathways to change. However, again, this rests on the strong assumption that 'solutions' are actually the goal, rather than diversionary strategies for maintenance of social control and the status quo. The interests of different stakeholders may not be aligned and may even be antithetical to one another (Leggon and McNeely 2012). Thus, attention to values and negotiations among actors in different positions and levels of power is critical for understanding and defining the parameters in which diversity can blossom — or not.

As discussed above, optimization and access to employment opportunities in this context present challenges to education and training relative to skill matching and attainment. Talent availability largely depends on education and skill training, and barriers to relevant educational attainment prevent possible workforce development at levels to drive innovation. The development and nurturance of relevant talent are essential to a community's vitality, pointing to the crucial role of academia (NAS 2016), but the lack of credentials and requisite skills to obtain and succeed early in S&T careers are especially acute among minorities and women who, accordingly, remain significantly underrepresented in S&T degree fields and in the S&T workforce.

From a practical perspective, talent must be developed in order to leverage it as a contribution to innovation, productivity, and growth. Attention to divergent labour requirements and needs stresses the impact of culture and identity on opportunity and access. Also, looking beyond businesses, organizations such as professional associations and labor unions bring legitimacy, ideas, and insights to the process (Hart 2010), and could help to develop cooperative mechanisms for ameliorating related problems and for providing value and benefit across levels and units of analysis. Furthermore, insights can be drawn from approaches used in different parts of the world to stimulate analytical thinking about principles and processes for the development and implementation of policies aimed at increasing S&T access, opportunities, and participation (Leggon *et al.* 2015).

As an example, again looking to the Nordic countries for lessons learned in reference to gender relations and diversity, the countries all have adopted policies and practices aimed at promoting equity and equality. Also, in Europe more generally since the 1990s, the European Commission has supported special initiatives on gender equality and to increase the proportion of women in academia, as well as incorporating gender-sensitive perspectives in research (EC 2000, 2008, 2009). Although varying in effectiveness, these examples offer policy lessons for invoking ways forward to increased workforce diversity. Related policy logics and rationales indicate directions for enhancing processes of inclusion, social justice, and progress for organizational and societal benefit.

Institutional constructs and applications

Even in the face of demands for innovation and productive contribution, institutionalized discrimination and bias pose barriers to S&T practice not only in regard to labor market structural change, but also to broader access and participation. Accordingly, questions of equity, access, and opportunity frame related issues over and above simple utility-based numbers. Such issues involve changes in the allocation of roles, resources, and power, taking the form of increasing employment opportunities, upgrading skills, generating income, and changing the 'diversity equation' (cf. Etzkowitz *et al.* 2010, p. 90; O'Brien 2014). Frankly, at a time marked by budget constraints and waning public investments in research and development in some countries (e.g., the U.S.), underrepresentation and disparities have been noted particularly in areas of S&T workforce development (Carey *et al.* 2012). However, innovation-intensive developments rely on organizations such as research universities and firms that thrive and depend on capacities for knowledge creation and the availability of knowledge workers. Thus, arguably, reducing and lifting barriers to participation and changing organizational (and societal) cultures can operate to add needed human resources, improve performance, and expand productivity.

Thus, profound questions have been raised about how to engage policy lessons and institutional constructs to provide protection for workers while exploiting innovative potential (WEF 2013). That is, what strategies can be engaged to develop and retain diverse talent? How can a more inclusive S&T community be constructed to incorporate broader participation and representation in the related workforce? To address such questions, it is incumbent to look beyond essentialist views of diversity and labor market inequality. As mentioned, relevant strategies should include adopting policies that specify goals and objectives, and that provide implementation strategies (Leggon et al. 2015). Also, solutions arguably must reflect a comprehensive and systemic perspective, characterized by multi-directional links that depend on labour market capacities, dependence on educational attainment and knowledge spill-overs and incorporation, general diffusion processes attached to innovation, and the interconnectedness and interdependence of technological change processes (cf. Aghion *et al.* 2008).

These points make pragmatic sense. However, they too depend on arguments for rationalized economic utility, which can be problematic in light of societal contexts reflecting ascriptive bias. Thus, to address the complexity attending issues related to the underrepresentation of minorities and women, various interrelated 'action areas' have been identified for policy and programmatic intervention, including academic preparation, psycho-social support, professional development, and leadership affect (cf. Leung and McNeely 2015). These action areas rely on an account of organizational cultures as integrative and dynamic and on sensitizing behaviour to different contextual motivators and determinants of opportunities and performance, reflecting a systemic approach to broadening S&T participation and inclusion, as previously discussed. They require looking beyond mere technocratic intervention to address more culturally substantive transformation. Inclusion and participation, as contributive factors, require an overarching multi-dimensional and multi-directional approach that will intervene in innovation processes and relations.

Note too that these notions do not support cooptation as inclusion, which actually would maintain social organizational and discriminatory hierarchical structures and practices. Rather, they posit a broadly encompassing and inclusionary position in S&T environments. More to the point, as argued above, a transformative strategy is required. Any transformative effort must ultimately address not only underrepresented individuals and groups, but should aim for change in attitudes, values, and behaviours across all stake-holders and structures, including (and even especially) those who occupy 'dominant' categories. A coherent strategy that considers relevant analytical and programmatic dimensions is needed to identify both opportunities and barriers, focusing on education and skills and on relevant sectors, occupations, and functions (cf. Miller and Atkinson 2013). However, such a strategy will only work if cultural and structural dynamics are transformed, that is, reconfigured to democratize the processes that determine educational and occupational attainment and opportunity and to privilege merit and capability over ascriptive entitlements.

The transformative impetus

Broadening participation and inclusion indicates a transformation of funda-mental relations, attitudes, and values of *both dominant and subordinate groups* in society. The complexity of this notion cannot be overstated given the deeply embedded nature of discrimination and stratification in cultural and institutional dynamics and structures. Accordingly, issues of social justice and equity are highly salient to questions of S&T workforce diversity. More superficial understandings and analyses of related conditions do not consider the *cumulative* and *reflexive* nature of determinant processes and conditions. Dedicated attention to both internal and external factors is required to construct action strategies for societal transformation. However, therein lies the problem.

One cannot assume agreement on the goal of societal transformation or on what it means in the first place. Moreover, it refers to an ultimately *essential* transformation that strips away fundamental, historically bound relational structures. This kind of change suggests that, while diversity is positively related to innovative capacity, it requires fundamental cultural and institutional disruption. Otherwise, participation simply becomes a basis for broadening exploitation. That is, *diversity has a proto-innovative basis that requires reforms and social change*, as opposed to typical social reproduction. Innovative capabilities are front and center in this regard, calling for changes in the nature and social organization of work and in the significance of workforce profiles and skills. Such issues are crucial for strengthening the capacity for innovation, and relevant stakeholders include both individuals and organizations across the social and institutional spectrum.

The aforementioned analytical dimensions and intervention areas are aimed at building an organizational and cultural infrastructure that will support broadening participation and inclusion. The ultimate goal is to 'normalize' diversity, i.e., to make diversity routine and to establish a fair balance between the affected parties such that S&T engagement and societal well-being are enhanced. Of course, the spirit of equality 'can only ever truly be promoted by challenging underlying basic assumptions including stereotypes and social expectations' (Trübswetter *et al.* 2016, p. 61). Doing so means attending to internal structures and external interaction among related processes. However, systems of inequality and discrimination encompass highly adaptable, deeply embedded, and dynamic processes, making them resistant to fundamental change (Coates 2012; Omi and Winant 1994). Especially telling are questions of access and retention that remain relevant, even when requisite qualifications are met, for determining employment participation profiles and levels. Such scenarios encompass structural and cultural challenges represented in hierarchical participation and interaction. Again, related outcomes reflect complex multidimensional processes that interact to determine opportunity and access and to sort and select who will succeed (or not) in related careers.

Transforming relevant processes and outcomes require a paradigmatic break in societal organization and relational practice — a fundamental shift in institutional and cultural principles, attitudes, behaviours, and structures. Inclusion here suggests that S&T participation and related values are constructed through interactive processes embedded in broader socio-cultural systems (Bonder 2015). Thus, improving inclusion in S&T means interrogating the ontology, structure, and legitimacy of those systems, that is, examining their essential nature, organization, and value as central operating and relational features. Indeed, in regard to traditionally underrepresented groups, 'inclusion requires a culture where differences are valued and individuals can remain authentic to themselves while still being a part of a productive team' (Insights 2013, p. 1).

A value-added diversity

Discrimination and bias are in sharp contradiction to market logic, reducing the contributions and productive power that generate higher values added. A workforce marked by narrowly homogeneous and limited relationships reflects an inherent risk of insularity and can be a hindrance in the increasingly dynamic production environment (RRA 2009). Maximizing workforce capacity requires developing a wide and diverse talent pool, such that higher education and training are increasingly important for effective innovation and value creation (NAS 2015, p. 104). Advancing education and preparing high-skilled workers arguably can lead to large returns and increased productivity, with estimates as high as 100–200 percent (NAS 2015). These workers represent opportunities for value-added and sustained contribution and advancement.

However, educational attainment and training alone, while necessary, are not sufficient to effect needed change. Even when educational barriers are overcome, employment and career disparities remain rampant. To achieve socio-economic development based on innovation, societal change is needed to match labour demands and overcome the institutionalized contradictions. Cultural and structural features and dynamics must be addressed to provide opportunities and equitable access and mobility. Identifying bias and discrimination (and reactions to them) in rhetoric and practice is crucial in this regard. Thus, for example, even when market concerns and accommodations take precedence, value can be added by making research more responsive to societal needs, thus reflecting a mutually reinforcing dynamic: *Innovation can create social change and social change can induce innovation.*

Underrepresentation in this sense is a limitation to innovation, such that overcoming it introduces more innovation and development based on the higher values added. As previously noted, research shows that more diverse organizations are both more profitable and more sustainable. However, the benefits of diversity and inclusion are not automatic. *Organizations must do the work of normalizing diversity in their cultures, of changing how they think about, engage, and enact diversity and what it means.* Diversity is not just an issue of increasing numbers of underrepresented individuals and groups. Success depends on transforming attitudes and behaviours of all involved, individuals and groups, including those who are currently privileged or advantaged, embraced by leadership and permeating the entire organization, with accountability at all levels (Butler *et al.* 2009). This is no mean feat, especially given the broadly institutionalized internal and external relations and dynamics that come into play for maintaining socially enduring ascriptive biases. Analytically, it demands a systematic theoretical and methodological engagement and understanding of innovation as socially contextualized, moving beyond typical incomplete and reductive interpretations.

Strategic mainstreaming

Again, this is not a mere numbers game. An action orientation to realizing inclusion points to transforming disciplinary and organizational cultures in both instrumental and intrinsic terms. Here, lessons might be taken from advances in gender mainstreaming and research on gender-based S&T workforce discrimination and bias. Despite efforts to remove gender disparities, women remain underrepresented in S&T educational attainment, careers, research and development, and decision-making positions (UNESCO 2003, 2004). As a result, gender mainstreaming has been introduced as a more comprehensive approach across levels of analysis to address these problems. Gender mainstreaming refers to the treatment of gender and gender perspectives as integral to the design, implementation, monitoring, and evaluation of policies and programmes in all political, economic, and social spheres (UN 1997). In fact, gender mainstreaming has been front and center in world-level discussions of the United Nations Millennium Development Goals and current Sustainable Development Goals attached to promoting gender equality and empowering women.[2]

Can this idea be extended to address other forms of participation and group dynamics? Can it be translated into a more broadly encompassing 'diversity mainstreaming'? As a general approach, mainstreaming encompasses adaptable rationales, principles, and processes that can be applied on different levels in various organizations and contexts. Mainstreaming in this instance would indicate the integration of diversity and equity into all systems and structures, policies, programmes, processes, and projects — into ways of seeing and doing, and into ways of understanding and conducting S&T (cf. Rees 2002). Embracing the discourse and approach of mainstreaming as a strategy for integrating and institutionalizing broader diversity and equity considerations in standard organizational operating procedures and activities is the point — but not a straightforward or easy task. Effective policies must be flexible and adaptable to different cultural contexts and population profiles. At the very least, analytic considerations must include 1) the extent to which mainstreaming processes are incorporated in policy and practice, 2) the ways in which different structural and cultural elements are understood and recognized as affective educational and workforce determinants, and 3) the role of social specifications and identities relative to broader representation and participation.

In other words, diversity mainstreaming policies are strategies for more sustainable workforce development (cf. Cohen 2006). In particular, while mainstreaming currently has been applied principally to gender, the same idea might be directed more broadly to race and ethnicity and other bases of discrimination to incorporate broadening and normalizing participation as integral to the design, implementation, monitoring, and evaluation of policies and programmes across political, economic, and social spheres (cf. UN 1997). In this sense, diversity mainstreaming is a strategy for integrating equity considerations in standard S&T practices and relations. Furthermore, to mainstream diversity — to make it an integral policy component — relevant strategic actions and institutional processes should be adopted in both public and private arenas. Diversity mainstreaming in S&T aims to transform discriminatory disciplinary and social institutions that are embedded in cultural norms and organizational practices.

Future challenges and prospects

As discussed here, underrepresentation in the S&T workforce is more than just a question of numbers and statistical density. It is a fundamental theoretical question of how social structures and relations are central to development and innovation. Innovation is a function of social change, and denying it from whatever source means less than optimal dynamic growth. Accordingly, recognizing the innovative capacity and contribution indicated by increased participation, what is needed is a complex systemic and structured approach that considers the intersections and interactions of social inequalities in innovation. Workforce diversity indicates different competencies and opportunities for participation in different processes and in different combinations, such that a diverse workforce is itself an innovative input in the production process.

Indeed, where diversity is found, there is a greater likelihood of innovation (RRA 2009, p. 9; WEF 2013). This is not mere rhetoric. Even in terms of business, research shows that diversity just makes good sense, in addition to furthering causes of social justice and societal well-being. However, this point does not stand by itself. Inclusion does not just happen. Diversity must be considered relative to the cohesion and community building that mark the more inclusive approaches that have been found to benefit organizations (cf. RRA 2009). As noted, 'in a world that is both diverse and deeply interconnected, companies and institutions with greater levels of diversity are achieving better performance' (Hunt et al. 2015, p. 17). That is, *diversity has become a strategic imperative.*

From this perspective, broadening participation refers to broadening contribution and can be interpreted as building creative pathways for innovation based on developing strategic relationships for enhancing organizational performance and productivity. As advanced economies become more diverse, embracing diversity can give companies an advantage in competing for talent. Indeed, economic and demographic shifts are forcing new views concerning the workforce inclusion of minorities and women. Diversity is a critical consideration for understanding the current and future skill supply and labour relations, and underrepresented groups targeted by diversity efforts are important sources of desirable talent (Hunt et al. 2015).

Analytically, the logic of diversity is applicable in broader terms, extended to individuals and groups who have faced social discrimination and bias in access and mobility. In this sense, building upon and expanding the idea of mainstreaming, the principal policy aim is the systematic incorporation of diversity and inclusion into research, analysis, and application to create 'Diversities of Innovation'. More to the point, diversities of innovation can be captured by facilitating change toward an inclusive S&T workforce (Butler *et al.* 2009). Harnessing representation and diversity will create a more productive environment based on inclusion and achievement. Indeed, as research has revealed, diversity drives innovation, maximizing opportunities and creating new markets (Cárdenas and Treuhaft 2013).

Of course, recognizing that related factors are confounded by social dynamics and structures requires an awareness of the complexity involved with developing workforce profiles that reflect equitable processes. Also, labour market and workforce demands and profiles are fluctuating in response to dramatic technological changes affecting the very nature of innovation and organization of work (cf. OECD 2016). For example, arguments abound positing the creation of new jobs and opportunities in response to Industry 4.0 technological changes (Langdon *et al.* 2011; Sirkin 2016). In fact, in today's highly globalized, technologically driven knowledge economy, S&T jobs are among the fasting growing of all types. Whether in academia, government, or industry sectors, or collaboration across them, organizations need skilled workers in order to remain competitive and enhance well-being. This requires not only developing and attracting top talent, but also leveraging diversity to achieve better performance and productivity (cf. NAS 2015, p. 6). However, related approaches often reflect only a superficial and generally non-contextualized understanding of skill development and worker mobility. Given the circular relationship among education, workforce, and societal discrimination and disparities, some groups are overlooked as part of an innovative future with higher values added based on participation. As such, practices and attitudes that support inequality and disparities depress the participation and contribution of minorities and women. Such positions are ultimately harmful not only to S&T advancement, but to economic, national, and societal advancement as well. Accordingly, *inequalities that depress diversity in S&T participation depress contributions to knowledge, productivity, and innovation.*

Indeed, policymakers should take note that, in order to maximize productive potential and competitiveness — and, more, for general societal well-being and stability — countries should strive for equity in opportunities and access to education and workforce participation (cf. WEF 2013). More than ever before, in the growing information and knowledge society, the underrepresentation of minorities and women and of other selected groups in S&T fields translates into a significant loss of human capital for development and progress (UNESCO 2007). Indeed, 'when we lose their intelligence and their energy, the impact is felt in reduced innovation and growth across whole economies and whole cultures'.[3] Transforming disciplinary and professional cultures and creating environments for equity and access in the S&T workforce and, more, for supporting contribution to productivity and innovation require explicit and direct, bottom-up and top-down attention to broadening participation now.

Notes

1 Thus, for example, technological development is critical to meet productive capacity-building objectives in developing countries (UNCTAD 2007), and evidence indicates that one of the highest returns for a developing economy comes from investing in education for girls and women (World Bank 2012).
2 www.un.org/millenniumgoals
3 E.W. Lempinen of TWAS, in OWSD 2013.

References

Aghion, P., Algan, Y. and Cahuc, P. 2008: Can Policy Influence Culture? CEPREMAP/ Docweb no. 0801. http://www.tinyurl.com/l8eprzu

Bhavnani, K., and Talcott, M. 2014: Interconnections and Configurations: Toward a Global Feminist Ethnography. In: Hesse-Biber, S.N. (Ed.). *Handbook of Feminist Research: Theory and Praxis*. Thousand Oaks, CA: Sage, 135-153.

Bonder, G. 2015: Foreword. In: Pearson et al.

Butler, R., Oldham, M. and Verderese, J. 2009: Why Diversity, Why Now? Creating Sustainable Competitive Advantage Through Diversity and Inclusion. *Pricewaterhouse-Coopers View* (Spring), 46–53.

Cárdenas, V. and Treuhaft, S. (Eds.). 2013: All-In Nation: An America that Works for All. Center for American Progress/PolicyLink. https://www.americanprogress.org/ issues/race/reports/2013/07/24/70540/all-in-nation-an-america-that-works-for-all

Carey, D., Hill, C., and Kahin, B. 2012: Strengthening Innovation in the United States. Economics Department Working Paper No. 1001, Organization for Economic Cooperation and Development.

Catalyst. 2014: *The Gender Divide in Tech-Intensive Industries*. New York, NY: Catalyst.

Coates, R.D. 2012: *Covert Racism*. Chicago, IL: Haymarket Books.

Cohen, J.E. 2006: Human Population: The Next Half Century. In: Kennedy, D. (Ed.): *Science Magazine's State of the Planet 2006-7*. London: Island Press.

Craig, E., Thomas, R.J., Hou, C. and Mathur, S. 2011: No Shortage of Talent: How the Global Market Is Producing the STEM Skills Needed for Growth. In: *Accenture*.

DiTomaso, N., Post, C., and Parks-Yancy, R. 2007: Workforce Diversity and Inequality: Power, Status, and Numbers. In: *Annual Review of Sociology* 33, 473–501.

Etzkowitz, H., Gupta, N., and Kemelgor, C. 2010: The Gender Revolution in Science and Technology. In: *Journal of International Affairs* 64 (1), 83-100.

European Commission (EC). 2000: *Science Policies in the European Union: Promoting Excellence Through Mainstreaming Gender Equality*. Brussels: EC.

European Commission (EC). 2008: *Benchmarking Policy Measures for Gender Equality in Science*. Brussels: EC.

European Commision (EC). 2009: *The Challenge in Research Funding: Assessing the European National Scenes*. Brussels: EC.

European Commission (EC). 2012a: *EU Skills Panorama Information and Communications Technologies (ICT) Sector Analytical Highlight*. Brussels: EC.

European Commission (EC). 2012b: *EU Skills Panorama STEM Skills Analytical Highlight*. Brussels: EC.

European Commission (EC). 2013: ICT for Competitiveness and Innovation. http:// ec.europa.eu/enterprise/sectors/ict/index_en.htm.

European Union (EU). 2005: *The Business Case for Diversity: Good Practices in the Work-place*. Luxembourg: EU.

Forbes. 2011: Global Diversity and Inclusion: Fostering Innovation Through a Diverse Workforce. *Forbes/Insights*.

Frehill, L., McNeely, C.L., and Pearson, W., Jr. 2015: An International Perspective on Advancing Women in Science. In: Pearson et al.

Gardiner, J. 2000: Gender and Family in the Formation of Human Capital. In: Cook, J., Roberts, J. and Waylen, G. (Eds.): *Towards a Gendered Political Economy*. Seffield: PERC, 61–76.

Goertz, G. and Mazur, A. 2008: Mapping Gender and Politics Concepts: Ten Guide-lines. In: Goertz, G. and Mazur, A. (Eds.): *Politics, Gender, and Concepts: Theory and Methodology*. Cambridge: Cambridge University Press, 14–43.

Hart, D. 2010: Introduction. In *Review of Policy Research* 27 (4), 387-388.

Herring, C. 2009: Does Diversity Pay? Race, Gender, and the Business Case for Diversity. In: *American Sociological Review* 74 (2), 208–224.

Hewlett, S.A., Marshall, M., and Sherbin, L. 2013: How Diversity Can Drive Innov-ation. In: *Harvard Business Review* (December).

Hilpert, U. 2012: Networking Regionalized Innovative Labour Markets: Towards Spatial Concentration and Mutual Exchange of Competence, Knowledge, and Synergy. In: Hilpert, U. and Lawton Smith, H. (Eds.): *Networking Regionalized Innovative Labour Markets*. London: Routledge, 35–57.

Hilpert, U. (Ed.). 2016: *Routledge Handbook of Politics and Technology*. London: Routledge.

Hunt, V., Layton, D. and Prince, S. 2015: *Diversity Matters*. In: McKinsey and Company.

Husu, L. 2015: A Comprehensive National Approach to Promote Gender Equality in Science: The Case of Norway. In: Pearson et al.

Insights. 2013: Fostering Innovation Through Diversity and Inclusion. The Insights Group.

InterAcademy Partnership (IAP). 2015: *Women for Science: Inclusion and Pariticipation in Academies of Science*. Pretoria: Academy of Science of South Africa.

International Labour Organization (ILO). 2012: *Global Employment Trends for Women*. Geneva: ILO.

International Labour Organization (ILO). 2016: *World Employment Social Outlook: Trends 2016*. Geneva: ILO.

Kandola, R. and Fullerton, J. 1998: *Diversity in Action*. London: Institute of Personnel and Development.

Kapur, D., and McHale, J. 2005: *Give Us Your Best and Brightest: The Global Hunt for Talent and Its Impact on the Developing World*. Washington, DC: Center for Global Development.

Lamberts, M., Ode, A., and Witkamp, B. 2014: *Racism and Discrimination in Employment in Europe*. ENAR Shadow Report. Brussels: European Network Against Racism.

Langdon, D., McKittrick, G., Beede, D., Khan, B., and Doms, M. 2011: STEM: Good Jobs Now and for the Future. Economics and Statistics Administration, Issue Brief No. 03-11 (US Department of Commerce).

Leggon, C., and McNeely, C.L. 2012: Promising Policies. In: Pearson, W., Jr., Frehill, L., and C. Didion (Eds.). *Blueprint for the Future: Framing the Issues of Women in Science in a Global Context*. Washington, DC: National Academies Press.

Leggon, C., McNeely, C.L., and Yoon, J. 2015: Advancing Women in Science: Policies for Progress. In: Pearson et al.

Leung, M.A., and McNeely, C.L. 2015: Opening Doors to Communities of Practice: Programmatic Interventions for Inclusion in the Computing Sciences. In: *IEEE Xplore/RESPECT* 2015. https://ieeexplore.ieee.org/document/7296520

Lund, S., Manyika, J., and Ramaswamy, S. 2012: Preparing for a New Era of Work. In: *McKinsey Quarterly* (November).

Mazur, B. 2010: Cultural Diversity in Organizational Theory and Practice. In: *Journal of Intercultural Management* 2 (2), 5–15.

McNeely, C.L., and Camacho, E.T. 2010: Conceptualizing STEM Workforce Migration in the Modern World Polity. In: *Labor: Supply and Demand eJournal*/ERN Public Policy Institutes Research Paper Series 2 (3). http://ssrn.com/abstract=1593393

McNeely, C.L., and Schintler, L. 2016: Recognizing Opportunities for S&T Workforce Development and Productivity: The Gendered Resource. In: Hilpert.

Milkman, K.L., Akinola, M. and Chugh, D. 2015: What Happens Before? A Field Experiment Exploring How Pay and Representation Differentially Shape Bias on the Pathway into Organizations. In: *Journal of Applied Psychology* 100 (6), 1678–1712.

Miller, B. and Atkinson, R.D. 2013: Are Robots Taking Our Jobs, or Making Them? In: *Information Technology and Innovation Foundations* (September). www2.itif.org/2013-are-robots-taking-jobs.pdf.

National Academy of Sciences (NAS). 2015: *Making Value for America: Embracing the Future of Manufacturing, Technology, and Work.* Washington, DC: National Academies Press.

National Academies of Sciences (NAS). 2016: *Promising Practices for Strengthening the Regional STEM Workforce Development Ecosystem.* Washington, DC: National Academies Press.

National Science Foundation (NSF). 2016: *Science and Engineering Indicators.* Arlington, VA: NSF.

New America. 2015: Technology for the People, By the People. Open Technology Institute. www.newamerica.org/oti/technology-for-the-people-by-the-people

O'Brien, J. 2014: The Diversity Equation: How Inclusiveness Is Driving Workplace Engagement. American Express Open Forum. www.americanexpress.com/us/small-business/openforum/articles/diversity-equation-inclusiveness-driving-workplace-engagement.

Omi, M. and Winant, H. 1994: *Racial Formation in the United States.* New York, NY: Routledge.

Organization for Economic Cooperation and Development (OECD). 2012: *Closing the Gap.* Paris: OECD.

Organization for Economic Cooperation and Development (OECD). 2015: *The Future of Productivity.* Paris: OECD.

Organization for Economic Cooperation and Development (OECD). 2016: Policy Forum of the Future of Work, Employment and Ministerial Meeting, 15 January 2016. www.oecd.org/employment/ministerial/policy-forum.

Page, S.E. 2007: *The Difference: How the Power of Diversity Creates Better Groups, Firms, Schools, and Societies.* Princeton, NJ: Princeton University Press.

Pearson, W., Jr., Frehill, L., and McNeely, C.L. (Eds.). 2015: *Advancing Women in Science: An International Perspective.* London: Springer.

Pennsylvania Institute of Certified Public Accountants (PICPA). 2015: *More Clients, More Talent, More Revenue: The Business Case and Toolkit for Diversity.* www.picpa.org.

Plan. 2009, 2015: *The State of the World's Girls.* plan-international.org/becauseiamagirl

Rees, T. 2002: *National Policies on Women and Science in Europe: A Report about Women and Science in Thirty Countries.* Luxembourg: Office for Official Publications of European Communities.

Root, H. 2013: *Dynamics Among Nations: The Evolution of Legitimacy and Development in Modern State.* Cambridge, MA: MIT Press.

Rothwell, J. 2013: The Hidden STEM Economy. Metropolitan Policy Program, Brookings Institution.

Ruggie, J.G. 2003: Taking Embedded Liberalism Global: The Corporate Connection. In: Held, D. and M. Koenig-Archibugi (Eds.): *Taming Globalization: Frontiers of Governance*. Cambridge: Polity Press.

Russell Reynolds Associates (RRA). 2009: *Different Is Better — Why Diversity Matters in the Boardroom*. New York: RRA, Inc.

Ryan, J., Hawdon, J. and Branick, A. 2002: The Political Economy of Diversity: Diversity Programmes in Fortune 500 Companies. In: *Sociological Research Online* 7 (1). www.socresonline.org.uk/7/1/ryan.html.

Schiebinger, L. and Schraudner, M. 2011: Interdisciplinary Approaches to Achieving Gendered Innovations in Science, Medicine, and Engineering. In: *Interdisciplinary Science Reviews* 36 (2), 154–167.

Schwab, K. 2016: *The Fourth Industrial Revolution*. Geneva: World Economic Forum.

Sirkin, H.L. 2016: Advanced Manufacturing Is Not a Job Killer, It's a Job Creator. *Forbes Magazine Online*. https://goo.gl/xfCcvL

Skerry, P. 2002: Beyond Sushiology: Does Diversity Work? In: *Brookings Review* 20 (1), 20–23.

Smyth, F.L. and Nosek, B.A. 2015: On the Gender-Science Stereotypes Held by Scientists: Explicit Accord with Gender-Ratios, Implicit Accord with Scientific Identity. In: *Frontiers in Psychology*. Doi: 10.3389/fpsyg.2015.00415.

Teitelbaum, M.S. 2014: *Falling Behind? Boom, Bust, and the Global Race for Scientific Talent*. Princeton, NJ: Princeton University Press.

Trübswetter, A., Genz, K., Hochfeld, K. and Schraudner, M. 2016: Corporate Culture Matters — What Kinds of Workplaces Appeal to Highly Skilled Engineers? In: *International Journal of Gender, Science, and Technology* 8 (1), 46–66.

United Nations (UN). 1997: *Report of the Economic and Social Council for 1997*. New York: UN.

United Nations Conference on Trade and Development (UNCTAD). 2007: *Trade and Development Report, 2007*. Geneva: United Nations.

United Nations Educational, Scientific, and Cultural Organization (UNESCO). 2003: *Assessment of Resources, Best Practices, and Gaps in Gender, Science, and Technology in the Asia-Pacific Region*. Jakarta: UNESCO.

United Nations Educational, Scientific, and Cultural Organization (UNESCO). 2004: Comparative Study on Gender Dimension of Policies Related to the Development and Application of Science and Technology for Sustainable Development. In: *Regional Secretariat for Gender Equity in Science and Technology*. Jakarta: UNESCO.

United Nations Educational, Scientific, and Cultural Organization (UNESCO). 2007: *Science, Technology, and Gender: An International Report*. Paris: UNESCO.

World Bank. 2012: *World Development Report: Gender Equality and Development*. Washington, DC: World Bank.

World Economic Forum (WEF). 2013: *The Global Gender Gap Report*. Geneva: WEF.

Wrench, J. 2014: Ethnic Discrimination and Anti-Discrimination in Employment: A Comparative European Perspective. Presented at the Principles of Equality and Challenges of Discrimination: Problems and Effective Remedies/Global Governance Program, EUI Florence.

6 Postsecondary education and the development of skilled workforces

Comparative policy innovation in
Brazil and the U.S.

Paul M.A. Baker, Matej Drev and Mariza Almeida

Introduction

It has become fairly common in developed economies for industrial concerns to maintain research and design expertise in centers of innovation, and move actual production and manufacturing offshore to other countries (NRC 2012). While there are certain efficiencies to this approach, it raises questions about what might be lost in the hollowing out of the production of goods that depend on advanced and specialized skills, as well as what efficiencies might be lost, especially in nascent complex product industries, due to a widening geographical gap between research, design, and manufacturing. A number of occupations (i.e. "middle-skill") are increasingly requiring advanced skills that historically have been considered technical or vocational (Handel 2015; Holzer & Lerman 2009). These skills fall somewhat between those generally acquired in a higher educational setting and more traditional vocational training. It is not uncommon to frame labor force adaptive innovation as a consequence of top-down corporate innovation, but less recognized is bottom-up innovation, particularly in manufacturing settings, that comes from the characteristics and experience of the labor force with significant tacit knowledge of production processes, and which can influence industry sector innovation. We believe that this represents a relatively untapped source of innovation that can be developed. Evidence of this lies in the significant difference in importance of this kind of innovation that occurs as a consequence of geographic, cultural and policy variation (Hilpert 2006).

From a supply standpoint, in many industrialized countries, workforces are increasingly clustering along an educational gradient into unskilled, basic labor, at one end, and highly educated, specialized, research and design focused knowledge workers at the other. As an (inadvertent) outcome, the middle-skill space along this gradient – the neglected highly skilled trades, critical to advanced manufacturing – have been allowed to decline, especially in the United States. While this trend of patchy workforce development has been observed by a number of scholars (e.g. Holzer 2015), most of the remedies to date have focused on tweaking traditional higher education (colleges and universities) to produce a better fit between higher education and employer needs. This somewhat ad hoc "fix", while potentially useful in the short term, may be targeting symptoms rather than underlying causes.[1] Put within a context of innovation as diverse and multi-dimensional, there is an opportunity to design more targeted policy interventions in a way which help support the development of skilled workforces which are adaptable to the changing needs of industry and research as well as capable of upgrading their skills as needed by the changing economy. With this in mind, in this paper we explore policy strategies for workforce development from two distinct industrialized economies, United States, and Brazil that offer perspectives for effective workforce development strategy for the coming decades.

Skill and education

While equating "skill" with educational attainment in traditional economics literature serves as a useful heuristic, it is also somewhat representative of the dysfunction present in current policy approaches aimed at fixing the problem of workforce divergence. Even the most prominent recent economic studies of the technology-driven splintering of the workforce along skill distribution conflate worker skill with college attendance or completion (e.g. Acemoglu & Autor 2011; Goldin & Katz 2010). However, participation in university education is not necessarily the sole, or even most appropriate representation of worker skills, especially in the most dynamic segments of the labor market, that of younger workers (Baker, et al., 2015). There has been a recent trend for highly skilled software developers to forgo formal university education in favor of coding training, alternative credentialing and other postsecondary skills acquisition (Waters 2015). A number of successful high-tech entrepreneurs are college dropouts. This is not an unknown condition. Artisans in service industries (e.g. chefs, make-up artists, musicians, video producers) might have little-to-no *formal* college-level education, even though they possess significant highly specialized skills that markets value. The same argument could be made for certain manufacturing workers, such as welders and machinists, that is, the acquisition of highly specialized skills can occur through, in-person, experience-based learning. This underscores the importance of tacit knowledge and experience, which are disembodied and acquired as a consequence of work being done. Alternatively, skills acquisition can occur through non-university-based postsecondary education as characterized by the German apprenticeship model (Gerlach & Ziegler 2015). Also, referred to a dual training, trainees split their days between classroom instruction at a vocational school and on-the-job time at a company.

> The theory they learn in class is reinforced by the practice at work. They also learn work habits and responsibility and, if all goes well, absorb the culture of the company. Trainees are paid for their time, including in class. The arrangement lasts for two to four years, depending on the sector.
>
> (Jacoby 2014)

Thus, given the observation that worker skills and educational attainment are increasingly becoming decoupled, then the focus on addressing labor market characteristics and supply via tweaks to the traditional higher education system might not be an optimal policy approach. Diverse approaches to policy innovation are called for, which recognize, in addition to the utility of traditional apprenticeship approaches (Lerman 2014), the value of innovative, alternative (e.g. information technology driven) learning environments made up of non-traditional postsecondary partnerships of various stakeholders, including employers, public institutions, employees (e.g. trade unions), and non-profit organizations (Auguste & Mariani 2015).

Technological change, innovation and workforce trends

What were the causes of the trend of clustering of the workforce into the highly skilled and low-skilled polarities? A key explanation is technological change. Recent literature in economics suggests that in the last few decades, technological change simultaneously raised the demand for skill and automated routinized worker tasks, creating a polarized equilibrium in the labor market. On the one hand, the demand (and price for) the most highly skilled workers and least-skilled workers increased, while the demand for workers in the middle of the skill spectrum decreased precipitously (e.g. Acemoglu & Autor 2011, among others). Advances in information and communication technology made mid-skill routinized tasks easy to automate (e.g. repetitive and highly-structured clerical and manufacturing work), lowering the labor market demand for affected individuals. At the same time, the return to knowledge and design focused work increased.

Another factor present, particularly in the U.S. and U.K. economies, was the influence of neoliberal economic philosophies, resulting in economies characterized by relatively flexible labor markets that allow rapid adjustments within a global economy, capital markets favoring replacement of labor with technology, or conversely, outsourcing labor needs to cheaper alternatives, and a focus on market operation rather than government intervention. Manufacturing jobs declined as the combination of technological innovation and cheaper labor made it more cost- effective to offshore jobs. As the industrial capability significantly weakened there were fewer jobs for the "middle skilled" and consequently no demand for improving their skills. This feedback loop resulted in fewer middle-skilled workers, and hence decreasing capacity to manufacture in the U.S. and of course, reducing demand for labor. In contrast, a number of European countries (e.g. Germany and the Scandinavian countries) took an alternative approach and invested heavily in re-skilling and modernizing the workforce to adapt to such changes. This allowed for example, for structural change in traditional heavy manufacturing regions based on investment in human capital. Currently, the German recognition of the importance of comprehensive industry policy (such as Industry 4.0 approach) recognizes the importance of manufacturing innovation, and the resultant investment in both automation as well as skills development, has maintained the leading edge in manufacturing processes (Gerlach & Ziegler 2015).

Absent these structural interventions, the composition of the workforce thus changes to one that is skews highly skilled and analytic – typically university-trained workers, and to lower-end service jobs, which are difficult or not particularly cost-effective to outsource. This least-skilled work contains a significant share of non- routinized tasks (e.g. preparing a meal, driving a delivery truck, installing a window frame). Further, the application of information and communication technologies (ICT) in control systems allows for the disaggregation of some advanced manufacturing skills from the locus of production (the factory floor) to a centralized or even non- local place, reducing the need for highly skilled industrial workers.

Another technology facilitated change is the re-conceptualization of the nature of work. Historically, work generally consisted of a worker completing a set of tasks at a fixed location – the workplace. The application of ICTs has allowed work to be deconstructed into a set of activities or tasks that occur at the point in time when they are needed to complete an objective. The work may or may not be done by a single agent who might or might not be co-located with other elements of the work process. While this virtualization of work promises economic efficiencies, there are also significant social and economic consequences to workplaces and communities. (Baker, Moon & Ward 2006, Moon, et al., 2014). A consequence of this is the rising "Gig economy" (Torpey & Hogan 2016) which matches a specific set of skills or work to a short-term specific need. This may be appealing to those with an entrepreneurial mindset, or high-risk tolerance for uncertainty and the desire to be in full control of their workflow, but when applied in enterprise settings transfers risk (such as loss of job protection and benefits) to the individual. In this way, the shrinking of the mid-range of the skills distribution may be considered an inevitable result of exogenous technological trends.

In fact, this trend is visible in many industrialized countries, including in the United States, Canada, and some countries of the European Union (Antonczyk, DeLeire & Fitzenberger 2010; Boudarbat, Lemieux & Riddell 2010). However, this thinking obscures three crucial facts: 1) the effect of this uneven workforce distribution on the efficiency of the innovation process; 2) the importance of place – the context of work locale; and 3) the potential for targeted public policy interventions to affect the equilibrium workforce distribution.

In addition to capital availability, and organizational cultures that recognize the advantages of flexibility, and innovative processes, successful adoption of innovation requires access to, and flow of workers across, the various levels of the skill pyramid (Acemoglu, Mostagir & Ozdaglar 2014; Arora, Branstetter & Drev 2013; Garicano & Rossi-Hansberg 2006). Especially in advanced manufacturing, skilled trade workers and technical machinists play an essential role in this process, as they provide rapid prototyping capabilities, and efficient implementation of inventions into the manufacturing process. In addition, they are vehicles for incremental process innovation, as they have the ability to rapidly observe and address inefficiencies in the manufacturing process. Their shrinking ranks, in many developed economies, due primarily to skill-biased technological change (and globalization), can therefore distort the optimal allocation of labor as an input into the innovation process, and lower its efficiency.

Policy approaches to human capital and workforce development

What kinds of innovation related policy interventions can restore a balanced workforce development for the future? We argue that the current focus on tweaking traditional postsecondary education may be suboptimal as it is trying to fix the problem of "missing skills" by bolstering traditional education. Instead, novel alternative approaches are needed, including a shift from a focus primarily on bachelor's and master's degree attainment to a broader array of policy objectives including multiple postsecondary credentials and advanced skills development opportunities (Van Horn, Greene & Edwards 2015; National Academy of Sciences 2013). In what follows, we document and compare innovative workforce development policy approaches in two different industrialized countries: United States, a technologically advanced country with a strong educational system, and Brazil, a newly industrialized country characterized by global competitiveness in several highly specialized industries. We also point out best practices whose wider adoption might significantly reduce the problem of shrinking ranks of middle-skill trade workers and technical machinists.

Another dimension relates to the impact of broader institutional (in this case, non-public sector) engagement in workforce development. As they have done since their inception in the late 19th and early 20th century, labor unions continue to be an important provider and stakeholder in worker's education and workforce development (Stuart, Huzzard & Oup 2015). However, the degree of union involvement differs substantially across countries, with some (e.g. Germany) actively fostering union-led (highly skilled) workforce development, while others (e.g. United States) exhibit declines in unionization rates and union strength. Not surprisingly, the International Labor Organization (ILO) emphasizes the need for labor union initiative in "encouraging innovative pedagogical approaches, delivery instruments and partnerships which promote the creation of new educational programs, curricula and course materials based on the needs and aspirations of workers and their unions." (ILO 2007). Other, increasingly important actors in the rethinking of the workforce development, are third sector, NGO, and corporate interests which have invested resources in the rethinking and redesign of postsecondary education. These range from large foundations such as the Bill and Melinda Gates and Lumina Foundations, institutions with interest in higher education change, such as the Clayton Christensen Institute, The Aspen Institute and New America, as well as technology developers with and interest in innovation in educational processes.

Historically, in many parts of the world, postsecondary education policy has tended to be a top-down, public sector-driven construct (Altbach, Reisberg & Rumbley 2009). While in the United States, this generally has been at a subnational (state level), and at federal or national level in other countries. In implementation, this varies from a fairly regimented approach of state driven policy objectives (e.g. enrolment quotas, program/field specific funding, curriculum mandates) to a more open system of guidance and cooperative policy in which institutions, while relatively independent, are incentivized through the use of public sector programs, or conversely, discouraged through the loss of public sector funds.

Conceptual model of postsecondary policy driven innovation

Given the complexities of policy articulation, regardless when considered as an independent (facilitating) variable, or, alternatively, as a dependent variable, as a consequence of stakeholder input, it is useful to construct a working model to help put various factors of the problem into conversation. The model (see Figure 6.1) attempts to capture the influence of various components of workforce development, which too frequently are examined in isolation rather than as an interconnected system that can result in suboptimal policy solutions.

Context and level: For instance, looking at postsecondary interventions from a macro level, the context of the particular workforce under consideration becomes important. At what level is policy conceptualized and developed and how does this translate into implementation. Is policy crafted at a state (i.e. national or federal level), is it crafted at a more regional/local level, or a combination of these? Economic conditions also are important here in that

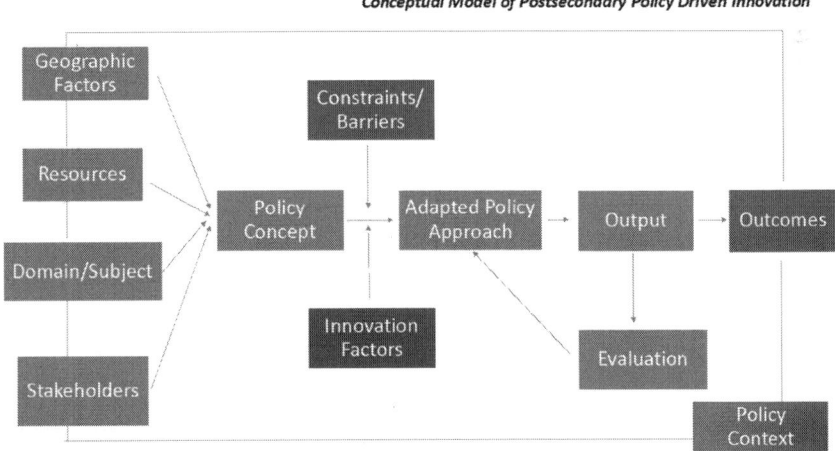

Figure 6.1 Conceptual Model of Postsecondary Policy Driven Innovation

while innovation frequently has been linked to economic growth (as a driver), the conditions for the emergence of technological innovation is less clear, but appears related to a variety of factors including geography, state policy initiatives, and networks of intellectual and human capital and economies that have capacity to take advantage of emergent scientific and technological advancements (Abramovitz 1986; Greenhalgh & Rogers 2012; Nelson 1995; Romer 1994). Hence post-secondary *policy* innovation (that is, one that explores new approaches) as well as policy *addressing* innovation, are both drivers of change, as well as a consequence of beneficial underlying social, economic, and political conditions. These policies can be applied in several ways, for instance, one in which a policy objective could be used to leverage an extant underutilized existing workforce. This might take the form of tax subsidies to hire a given set of highly skilled workers, or to enhance growth in a targeted sector, such as aviation. Conversely, policy instruments could target *development* of labour – such as policy incenting or supporting development of workers with advanced skills training – to address the concern that "there are no workers qualified to produce the desired manufactured products." *Domain:* Another set of considerations relates to the object being guided. For instance, postsecondary education policy covers the provision of higher education, specifically, as well as the development of technical/professional advanced skills (e.g. apprenticeship type approaches), and occupation specific skills including professional development. These each have overlapping interests involved and consequently, potentially competing policy objectives.

Resources: This ranges from public sector funding (Federal/national, regional, local), to public-private partnerships, to private corporate (mostly training oriented), and increasingly, to third sector funding. An example of this could be an industry supported apprentice program, or a state economic development-oriented training program.

Actors/stakeholders: who (and what) are the interests involved – institutions, students, employers, governments, among others. It is not enough to simply identify these interest, empirical data collection is critical to be able to evaluate efficacy of policy interventions.

Approaches: What are the delivery modalities (higher education, private [proprietary] schools, training specific [short-term] options, technology-driven ["Do it yourself"] and traditional apprentice-based programs).

Barriers: These include such factors as cost, both to the learner as well as to other stakeholders, technological barriers, awareness of system constraints, resistance to change, risk aversion, among others.

Policy feedback mechanisms: Various measure of efficacy, including learner performance, and the application of "big data" and data analytics in measuring efficacy, changes in workforce composition, employer satisfaction, among others.

Applying our model, then, analysis yields three main lessons for effective workforce development: (1) for maximum workforce development impact, policy interventions should be open to a wider range of possibilities than have historically been employed; including alternative learning/training approaches (e.g. information technology driven, alternative delivery and participation modalities) including new learning environments and opportunities, (2) workforce development should have an intentional focus on broadening postsecondary partnerships of various stakeholders, including employers, public institutions, employees (e.g. trade unions), and non-profit organizations, and (3) re-examination of the nature and range of work related activities, and exploration of new approaches to develop a better fit between technology enabled work (and work contexts) and the skills and availability of 21st century workforces.

Approaches to Developing 21st Century Workforces – Comparative Case Examples

It is helpful to present some comparative statistics for context. Target science and technology workforce indicators vis-à-vis the innovation level in the international context provide a useful comparative country innovation level perspective. Table 6.1 (below) presents the Global Innovation Index (GII) 2016 rank and chosen input and output scores for selected countries in order to provide a picture that allows comparisons in order to understand the country's context.

While a cursory examination of the rankings indicates that the U.S. and Brazil are relatively far apart, with respect to innovation, the size of the Brazilian economy (9th in the world) suggests that resources are available in Brazil to address the underlying conditions reflected in these indicators. Further, certain key indicators such as infrastructure and per capita GDP fall within the upper half of countries represented. Taking a more focused look, the globally competitive nature of certain industries (e.g. aviation, agriculture, and energy) suggests that innovative industrial activities could be amplified by a proactive focus on postsecondary, industry-based, workforce development. The following sections describe some policy-related approaches to postsecondary workforce development currently in place in the U.S. and Brazil, and outline some potential areas that might be reasonable approaches to enhance the impact of innovation relate to workforce transformation.

U.S. – policy innovation in delivery of training and education

In the U.S. workforce development, and associated policy, not surprisingly is complicated by the somewhat distributed nature of postsecondary education. As a rule, postsecondary education has been generally the domain of the states, with the federal role generally concerned with funding financial aid or stimulating university level research. However, changing public perspectives on the cost, efficacy, and value of higher education have prompted the federal government to step beyond these roles and pursue a more aggressive strategy of funding approaches to increase degree completion and demand accountability for use of diminishing federal funding. In this sense, postsecondary education can best be thought of as a system with a variety of stakeholder interests: federal, state, and local governments, individual institutions, educational technology and service providers, employers and last but not least, the learner.

Table 6.1 Key science and technology workforce indicators

Country	GII Rank	Score (Rank)		Education Scores (Rank)		Knowledge worker Scores (rank)		
		Regulatory Environment (Quality)	Government Effectiveness	Graduates in science & engineering	Researchers	Employment in knowledge-intensive services	Females employed with advanced degrees	Growth rate of GDP per person engaged
UK	3	90.1 (7)	83.9 (14)	48.9 (29)	51.4 (17)	75.9 (8)	64.2 (18)	55.3 (72)
US	4	76.2 (19)	79.5 (20)	26.6 (85)	48.6 (21)	60.5 (26)	n/a	56.1 (70)
Finland	5	91.9 (4)	95.1 (3)	54.8 (14)	84.6 (3)	72.2 (12)	76.8 (7)	53.6 (80)
Singapore	6	100 (1)	100 (1)	n/a	80.7 (6)	85.0 (2)	67.1 (14)	52.8 (82)
Ireland	7	88.2 (11)	83.5 (15)	45.9 (33)	45.1 (23)	64.3 (23)	74.1 (9)	69.8 (27)
Germany	10	86.7 (13)	87.2 (12)	n/a	54.0 (16)	69.5 (17)	36.6 (53)	55.6 (71)
Korea	11	72.2 (26)	71.7 (23)	63.6 (7)	83.5 (4)	33.8 (64)	n/a	58.1 (64)
Canada	15	90.1 (6)	87.9 (11)	n/a	54.7 (13)	69.8 (16)	48.1 (36)	62.2 (42)
China	25	38.1 (34)	48.5 (49)	n/a	13.4 (46)	n/a	n/a	72.1 (20)
Spain	28	64 (37)	71.1 (25)	42.5 (41)	31.9 (33)	52.6 (40)	63.4 (20)	51.6 (87)
Italy	29	61.1 (43)	49.5 (48)	38.1 (54)	24.2 (36)	56.7 (36)	32.6 (60)	47.0 (97)
Russian Fed.	43	34.7 (97)	36.9 (74)	55.3 (11)	37.5 (28)	70.6 (14)	97.4 (2)	53.6 (81)
Chile	44	82 (17)	70.8 (26)	35.9 (61)	5.0 (61)	39.1 (55)	45.7 (38)	52.0 (86)

Country								
South Africa	54	52.7 (59)	48.2 (51)	35.5 (63)	4.8 (62)	39.0 (56)	29.9 (62)	48.6 (94)
Mexico	61	55.4 (53)	44.3 (59)	56.6 (17)	3.8 (65)	30.4 (73)	20.0 (69)	61.8 (43)
Colombia	63	57.2 (51)	36 (75)	43.6 (37)	1.7 (78)	26.1 (83)	38.8 (46)	65.6 (34)
India	66	33.6 (99)	33.4 (82)	57.5 (8)	1.8 (77)	n/a	n/a	82.1 (6)
Brazil	**69**	**42.9 (75)**	**34.8 (79)**	**20.2 (96.0)**	**8.3 (52)**	**33.9 (63)**	**26.9 (67)**	**52.5 (85)**
Argentina	81	18 (124)	34 (81)	25.0 (89)	14.3 (43)	37.6 (59)	48.5 (35)	44.1 (103)

Source: Cornell University, INSEAD & WIPO 2016, Acs, Szerb and Autio (2016). The global entrepreneurship and development index. In Global Entrepreneurship and Development Index 2015(pp. 11–31). Springer International Publishing. www.globalinnovationindex.org/analysis-economy

The current economic climate of the United States, as it recovers from the recession of the early part of the 21st century, has had several consequences with respect to postsecondary education. Given the reduced tax revenues of many states, funding for public postsecondary education competing with other demands on the government has been cut significantly. Forty-seven states – spent less per student in the 2014–2015 school year than they did at the start of the recession, adjusted for inflation. (Mitchell & Leachman 2015). This reduction in resources coupled with other institutional changes such as the demand for premium facilities, increase in administrative staff in some areas and addressing of deferred infrastructure, pressured postsecondary institutions to increase tuition. In the U.S. tuition in 4-year public colleges and universities rose approximately 29% since the 2007–2008 school year, after adjusting for inflation (Mitchell & Leachman 2015). Similar proportional increases have occurred at community and technical colleges and other venues for postsecondary education, where it is more problematic as the focus on instruction rather than research means the cost of institutional running relies on tuition and student related revenues, where not much margin exists for increase.

On the demand side, rising costs have led students to consider whether the return on investment in education is sufficient to take on increased debt loads to be able to afford postsecondary education. Conversely, employers have indicated that today's college graduates are not especially well prepared with the analytic skills to complete tasks that they view as important, that is, they are not "workplace ready" when they complete their education.[2] As a consequence, there is increasing pressure on postsecondary education providers, to be more cost-effective, and to more closely tailor the instructional curriculum to meet the needs of students and employers. This is why innovative approaches to postsecondary education have become of such significant interest.

Policy innovation then, in terms of U.S. postsecondary education, occurs at several levels and uses several different mechanisms. At the delivery level – the institutions – much of the innovation has been related to achieving cost savings and increasing efficiency while avoiding damaging the quality of the educational and learning experiences. Here, in some cases, it is a response to several pressures: 1) the demand from students that education prove its value, and meet their needs, 2) the need to demonstrate to the public funders (states) that they are "educating students" in an effective manner, and that they are achieving college completion objectives, 3) the increasing competition not only from peer traditional institutions of higher education, but increasing from alternative providers of education and certification of learning and advanced skills training (e.g. "coding academies").

At a state and regional level policy development occurs in response to the influence of state regulatory and funding institutions (which might be respectively the department of education, the governing boards of the postsecondary educational institutions) and through regional compacts of agreements of cooperation and best practices exchange, as well as through innovative application of data collection (Zinn & Van Kluenen, 2014).

At the federal level, policy influence occurs through several mechanisms. As a rule, the U.S. Federal government does not directly steer national education policy through strict guidance; it does exert guidance through a combination of funding incentives: some direct institutional subsidies, through incentive and innovation programs, through a large federal financial aid system, and the funding of institutional research. Innovation steering also occurs via some regulation, typically through manipulation of the federal financial aid system, with a host of regulatory strings attached (Brewer & Tierney 2011). This serves to restrict some potential competitors for federal funds, and by restricting the entry of potential competitors to the mix, is ostensibly to protect against unscrupulous or unqualified operators. However, as such the government may also be erecting barriers to educational innovation.

Finally, another critical component of the U.S. postsecondary system are the regional and professional accrediting bodies that certify that an institution is recognized as being a reputable organization. While not required, without accreditation (certification) students from a potential provider of learning would not be eligible for student loans, a significant barrier in the states, given the cost of education. While well intentioned, the standardization that occurs in this context has a potentially stifling effect on innovation outside of the tradition patterns of delivery of education in the credit-hour system based on face to face, in person "seat time."

So, in what forms can innovation occur under favourable policy approaches? Broad categories include 1) relaxing regulation with respect to the time and manner it takes to achieve a degree (process), including online and collaborative delivery of material, 2) alternative evaluation methods (competency-based education and evaluation, alternative portfolios instead of transcripts), 3) alternative financing mechanisms (a portable funding stream controlled by the learning rather than one tied to a given institution), 4) alternative delivery methods – increasing the number and type of modes of learning and training, 5) incenting innovation in educational technologies of production, learning, and assessment of learning (e.g., learning analytics).

Examples of policy innovation include encouraging new approaches to educational delivery including recognition of alternative delivery modes in a way which does not run up against accreditation boundaries – here the U.S. department of education has pilot programs that specifically allow for experimental approaches, an example being the online program offered by Southern New Hampshire University, encouraging new partnerships delivering of alternative programs – for example Western Governors University, a private, non-profit, online U.S. university founded by 19 U.S. governors in 1997, using a competency-based learning model, with students working online. The U.S. also has specific programs targeted at innovation, and the Office of Innovation and Improvement (OII), whose mission is to identify and develop solutions to educational challenges, make investments in innovative educational programs and practices, and administer discretionary grant programs.[3]

More indirectly, U.S. policy is developed in consultation with other policy actors such as the Bill and Melinda Gates Foundation, the William and Flora Hewlett Foundation, the Lumina Foundation, and the MacArthur Foundation, as examples. The foundations both provide valuable external insights into innovation, as well as an informal manner of policy guidance through funding streams that encourage alternative approaches to education and institutional operations (Baker, Bujak & DeMillo 2012).

Alternative approaches to postsecondary education include, aside from the competency-based educational approaches mentioned above, certification of learning in lieu of formal education (e.g. online educational platforms such as MOOCs, learning "badges", competency-based testing, etc.). These have been offered by collaborative partnerships such as Coursera, Udacity, and EdX, as well as through options such as Degreed (a company which developed methods of evaluating alternative learning approaches), the Open Badges Program (https://openbadges.org/), or the American Council on Education's prior learning assessments program (www.acenet.edu/higher-education/topics/Pages/Credit-for-Prior-Learning.aspx). Increasing attention has been paid to rethinking traditional approaches such as apprenticeship programs which are beginning to regain favour. Aside from a focus on fine-tuning the technical and community college systems to teach work readiness, calls are being heard to increase formal national investment by government and employers in on-the-job apprenticeship training. Efforts such as the U.S. Office of Apprenticeship (OA), part of the U.S. Department of Labor, which works in conjunction with independent State Apprenticeship Agencies (SAAs) to administer ApprenticeshipUSA, a program in conjunction with employers to encourage apprenticeships. Also, training programs and apprenticeships efforts by the unions, such as the AFL-CIO, and the American Institute for Innovative Apprenticeship (http://innovativeapprenticeship.org/) have been established to expand and maintain high quality apprenticeship programs in the United States. And in a purely private sector approach, many companies have started their own target training programs to develop skilled workers suited to their needs. An example of the latter is the pilot apprenticeship programs established by Siemens, as well BMW and Volkswagen, oriented to supplying training to address the skills gap – while the investment is significant, they feel that results are well worth the cost (Peralta 2015).

A further aspect is that different types of apprenticeships have different objectives. There are those that sharpen and focus skills (tactical), as opposed to those with more strategic approaches designed to expand worker horizons and produce flexible, competent and fluid workers. This latter approach, while more expensive, produces a workforce which, while perhaps less advantageous to a specific *individual enterprise* at a given point in time, actually might be of greater benefit to a regional or national economic structure. From a policy aspect, this gets to whether the focus is on the social equivalent of short term "quarterly profit", or takes the longer view, with social policy focused on workforce "sustainability". While the enterprise tends to focus on short term benefits, trade unions and other professional organizations can be said to have a different focus, both longer term and more global in nature. Rather than individual gain, the emphasis on achieving gains that improve and enhance the profession or discipline, rather than the individual (or a specific company).

Overall, in the U.S. workforce development, and associated policy, over the last decade, has been less a matter of formal direction and governance, but rather an emergent mosaic of approaches, actors, and incentives that has been more open change and experimentation, and devolve regulation and control to subnational entities (states and regional authorities). As of 2017, this can be expected to continue under the new Trump administration.

The positive outcome of this approach is that a variety of possibilities exists, however the lack of guidance runs the risk of less than efficient use of public resources, at the funding end, and environment which places a significant load on the learner to determine the best options in terms of cost, approach, and outcomes. Further, an additional consequence might be that imperfect signalling in the "market" for education and training results in a mismatch between (industry) desired skills and those possessed by workforce participants. Looking to see what has been effective in competitive economies globally, might yield interesting insights and the potential for policy "hedging", to borrow a financial concept where experimenting with different type of approaches might general unanticipated positive workforce outcomes.

Brazil – manufacturing specialization and unmet opportunities

In Brazil, education has been shaped through different programs over time, in response to changing social and political objectives. In general, there has been a tendency to separate technical education from more academically oriented secondary school education. This approach could be interpreted as a strategy that considers secondary education to be the final stage of basic education, whereas *technical* (or "vocational") education is an alternative postsecondary path (Herran & Rodriguez 2000). The federal government plays a key role in providing guidelines and incentives to implement the courses, as in general, the federal government has oversight for higher (and postsecondary) education.

Brazil faces several challenges related to education policy, especially with regard to issues of access and quality. Since 2003, there has been an increased focus on social inclusion and poverty reduction, which includes programs aimed at promoting education access to disenfranchised population groups, rather than on development of targeted advanced skills. Further, the role of innovation and support of new technologies as a component of industrial policy, which could be enhanced via target educational initiatives appears to be absent. These programs targeted at basic educational literacy, have been relatively successful, as marked by an increase in the average number of years of schooling from 4.9 in 2000 to 7.6 in 2013, and which corresponds in the same period to an increase in income for workers (IPEA 2013). The focus though is still on basic literacy rather than on development of advanced skills training. Despite these improvements, Brazil is still plagued by significant inequality in all realms of educational access and attainment.

Analysis of Brazilian science and technology workforce vis-à-vis the innovation level in the international context indicates that its industry in not highly innovative (see Table 6.1 above). Although Brazil is considered the 9th largest economy in the world, behind the United States, China, Japan and leading European Union countries, it ranks 69th in the World Economic Forum's Global Innovation Index 2016, behind some similar economies, such as the Russian Federation, India, and China. The investment level has increased from 2004 to 2014, but the relatively low level in previous decades have led to a technological gap. This position is also behind middle-level European countries like Italy and Spain, and some Latin American (e.g. Chile, Mexico, Colombia), and Asian countries (e.g. Singapore and Korea), despite this lagging result, Brazil leads other South American countries in the S&T arena. Several nodes of innovation exist, notable in the aviation, agriculture, and energy industries, which indicate that globally competitive innovation nodes are possible, and indicates the value of appropriately skilled workforces.

Recognition of the importance of public support for industrial innovation resulted in passage of the Innovation Law in 2004, leading to the creation a set of instruments designed to foster innovation in companies, particularly small- and medium-sized enterprises, such as "Tax Incentives for R&D", "Direct Support to R&D and Innovation in Firms", and "Access to Finance/Public Support for Venture Capital and Loan Guarantees", to cite a few examples. It also encouraged the diffusion of research activities from public institutions (universities or research centres) to fuel technological development (Páscoa 2004) by supporting collaborative research projects between university and companies, providing stimulus to create/increase activities in science parks and incubators, and establishment of Technology Transfer Offices (TTO) inside universities. Considering the recent implementation of this policy there are no conclusive results about their impact, as many of the supported projects have not yet been fully developed and the results are yet to appear in the economic indicators. However, based on previous results observed by De Negri, Negri & Lemos (2009) in inducing investment in most of the sectors, there are indications that this should be an effective approach. Additionally, studies on a local scale in companies that received support from government programs to innovate were carried out, and results include an increase in company revenues, patent applications, diversification of production and exports (CGEE 2009; INEP 2014; Salles-Filho, et al. 2011). According Cirera et al. (2015) the innovation and diversification of exporting companies in the period 2000–2008 led to increased revenue and foreign market share.

There are some internal aspects of Brazil's economic context that can explain the relatively late emphasis on advanced skills training and workforce development rather than on primary social/literacy-based direction. The country's early industrialization was driven by government policies based on import substitution (1940/1950), with the help of foreign investment and foreign technology. The state intervened in areas considered to be strategic, such as energy and oil (off-shore drilling), telecommunications, information technology, aviation, agriculture, and defence (Coutinho 1994). Only in the 1970s were research activities introduced to Brazilian universities, which led to the creation of graduate courses and additionally trained scientists, engineers, and researchers (Freeman 2002).

After a period of pronounced industrialization, the opposite trend, *general* de- industrialization, and increasing industrial *specialization* has become evident. The key characteristic of this trend in Brazil's economic development is the specialization of production and export activities based on the exploitation of natural resources (minerals, energy, and food) and low-tech services, outside of certain highly skilled industrial sectors. This suggests a role for the development of target and appropriate skills enhancement that might increase the efficacy and competitiveness of these sectors, increasing the diversity and competitiveness of Brazil's industrial base.

As a consequence, between 2000 and 2013 there was a 53.1% increase in the share of primary products in Brazil's exports, in parallel with significant decreases in the share of manufacturing industry products in Brazil's exports (22%) and a drop in their value added from 17.2% to 13% (Pinto & Macedo Cintra 2015). In terms of knowledge workers (% of workforce) the Global Innovation Index indicates that Brazilian ranking in graduates in science and engineering, employment in knowledge-intensive services, females employed with advanced degrees is not only below that of OECD countries but also behinds other BRIC countries. This raises an interesting question of whether the decline in advanced manufacturing industry exports is a consequence of the lack of a sufficiently trained and available workforce, or whether the lack of available individuals with advanced skills is a consequence of perceived lack of jobs, and hence, incentive to continue education/training.

The decline in advanced manufacturing industry exports may be related to structural changes in the Brazilian economy since 1990 when it started to increase its integration with the global economy. In addition, the industrialization in some peripheral countries since the 90s has been due to their integration in global value chains. The fractionalization of production, established in these countries, tends to be labour intensive and lower value production, due to the lower wages in comparison to other developing countries, and for this reason the Asian countries are preferred instead of Latin America. Other occurrences include the fact that microelectronics and information technology sectors, important in global economic chains, lost ground in the industrial mix as import substitution was reduced as a meaningful policy objective.

Structurally, Brazil's educational system is split into two parts: (a) the traditional education system and (b) the technical education system, with two separate educational and training trajectories for students. At the postsecondary education level, both systems have been marked by a pronounced trend, a strong focus on a particular type of curriculum: technology courses provided by universities and aimed at technologists and/or bachelor's degree students that can be followed by graduate school. These technology curricula were created in the 1970s because of the need for training and qualification of workers who could meet the demand of business (Amorim & Schwartzman 2014). This was a profoundly new perspective for higher education in Brazil, more closely matching what already existed at the time in other countries (CNE 2001). The percentage of the population in the 18–24 cohort who attended or have completed higher education increased from 9.8% in 2003 to 15.10% in 2012, which represents approximately 30% of this age group. Of all postsecondary students enrolled, 67% are pursuing bachelor's degrees, while 18.9% work toward teaching credential courses and 13.62% are following technologist curricula (INEP 2014). This approach, however, may not produce the range of flexible, highly skilled workers needed in high-growth, innovation-driven industrial sectors.

Historically, some resources have been directed toward workers through initial and continuing education courses or professional qualification, starting with initial offerings in 1963 (Castioni 2013). The formal education system, in the past, however, placed little weight on developing job skills, relying on business/industry provided on-the-job training beyond the basic skills acquired through formal education. Further, there is still a perception of education for work associated with vocational training as being directed to underprivileged classes. In part to address this, several programs have been established in the country in recent decades sought to create professional courses for various levels of workers in order to meet the demand for qualified human resources (Castioni 2013) in a context where technological innovation started to require more and more workers with more than the basic continuing vocational qualification (Takahashi & Wünsch 2010). Thus, many larger, Brazilian firms spend significant time training employees despite the high-labour turnover, which reduces incentive to provide training (Gupta et al. 2013). An additional observation may be due to limited availability of resources, since most of the private business in Brazil are microenterprises and SMEs (Mazzucato & Penna 2016), then enterprises are focused on immediate survival rather than forward looking innovation. Given this, then industry and business driven workforce development will need to come from the larger state-owned enterprises.

In this context, Brazilian 15–29 year-olds spend more time employed (6.6 years) than in education (5.4 years), compared to the OECD average of 5.5 years employed and 7.2 years in education, with the consequence that hiring youth is expensive and employers have little incentive to hire apprentices (OECD 2013). Here is one possibly unexploited avenue to enhancing available workforce, implementing formal advanced skills training programs.

Policy related to technical and vocational education has varied over time, with the federal government playing a key role in providing guidelines and incentives to implement major programs and approaches. From 1995 to 2002, the National Plan of Workers' Qualification (Planfor)/(Plano Nacional de Qualificação do Trabalhador) was implemented under coordination of the federal government, but in a decentralized implementation with participation of state government, stakeholders from the civil society, such as NGOs and trade unions, particularly the Unified Workers' Central (Central Única dos Trabalhadores (CUT), Union Strength (Força Sindical (FS), and General Confederation of the Workers (Confederação Geral dos Trabalhadores (CGT). From 1995–2000, 2.3 million workers took part in the program, the majority of them were unemployed with a low level of education representing a range of economic sectors: construction, tourism, maintenance/repair services; personal (health, beauty, wellness); cultural, leisure, sports; handicrafts associated with tourism; and agriculture (Almeida 2003). This program, was replaced by National Training Plan (Plano Nacional de Qualificação [PNQ]), developed from 2003 to 2012, which was divided into three different strategies: 1) ones at the state level taking into consideration the regional differences, 2) special projects, and 3) by industry sector. In total, 2.9 million workers received professional education. The established priority was defined for vulnerable populations, women, young people between 16–24 years; the majority of which had not completed secondary education.

In 2013, the federal government established the National Program for Access to Technical Education and Employment (Programa Nacional de Acesso ao Ensino Técnico e Emprego [Pronatec]) under the Ministry of Education. Aside from the large-scale programs described above, the educational and vocational policies have been influenced by a number of additional considerations. On the one hand, the government's objective was to increase the number of students graduated from high school seeking to continue their studies at the postsecondary level (CNE/CES 436/2001). On the other hand, is a renewed focus on fostering technological innovation and diminishing poverty. Pronatec's objective is to expand and democratize the supply of vocational and technical education courses targeted at improving the quality of secondary education for young people, workers, and beneficiaries of income transfer programs. The federal government is responsible for student enrolment, and monitors quality, student attendance and other variables, using an online system. This is an important initiative given the fact that overall "the Brazilian system of vocational education and adult training is not fully developed and is insufficient to meet the demands of industry", and the mismatch between skills and the kinds of training offered by these institutions and the demands of the productive sector, which may be due to the lack of a proactive attitude by business enterprises regarding training and capacity-building (Cassiolato 2015).

Under this program, various courses were offered to groups of workers with different levels of education focusing on either social inclusion or technological innovation. The courses are defined based on priorities selected by local entities composed by representatives of local government, educational institutions, employers, and NGOs in order to meet the demand from manufacturing and services sectors through educational institutions. The total number of enrolment was 8.1 million between 2011–2014.[4] The courses are divided into five areas: Management and Business, Information Technology, Industrial Production, Cultural Production and Design, Tourism and Leisure. The subject areas selected for course development was made taking into consideration local opportunities in labour market in 65% of the municipalities.

The social inclusion focus was organized as a mechanism that prioritizes the reduction of extreme poverty by carrying out the Brazil Without Extreme Poverty Plan (Plano Brasil Sem Miséria), that includes in its objectives a set of instruments for "productive inclusion" that give the poor access to earning professional qualifications through vocational training courses, labour intermediation, and microfinance loans. The majority of the courses participants were considered the poorest group of Brazilian population and with more barriers to participation in the labour market: 63% of participants were included in the Unified Registry, target population in the social programs, like Family Grant, Food Purchase; another indicator is that 66% are young people between 18–29 years have less opportunity to find a job in the labour market; and 60% are women. The proportion of participants that complete the course and passed the final exam was higher than in similar previous initiatives and participants from other social programs, Unified Registry and Family Grant, performed better than the average of the other social groups (MDS 2014).

Pronatec vocational training courses under Plan Brazil Without Extreme Poverty are offered free of charge due to government support by educational institutions such as the Federal Institutes for Education, Science, and Technology and institutions linked to business associations as SENAC (National Commercial Training Service) and SENAI (National Industrial Apprenticeship Service). From 2011 to 2014, 1.6 million workers were enrolled in the program, out of which 67% of participants are young women between 18 and 29 years old (MDS (Ministério do Desenvolvimento Social e Combate à Fome) 2014).

The economic and political crises that started in 2014 have affected the programs due the reduction of financial resources directed to the program implementation. Budget cuts occurring in strategic areas like science and education programs are affecting the medium and long-term future of country's development. The fiscal austerity also has had an impact on health and social inclusion programs like Pronatec by reducing the wage subsidies, important to training programs. Considering both the significant level of social inequalities in the country, and the mismatch between skills and the kinds of training offered by these institutions and the demands of the productive sector, the key policy challenge is to incorporate workers with low level of education into the system by providing better possibilities of inclusion in the labour market through education and training programs. Looking beyond the immediate financial situation an investment focused strategy for innovation related workforce development is one which leverages the different interests in the innovation systems (Mazzucato & Penna 2016). Given the investments being made by other competitive economies (i.e. East Asian NICS), not making investments in workforce preparation either directly or in partnership is private/corporate or NGO entities may result in Brazil missing a window of opportunity for exploiting industrial innovation.

In summary, Brail is not lacking in basic resources (in terms of natural or human resources) and adoption of effective workforce development strategies developed elsewhere, *in conjunction with input and buy-in from internal actors* seems to be a viable approach. As noted by several observers, scientific research efforts have substantially improved recently and is producing frontier knowledge in some key areas, with "islands of productive excellence" in sectors such as oil and gas, aviation, agriculture, health, and, to a lesser extent, banking automation (Mazzucato & Penna 2016). These represent potential nodes upon which to build an industry-driven workforce that can thrive. The synergistic combination of postsecondary education initiatives, as informed by new partnerships across industrial sectors and with institutions of postsecondary education, seems to be an exploitable under-utilized potential which could be enhanced by the development of new networks of innovation and advanced skill development.

Comparative case analysis and summary

Looking across the cases Table 6.2 presents certain common themes appear and certain significant differences:

A number of insights arise from the cross-country comparison of postsecondary workforce development efforts. For instance, the importance of taking into account the ability of the workforce itself to contribute to innovation could be more explicitly emphasized. This is best illustrated by the sector innovation in Brazil's aviation industry. Secondly, the quality and nature of education both general, and skill specific is important, not just the number of degree holders. Innovative industries express demand for well-educated/skilled personnel with preparation in advanced skills as well as in the capacity for problem-solving and ability to update and retrain. Innovation itself may be too narrowly understood; here the diversities of innovation framework has applicable value, taking into consideration contextual variables such as industrial institutions and their capability to modernize, a well-prepared and motivated workforce ready to take advantage of innovative opportunities or to generate new opportunities, and research and teaching institutions which provide richer diversity of innovation (in the region or country). Finally, government policies can drive future areas of innovation not just by traditional industrial targeting policy, but by encouraging the development of underlying skills and workers critical to globally competitive industry.

In terms of understanding either existing or potential policy implementations it is valuable to consider the context of the policy along several dimensions. This can include social and political contexts, regional or geographic contexts, as well as sector-specific considerations. An additional consideration is the

Table 6.2 Postsecondary policy innovation model

Factor	Brazil	US	Comparison
Policy Level (Central/ Distributed)	Most postsecondary education under the control of the federal government.	Mixed: Education is most administered and regulated at a state or via regional accreditors, national educational policy innovations mostly implemented via federal financing and grant programs.	Central control has the advantage of uniformity and consistence of approach. A decentralized approach sacrifices the predictability of application but allows for localized and more targeted innovation to occur and greater input from local interests.
Policy Context	Although policy is a national program, the local economic context influences the selection of courses.	Federally, primarily focused on incenting innovation via financial mechanisms, and suggested goals, with state level regulation. Philosophically focused on recognizing variation that occurs in the 50 states.	In both cases the federal government has a significant influence on policy, with the Brazilian approach reflecting adjustments made to address local conditions, and the U.S. approach one that takes a decentralized approach encouraging subnational (state and local) innovation.
Domains/ Focus	Technical/professional advanced skills and occupation specific skills.	Historically, focused on higher education at a federal level, with broader postsecondary (and training/vocational options) at the state level. Increasingly, in response to employer and learner needs, focused on alternative certification training approaches.	The Brazilian approach is characterized as policy shifting in response to social and economic requirements. While still very top down, more recent approaches recognize the importance of adaptability to context-based needs. The U.S. approach tends to focus primarily on postsecondary in a tertiary (that is higher education) manner. Recently, a combination of technological innovations in learning technologies and larger social/employer factors are producing a range of alternative learning and training approaches.

(Continued)

Table 6.2 (Cont.)

Factor	Brazil	US	Comparison
Resources/ Funding	Public	Public (federal and state) and for innovation initiatives, foundation and NGOs. Private funding by unions and corporations for internal training.	In both cases most workforce related development is funded via public sector education and training. In the U.S. there are increasingly alternatives (such as apprentice programs) and local-level public/private partnerships which show promise for innovation in workforce preparation.
Actors	Government (federal, regional and local levels), educational institutions, business associations, trade unions, civil society organizations, employers.	Institutions of education and training, federal governmental agencies (primarily Department of Education and Department of Labor), state regulatory agencies, regional and professional accreditation agencies, foundations, educational technology and service providers, unions and multi-actor partnerships.	In Brazil, most actors have been institutional (primarily government) entities but industry and industry/university collaborations are beginning to be more evident. In the United States, much higher education is public sector based, but increasingly a focus is developing on postsecondary education and training that is technical and specialized in nature and via alternative (non-university) channels.
Approaches	Technical colleges, short-term training in specific areas.	Generally oriented toward allowing for localized decision-making with federal policy focused on broad goals rather than specific, target outcomes. Increasingly partnerships that work across institutional boundaries and the use of alternative recognition of learning approaches.	Brazil uses a traditional technical training approach, but increasingly is taking advantage of synergies made possible by multi-stakeholder collaborations. The U.S. has focused on tertiary preparation to the disadvantage of more technical, training. Technology-driven approaches, and employer feedback has raised the importance of the issue.

(*Continued*)

Table 6.2 (Cont.)

Factor	Brazil	US	Comparison
Barriers	Continuous source of resources.	Decentralized system allows for innovation but also tends to underfund key elements. Institutional actors (such as accrediting agencies) can be resistant to experimental approaches. The relative neglect of non-higher educational approaches (e.g. training and apprenticeship) has reduced the potential contribution of this component.	Sufficient resources are almost a universal problem. Awareness of the importance of a commitment to advanced skills training and a growing recognition of the consequences of the coupled loss of manufacturing base, and specialized workforces has refocused the need for policy innovation in these areas.
Policy feedback mechanisms	Minister of Education established an online system to control student enrolment and course monitoring.	Response to public concern about efficacy and value of postsecondary workforce development has been to explore new options and approaches and to be more open to innovation.	A variety of interests have begun to raise the level of discourse in the area, and the availability of newer communication tools allows for more efficient coordination as well as the use of social media to mobilize public awareness.
Innovation Mechanisms	Social inclusion focus directing the majority of courses vacancies to the participants of Plan Brazil without extreme poverty.	Public private partnerships, alternative certification mechanisms, learner-oriented system delivery, new focus on training, apprenticeships and new approaches skill development.	Top down policy innovation is increasingly occurring in Brazil especially as sector interests begin to engage. In the U.S. much innovation is technology driven, and operates by opening new opportunities for employment. However, in both places opportunities for "not-developed-here" policy (drawing on the diversities of innovation theme) suggests that there are other models for workforce development which can be effectively adapted to local needs.

characteristics of the stakeholders (e.g. corporations, trade unions, workers, as well as the consumer), when matching mechanisms to change barriers. Several themes thus emerge for policymakers: (1) new policy interventions can focus on developing alternative learning/training approaches (e.g. information technology driven, alternative delivery and participation modalities), including new learning environments and opportunities, (2) multi-sector approaches, rather narrow sector-based interests, focus workforce development on postsecondary partnerships of various stakeholders, including employers, public institutions, employees (e.g. trade unions), and non-profit organizations, (3) re-examination of the *nature* and range of work related activities, and exploration of new policy and regulatory innovations to facilitate better fits between technology-enabled work and the skills and availability of 21st century workforces.

On the surface, innovation is frequently thought of as operating at the firm or industry level. However, one of the most useful aspects of the diversities of innovation approach (discussed in other chapters), be it regional, structural or by stakeholder, is the intriguing range of options made possible by shifting analytic context. Innovation in the development of highly skilled workforces is iterative – policy can drive, or incent workforce and industry innovation practices, but conversely, *policy innovation* itself can occur by applying the lens of diversities of innovation. Policy innovation can arise by incorporating a wide set of options and contextual practices.

In the U.S. postsecondary policy innovations include encouraging new approaches to educational delivery including federal innovations supporting alternative training and delivery modes that supplement existing higher education avenues such as the Office of Innovation and Improvement (OII). Additionally, U.S. policy is developed in consultation with other policy actors such as foundations which provide valuable external insights into innovation, as well as an informal manner of policy guidance through funding educational experiments, and non-profits and trade organizations which represent sector interests. The positive outcome of this approach is that a variety of possibilities exists, however the lack of coordinating guidance runs the risk of less than efficient use of public resources, at the funding end. Further, this could result in an environment which places a significant load on the learner to determine the best options in terms of cost, approach, and outcomes.

In Brazil, while challenges exist in terms of economic unpredictability, the success of certain specialized manufacturing industries represent possibilities for sector specific innovation and policies innovation targeting more formalized matching of sector needs to development of highly skilled workforces. Further, an expanded emphasis on university-industry partnerships represents another opportunity for synergistic innovation.

Overall, advances in information and communication technology as well as the increasing ability of artificial intelligence (AI) based technologies go past taking on mid-skill routinized tasks to non-routine, context variable tasks, and further reduce the labour market demand for a wider range of middle-skill individuals. This suggests that a policy response applying the diversities of innovation framework drawing on regional variation, and the enhancement of highly skilled workforces can broaden a country's innovation base and increase its competitiveness. Some types of industrial innovation are less successful when they solely are driven by technology, divorced from associated soft-engineering processes related to workers and bottom-up innovation approaches. In advanced manufacturing, skilled trade workers play an essential role in innovation processes, as they provide rapid prototyping capabilities, and offer the ability to rapidly observe and address inefficiencies in the manufacturing process. While specific skill-based job training might provide short-term benefits, it is unclear whether the individual and the public are better off with education systems that practices this separation and locks a subset of the population into a specific track. An alternative approach to workforce development focuses on continuous lifelong learning opportunities, as well as opportunities that can enhance and increase the innovation of regional economies and workforces and draw on a wide array of actors and partnership that leverage the comparative strengths of their sectors.

Notes

1 An additional consideration, although one beyond the scope of this chapter, are the dimensions of the demand component, from students and learners on one side, and from employers on the other. One of the key changes being observed in policy innovation is the intentional inclusion of these stakeholders in developing workforce preparation solutions. Understanding student needs and perceptions is important to designing approaches that speak to the needs of the primary consumers of postsecondary education (Kunz & Staub 2016). Another change is the recognition that non-traditional (i.e. university) higher education is falling short of meeting the increasing complex skills needed by industry (Carew 2016).
2 (Hart Research, www.aacu.org/sites/default/files/files/LEAP/2015employerstudent survey.pdf).
3 https://sites.ed.gov/oii/
4 http://portal.mec.gov.br/index.php?option=com_docman&view=download&a lias=22071-24092015-lancamento-estudos-pronatec-setec-pdf&category_slug=abril-2010-pdf&Itemid=30192)

References

Abramovitz, M. 1986: Catching Up, Forging Ahead, and Falling Behind, *The Journal of Economic History*, 46 (2), 385–406.
Acemoglu, D. & Autor, D. 2011: Skills, Tasks and Technologies: Implications for Employment and Earnings, *Handbook of Labor Economics*, 4 (B), 1043–1171.
Acemoglu, D., Mostagir, M., & Ozdaglar, A. 2014: Managing Innovation in a Crowd, NBER Working Paper #19852.
Acs, Z.J., Szerb, L., & Autio, E. 2016: *Global Entrepreneurship and Development Index 2015*. London: Springer International Publishing.
Almeida, M.L.D. 2003: Da formulação à implementação: análise das políticas governamentais de educação profissional no Brasil. PhD Thesis, University of São Paulo. Available at: www.bibliotecadigital.unicamp.br/document/?code=vtls000308412

Altbach, P.G., Reisberg, L., & Rumbley, L.E. 2009: *Trends in Global Higher Education: Tracking an Academic Revolution*. Paris, France: United Nations Educational, Scientific and Cultural Organization (UNESCO). Available at: www.uis.unesco.org/Library/Documents/trends-global-higher-education-2009-world-conference-en.pdf

Amorim, E. & Schwartzman, S. 2014: Educação Técnica e Vocacional nos Estados Unidos. In: Oliveira, M.P.P. et al. *Rede de Pesquisa Formação e Mercado de Trabalho Educação Profissional e Tecnológica*, Vol. 3. Brasília: IPEA/ABDI. (44–76).

Antonczyk, D., DeLeire, T., & Fitzenberger, B. 2010: Polarization and Rising Wage Inequality: Comparing the U.S. and Germany, University of Freiburg Working Paper, March 2010.

Arora, A., Branstetter, L., & Drev, M. 2013: Going Soft: How the Rise of Software-Based Innovation Led to the Decline of Japan's IT Industry and the Resurgence of Silicon Valley, *The Review of Economics and Statistics*, 95 (3), 757–775.

Auguste, Bryon & Mariani, Tyra. 2015. We Need to 'Rewire' the Labor Market. April 30, New America Foundation. https://context.newamerica.org/we-need-to-re-wire-e2ea173d6b31#.cblav8dk9

Baker, P.M.A., Breznitz, S., Seavey, A., & Bujak, K.R. 2015: 21st Century Universities as Drivers for Innovation: The Key Facets of Learning, Research, and Collaboration. In: Hilpert, U. (Ed.), *Handbook on Politics and Technology*. London: Taylor & Francis Ltd: Routledge. pp. 236–248.

Baker, P.M.A., Bujak, K.R., & DeMillo, R.A. 2012: The Evolving University: Disruptive Change and Institutional Innovation. In proceedings of the 4th International Conference on Software Development for Enhancing Accessibility and Fighting Info-exclusion. In: *Elsevier Procedia Computer Science*, Vol 14. Porto, Portugal, 330–335.

Baker, P.M.A., Moon, N.W., & Ward, A.C. 2006: Virtual Exclusion and Telework: Barriers and Opportunities of Technocentric Workplace Accommodation Policy, *WORK: A Journal of Prevention, Assessment and Rehabilitation*, 27 (4): 421–430.

Boudarbat, B., Lemieux, T., & Riddell, W. 2010: The Evolution of the Returns to Human Capital In: *Canada*, 1980–2005, IZA Working Paper No.4809, March 2010.

Brewer, D.C. & Tierney, W.G. 2011: Barriers to Innovation in U.S. Higher Education. In Wildavsky, B., Kelly, A.P., & Carey, K. (Eds.), *Reinventing Higher Education: The Promise of Innovation*. Cambridge, MA: Harvard Education Press. (11–40).

Carew, D. 2016: Young Workers without College Degrees Face Uncomfortable Truths. The Hill Blog. June 23, 2016. Available at: http://thehill.com/blogs/pundits-blog/economy-budget/284569-young-workers-without-college-degrees-face-uncomfortable

Cassiolato, J.E. 2015: Evolution and Dynamics of the Brazilian National System of Innovation. In: Shome, P. & Sharma, P. (Eds.), *Emerging Economies*. New Delhi: Springer. (265–310).

Castioni, R. 2013: Planos, Projetos e Programas de Educação Profissional: Agora é a vez do PRONATEC, *Revista Sociais E Humanas*, 26 (1), 25–42.

Cirera, X., Marin, A., & Markwald, R. 2015: Explaining export diversification through firm innovation decisions: The case of Brazil. *Research Policy*, 44(10), 1962–1973.

CGEE (2009). *Os Novos Instrumentos de Apoio À Inovação: Uma Avaliação Inicial*. Brasília: Centro de Gestão e Estudos Estratégicos—Associação Nacional de Pesquisa e Desenvolvimento das Empresas Inovadoras.

Conselho Nacional de Educação (CNE). 2001: *Diretrizes Curriculares Nacionais para a formação de Professores da Educação Básica*. Brasilia: MEC.

Cornell University, INSEAD, and WIPO. 2016: *The Global Innovation Index 2016: Winning with Global Innovation.* Ithaca, Fontainebleau, and Geneva.

Coutinho, L.E. 1994: *Estudo da Competitividade da Indústria Brasileira. 4ª Edição.* Rio de Janeiro: Papirus.

De Negri, F., Negri, J. A., & Lemos, M. B. 2009: Impactos do ADTEN e do FNDCT sobre o desempenho e os esforços tecnológicos das firmas industriais brasileiras. *Revista Brasileira de Inovação*, 8(1), 211–254.

Freeman, C. 2002: Continental, National and Sub-National Innovation Systems – Complementarity and Economic Growth, *Research Policy*, 31, 191–211.

Garicano, L. & Rossi-Hansberg, E. 2006: The Knowledge Economy at the Turn of the Twentieth Century: The Emergence of Hierarchies, *Journal of the European Economic Association*, 4, 396–403.

Gerlach F. & Ziegler, A. 2015: From Problem Child to Poster Boy: The New Image of German Industry and Industrial Policy. In: Gerlach, F., Schietinger, M., & Ziegler, A. (Eds.), *A Strong Europe – But Only with a Strong Manufacturing Sector: Policy Concepts and Instruments in Ten EU Member States.* Düsseldorf: Schüren Verlag. (58–79).

Goldin, C. & Katz, L. 2010: *The Race between Education and Technology.* Cambridge, MA: Harvard University Press.

Greenhalgh, C. & Rogers, M. 2012: *Innovation, Intellectual Property, and Economic Growth.* Princeton, NJ: Princeton University Press.

Gupta, N., Weber, C., Pena, V., Shipp, S.S., & Healey, D. 2013: *Innovation Policies of Brazil (No. IDA-P-5039).* Alexandria, VA: Institute For Defense Analyses.

Handel, M.J. 2015: *The Future of Employment, Wages, and Technological Change. Emerging Trends in the Social and Behavioral Sciences: An Interdisciplinary, Searchable, and Linkable Resource.* John Wiley and Sons. doi:10.1002/9781118900772.etrds0338

Herran, C. & Rodriguez, A. 2000: Secondary Education in Brazil: Time to Move Forward, InterAmerican Development Bank, Report No. BR-014, World Bank, Report No, 19409-BR.

Hilpert, U. 2006: Knowledge in the Region: Development Based on Tradition, Culture and Change, *European Planning Studies*, 14 (5), 581–599.

Holzer, H. 2015: *Higher Education and Workforce Policy: Creating More Skilled Workers (and Jobs for Them to Fill).* Washington, DC: Brookings Institution. Available at: www.brookings.edu/~/media/research/files/papers/2015/04/workforce-policy-briefs-holzer/polarization_jobs_policy_holzer.pdf

Holzer, H.J., & Lerman, R.I. 2009: *The Future of Middle-Skill Jobs (Vol. 41).* Washington, DC: Brookings: Center on Children and Families.

INEP (Instituto Nacional De Estudos E Pesquisas). 2014: *Censo da Educação Superior 2012: Resumo Técnico.* Brasília: Instituto Nacional de Estudos e Pesquisas Educacionais Anísio Teixeira. Available at: http://download.inep.gov.br/download/superior/censo/2012/resumo_tecnico_censo_educacao_superior_2012.pdf, accessed on November, 23, 2015.

International Labour Organization. 2007: *The Role of Trade Unions in Workers' Education: The Key to Trade Union Capacity Building*, Background Paper ISRTU/2007.

IPEA (Instituto de Pesquisa Econômica Aplicada). 2013: *Duas décadas de desigualdade e pobreza no Brasil medidas pela Pnad/IBGE. Comunicado 159.* Brasília: Instituto de Pesquisa Econômica Aplicada. Available at: http://ipea.gov.br/portal/images/stories/PDFs/comunicado/131001_comunicadoipea159.pdf

Jacoby, T. 2014: Why Germany Is So Much Better at Training Its Workers, In: *The Atlantic*. October 16, 2014. Available at: www.theatlantic.com/business/archive/2014/10/why-germany-is-so-much-better-at-training-its-workers/381550/

Kunz, J.S. & Staub, K.E. 2016: Subjective Completion Beliefs and the Demand for Post-secondary Education (February 22, 2016). University of Zurich, Department of Economics, Working Paper No. 218. Available at: http://ssrn.com/abstract=2736955

Lerman, R. 2014: Expanding Apprenticeship Opportunities in the United States. In: M. Kearney and B. Harris (Eds.), *Policies to Address Poverty in America*. The Hamilton Project. Washington, DC: Brookings Institution, pp. 79–86.

Mazzucato, M. & Penna, C. 2016: *The Brazilian Innovation System: A Mission-Oriented Policy Proposal*. Brasília, DF: Centro de Gestão e Estudos Estratégicos. Available at: www.cgee.org.br/documents/10195/1774546/The_Brazilian_Innovation_System-CGEE-MazzucatoandPenna-FullReport.pdf

MDS (Ministério do Desenvolvimento Social e Combate à Fome). 2014: *Plano Brasil Sem Miséria. Caderno de Resultados*. Brasília: MDS. Available at: www.mds.gov.br/webarquivos/publicacao/brasil_sem_miseria/cadernodegraficosbsm-35anos.pdf, accessed on November, 23, 2015.

Mitchell, M. & Leachman, M. 2015: *Years of Cuts Threaten to Put College Out of Reach for More Students*. Washington, DC: Center on Budget and Policy Priorities.

Moon, N. W., Linden, M. A., Bricout, J. C., & Baker, P. 2014: Telework rationale and implementation for people with disabilities: Considerations for employer policymaking. *Work*, 48(1), 105–115. doi:10.3233/WOR-131819.

National Academy of Sciences. 2013: *Education for Life and Work: Developing Transferable Skills and Knowledge for the 21st Century*. Washington, DC: National Academies Press.

National Research Council (US) Committee on Comparative National Innovation Policies: Best Practice for the 21st Century. 2012: *Rising to the Challenge: U.S. Innovation Policy for the Global Economy*. Wessner, C.W., Wolff, A.W., (Eds.), Washington, DC: National Academies Press (US). Available at: www.ncbi.nlm.nih.gov/books/NBK98691//10.17226/13386

Nelson, R. 1995: Recent Evolutionary Theorizing About Economic Change, *Journal of Economic Literature*, 33 (1), 48–90.

OECD. 2013: Education Policy Outlook: Brazil. Available at: www.oecd.org/education/policyoutlook.htm

Páscoa, A. 2004: In Search of an Innovative Environment – The new Brazilian Innovation Law. World Intellectual Property Organization. Available at: www.wipo.int/sme/en/documents/brazil_innovation.htm

Peralta, K. 2015: Apprenticeships Could Be Gateway to Middle Class – European Style Earn-as-You-Learn Programs Are Gaining Traction in the U.S. In: *U.S. News* (January 12, 2015). Available at: www.usnews.com/news/articles/2015/01/12/apprenticeships-could-provide-a-pathway-to-the-middle-class

Pinto, E.C. & Macedo Cintra, M.A. 2015: América Latina e China: Limites econômicos e políticos ao desenvolvimento. Available at: www.ie.ufrj.br/images/pesquisa/publicacoes/discussao/2015/TD_IE_017_2015_PINTO_GONALVES.pdf, accessed on July, 15, 2015.

Romer, P. 1994: The Origins of Endogenous Growth, *Journal of Economic Perspectives*, 8 (1), 3–22.

Salles-Filho, S., Bonacelli, M. B., Carneiro, A. M., De Castro, P. F. D., & Santos, F. O. 2011. Evaluation of ST&I programs: a methodological approach to the Brazilian Small

Business Program and some comparisons with the SBIR program. *Research Evaluation*, 20(2), 159-171.

Stuart, M., Huzzard, T., & Oup, S. 2015: Unions, the Skills Agenda and Workforce Development. In: Buchanan, J., Finegold, D., Mayhew, K., Warhurst, C. (eds) *Oxford Handbook on Skills and Training*. Oxford: Oxford University Press.

Takahashi, A. & Wünsch, R. 2010: Cursos superiores de tecnologia em gestão: reflexões e implicações da expansão de uma (nova) modalidade de ensino superior em administração no Brasil, *Revista de Administração Pública*, 44 (2), 385–414.

Torpey, E. & Hogan, A. 2016: *Working in a Gig Economy*. Washington, DC: U.S. Bureau of Labor Statistics (May). Available at: www.bls.gov/careeroutlook/2016/article/what-is-the-gig-economy.htm

Van Horn, C., Greene, T., & Edwards, T. Eds. 2015: *Transforming U.S. Workforce Development Policies for the 21st Century*. Washington, DC: Federal Reserve Bank and the W.E. Upjohn Institute.

Waters, J. 2015: How Nanodegrees Are Disrupting Higher Education: New "micro" online certification programs are changing the educational pathways to success in certain industries. Campus Technology (08/05/15). Available at: https://campustechnology.com/articles/2015/08/05/how-nanodegrees-are-disrupting-higher-education.aspx

Zinn, R. & Van Kluenen, A. 2014: *Making Workforce Data Work: How States Can Use Education and Workforce Data to Develop Skilled Workers and Strong Economies*. Washington, DC: National Skills Coalition.

7 Underemployment of middle-skilled workers and innovation outcomes

A cross-country analysis

Francesco D. Sandulli and Elena Gimenez Fernandez

Introduction

Most of the economic growth over the last 50 years in most modern economies reflects the interaction between higher innovation outcomes and educational attainment (Fernald and Jones 2014). However, on one the hand, the growth of the relative demand for highly skilled workers has accelerated compared to the rest of the workforce over the last two decades. On the other hand, jobs for middle-skilled workers have declined along with their wages. These major declines in employment growth and wages for jobs in the middle of the skills demand distribution have been happening since the late 1980s (Autor 2010). Previous literature shows that the main causes for the reduction of middle-skilled jobs were the automation of routine tasks and the impact of global trade on manufacturing jobs (Sandulli et al. 2013).

One of the main impacts of this crisis in the labor market for middle-skilled workers is that these workers who lost their jobs had to apply for low-skilled jobs. For instance, Dolado et al. (2013) have observed in Spain that middle-skilled workers with more difficulties in finding jobs which adequately match their skills will tend to apply for low-skilled jobs. Because of this mismatch in labor markets, in 2015, 9.5 million middle-skilled workers in the European Union had a low-skilled job according to official statistics from Eurostat. In turn, the shift of middle-skilled workers from middle-skilled jobs to low-skilled jobs provoked an excess supply of workers in low-skilled jobs and created a crowding out effect by expelling low-skilled workers from the job market. In fact, according to Eurostat statistics, the unemployment rate for workers with an educational attainment below a lower secondary education rocketed from 10.6% in 2007 to 17.4% in 2015.

Therefore, the new structure of the job market has created serious challenges such as underemployment of middle-skilled workers and unemployment of low-skilled workers. Moreover, job polarization combined with increasing migration flows produced downward pressure on the relative wages of workers at the low end of the income distribution (Gould 2015). The impact of these transformations in the labor market may go beyond the economic field. For instance, recent evidence suggests that these changes in the labor market may also have broader political impacts. Autor et al. (2016) shows a negative relationship between the likelihood of voting in moderate politicians in the United States and the exposure of local labor markets and China imports that utterly may lead to a hollowing out of the market for middle skills. Dippel et al. (2015) found a similar relationship in Germany.

Innovation seems to be signaling the way out to the problem of job polarization. Recent evidence shows that innovation and intangible capital is the largest source of growth in the US (Hulten and Ramey 2019). However, while most of the research has focused so far on studying the existence and reasons for job polarization, so far little research has studied the impact of the new structure of employment on innovation. Only recently, Autor et al. (2016) have found a strong negative impact of import exposure on domestic innovative outcomes such as patents. Skills endowment and distribution are critical to the innovation activities of most countries.

Most of the existing research has focused on the impact of global trade and skill- biased technological change on the two extremes of the labor distribution, high and low-skilled workers. However, the behavior of middle-skilled workers and the impact of their choices in the job market are still unclear. This chapter tackles this gap by studying the phenomenon of underemployment in middle-skilled workers. More precisely, this research studies the relationship between the underemployment of middle-skilled workers and the innovation output of European economies. Skills endowment is typically associated with countries' innovation capabilities. This relationship between innovation and skills is quite straightforward in the case of high-skilled and middle-skilled workers. However, the role played by underemployed middle-skilled workers on innovation is still unclear. On the one hand, firms may seek to hire underemployed middle-skilled workers to hinge upon their skilled premium to promote innovation from low-skilled jobs. On the other hand, innovation literature suggests that underemployment is associated with dissatisfaction, limiting the innovative attitudes of the employees. In fact, recent research suggests that job satisfaction is a necessary condition for innovation, where individual attitudes of the employees towards change in organizational routines that transform knowledge into new products may define the success or failure of the innovation process. Where a majority of employees experience job satisfaction they will endorse rather than resist innovation, will promote cooperation and will generate creative ideas (Shipton et al. 2006). In those organizations, industries and regions with lower levels of underemployment, we would expect more positive attitudes towards innovation and therefore a stronger innovation performance.

This paper contributes by solving this gap through the study of the contribution of underemployed middle-skilled workers to the innovation output of European countries. The chapter is structured as follows. First, we will describe the sources of underemployment of middle-skilled workers. Then, the relationship between innovation and skills, with a special focus of the theoretical arguments that explain the role of underemployed middle-skilled in innovative activities. The chapter continues with the description of the empirical model to test the relationship between underemployed middle-skilled workers and the innovative outcome in European countries. Finally, results of the empirical analysis are discussed, and conclusions are drawn.

Middle-skill workers and job polarization

Recent research emphasizes the impact of global trade and technological change on the changes in the structure of employment by producing job polarization. Job polarization is defined as a rising employment share for the lowest- and highest-paid occupations and a fall for the middling occupations (Goos and Manning 2003). Recent research confirms that job polarization has hollowed out the overall demand for middle-skilled workers in all sectors, while increasing the supply of workers in both high-skilled and low-skilled jobs (Autor and Dorn 2013). High-skilled jobs are being fulfilled by larger cohorts of highly skilled workers. For instance, according to Eurostat data population with tertiary education in the European Union has grown from 54 million in 2002 to 87 million in 2015. This trend explains the growing share of tertiary education workers in the EU job market shown in Figure 7.1.

On the one hand, an increasing participation in world import flows from low labor-cost countries such as China, Vietnam or Indonesia produces substantial adjustment costs and distributional consequences in those

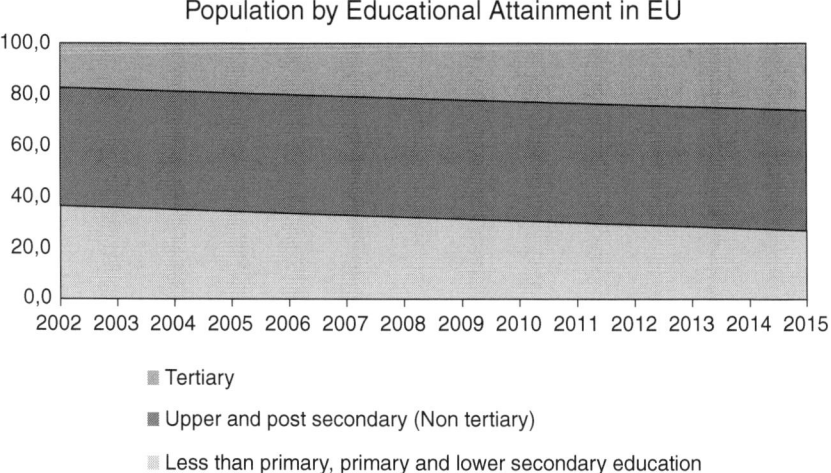

Figure 7.1 Evolution of EU population distribution by educational attainment level, 2002–2015

Source: Eurostat (2016)

industries more exposed to foreign competition. Autor et al. (2016) find that China competition depresses wages and raises unemployment rates for at least a full decade after the China trade shock commences, and what is even more significant, offsetting employment gains in other industries is remarkably slow.

On the other hand, the development of information technologies has produced decades of machine displacement of human labor. In several industries, endogenous technological change has produced the simultaneous growth of high-education, high-wage and low-education, low-wages jobs. This job polarization has been linked to the decline in the demand for routine or codifiable of both manual and cognitive tasks (Acemoglu and Autor 2011; Goos et al. 2013; Sandulli et al. 2014). In fact, occupations with the largest shares of highly educated workers and those with the highest shares of low-educated workers have low scores on routine cognitive tasks.

Table 7.1 shows that these groups also have typically low scores on routine manual tasks. By contrast, occupations with high shares of middle-educated workers typically score high on both routine cognitive and routine manual tasks (Michaels et al. 2014).

Recent evidence suggests that skill-biased technological change may also increase the demand for low-skilled jobs compared to moderately skilled jobs. Larger proportions of highly skilled workers should boost relative labor demand for the least-skilled workforce, because highly skilled workers will demand more services which are low skills intensive (Mazzolari and Ragusa 2013) and because in these services automation is more complex (Autor and Dorn 2013). However, instead of lower-skilled workers, moderately skilled workers may fulfill this excess demand for low-skilled jobs. In fact, despite the reduction of middle-skill jobs, the share of middle-skilled workers in the EU has remained relatively stable over the last decade at the expense of low-skilled workers. Lower-skilled workers are being displaced from middle-skilled jobs to low-skilled jobs as shown by the growing share in the EU of overskilled middle-skilled workers[1] (Figure 7.2). This process is creating a crowding out effect since low-skilled workers are being expelled from the job market (Figure 7.3).

Table 7.1 Task distribution by educational attainment level

	Highly educated	*Middle educated*	*Low educated*
Routine Cognitive Tasks	Low	High	Low
Routine Manual Tasks	Low	High	Low
Non-routine Cognitive Tasks	High	Average	Low
Non-routine Manual Tasks	Low	Average	High

Source: Own Elaboration from Michaels et al. (2014)

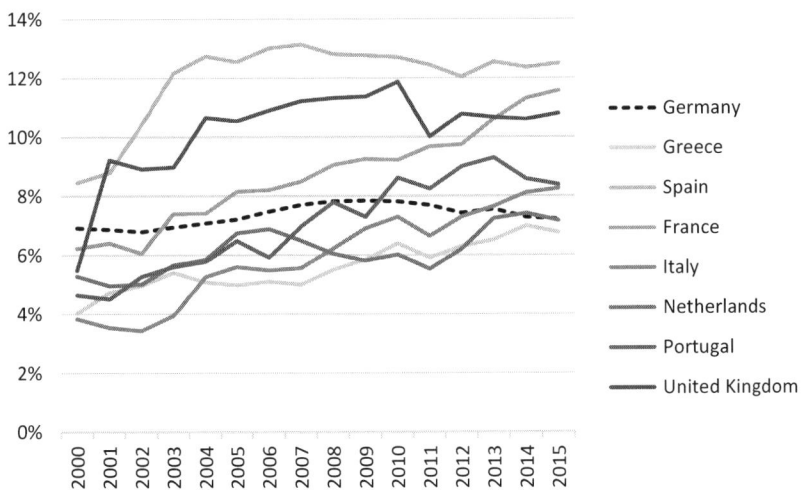

Figure 7.2 Evolution of the share of underemployed middle-skilled workers in EU countries, 2002–2015
Source: Eurostat (2016).

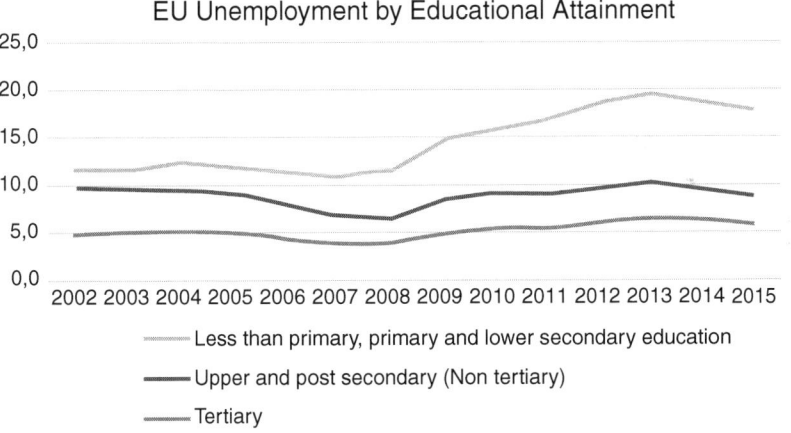

Figure 7.3 Evolution of EU unemployment by educational attainment level, 2002–2015
Source: Eurostat (2016)

The reaction and adjustment of moderately skilled workers to job polarization is one of the most interesting questions regarding labor markets in the near future. Moderately skilled workers will have two choices in a polarized labor market. In first place, they may apply for high skills jobs. In this case, moderately skilled worker will be overemployed. Recent research suggests that this will be the case in the early stages of technologies where the education system had no time yet to deliver the new skills required by new technologies. However, as long as the educational system adjusts to the new technologies and their corresponding skills, moderately skilled workers will be more unlikely to find a highly skilled job (Vona and Consoli 2015). Overemployed middle-skilled workers may benefit from a wage premium compared to other moderately skilled workers in low skills jobs (Strauss and De la Maisonneuve 2009).

However, the chances to find a high skills job will depend on some structural characteristics. In first place, middle-skilled workers will find more difficulties in finding a high-skilled job in labor markets with larger endowments of highly skilled workers (Hamersma et al. 2015). In second place, the industrial structure will likely define the shift towards one side or the other of the skill continuum. In countries where industries are more likely to be offshored such as low technology manufacturing industries, polarization will produce middle-skilled workers to move towards low value services (Oldenski 2014) or middle-skilled services (Holzer 2015).

Moderately skilled workers will have more chances of finding a job if they apply for low skill jobs. They may enjoy a wage premium compared to workers with lower skills in their same positions (Brynin and Longhi 2009). However, this excess supply of moderately skilled workers for low skill positions may produce a crowding out effect for low-skilled workers as shown above. This problem is characteristic of some European countries such as Spain where most of the youth unemployment may be explained by this process (Dolado et al. 2013).

Skills distribution and innovation

Innovation literature would suggest that larger cohorts of highly skilled workers would favor the creation of new products and services (Bartel and Lichtenberg 1987). High technical skills are a complementary asset with R&D collaboration and product and process innovation. Moreover, high technical skills foster the capacity to absorb and integrate external knowledge into the firms (Leiponen 2005). Job polarization may favor innovation. The reason is that skills and R&D are complementary factors, and therefore raising the supply of highly skilled workers increases the attractiveness of investing in R&D (Acemoglu 1998).

Middle-skilled workers may also contribute to innovation. These workers are a key source of incremental innovations (Freeman 1995; Toner 2011). Middle-skilled workers may have a direct effect on innovation because they may generate ideas that flow up to upper management (Bradley et al. 2016), and also because they are a key element in absorbing and adapting external knowledge to internal routines and knowledge (Ozgen et al. 2013).

Incremental innovations, which involves innumerable small modifications in existing products rather than basic R&D development, may collectively have a greater immediate impact on innovational growth than the initial introduction of technology developed by R&D (Baumol 2004).

Middle-skilled workers may also increase absorptive capacity (Makkonen and Lin 2012) or facilitate the implementation of innovation (Huiban and Bouhsina 1998). In some industries such as low-technology industries, the contribution to innovation of middle-skilled workers is larger than the contribution of high-skilled workers (Freel 2003).

It has been frequently mentioned in the innovation literature, that innovation requires the previous development of organizational learning capabilities. Innovation involves the construction of a conceptual framework which shapes the interaction between firms' internal resources and the environment in terms of knowledge acquisition, transformation and dissemination. Typically innovation requires effort from the workers to engage with these knowledge-related activities beyond their routine tasks. However, workers will not engage with these tasks unless they are rewarded, independently of their nature, either monetary or intrinsic rewards. Therefore, worker satisfaction is key for organizational learning, and consequently, innovation. In fact, job satisfaction is a strong predictor of organizational innovation (Shipton et al. 2006).

Underemployment may affect the contribution of middle-skilled workers to innovation. Underemployment produces job dissatisfaction (Fine and Nevo 2008; Erdogan and Bauer 2009) and the perception of unfair rewards (Agut et al. 2009). Underemployment is also associated with lower levels of psychological well-being (Feldman 1996; Heyes et al. 2016) and more likely intent to leave (Maynard et al. 2006). These negative attitudes may influence organizational innovation. Evidence from Spain shows that overqualification relates positively with employee demotivation and negatively to the personal attitudes towards innovation (Agut et al. 2009). This result shows that while one of the expectations of firms when hiring overqualified employees is to boost innovation (Erdogan et al. 2011), firms need to find procedures and incentives to ignite this innovative process. Existing literature suggests that proactive attitudes of overqualified workers towards innovation may depend on the job specifications. For instance, Luksyte and Spitzmueller (2015) show how overqualified workers will be more creative when they feel supported and appreciated by supervisors. Similarly, Zhou and George (2001) observe that job dissatisfaction, a typical feature of underemployment, may ignite individual creativity if driven by supportive organizations and work environments. Wu et al. (2017) describe how overskilled workers will be more likely to develop adaptive behaviors in more autonomous jobs. Organizational identification may also benefit the individual creativity of overskilled workers when a perceived skill mismatch is not too extreme (Lin et al. 2017).

Nevertheless, if firms do not to put in place these mechanisms we should expect a negative impact of underemployment of middle-skilled workers on innovation.

Empirical model and data

The main goal of this chapter is to study the relationship between under-employed middle-skill workers and innovation in European countries. From an empirical point of view, we will test these relationships using panel data at a country level. There is empirical evidence showing that polarization reached different levels across Europe. Moreover, the impact of polarization on innovation may be different depending on the different structures of national systems of innovation. This paper will explore the relationship between larger shares of underemployed middle-skill workers and innovation activity. The empirical model is defined as follows:

$$
\begin{aligned}
Y_{it} = {} & GDP_{it} + RD_{it} + High_{it} + Intangible_{it} + Mid\_ov_{it} \\
& + (Mid\_ov_{it})^2 + Manufacturing_{it} + u_i
\end{aligned}
\tag{1}
$$

being u_i the individual-specific time-invariant effects[2] and where for country i and time t our dependent variable Y_{it} will be the innovation output. The analysis employs two measures of innovation output. First, we will study the relationship between the proportion of underemployed middle-skill workers and the log of the number of patents granted per active worker. However, not all innovation output produces patents. In some cases, patenting implies some risk of knowledge disclosure that some firms are not willing to take. In some other cases, regulation simply does not allow for the transformation of new knowledge into patents. This is the case of most process innovations or the intellectual capital developed through experience and time-based learning. For this reason, the study employs the log of registered trademarks per habitant as a second measure of innovation output.

The model comprises a number of control variables. It takes into account that innovation resources are an important determinant of innovation output. Innovation resources are measured in terms of R&D investments (RD_{it}), intangible assets ($Intangible_{it}$) and human capital ($High_{it}$). R&D resources are characterized by strong cumulativeness. This is the "technology-push" hypothesis, which considers that R&D activities are path-dependent (i.e. Nelson and Winter 1982). The variables RD_{it} and $Intangible_{it}$ will capture this technology push effect. Innovation investment is measured by the log of the level of R&D expenditure per active population while the log of fixed intangible assets as a share of total GDP measures intangible assets. Another important innovation resource is human capital. As discussed above, we would expect that high-skilled labor force improves innovation. In this sense, larger cohorts of highly educated workers ($High_{it}$) produced by job polarization should boost innovation. The proxy measure used for high-skilled human capital in this research is the log of the share of human resources with tertiary education on total employment.

Additional to the "technology push" hypothesis, former innovation literature suggests that a growing economy can boost innovation activities by increasing the profitability and appropriability of innovations as well as by reducing financial constraints (i.e. Kleinknecht and Verspagen 1990; Piva and Vivarelli 2007). Therefore, we put forward a dynamic specification of the innovation results that take into account the log of the GDP per capita (GDP$_{it}$) to measure the "demand pull", expecting that growing GDPs will be positively related to innovation activities and outcomes.

Additionally, the model will use recent mismatch measures (for over and under qualification of middle-skilled workers) to understand how innovation reflects changes in the employment structure. More precisely, the model will measure the impact of underemployed middle-skill workers (Mid_ov$_{it}$) by the log of the share on total employment of middle-skill workers performing low-skilled occupations.[3] Finally, we measured the shared of the GDP produced by manufacturing industries, since patent production tends to be biased towards these industries compared to service industries. The measures for the variables in the analysis are summarized in Table 7.2.

The model has been estimated at a country level using Eurostat data for a data set from 2006 to 2014. The sample comprises 28 countries from the European Union plus Norway, Iceland and Switzerland. Hausman test results advocate for fixed-effects panel analysis.

Results

The analysis focus on the economic relationship between underemployed middle-skill workers and innovation in Europe. The results in Table 7.3 confirm the negative relationship between the proportion of underemployed middle-skill workers and innovation for both patents (Mid_ov$_{it}$ = −1.098;

Table 7.2 Variable description

Variable	Description	Measurement
Y$_{it}$	Patents	Log Patents granted per active capita in country i during year t
		Log Trademarks granted per capita in country i during year t
GDP$_{it}$	GDP	Log Real GDP per capita in country i during year t
RD$_{it}$	RD	Log Real R&D Expenses/capita in country i during year t
High$_{it}$	Highly Skilled Workers	Log Persons with tertiary education and employed per capita in country i during year t
Mid_ov$_{it}$	Middle-overskilled	Log Proportion of Middle-skilled workers in Elementary Jobs in country i during year t
Manufacturing$_{it}$	Middle-underskilled	Log of Proportion of GDP produced by Manufacturing Industries in country i during year t
Intangible$_{it}$	Job Mismatch	Log of Proportion of GDP invested in Fixed Intangible Assets

Table 7.3 Model estimation

	Model I Patents	Model II Trademarks
	Coefficients (S.D.)	Coefficients (S.D.)
GDP_{it}	2.514*** (0.178)	6.552*** (0.330)
RD_{it}	0.451*** (0.100)	−0.163 (0.181)
$HIGH_{it}$	0.415*** (0.143)	1.141*** (0.282)
Mid_ov_{it}	−1.098* (0.645)	−4.336*** (1.151)
$Mid\_ov_{it}^{2}$	−0.213* (0.111)	−0.815*** (0.200)
$Intangible_{it}$	−0.150** (0.062)	0.097 (0.113)
$Manufacturing_{it}$	0.646*** (0.172)	1.760*** (0.306)
Constant	−23.456*** (1.771)	−69.833*** (3.316)
Yearly dummies	Significant***	Significant***
R^2	0.87	0.87
N	413 (25 groups)	396(26 groups)

*p<0.1; ** p<0.05; ***p<0.01

$p< 0.1$) and trademarks ($Mid\_ov_{it} = -4.336$; $p< 0.01$). The coefficient is larger and more significant for trademarks. This result may be explaining the relevance of job mismatch of middle-skill workers in those industries and countries that are less patent intensive. For both models the quadratic effect for underemployed middle-skill workers is negative. This result suggests that the more the proportion of underemployed middle-skill workers the worse the impact on the innovative capability of a country.

Control variables confirm both technology push-and-demand pull hypothesis, since both innovation resources ($RD_{it} = 0.451$; $p< 0.01$ and $HIGH = 0.415$; $p< 0.01$) and GDP ($GDP_{it} = 2.514$; $p< 0.01$) contribute positively to the patent generation of the economy. For trademarks, technology push assumption is only confirmed for high-skilled workers while demand pull assumption is fully confirmed. For both models, economies with stronger manufacturing industries tend to be more innovative.

Discussion and conclusion

The main contribution of this research to the study of diversities of innovation is to explore how innovation outcomes depend on the structure and correct functioning of labor markets. The results reveal that those economies with more inefficient labor markets for middle-skill workers tend to be less innovative. The results of this research have significant implications for the future of developed economies since underemployment of middle skill workers might undermine the most important driver of economic growth. From a theoretical point of view, these results are in line at the country level with the literature at the firm- evel (Agut et al. 2009; Erdogan et al. 2011) that suggests that underemployment hampers innovation. Moreover, despite the existence of some evidence at the firm level that suggests that proper organizational mechanisms and human resource practices may reverse this negative relationship between underemployment and innovation (Zhou and George 2001; Lin et al. 2017), our results confirm the negative relationship between underemployment and innovation, probably because at the country level these mechanisms have not widely implemented. This is a novel and interesting contribution of this research to innovation policies, which have typically been focused on the hard part of the innovation process, basically knowledge generation and dissemination, and have neglected the soft part of the innovation process, more related to internal conditions that favor organizational learning, such as job satisfaction, human resources policies or the development of innovative cultures. Within this soft part, this research focused specially on the impact of job mismatch as a frequent ignitor of job dissatisfaction and therefore a deterrent of innovation, as shown by the results of our analysis.

To some extent, job mismatch is a frequent phenomenon in labor markets. It may take some time to adjust the supply of skills to occupational changes resulting from technological changes or new economical frameworks. For instance, part of the underemployment of middle skill workers may be explained by the shift from manufacturing-driven economies to services-driven economies. In this context, former employees in manufacturing industries lost their jobs and had to look for alternative revenue sources in less qualified employments in the services industries. The efforts to reindustrialize some geographical areas may try to revert this trend with the goal of decreasing the proportion of dissatisfied workers and fostering innovation. After some time, the labor market would tend to the equilibrium and skills premium would tend to disappear (Kuznets 1955; Greenwood 1997; Autor 2015). Nevertheless, some aspects of the current behavior of labor markets in several economies remain serious causes for concern. First of all, the magnitude of underemployment suggests that economic and social impacts might be pervasive. In fact, in the European Union underemployed middle skill workers are close to 10 million. However, these underemployed workers are not evenly distributed among European countries and regions. As shown in Table 7.4, for instance the different stages in the transition from manufacturing to services economies reflects that some countries with a strong reduction of the contribution of the manufacturing industry to the GDP, such as Belgium, Latvia, Spain or France tend to have large proportions of underemployed middle-skilled workers than countries with weaker contractions of the manufacturing industry. Similarly, educational policies may explain those differences. For instance, countries with a strong tradition in dual vocational training such as Austria, Germany or Switzerland tend to have lower proportions of underemployed middle-skilled workers.

In second place, the growing trend behind this phenomenon suggests that the impact of underemployment could increase in the following years. In fact, global trade and skill-biased technological change, the external shocks that provoked job polarization in developed economies, are quite likely to be more intensive in the following years (Brynjolfsson and McAfee 2014). The combination of both large magnitude and long persistence might be

Table 7.4 Proportion of underemployed middle-skilled
workers in Europe (2016)

Latvia	15,5%
Lithuania	12,8%
Spain	12,5%
Belgium	12,3%
France	11,6%
Ireland	11,3%
United Kingdom	10,8%
Bulgaria	10,5%
Estonia	10,0%
Denmark	9,7%
Finland	8,7%
Romania	8,6%
Hungary	8,6%
Poland	8,4%
Portugal	8,4%
Slovakia	8,3%
Italy	8,3%
Austria	7,4%
Germany	7,2%
Netherlands	7,2%
Slovenia	6,8%
Greece	6,8%
Czech Republic	6,0%
Iceland	5,8%
Sweden	4,6%
Norway	4,0%
Switzerland	3,7%

Source: Eurostat (2016)

producing a deep impact in social and political structures (Dippel et al. 2015; Autor et al. 2017). Governments have serious concerns regarding by this problem, which is impoverishing large shares of the population and putting at risk future growth. Therefore, some governments are trying different measures to solve the underemployment problem of middle-skilled workers. For instance, US government has tried to deal with this process from both the demand side and the supply side of the labor market. Regarding the demand side, the US government under Obama's administration has devoted between 2013 and 2016, one billion dollars to the National Network of Manufacturing Innovation (NNMI). Following the model of German Fraunhofer Institutes, this initiative is creating across the US a network of R&D consortia with public and private partners to advance innovation in manufacturing industries.[4] Thus, NNMI is trying to fight middle skill underemployment by recovering the middle-skilled jobs that have been lost over the past decades. On the other hand, US government needed to smooth the workforce transition from old to new manufacturing industries. To reach this goal, US government set up several programs such as ApprenticeshipUSA, Youth Career Connect, American Technical Training Funds or Americas College Promise to foster the development of the skills for the future manufacturing industries.[5] Recent analysis supports the development of an effective Talent Supply Chain where firms and educators would work together to fix the skill gap of middle skill workers (Accenture 2014). However, changes in educational systems to readjust education supply with skills demand tend to be slow (Vona and Consoli 2015). Overall, either solutions based on fostering the demand for middle skill workers or skill adjustments of these workers require long times. Meanwhile the problem grows in magnitude. For this reason, some governments are discussing some short-term measures to buy some time as long-term solutions mature. These measures try to mitigate the shocks produced by global trade and skill-biased technological change. For instance, some governments, such as President Trump's administration in the US, are trying to limit international trade to reduce job erosion in those industries more exposed to imports. While measures to slow down skill-biased technological change are more difficult to implement, there are some political initiatives in that direction. For instance, the European Parliament is discussing to give robots legal status as "electronic persons", which among other implications would likely involve some degree of new taxation on robots' operations. Future research will probably address whether these short-term measures will have collateral negative consequences on the competitiveness of the countries. The cure could prove worse than the middle skill underemployment. Finally, there is some consensus on the need for innovative social safety nets that could allow middle-skilled workers and low-skilled workers to adapt to this framework without slipping into poverty or marginalization. This research, by connecting middle-skilled underemployment and innovation underperformance, contributes to the existing arguments, which point out the urgent need to mitigate underemployment of middle skill workers and to invest into the development of new economical, educational and social institutions to face the main challenge of most economies in the near future.

Notes

1 We defined overskilled middle-skilled workers as workers with upper and post-secondary educational levels employed in an elementary job.
2 Hausman test confirmed the convenience of fixed effects estimation in this sample.
3 We would consider middle-skill workers as those workers with a Upper and Post secondary (Non tertiary) Educational Level.
4 US President Donald Trump seems to embrace a similar point of view, since he has heralded a "new industrial revolution" during his campaign and first months of mandate in 2017. Similarly, in Europe some countries adopted similar plans to increase the demand for middle-skill workers in the industry such as Platform Industrie 4.0 in Germany or the Alliance Industrie du Futur in France.
5 While NNMI was supported by the US Congress, most of the programs to foster new skill development have found strong resistance by the Republican majority in the US Congress.

References

Accenture. (2014): *Bridge the gap: Rebuilding America's middle skills.* Burning Glass, Boston.

Acemoglu, D. (1998): Why do new technologies complement skills? Directed technical change and wage inequality. The Quarterly Journal of Economics, 113(4), 1055–1089.

Acemoglu, D. & Autor, D. (2011): Skills, tasks and technologies: Implications for employment and earnings. Handbook of Labor Economics, 4, 1043–1171.

Agut, S., Peiró, J. M. & Grau, R. (2009): The effect of overeducation on job content innovation and career-enhancing strategies among young Spanish employees. Journal of Career Development, 36, 159–182.

Autor, D. (2010): *US labor market challenges over the longer term.* Federal Reserve Board of Governors.

Autor, D. (2015): Why are there still so many jobs? The history and future of workplace automation. The Journal of Economic Perspectives, 29(3), 3–30.

Autor, D. & Dorn, D. (2013): The growth of low-skill service jobs and the polarization of the US labor market. The American Economic Review, 103(5), 1553–1597.

Autor, D., Dorn, D. & Hanson, G. H. (2016): The china shock: Learning from labor market adjustment to large changes in trade (No. w21906). National Bureau of Economic Research.

Autor, D., Dorn, D., Katz, L. F., Patterson, C. & Van Reenen, J. (2017): Concentrating on the fall of the labor share (No. 23108). National Bureau of Economic Research.

Bartel, A. P. & Lichtenberg, F. R. (1987): The comparative advantage of educated workers in implementing new technology. The Review of Economics and Statistics, 69(1), 1–11.

Baumol, W. J. (2004): Education for innovation: Entrepreneurial breakthroughs vs. corporate incremental improvements (No. w10578). National Bureau of Economic Research.

Bradley, D., Kim, I. & Tian, X. (2016): Do unions affect innovation? Management Science, 63(7), 2251–2271.

Brynin, M. & Longhi, S. (2009): Overqualification: Major or minor mismatch? Economics of Education Review, 28(1), 114–121.

Brynjolfsson, E. & McAfee, A. (2014): *The second machine age: Work, progress, and prosperity in a time of brilliant technologies.* WW Norton & Company.

Dippel, C., Gold, R. & Heblich, S. (2015): Globalization and its (dis-) content: Trade shocks and voting behavior (No. w21812). National Bureau of Economic Research.

Dolado, J., Jansen, M., Felgueroso, F., Fuentes Hutfilter, A. & Wölfl, A. (2013): Youth labour market performance in Spain and its determinants: A micro-level perspective (No. 1039). OECD Publishing.

Erdogan, B., & Bauer, T. N. (2009): Perceived overqualification and its outcomes: The moderating role of empowerment. Journal of Applied Psychology, 94(2), 557.

Erdogan, B., Bauer, T. N., Peiró, J. & Truxillo, D. M. (2011): Overqualified employees: Making the best of a potentially bad situation for individuals and organizations. Industrial and Organizational Psychology, 4(2), 215–232.

Fernald, J. G. & Jones, C. I. (2014): The future of US economic growth. The American Economic Review, 104(5), 44–49.

Fine, S., & Nevo, B. (2008): Too smart for their own good? A study of perceived cognitive overqualification in the workforce. The International Journal of Human Resource Management, 19(2), 346–355.

Feldman, D. C. (1996): The nature, antecedents and consequences of underemployment. Journal of Management, 22(3), 385–407.

Freel, M. S. (2003): Sectoral patterns of small firm innovation, networking and proximity. Research Policy, 32(5), 751–770.

Freeman, C. (1995): The 'National System of Innovation' in historical perspective. Cambridge Journal of Economics, 19(1), 5–24.

Goos, M. & Manning, A. (2003): McJobs and MacJobs: The growing polarisation of jobs in the UK, in: Dickens, R., Gregg, P., Wadsworth, J. (eds.) The Labour Market Under New Labour. Palgrave Macmillan, London.

Goos, M., Salomons, A. & Vandeweyer, M. (2013): Job polarization during the great recession and beyond. Euroforum policy paper 2, KU Leuven.

Gould, E. D. (2015): Explaining the Unexplained: Residual Wage Inequality, Manufacturing Decline, and Low-Skilled Immigration. CEPR Discussion Paper No. DP10649. Available at SSRN: https://ssrn.com/abstract=2615909.

Greenwood, J. (1997): The third industrial revolution: Technology, productivity, and income inequality (No. 435). American Enterprise Institute.

Hamersma, M., Edzes, A. & van Dijk, J. (2015): Underqualification as an opportunity for low-educated workers. Environment and Planning C: Government and Policy, 33(1), 83–103.

Heyes, J., Tomlinson, M. & Whitworth, A. (2016): Underemployment and well-being in the UK before and after the great recession. Work, Employment & Society, 31(1), 71–89. doi:10.1177/0950017016666199.

Holzer, H. (2015): Job market polarization and US worker skills: A tale of two middles. Brookings Institution Economic Studies Working Paper, April, 6.

Huiban, J. P. & Bouhsina, Z. (1998): Innovation and the quality of labour factor: An empirical investigation in the French food industry. Small Business Economics, 10(4), 389–400.

Hulten, C. & Ramey, V. (2019): Introduction: Skills, education, and US economic growth: Are US workers being adequately prepared for the 21st century world of work? in Hulten, C. & Ramey, V. (eds.) Education, skills, and technical change: Implications for future US GDP growth. University of Chicago Press. Chicago.

Kleinknecht, A. & Verspagen, B. (1990): Demand and innovation: Schmookler re-examined. Research Policy, 19(4), 387–394.

Kuznets, S. (1955): Economic growth and income inequality. The American Economic Review, 45(1), 1–28.

Leiponen, A. (2005): Skills and innovation. International Journal of Industrial Organization, 23(5), 303–323.

Lin, B., Law, K. & Zhou, J. (2017): Why is underemployment related to creativity and OCB? A task crafting explanation of the curvilinear moderated relations. Academy of Management Journal, 60(1), 156–177.

Luksyte, A. & Spitzmueller, C. (2015): When are overqualified employees creative? It depends on contextual factors. Journal of Organizational Behavior, 37(5), 635–653.

Makkonen, T. & Lin, B. (2012): Continuing vocational training and innovation in Europe. International Journal of Innovation and Learning, 11(4), 325–338.

Maynard, D. C., Joseph, T. A., & Maynard, A. M. (2006): Underemployment, job attitudes, and turnover intentions. Journal of Organizational Behavior: The International Journal of Industrial, Occupational and Organizational Psychology and Behavior, 27(4), 509–536.

Mazzolari, F. & Ragusa, G. (2013): Spillovers from high-skill consumption to low-skill labor markets. Review of Economics and Statistics, 95(1), 74–86.

Michaels, G., Natraj, A. & Van Reenen, J. (2014): Has ICT polarized skill demand? Evidence from eleven countries over twenty-five years. Review of Economics and Statistics, 96(1), 60–77.

Nelson, R. R. & Winter, S. G. (1982): The Schumpeterian tradeoff revisited. The American Economic Review, 72(1), 114–132.

Oldenski, L. (2014): Offshoring and the polarization of the US labor market. Industrial & Labor Relations Review, 67(3 suppl), 734–761.

Ozgen, C., Nijkamp, P. & Poot, J. (2013): The impact of cultural diversity on firm innovation: Evidence from Dutch micro-data. IZA Journal of Migration, 2(1), 18.

Piva, M. & Vivarelli, M. (2007): Is demand-pulled innovation equally important in different groups of firms? Cambridge Journal of Economics, 31(5), 691–710.

Sandulli, F. D., Baker, P. M., & López-Sánchez, J. I. (2013): Can small and medium enterprises benefit from skill-biased technological change? Journal of Business Research, 66(10), 1976–1982.

Sandulli, F. D., Baker, P. M., & López-Sánchez, J. I. (2014): Jobs mismatch and productivity impact of information technology. The Service Industries Journal, 34(13), 1060–1074.

Shipton, H. J., West, M. A., Parkes, C. L., Dawson, J. F. & Patterson, M. G. (2006): When promoting positive feelings pays: Aggregate job satisfaction, work design features, and innovation in manufacturing organizations. European Journal of Work and Organizational Psychology, 15(4), 404–430.

Strauss, H. & De la Maisonneuve, C. (2009): The wage premium on tertiary education: New estimates for 21 OECD countries. OECD Journal: Economic Studies, 2009, 183–210.

Toner, P. (2011): Tradespeople and technicians in innovation. In Fostering enterprise: The innovation and skills nexus–research readings, 127.

Vona, F. & Consoli, D. (2015): Innovation and skill dynamics: A life-cycle approach. Industrial and Corporate Change, 24(6), 1393–1415.

Wu, C. H., Tian, A., Luksyte, A. & Spitzmueller, C. (2017): On the association between perceived overqualification and adaptive behavior. Personnel Review, 46 (2), 339–354.

Zhou, J. & George, J. M. (2001): When job dissatisfaction leads to creativity: Encouraging the expression of voice. Academy of Management Journal, 44(4), 682–696.

Part IV

Divergent strategies and problems of new technological powers in a changing global situation

8 Diverse patterns of innovation in India for broader impacts

Torsten Schunder and Sharmistha Bagchi-Sen

Introduction

New innovation spaces are emerging in economies characterized by a large share of poor or low-income population with limited capacities to become producers or consumers in the globalized marketplace. Innovations to serve this population segment have to consider resource scarcity and develop efficient production methods. Companies interested in this segment generate innovation not only for the benefit of the target market but also to add to the competitive advantage of the firm in the form of reduced production costs, gains via corporate social responsibility, and access to new technologies or solutions applicable to other parts of the world. In emerging market economies, innovation opportunities involving new types of customers as well as new non-traditional stakeholders are arising to support sustainable livelihoods through organizational innovation in product delivery differing considerably from established pathways of innovation (Doh and Teegen 2002; Lambell et al. 2008; Yaziji and Doh 2009; Aoyama 2012; Parthasarathy et al. 2015).

The population segment served is commonly referred to as the Bottom or Base of the Pyramid (BOP) and is characterized by low individual purchasing power, limited access to finance, poor infrastructure, and neglect from traditional forms of business. In aggregate terms, the purchasing power of the BOP is high and the BOP is constituted of "about 3 billion people, representing 70 percent of the developing world population" (Prahalad 2009, p. 35) with a net GDP of $12.5 trillion (Prahalad 2009). Prahalad proposed that serving the enormous market constituted by the BOP will help alleviate poverty by providing them with consumption choices and creating more entrepreneurial opportunities. After the initial acceptance of the concept, critiques noted that seeing the BOP as consumers is exploitative. However, incorporating the BOP as partners with ideas and inputs in the broader production and innovation systems is a better goal (Karnani 2006, 2007). The definition used to delineate the group (i.e., earning two dollars per day or 2000 dollars per year) vary considerably among interest groups—therefore, the market size at the BOP might be grossly overestimated considering that a large proportion of their income is probably spent, according to Maslow's pyramid of needs, on essential goods (Fletcher 2005), reducing the amount of available money for non-essential goods and services.

Innovation is often high-tech, as discussed in the literature, and occurs in a formal environment to serve relatively affluent consumers. In contrast, innovation at the BOP is often low tech, adapted to the environment of the consumer requiring additional organizational innovation for product delivery. The social perspective is an integral part of this type of innovation and profit margins are low considering the low purchasing power of the BOP. The global value of innovation at the BOP, whether in health care or other areas, is that less resource-intensive solutions are created to help with global issues of resource scarcity, poverty (whether in emerging or developed economies), and excessive health care costs in developed economies.

Multinational enterprises struggle to access and serve the BOP. Successful and profitable engagement in this consumer segment requires close interaction between consumers and producers as well as intermediaries facilitating this exchange. Innovation at the BOP is additionally driven by government organizations, non-profit organizations, academic entities, and social entrepreneurs. Inclusive innovation might be a way for companies and entrepreneurs to engage with the BOP facilitating new modes of interactions among various constituents: the MNC, the community, NGOs, potential users, and so on. New modes of cooperative interaction are expected to enable companies and entrepreneurs to acquire knowledge from relevant (potential) customers, generate innovation balancing the interest of companies and entrepreneurs, and, at the same time, serve the target market. This kind of engagement goes beyond creating cheap products or services based on existing designs. New technologies and creative applications require a product development approach aligned with the social, technological, and infrastructural environment combined with product marketing and delivery innovations to create goods with high value proposition (Kolk et al. 2013; Parthasarathy et al. 2015).

This chapter examines inclusive innovation in India at the BOP as an example of the diversity of innovation processes at the bottom of the pyramid. The discussion below focuses on contrasting various stakeholders and their modes of involvement and interaction with traditional innovation processes using cases in the health care industry.

Innovation

In a general sense, innovation is something new and is mostly related to industrial companies (Hauschildt and Salomo 2011). Innovation in an industrial context is seen as a process leading to the development of proprietary rights and subsequent exploitation of those rights.

> The invention process covers all efforts aimed at creating new ideas and getting them to work. The exploitation process includes all stages of

commercial development, application, and transfer, including the focusing of ideas or inventions towards specific objectives, evaluating those
objectives, downstream transfer and/or development results, and the
eventual broad-based utilization, dissemination, and diffusion of the
technology-based outcomes.

(Roberts 1987, p. 3).

In this context, innovation is seen as technology-based and the end result is
a product. With the emergence of the service industry, a broader definition
of innovation is used. In management theory, innovation is separated into
three different functional types of innovation expanding the technological
perspective (Zahn and Weidler 1995):

1) technical innovation relating to product and process innovation as well as
    (technical) knowledge;
2) organizational innovation including changes in corporate structure,
    culture, systems, and management; and
3) business innovation including changes in the business model, market
    structure, and separation.

In large companies, like western multinational corporations (MNCs), the
process of innovation is institutionalized and structured to minimize uncertainty. To achieve a certain predefined goal with a defined resource allot-
ment, alternatives to the current state of knowledge plans are developed. To
be successful, a company needs market intelligence to successfully design
a product and identify a problem/niche that will solve/serve. This process
relies on formal inputs from skilled employees, academics or researchers,
user-feedback, and standardized off-the-shelf resources. The subsequent marketing of an innovation relies on well-established channels (e.g., advertising
through media outlets).

A broad interpretation of innovation also includes social innovations, such
as, policies, lifestyles, and social technologies (Zapf 1989). Kallen (1973)
defines innovation as:

the transformations in food, shelter, defense against enemies and
disease, tools and technologies of production and consumption, forms
of play and sport, rituals and liturgies of religion, precedents of law,
inventions in science and thought, style and attitudes in literature and
arts.

(Kallen 1973, p. 447).

This definition encompasses social innovation and greatly expands the
stakeholders in the innovation process from businesses to governments,
policies, social organizations, and so on.

Innovation at the bottom of the pyramid

The innovation environment at the BOP is often informal. Members of the BOP are not part of usual economic exchanges and are often overlooked as a source of innovation given their lack of involvement in official labor markets or processes of consumption. Servicing the BOP as well as incorporating them in the knowledge creation or production process requires overcoming various challenges. At the BOP, where purchasing power is low and life is determined by the acquisition of necessities, companies are competing against broader challenges (Agnihotri 2012). To successfully convince customers at the BOP to purchase a product and/or take on debt to purchase, a product has to significantly enhance production capacities, income potential, or the ability to fulfill basic needs of the BOP, while being at the same time characterized by affordable pricing, low maintenance cost, high reliability, and long-term benefit. Aside from the value represented by the product itself, the BOP has limited access to financing options and does not have access to convenient communication channels, roads, and electricity. To successfully exploit an innovation at the BOP, access to finance (e.g., microfinance) enabling buyers to obtain credit is critical (Agnihotri 2012). Additionally, the financial constraints at the BOP strongly limit the achievable profit margin. Access affects innovation in several ways. Access to electricity defines the product properties which have to be adapted to the local conditions or require the simultaneous introduction of energy sources. Limited access to communication channels limits the ability to market a product and affects the ability to incorporate local knowledge into the product design. In both cases, intermediaries are helpful to bridge the divide providing access to knowledge or serving as marketing instrument. Trust is an important currency not only between company and intermediary, intermediary and the BOP, but also between the company and the BOP based on the company's brand reputation.

As mentioned above, providing a product with a high value proposition is challenging but in addition, functioning markets do not always exist. The limited availability of information, a lack of competition, or the dominance of a small number of local vendors imposing limitations in distribution systems and marketing channels are some of the reasons inhibiting market formation. Establishing a distribution system or applying traditional marketing methods often makes it difficult to introduce a product operating with a very limited profit margin. Coupled with a lack of financing options, a large part of the BOP can be excluded from the market. Therefore, alternative business models offering innovative financing, delivery, and marketing systems are required. This might involve cooperation with NGOs, other related institutions (e.g., microfinance), or the implementation of pay-per-use solutions to successfully supply the BOP and potentially enhance its function as users and potential producers (Karnani 2006, 2007).

BOP consumers have not been necessarily exposed to advanced technologies—therefore, simplicity and reliability of use are important product properties. Similarly, less complex devices can be used by less-skilled staff reducing potential cost in the field. While price sensitivity is an important characteristic, BOP consumers are brand conscious (Agnihotri 2012). In India's health system, for example, expensive foreign devices are used and consumers associate these with higher degrees of quality than nationally produced devices, which subsequently lack acceptance by the BOP or hospitals despite their comparable quality, better pricing, and affordability by lower income groups. Promoting wider acceptance requires intensive lobbying with governmental organizations and NGOs to increase the acceptance of methods and devices (Parthasarathy et al. 2015).

Inclusive innovation

Several innovation concepts have been identified in the literature to serve the BOP. Pro-poor innovation originated mostly within traditional R&D facilities, which often did not embed the poor directly in the product development process. Pro-poor innovations focus on cost reduction through the removal of features or making changes in packaging (Karnani 2006). Reducing package size (e.g., shampoo) is seen as a way to create affordable units of products; however, considering that large packages offer lower per unit costs, the success of this approach is questionable (Fletcher 2005; Karnani 2006; Agnihotri 2012). The appropriateness of the approach is also questioned given the lack of involvement of the poor. Producing cheap less functional products and emphasis only on the low price may lead to non-acceptance within the intended target group. Quality and longevity of products are valued but these characteristics do not necessarily characterize cheap products.

Grassroots innovations, in contrast, represent innovations that are created by the poor themselves out of necessity and are characterized by the creative application of limited resources to overcome obstacles and are often a reactive approach towards innovation. An example is the Jaipur foot invented in the context of artificial limbs—the lack of affordability affected the market for artificial limbs because of pricing ($45) (Bound and Thornton 2012). Jaipur foot-type innovations happen on a micro-level and adaptation on larger scales can be difficult especially for service innovations, which are solutions to local problems (Seyfang and Smith 2007; Paunov 2013). These innovations emerge within the informal sector and outside of traditional firms or formal R&D divisions. To bring these innovations to a larger market, cooperation between local entrepreneurs and corporations might be fruitful; however, this cooperation is unlikely in the absence of intermediaries (Utz and Dahlman 2007). Local (micro) entrepreneurs, familiar with the local context and available technologies, might be valuable knowledge sources for larger companies to adapt or develop product specifications for a specific local context (Paunov 2013).

Inclusive or frugal innovation represent a wider approach than providing cheap goods. The idea aims at creating for the BOP useful high performance and high quality goods at affordable prices and is able to incorporate the ideas of pro-poor and grassroots innovation. "Jugaad", a term widely used in the Indian context of frugal innovation, is based on improvisation due to resource constraints and lack of affordable solutions (Tiwari and Herstatt 2012a). In addition to considering price, usefulness, and quality, these innovations are not only related to technological innovation but incorporate technical change and bundle the innovation with new business models and changes in the organizational structure enabling companies to overcome constraints in marketing, financing, and distribution. Inclusive Innovation is requiring new forms of cooperation and interaction between the public sector, private sector, and non-traditional partners such as the poor/user and NGOs. The inclusion of the poor within the production process either as source of knowledge or innovators themselves is useful to create products that are acceptable (Guth 2005; Utz and Dahlman 2007; Lundvall 2009; Paunov 2013). Another potential type of innovators are NGOs and governments receiving an increasing scholarly interest as drivers of social change (Madsen 1997; Bach and Stark 2002; Mitlin et al. 2007; Mulgan et al. 2007). Embedded and familiar with the local context, these organizations can enjoy not only access to knowledge but also higher levels of trust thereby enabling easier product adoption and distribution among the BOP by knowing the realities of life in a specific region. Their motivation is driven by social transformative rather than financial goals and generally create value by creating benefits for the society by solving a societal problem more efficiently and/or more sustainable than previous actors without being bound by traditional ideas about innovation, organizational and stakeholder pressure, and able to pursue new approaches incorporating different perspectives in generating alternatives, which is often referred to as social innovation (Bach and Stark 2002; Mitlin et al. 2007; Mulgan et al. 2007). NGOs as innovators profit often from their relations with governments as well as the potential to receive outside funding from private entities. Though often pursuing more complex goals of greater social transformation than a specific innovation (Mulgan et al. 2007) by social ideals driven innovations compete when it comes to deployment and distribution with businesses at the bottom of the pyramid creating a more complex environment for corporations to engage with the BOP as earning potentials might be divided between NGOs, governmental providers, and private providers.

In sum, the idea of innovation by companies and organizations for and at the bottom of the pyramid needs a broader conceptualization combining technological, organizational, business, and social innovations. Characteristics of successful inclusive innovation should be not only affordable but useful, scalable, robust, fault resistant, and have supportive marketing, delivery and financing options (George et al. 2012; Tiwari and Herstatt 2012a). The following cases from health care shows the basic principles of inclusion, economies of scale, adaption, and the discussion is generalizable to other sectors.

Cases of innovation to serve the BOP

Successful innovation at the BOP depends on knowledge, embeddedness, and the support of NGOs, local governments, and community leaders. The following examples, summarized in Table 8.1, showcase how knowledge can be generated and used by MNCs and non-profit organizations and how non-traditional partners become crucial elements in connecting the producer and the user. These cases demonstrate that understanding local demand and culture is necessary to develop a product that is affordable and also acceptable by the BOP. This requires innovators to gather intelligence through direct interaction with the BOP or intermediaries and successfully develop products or services, which are appropriate. New forms of financing and distribution to successfully adapt to the conditions at the BOP are equally important. The **Jaipur Foot**, currently distributed in India and 26 other low-income countries by the NGO "Bhagwan Mahavir Viklang Sahayata Samiti", for example is not only a product adapted to scarce local conditions by being repairable with readily available materials resulting in a low price, but allows users to squat, which is difficult with traditional prosthesis. Squatting is a culturally preferred mode and used in social gatherings potentially excluding traditional prosthesis users (Weidner et al. 2010; Bound and Thornton 2012). Additionally, to the established Jaipur Foot, the NGO develops together with companies (e.g., Dow Chemicals) and universities (e.g., MIT, Stanford University), product improvements and new prosthesis (e.g., Jaipur Knee)(Bound and Thornton 2012; Sengupta 2013).

To understand the needs of specific subgroups, direct interaction is important. While firms can be successful with creating formalized development processes (e.g., General Electric), the structure as well as value norms differ considerably between BOP development and traditional markets. A close connection with the served consumers and immersion with local conditions is advantageous to successfully develop products and services for the BOP. **Ayzh**, a social for-profit entrepreneurial endeavor in India, developed their clean birth kits interacting with rural underprivileged women to create a widely acceptable product engaging additionally in cooperation with universities to improve the kit after the initial product inception (e.g., RTBI Incubator from IIT-Madras, MIT) (Aziz et al. 2013; Sengupta 2013). By additionally relying on rural underprivileged women in the production process offering them economic opportunities, the company increased its legitimacy and reach (Zelenika and Pearce 2011). **Arogya Parivar** and **Aravind** both rely on local personnel to gather the necessary knowledge and adapt to the local conditions. Arogya Parivar, a social business founded by Novartis to decrease usual business pressure for the venture, uses in India locally recruited health educators to assess the therapeutical needs of a community to offer a localized portfolio while educating consumers about the benefits of the offered (Pfitzer et al. 2013; Sengupta 2013). Additionally, Arogya Parivar provides pharmacies and doctors with micro loans to finance

Table 8.1 Summary of observed cases and their involvement at the BOP

Company	Type	Product and/or Services	Location	Notes	Partners	Economies of scale
General Electric	MNC	Baby Warmer "Lullaby", "Lullaby LED PT" against infant jaundice; developed to meet needs of BOP	India, 62 other countries	Developed in close cooperation with BOP, sold now in 62 different countries, success led to more investment by GE and expansion of involvement	Cooperation with NPOs as customer/technical help	Export
Embrace	Social Entrepreneur, NPO	Basic safe baby warmer, working on versions without use of electricity	India/Nepal	Designed from scratch for BOP	Result of "Design for Extreme Affordability" course at Stanford University	Sells good to large retailers, Cooperation with NPOs to increase reach
Narayana Hrudayalya	National company// MNC	Mass Heart Surgery, Telemedicine	India, Cayman Island	Opened hospital on Cayman Islands to serve US customers seeking to reduce treatment cost	Government Institutions, National Research Institutions to enable telemedicine network	Telemedicine, Physician network
Healing Fields Foundation	NPO	Health Education and Micro Health Insurance	Uttar Pradesh, Bihar, Orissa & Andhra Pradesh, Karnataka (India)	Has research unit to explore local needs, uses basic survey tools via phone	Private Insurers, State governments (facilitator for funding and development meeting local needs), NPOs	Local community workers

Arogya Parivar (by Novartis)	Social Business created by MNC	Health education, localized drug portfolio	India	Local health workers to develop trust and ensure that patients follow treatments; developed 11 new products to treat local problems	Microfinance institutions to enable local doctors/pharmacists to purchase products	Local adaption and community workers to educate potential customers
Bhagwan Mahavir Viklang Sahayata Samiti	NPO	Jaipur Foot, Jaipur Knee …	India + 26 other countries	For free, culturally embedded	Cooperates with national and international research/industrial partners (among others: Stanford University, MIT, Indian Institute of Technology, Jain Irrigation, Dow Chemicals …)	
Aravind Eye Care	NPO	Mass produced cataract and other eye surgeries; eye care and prevention education	South India	Has international education center exporting knowledge to other locations	Local sponsors and community workers essential to organize screening events	Local community workers, screening events in rural areas
AYZH	Social Entrepreneur, For-Profit	Clean Birth Kit	India, planned expansion to Africa	Developed, sourced and produced by local women providing economic opportunities	Various universities (RTBI Incubator from IIT-Madras, MIT, Colorado State University)	Export considered, relies on rural women to build trust and reach, sells to for-profit and non-profit health organizations

the acquisition of medicine overcoming the local resource scarcity (Pfitzer et al. 2013). Aravind Eyecare, a NGO operating in South India, relies on local community workers and the essential support of local sponsors (NGOs, governments, individuals) to connect consumers with their services by offering localized screenings and help rural consumers to reach treatment centers. Transportation to more central places can be expensive and time consuming. By offering local check-ups Aravind reduces the opportunity cost of using the offered services to the BOP requiring only patients in urgent need to travel (Rangan and Thulasiraj 2007).

The role of community engagement, NGOs, and governments is often of an enabling nature. **Embrace** operates in India and Nepal and produces a low-cost baby warmer requiring no constant access to electricity to operate. They rely on a twofold strategy selling their, from scratch for the BOP designed, baby warmer to large distributers of child goods and donating their baby warmer to rural NGOs thus enhancing the reach and acceptance of the product. Embrace, starting as a social business, merged with the Thrive Network, an international non-profit organization, to expand its reach (Misra 2013; Sengupta 2013; Embrace 2016).

Narayana Hrudayalya, an Indian corporation, works in Karnataka together with the state government to provide the poor with a micro health insurance allowing the poor to consume its services centering around telemedicine and mass heart surgery. Similarly, NGOs like the "Healing Fields Foundation" promote health savings groups and micro insurances to provide the poor with access to health care aside of also providing health care education (Sengupta 2013). The Healing Fields Foundation operates in the Indian states Uttar Pradesh, Bihar, Orissa & Andhra Pradesh, and Karnataka and works together with private insurers (insurer) and governments (funding) to create micro insurances. The organization serves also as intermediary between the population and the government employing local community workers to support their research unit with phone surveys to direct state funding towards projects the local community needs.

With the emergence of the state led Rashtriya Swasthya Bima Yojana (RSBY), a health insurance plan for the poor, health care is supposed to become affordable on a household level (RSBY 2009; Das and Sharma 2015). Aiming to insure, by 2017, 70 million households, the insurance relies on economies of scale and state support to allow the poor to acquire essential health care products and services. In this case, the state enables the poor to use health care services—even in cases where the health care product is already developed to fulfill the needs of the BOP financial constraints prevent often consumption requiring additional measures to enable the BOP to consume a service expanding the notion of innovation by other dimensions (e.g., financing).

Innovation at the bottom of the pyramid differs significantly from traditional, often formalized and expensive, innovation processes in corporations. Corporations, whether multinational or national, can use their engagement at the BOP to learn about markets and develop suitable products and services, which are developed considering the scarcity of resources. Additionally, their involvement can yield knowledge allowing the successful transfer of concepts and products into other markets, developed and developing, or positively affect the image of a company in a market conscious about social responsibility.

The health care division of the multinational corporation General Electrics (GE) established a program called "healthymagination" and developed with their Indian subsidiary Wipro GE health care for the Indian market including the baby-warmer "Lullaby" in close cooperation with the BOP using an R&D center in India (Agnihotri 2015), which was launched in 2011 with the aim to provide an affordable high quality product which could improve access to infant health care for the poor. GE sells the created product in 62 different countries including developing but also developed markets like the US (cf. Sehgal et al. 2010; Tiwari and Herstatt 2012a; Agnihotri 2015) showing the export potential of innovation at the BOP. Following the success of the product GE subsequently decided to invest US$50 million into development at the BOP expecting the launch of a variety of further products including the infant jaundice treatment device "Lullaby LED PT". GE entered partnerships with NPOs to distribute their product and additionally provides organizations like "Embrace" with technical assistance to create other BOP products.

Innovation at the BOP is for corporations a valuable source of knowledge leading potentially to internationalization of local corporations. Narayana Hrudayalya (mentioned above) specialized in heart surgery reducing prices via economies of scale generating between US$200 million in revenue in 2011–2013 (Sengupta 2013). Surgeries cost less than US$3000 and are discounted for poor patients. The company relies on a telemedicine network, enabled by the Indian national satellite agency, to connect doctors and patients in remote areas with its diagnostic units and works together with state governments to provide hospital beds for persons in need. Gathering experience in mass quality health care the company expanded with a US$70 million subsidiary to the Cayman Islands to offer un- and under-insured US customers affordable health care. The company plans overall a US$2 billion investment including a 2000-bed hospital and a medical university. The company does not operate in the US itself due to stringent institutional requirements and the founder sees those as deterrence for health care delivery innovations in the US (Anand 2009; Das 2014).

New business forms like social enterprises are beginning to serve the BOP. Novartis set up Arogya Parivar to deliver health care and pharmaceuticals to the BOP relying on locally recruited health educators to assess the therapeutical needs of a community to localize the local selection and educate them about the benefits of the offered services while additionally providing pharmacies and doctors with micro loans to finance the acquisition of medicine. Economies of scale are achieved via the vast network and access to over 50 million potential customers (Sengupta 2013). The localization led to the development of new therapeutic applications which can be potentially applied in other rural areas (Pfitzer et al. 2013). While created as individual unit to reduce business pressure and expecting a long time to recover initial investments, the company became profitable after 31 months (Pfitzer et al. 2013). Similarly, the NGO Aravind Eyecare screens annually 2.4 million potential patients directing patients in need to their highly standardized surgical centers in which, in 2013, 285,000 eye surgeries were conducted (Rangan and Thulasiraj 2007; Sengupta 2013). Due to their large degree of specialization Aravind became a leading provider in cataract surgery. Narayana Hrudayalya reaches out to its customers in several ways relying on telemedicine to connect patients with doctors in diagnostic hubs and direct them for treatment to their hospital facilities which are created in cooperation with state governments. Additionally, the company participates in a family physician network in which physicians can use a free software and NH-provided ECG devices to send ECGs to an NH specialist for assessment thus acquiring patients for their hospitals (Anand 2009; Das 2014; Parthasarathy et al. 2015).

Ayzh, a small for-profit social enterprise, produces a clean birth kit in India involving rural women in development and production; they distribute their product via for-profit and non-profit organizations to gain access to large numbers of underprivileged women and achieve economies of scale (Zelenika and Pearce 2011; Aziz et al. 2013). The company plans on expanding to Africa (Sengupta 2013). Aravind Eyecare has an international education center educating medical staff and NGOs about Aravind's operations—this effort potentially exports the gathered experience to other areas of the world enabling knowledge transfer to similar operations (Sengupta 2013).

Whether traditional companies or social enterprises, the above examples illustrate that engaging the bottom of the pyramid potentially yields new products and services adapted to the needs of the poor. Without expensive R&D by adapting to the resource constraints and specific needs of this specific markets companies can not only generate new products and achieve potential profits but may also gather the necessary experience and knowledge to enter other markets. MNCs engaging at the BOP may be able to apply and export the new concepts and products/services to other markets whereas those can be developing markets but also developed markets. Additionally, as the examples of Ayzh and Narayana Hrudayalya show, engaging at the BOP may be a pathway to internationalization for corporations.

The business and non-profit examples show that for successfully engaging at the BOP economies of scale are of crucial importance considering that profit margins are small and individual purchasing power is small. Economies of scale are achieved via several methods. Companies can rely on other companies or NGOs to use their distribution network and often access the trust-based network of NGOs to reach deep into rural areas as illustrated by Ayzh and Embrace. Those new partnerships enable organizations to achieve economies of scale by increasing the number of potential customers. Other cases such as

Aravind, Narayana Hrudayalya and Arogya Parivar rely on establishing local contacts by either localizing events (eye-screening—Aravind) or by setting up communication channels with the rural population. Those approaches can rely on direct involvement through community workers (Aravind and Arogya Parivar) or may connect rural customers via modern telecommunication channels using for example telemedicine (Narayana Hrudayalya). The end result is an expansion of the reach of the organization enabling customers to receive appropriate products or serve as intermediaries between customer and product/service. Ayzh goes further by incorporating its target group, rural underprivileged women, in their production process supporting additionally the acceptance and reach of the product. Exports may serve as an additional way to achieve economies of scale.

The stakeholders

The above cases show a large variety of involved partners pursuing different approaches to create and deliver products to the BOP. Acquiring knowledge or generally entering the BOP market can be challenging though the above cases show successful strategies facilitating alternative business models and social engagement outside the formal marketing and innovation process. Businesses have to recognize the BOP as a customer group with specific needs and demands to be successful and have to get involved in market research to explore and embed the needs of the local consumers in product development. Gathering this knowledge is essential to reduce the risk of non-acceptance by the BOP and hence the success or failure of a product. Companies cannot collect this information in usual ways hence the BOP is bypassed as a source of innovative ideas due to their low degree of participation in the economy. NGOs can serve in this role due to their trust-based access to local networks as the case of the "Healing Fields Foundation" shows, as intermediary between BOP and private insurers and government organizations. Embrace relied on public hospitals to gain access to rural neonatal conditions in Nepal useful in developing their design. But the case of GE shows that direct customer interaction can be successful as well. In the following section, ways how stakeholders engage with the BOP to deploy or facilitate innovation at the BOP are characterized.

Multinational corporations rarely target the consumer demographics represented by the BOP and the number of involved companies is low but with increasing saturation of established markets and limits to growth, transforming the accessibility of the BOP to goods and services can be a growth strategy for multinational corporations (Fletcher 2005; Karnani 2006). While this has potential for revenue growth, this strategy could endow companies with a competitive advantage based on the combination of creativity and efficiency necessary to serve the BOP. Traditional R&D models and innovation processes of MNCs require adjustment to be successful at the BOP hence companies struggle with established methods to enter local networks and gather knowledge. This includes the facilitation of new partnerships with local companies but also non-traditional partners (e.g., NGOs) and the creation of local capacity (Vermeulen et al. 2008). While GE is a more traditional actor relying on a development center and direct interaction with the BOP in designing their new products, the examples of Arogya Parivar, Aravind, and Narayana Hrudayalya show that building capacity via local community workers grants access to knowledge. MNCs have the ability and experience to scale up local products and can thus be valuable partners for entrepreneurs to distribute products as well as sources of knowledge as shown by the Jaipur Foot, Embrace baby warmer, and Ayzh.

Formal R&D is a potential mechanism of acquiring knowledge. Multinational corporations' entry mode decision can considerably impact their access to local knowledge (Reddy 2005; Narula and Dunning 2010). Greenfield developments comply with the corporate structure and strategy but require "time" to get accepted in the local context as well as in the scientific community in the host country. Acquiring an existing facility allows a company to rely on already established links to local suppliers and customers or to the community and so the alternative of acquiring a local establishment might help facilitate these relationships to gather market knowledge. It should be noted that the interaction between greenfield sites or acquisitions and the BOP remains limited without increasing the effort to cooperate. Establishing indigenous development units seem to be a way to relate product development to the locally available technologies (Reddy 2005). However, a working relationship with the potential consumers has to be established to ensure the creation of a suitable product and reduce the risk of failure (Reddy 2005). To effectively serve the BOP it is also not sufficient to recycle existing technologies and reduce their features (Sehgal et al. 2010). Only a new development process adapted to locally available capabilities and technologies has the potential of creating a successful product. Arogya Parivar, Aravind, and Narayana Hrudayalya rely all on strong interaction with local communities facilitating local community workers (Arogya Parivar, Aravind) or telemedicine to establish contact with the BOP, leading in the case of AP, to a locally adapted product portfolio.

While local companies, or MNCs originating in the emerging economy, might have easier access to government resources and local knowledge, their innovation process seems to follow a formal approach with customers who are more affluent than the BOP. This might imply that similar adjustments have to be taken by local (large) firms to tap into the knowledge at the BOP. MNCs have used distinct practices parallel to their existing capabilities showing a separation of formal R&D from innovating for the BOP (Vermeulen et al. 2008).

While less resource intensive modes of production or products exploitable in other markets are a competitive advantage for companies, companies can achieve other advantages. The idea of generating global corporate social responsibility and building brand recognition in a developing market segment to gain access to future consumers is entering company and innovation strategies (Agnihotri 2012; Tiwari and Herstatt 2012b; Ramani and Mukherjee 2014). Novartis, for example, mentions Arogya Parivar in multiple social responsibility reports as successful social business and used the experiences gained in the project to expand their social businesses to Vietnam, Kenya and Indonesia (Novartis 2014, 2016). Engaging in the BOP is a long-term strategic investment helping companies to create more resource efficient products, brand recognition, and indirect positive marketing effects in other countries.

Social entrepreneurs, whether with for profit or non-profit business models seem to be important innovators emphasizing the social aspects of business. These innovations can be conceived locally based on necessity (Jaipur Foot) or outside. These innovations are often place bound or small-scale innovations. The case of Ayzh shows that a local connection and cultural understanding are important contributors to derive successful innovation. The Embrace baby warmer started as a design project in a "Design for Extreme Affordability course" at the Stanford University—without direct exchange, the university served as mediator between the BOP and the entrepreneurs. Universities serve as a source of knowledge for innovators at the bottom of the pyramid helping BOP innovations to be developed further. In the case of the Embrace baby warmer, a university served as mediator between the entrepreneurs and the BOP and can be seen as incubator of the idea (Misra 2013; Embrace 2016). But it appears that in other cases of smaller social enterprises, Ayzh and the Jaipur Foot, universities got involved after a product launch helping the innovator to improve upon the good. This seems to be the case for the Jaipur Foot as well as Ayzh, which are both supported by local and international partners including well renown universities like the MIT (Sengupta 2013). The cases also show that access to the distribution system of (multinational) corporations and non-profit organizations increases the reach of products as stakeholders cooperate bringing together for profit and non-profit goals.

NGOs can serve in a multitude of ways in the innovation process. They can facilitate the interaction between companies and the BOP but can also serve as marketers and distributors of products whereas Embrace and Ayzh rely strongly on those channels. Aravind Eyecare relies on local partners to organize screening event. The cases of the Jaipur Foot and Aravind Eyecare also show that NGOs can serve as innovators either expanding on an idea (Jaipur Knee) or developing new processes adapted to the local needs of the population by combining health care education, screening, and treatment (Aravind). Given their committed engagement in a specific area, NGOs build social capital with the population providing the organization with access to information and local networks which can be facilitated in cooperation with businesses or other agencies allowing a partner to tap into knowledge at the BOP or rely on the NGO as a distribution and marketing partner (Tasavori 2013; SadreGhazi n.d.). The NGO "Healing Fields Foundation" is such a partner collecting data at the BOP to share them with government entities to ensure that scarce resources are used efficiently to achieve benefits for the BOP. Cooperation between for-profit and non-profit entities can be a necessity to upscale a service or product and the example of health insurance shows how important the interaction between different types of organizations are to successfully deploy health innovations at the BOP. But cooperation can be contentious given their different valuation of profit and may require companies to go to great lengths to build trust (Oetzel and Doh 2009). A successful cooperation requires a company to demonstrate its commitment to long-term goals rather than short-term profit.

Governments have a strong impact on innovation and business interaction by setting rules and norms and supporting/deterring developments via policies. Governments can help establish a supportive environment for BOP innovation supplying innovators with the resources to deploy innovations on a larger scale. Narayana Hrudayalya cooperates with state governments to create hospital wings suitable for heart surgery supplying the hospitals with the necessary equipment. Governments can affect knowledge discovery by supporting an inclusive innovation system not only supporting formal research but also providing grants and seed capital for the exploration of prototypes derived in the informal sector encouraging entrepreneurs as well as supporting the cooperation between informal and formal sector. Additionally, governments can allow access to communication technologies and potentially subsidize useful innovations. Narayana Hrudayalya for example cooperates with India's Satellite Research Organization (ISRO) to provide their telemedicine network (Sengupta 2013) technology unlikely to be available without government support. Successful development of innovation at the BOP requires the cooperation of government institutions, (MN)Cs, NGOs and the BOP itself as a source of entrepreneurs to ensure successful development, deployment and the social benefits of BOP innovations (Hietapuro 2011). As the Rashtriya Swasthya Bima Yojana shows governments are also important facilitators of health insurance directly influencing people's ability to access health care and other institutions like the NGO "Healing Fields Foundation" or even companies like Narayana Hrudayalya lobby for the creation of health insurances (Sengupta 2013). Without access to health insurance even low-cost services as provided, for example, by Narayana Hrudayalya might be not accessible for the BOP thus enabling consumers to use services but also allowing companies and NPOs involved with the BOP to achieve necessary economies of scale. The potential of the exploitation of the BOP and its entrepreneurs is a major concern and policies could be used ensure that the BOP is supported and enabled in its ability to partake as producer in market processes rather than encouraging consumption to reduce poverty (Karnani 2006). Governments can ensure that the interests of the BOP as innovator, producer, and user are protected when corporations and the BOP (Utz and Dahlman 2007).

Conclusions: implications for innovation at the BOP

The partners, innovators, and processes vary in successful product placement at the BOP. To generate successful innovations for the BOP providing long-term benefits and reducing poverty requires companies, governments, and NGOs to be flexible and willing to explore new non-standardized venues outside of formal company R&D. This includes the ability to compromise between different value systems (e.g., non-profit vs. for-profit) to create an environment in which knowledge can be exchanged and products can be distributed overcoming the challenges of innovation at the BOP. The types of organization involved at the BOP vary including NGOs and firms (e.g., social businesses) and they compete with each other potentially as innovators at the BOP for scarce resources. Comparing social innovative processes of NGOs with commercial oriented innovation processes of companies might yield further insights on how to successfully engage at the BOP.

But while the types of organization involved vary, a couple of commonalities can be identified across the presented cases. Gaining access and including the BOP or specific target groups within the BOP in the development process via direct exchange or intermediaries is crucial for success. While in some cases traditional innovation processes are used (e.g., GE), all cases are characterized by a high degree of interaction with the BOP to create useful products for the BOP. The cases discussed in this chapter go mostly beyond pure product development facilitating new ways of product distribution, production and marketing rather than developing only a cheap stripped-down product. NGOs and companies also rely on local connections as demonstrated by the cases of Aravind, Healing Fields, and the Novartis founded Arogya Parivar. Local connections are crucial in gathering knowledge, creating trust, and gaining access to the bottom of the pyramid. In this context, several organizations, NGOs, and social businesses rely on local customer education or screening introducing the benefits they provide while creating a market for their products. While it might be argued that the Jaipur Foot and Aravind started out as grassroot innovations, their increasingly holistic approaches show that principles of inclusive innovation have been incorporated. This indicates that inclusive innovation plays an increasingly important role to be successful at the BOP. In contrast to traditional products, products created at the BOP are low cost and target a large number of low-income population or low-income families in the case of health care. The demands of the customers regarding accessibility and affordability differ considerable from other normally observed consumers driving the creation of new innovative products or service delivery systems attractive for the target consumers as can be seen with the observed health care services and products. The understanding of local conditions and cultural context seems, in general, more important for success than capital intensive R&D processes or delivery systems.

Success is strongly dependent on the ability to meet the needs of the local population and provide a quality product with a high value proposition. NGOs can serve in this role due to their trust-based access to local networks as the cases of Embrace; however, the case of GE shows that direct customer interaction can be successful as well. Product adaption based on specific local market conditions has been very successful yielding further innovative potential as the new pharmaceuticals developed by Arogya Parivar or the success of the Jaipur Foot indicate. Considering the cultural context and needs of customers during product development, marketing and distribution is a further important component contributing to success. The Jaipur foot, in contrast to previous existing prosthetics, allowed consumers not only to maintain their prosthetics easily and locally, but also allows them to squat and thus to participate in normal social interactions which have contributing to its success. In the case of Ayzh's birth kits, understanding the local and cultural conditions and using their target customers in their production process greatly increased the company's acceptance and credibility contributing to its success.

Engaging at the BOP in social ventures can supply companies with knowledge adaptable in different context creating new business opportunities by exporting products or business concepts and can function as a pathway to internationalization. The latter is also valid for NGOs expanding their reach or spreading their knowledge by educating staff of other international organizations. The impact of innovation at the BOP on western economies and products are illustrated by several cases as well (e.g., lullaby by GE, Narayana Hrudayalya engaging in medical tourism between the USA and the Cayman Islands). Lessons learned from innovating for the BOP might be furthermore an important concept in supporting the urban poor as well as health care systems in crisis in Western economies. Overall the cases of Arogya Parivar, a Novartis subsidiary, GE and Narayana Hrudayalya show that engaging at the BOP can be very attractive for MNCs and contribute to the emergence of MNCs. While the case of Arogya Parivar shows that successful involvement can become profitable, the case of GE shows that innovations created for the BOP can be adapted to other, including developed markets, yielding further business opportunities encouraging GE to substantially expand its R&D efforts at the BOP. The case of Naryana Hrudayalya involvement at the BOP enabled the internationalization of the company based on principles learned at the BOP.

The application of information and communication technologies (ICT) are critical for the BOP as illustrated in the health care cases where firms found "a sweet spot" (Parthasarathy et al. 2015, p. 62) that permits meeting of the social goals of catering to the underserved and making the provision of the product or service a sustainable proposition (Parthasarathy et al. 2015). ICT applications allow less resource intensive modes of engagement and the opportunity to scale up operations.

Scale is an important factor for sustainable business considering the low profit margins at the BOP. Scaling up can be achieved by partnering with public and private organizations. All cases show that the product alone is not sufficient to be successful. Finding new innovative ways of distribution and marketing as well as providing easy access are crucial for acceptance—this can entail the provision of cost free equipment or screening or bringing services and products to consumers via new forms of distribution (e.g., telemedicine, NGOs as distribution network, consumer education) or government involvement (partnerships, health insurance). Specifically, the state is an important facilitator of innovation in health care by enabling health insurances for the BOP to use medical services. The state becomes additionally an important enabler for organizations involved at the BOP—it can grant organizations access to information technologies or services (e.g., Naryana Hrudayalya) at the BOP.

References

Agnihotri, A. 2012: Revisiting the debate over the bottom of the pyramid market. In: *Journal of Macromarketing*, **32** (4), 417–423.

Agnihotri, A. 2015: Low-cost innovation in emerging markets. In: *Journal of Strategic Marketing*, **23** (5), 399–411.

Anand, G. 2009: The Henry Ford of heart surgery. *The Wall Street Journal*. In: https://www.wsj.com/articles/SB125875892887958111.

Aoyama, Y. 2012: Geography of economic governance: Industrial dimensions of state-market relations.

Aziz, A., Sarason, Y. & Hanley, G. 2013: Ayzh at a crossroad: Maternal health for whom? In: WDI Publishing. Purchasable at http://wdi-publishing.com/casedetail.aspx?cid=1429329.

Bach, J. & Stark, D. 2002: Innovative ambiguities: NGOs' use of interactive technology. In: *Eastern Europe. Studies in Comparative International Development*, **37** (2), 3–23.

Bound, K. & Thornton, I. W. 2012: *Our frugal future: Lessons from India's innovation system*. Nesta, London.

Das, S. 2014: The Economic Times. Devi Shetty opens low-cost health care venture in Cayman Islands outside US regulatory reach. In: http://articles.economictimes.indiatimes.com/2014-02-24/news/47635802_1_devi-shetty-narayana-health-indian-doctors Accessed: 29.04.2016.

Das, S. & Sharma, Y. S. 2015: The Economic Times. Government shuts doors on private insurers in Rashtriya Swasthya Bima Yojana. In: http://articles.economictimes.indiatimes.com/2015-01-06/news/57748116_1_rsby-rashtriya-swasthya-bima-yojana-insurance-companies Accessed: 29.04.2016.

Doh, J. P. & Teegen, H. 2002: Nongovernmental organizations as institutional actors in international business: Theory and implications. In: *International Business Review*, **11** (6), 665–684.

Embrace. 2016: Embrace global. In: Company Website. http://embraceglobal.org/ Accessed: 29.04.2016.

Fletcher, R. 2005: International marketing at the bottom of the pyramid. In: ANZMAC 2005 Conference: Marketing in International and Cross-Cultural Environments. www.anzmac.org/conference_archive/2005/cd-site/pdfs/9-Marketing-Int-C-Cultural-Env/9-Fletcher.pdf Accessed: 27.07.2014.

George, G., McGahan, A. M. & Prabhu, J. 2012: Innovation for inclusive growth: Towards a theoretical framework and a research agenda. In: *Journal of Management Studies*, **49** (4), 661–683.

Guth, M. 2005: Innovation, social inclusion and coherent regional development: A new diamond for a socially inclusive innovation policy in regions. In: *European Planning Studies*, **13** (2), 333–349.

Hauschildt, J. & Salomo, S. 2011: *Innovationsmanagement*. Vahlen, München.

Hietapuro, M. 2011: Partnerships in BOP business. In: https://aaltodoc.aalto.fi/bitstream/handle/123456789/661/hse_ethesis_12529.pdf?sequence=1 Accessed: 29.04.2016.

Kallen, H. M. 1973: Innovation. In: Etzioni, A. Etzioni-Halevy, E. (Publ.), *Social change – Sources, patterns and consequences*. 2nd ed., Basic Books, New York, 447–450.

Karnani, A. 2006: Mirage at the bottom of the pyramid. In: http://deepblue.lib.umich.edu/bitstream/handle/2027.42/57215/wp835?sequence=1 Accessed: 27.07.2014.

Karnani, A. 2007: The mirage of marketing to the bottom of the pyramid. In: *California Management Review*, **49** (4), 90–111.

Kolk, A., Rivera-Santos, M. & Rufin, C. 2013: Reviewing a decade of research on the "base/bottom of the pyramid"(BOP) concept. In: *Business & Society*, **53** (3), 338–377.

Lambell, R., Ramia, G., Nyland, C. & Michelotti, M. 2008: NGOs and international business research: Progress, prospects and problems. In: *International Journal of Management Reviews*, **10** (1), 75–92.

Lundvall, B. A. 2009: Innovation as an interactive process: User-producer interaction to the national system of innovation: Research paper. In: *African Journal of Science, Technology, Innovation and Development*, **1** (2 & 3), 10–34.

Madsen, S. T. 1997: Between people and the state: NGOs as troubleshooters and innovators. In: Lindberg, S. & Sverrisson, A. (Eds.): *Social movements in development*, Palgrave Macmillan, London, UK, 252–273.

Misra, M. 2013: Warmth for newborns: The embrace infant warmer. In Satia, J., Misra, M., Arora, R. & Neogi, S. (Eds.): (2013). *Innovations in maternal health: Case studies from India*, SAGE Publications, New Delhi, India, 147–157.

Mitlin, D., Hickey, S. & Bebbington, A. 2007: Reclaiming development? NGOs and the challenge of alternatives. In: *World Development*, **35** (10), 1699–1720.

Mulgan, G., Tucker, S., Ali, R. & Sanders, B. 2007: Social innovation: What it is, why it matters and how it can be accelerated. Skoll Centre for Social Entrepreneurship.

Narula, R. & Dunning, J. H. 2010: Multinational enterprises, development and globalization: Some clarifications and a research agenda. In: *Oxford Development Studies*, **38** (3), 263–287.

Novartis. 2014: Corporate responsibility performance report 2013. Novartis AG 2014. In: www.novartis.com/sites/www.novartis.com/files/documents/cr-performance-report-2013.pdf.

Novartis. 2016: Corporate responsibility performance report 2015. Novartis AG 2016. In: www.novartis.com/sites/www.novartis.com/files/novartis-cr-performance-report-2015.pdf.

Oetzel, J. & Doh, J. P. 2009: MNEs and development: A review and reconceptualization. In: *Journal of World Business*, **44** (2), 108–120.

Parthasarathy, B., Aoyama, Y. & Menon, N. 2015: Innovating for the bottom of the pyramid: Case studies in health care from India. In: Hostettler, S., Hazboun, E. & Bolay, J.C. (Eds.): *Technologies for development*, Springer International Publishing, Cham, 55–69.

Paunov, C. 2013: Innovation and inclusive development. OECD Science, Technology and Industry Working Papers, 2013/01, OECD Publishing, Paris. http://dx.doi.org/10.1787/5k4dd1rvsnjj-en

Pfitzer, M., Bockstette, V. & Stamp, M. 2013: Innovating for shared value. In: *Harvard Business Review*, **91** (9), 100–107.

Prahalad, C. K. 2009: *The fortune at the bottom of the pyramid, revised and updated 5th anniversary edition: Eradicating poverty through profits*. Prentice Hall, New Jersey.

Ramani, S. V. & Mukherjee, V. 2014: Can breakthrough innovations serve the poor (BOP) and create reputational (CSR) value? Indian case studies. In: *Technovation*, **34** (5), 295–305.

Rangan, V. K. & Thulasiraj, R. D. 2007: Making sight affordable (innovations case narrative: The Aravind eye care system). In: *Innovations*, **2** (4), 35–49.

Rashtriya Swasthya Bima Yojana (RSBY). 2009: Rashtriya Swasthya Bima Yojana (RSBY). In: www.rsby.gov.in/about_rsby.aspx Accessed: 29.04.201654ii.

Reddy, P. 2005, R&D-related FDI in developing countries: Implications for host countries. In: *Globalization of R&D and developing countries*. United Nations, New York, 89-105.

Roberts, E. B. 1987: *Generating technological innovation*. Oxford University Press, New York, USA.

SadreGhazi, S. n.d.: Challenges of corporate involvement in pro-poor innovation. In: www.ungs.edu.ar/globelics/wp-content/uploads/2011/12/ID-359-Sadre Ghazi-Inclusive-Innovation.pdf Accessed: 27.07.2014.

Sehgal, V., et al. 2010: The importance of frugal engineering. In: *Strategy and Business*, **16** (59), 20–25.

Sengupta, R. 2013: Sustainable and inclusive innovations in health care delivery–A business model perspective. *GIZ India & CII-ITC Centre of Excellence for Sustainable Development*.

Seyfang, G. & Smith, A. 2007: Grassroots innovations for sustainable development: Towards a new research and policy agenda. In: *Environmental Politics*, **16** (4), 584–603.

Tasavori, M. 2013: The entry of multinational companies to the base of the pyramid: A network perspective. In: www.essex.ac.uk/ebs/research/working_papers/WP2013-8_Tasavori_multinational_companies.pdf Accessed: 27.07.2014.

Tiwari, R. & Herstatt, C. 2012a: Open global innovation networks as enablers of frugal innovation: Propositions based on evidence from India (No. 72). Working Paper, Technologie-und Innovationsmanagement, Technische Universität Hamburg-Harburg. In: www.econstor.eu/bitstream/10419/68261/1/733539696.pdf Accessed: 27.07.2014.

Tiwari, R. & Herstatt, C. 2012b: Frugal innovations for the 'unserved' customer: An assessment of India's attractiveness as a lead market for cost-effective products (No. 69). Working Papers/Technologie-und Innovationsmanagement, Technische Universität Hamburg-Harburg. In: www.econstor.eu/bitstream/10419/55862/1/687849292. pdf Accessed: 27.07.2014.

Utz, A. & Dahlman, C. 2007: Promoting inclusive innovation. In: Dutz, M. A. (Ed.): 2007: *Unleashing India's innovation: Toward sustainable and inclusive growth*, World Bank Publications, Washington DC, 105–128.

Vermeulen, P. A. M., Bertisen, J., Geurts, J. L. A., Kandachar, P., & Halme, M. 2008: Building dynamic capabilities for the base of the pyramid. In: Kandachar, P. & Halme, M. (Eds.): *Sustainability challenges and solutions at the base of the pyramid*, Routledge, London, 369-386.

Weidner, K. L., Rosa, J. A. & Viswanathan, M. 2010: Marketing to subsistence consumers: Lessons from practice. In: *Journal of Business Research*, **63** (6), 559–569.

Yaziji, M. & Doh, J. 2009: *NGOs and corporations: Conflict and collaboration*. Cambridge University Press, Cambridge.

Zahn, E. & Weidler, A. 1995: Integriertes innovations management. In: Zahn, E. (Ed.): *Handbuch Technologiemanagement*, Schäffer-Poeschel Verlag, Stuttgart, 351-376.

Zapf, W. 1989: Über soziale Innovationen. In: *Soziale Welt*, **40** (H. 1/2), 170–183.

Zelenika, I. & Pearce, J. M. 2011: Barriers to appropriate technology growth in sustainable development. In: *Journal of Sustainable Development*, **4** (6), 12.

9 South Korea as a new player in global innovation

Role of a highly educated labour force's participation in new technologies and industries

Sunyang Chung

Introduction

The South Korean economy has developed remarkably since the beginning of its industrialization. South Korea has moved from a very poor country to a developed country. There are two important factors in the successful development of South Korea: technological innovation and S&T manpower. It has accumulated its technological and innovation capabilities through the close collaboration between the government and industrial companies. South Korea is one of the representative successful cases that S&T and innovation play an essential role in economic and social development of a country.

An even more important factor is well-qualified S&T manpower, because R&D activities and technological innovations are generated, diffused and exploited by S&T manpower. At the beginning of its economic development, however, South Korea had a big problem with a shortage of S&T manpower. At that time South Korea was a poor agricultural country and it had no S&T-education infrastructure because it had experienced the Korean War from 1950 to 1953. However, South Korea has established the S&T education system, especially from the beginning of the 1970s and nurtured sufficient S&T manpower in a short-period.

Based on the accumulation of technological and innovation capabilities by South Korean S&T manpower, South Korean companies could produce and export their products and services to world markets. At the beginning of its industrialization, South Korea could export only low-tech products, but it could shift its export items to medium-tech and high-tech products in the course of economic development. In order to accumulate technological capabilities and produce more sophisticated products, South Korean innovation actors, i.e. industrial companies, public research institutes and universities, have increased the number of R&D personnel. In particular, South Korean companies have accumulated their R&D and innovation capabilities since the beginning of the 1980s. They have established their own research institutes and recruited many researchers and engineers and increased their R&D investments to a large scale.

The South Korean government has also played a pivotal role in nurturing S&T manpower and accumulating technological and innovation capabilities of South Korean innovation actors. It has enacted many relevant laws for nurturing and exploiting S&T manpower, established relevant education institutes and initiated a series of master plans for developing its national economy and S&T capabilities. It set very ambitious goals to nurture S&T manpower and attained, and even surpassed, the goals. These South Korean experiences on nurturing and developing S&T manpower in the development of the national economy will be of interest to other countries. This chapter will discuss the South Korean experiences in detail.

This chapter is composed of five Sections. After the introduction in Section 1, Section 2 will discuss the role of S&T manpower in accumulating indigenous technological capabilities in developing countries and review some literature on South Korean experiences. In Section 3, we will discuss the economic development of South Korea briefly. Here we will analyse the changes in South Korean industrial structures and S&T performance. In Section 4, we will analyse the historical development of S&T manpower since the beginning of South Korean economic development. Section 5 is about the role of the South Korean government in the development of S&T manpower. Here we will discuss the detailed initiatives of the South Korean government for nurturing and developing S&T manpower in the process of economic development. Finally, in Section 6, we will identify some meaningful implications, which will be interesting for international readers.

S&T manpower and economic development

There have been many discussions on the role of technological innovations in the economic development of developing and less-developed countries. However, it is not easy for developing countries to accumulate technological capabilities. Clark (1985) emphasizes that developing countries have two major problems with regard to their accumulation of technological capabilities. The first problem is the rigid political structures which hindered flexible allocation of S&T resources and a rapid response to demand conditions. The other one is the lack of policy measures to make technological development. His arguments indicate the importance of S&T infrastructure for developing countries.

The discussion on the role of technological innovations in the development of developing countries has been focused on the concept of *indigenous technological capabilities*. This concept is defined as a nation's capacity to absorb, digest, develop and appropriate its own technological innovations (Caillods, 1984; King 1984; Bell 1985; Clark 1985; OECD 1992a; Chung 2012). In particular, Bell (1985) emphsises that indigenous technological capabilities in developing countries could be well accumulated by sound governmental intervention and intentional investment of scarce S&T resources. This indicates that the governments of developing countries must have a strategic intent to accumulate technological capabilities. OECD (1992b) argues that developing countries have heavily focused on the supply side of technological innovations in their efforts to develop national economies. For example, they have focused on production, investment, engineering, and new technological development without fully considering the demand and domestic market conditions. Therefore, most developing countries have failed to accumulate indigenous technological capabilities.

Here we should consider the relationship between indigenous technological capabilities and S&T manpower (Figure 9.1). In general, the indigenous technological capabilities are embedded in S&T manpower through their in-house R&D activities and R&D cooperation with other innovation actors. At the beginning of the industrial development, developing countries heavily rely on technology imports from foreign advanced countries because they have no sufficient in-house R&D capabilities. These countries make a great effort to digest, adopt and appropriate foreign technologies. As they accumulate a certain level of technological capabilities through this process, they start to carry out their in-house R&D activities. When they are successful, in-house R&D activities become more important than technology adoption in their accumulation of indigenous technological capabilities. Based on this process developing countries can accumulate higher-level indigenous technological capabilities and they can attain the goal of national economic development.

South Korea has been exceptionally successful in accumulating indigenous technological capabilities. In the process of accumulation, S&T manpower has played a pivotal role. There have been many discussions on S&T resources in the development of national S&T and economic development. However, many discussions have been concentrated on S&T investment rather than S&T manpower (Chung 2003, 2016). Therefore, in this section, we will review a few discussions on the role of S&T manpower in a national innovation system particularly from a South Korean context.

The role of S&T manpower in the technological and economic development was well recognised even at the beginning of the S&T development of South Korea. The Asian and Pacific Centre for Transfer of Technology (APCTT) (1986) published a book titled *Technology Policies and Planning Republic of Korea*. This book made a comprehensive review of the South Korean S&T policies and system from the explicit recognition of technology

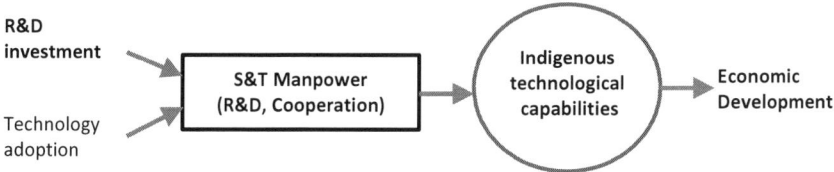

Figure 9.1 Process of accumulating indigenous technological capabilities

for economic development, organisational and administrative framework, technological manpower, policy measures, technological facilities, and technology capability as well as a sectoral review of the agriculture, communication, and construction sectors. It recognised that South Korea largely owed its high level of growth to its fostering S&T manpower. It discussed the very strong demand for S&T manpower in the economic development of South Korea. For example, the amount of S&T manpower in 1975 reached over one million and the South Korean government projected that the demand for this manpower would increase to two million. But in the early 1980s, the demand for S&T manpower outstripped the projection because of the active development of the heavy and chemical industries in the 1980s.

Westphal *et al.* (1984) ascribed the early success of South Korean industries to their efforts of acquiring indigenous technological capabilities through various forms of learning foreign technologies. According to them, a tremendous amount of know-how was accumulated by South Koreans returning from study or work abroad. South Korea followed a strategy of emphasising local technological effort and control. They stressed the role of South Korea's abundance of entrepreneurial resources not only in private and public sectors. These constituted the industrial dynamism of South Korea. According to them, South Korean manpower mastered the technologies that were transferred from foreign and advanced countries and thereby reduced the reliance on foreign technologies and fostered locally based innovation activities. In addition, Song (1990) emphasizes the role of well-qualified human resources in the rise of South Korean economy. He argued that the educational attainment in South Korean people continued to rise and they played an important role in the development of the South Korean economy.

The shortage of S&T manpower was a key issue in South Korean society in the early 2000s and therefore the South Korean government has been implementing various policy measures. In this regard, Eom and Park (2007) investigated the factors that cause a shortage of S&T manpower by looking at a recent survey on the actual employment conditions in manufacturing and major service industries. According to them, enterprises are more exposed to the problems of S&T manpower shortage when they perform R&D more proactively and their innovation activities are more organised. In addition, they identified that R&D and internal demand variables are more eminent to the shortage problem on skilled manpower and the shortage is not only caused by the quantitative aspects but also the qualitative aspects such as skill obsolescence and mismatch in the South Korean labour market.

Jeong *et al.* (2010) identified the determinants that affect the compensation satisfaction of South Korean S&T manpower. According to them the compensation satisfaction of S&T manpower was influenced by job accomplishment, monetary compensation and social compensation in order. Based on this conclusion they recommended that the job accomplishment of South Korean S&T manpower should be enhanced by endowing more discretionary authority to conduct R&D activities. Min (2012) also analysed the compensation level and portfolio of South Korean advanced S&T manpower. He identified that South Korean advanced S&T manpower preferred not only economic rewards but also non-economic rewards such as social recognition and self-satisfaction. In this study he also analysed the difference in preferred rewards among university professors, researchers in South Korean government-sponsored research institutes and researchers in industrial companies. According to him, the former preferred research environment, researchers in government-sponsored research institutes wanted job stabilisation, and researchers in industrial companies wanted to have a higher monetary reward. In addition, two main factors of changing occupations for South Korean advanced S&T manpower were monetary reward and social reputation.

Chung (2012) discussed the role of R&D manpower in the attainment of the competitive advantage of industrial companies. He argued that a company needs not only well-qualified researchers but also good technicians and research assistants in order to produce good R&D results. He also argued that this logic is also well applicable to a nation's accumulation of S&T and innovation capabilities.

Lately there have been many discussions worldwide on the role of S&T manpower in S&T and economic development. A good example which deals with the role of S&T manpower is the famous report called *Rising above the Gathering Storm*, which was published by the National Academy of Science, *et al.* (2005) in USA. The report suggested a series of concrete action plans to be applied for securing national prosperity and enhancing the quality of life of US citizens through S&T and innovation. The report suggested four broad action recommendations for this purpose: K-12 education (10,000 Teachers, 10 Million Minds), research (Sowing the Seeds), higher education (Best and Brightest) and economic policy (Incentives for Innovation). It implies that the US has focused on nurturing, developing, and securing well-qualified S&T manpower, as the two major action plans of these four are related to S&T manpower. This report suggested 20 detailed implementation steps according to these four recommendations. Also Florida (2002, 2005) emphasizes that there has been fierce competition in recruiting and maintaining creative talent as we are entering a creative economy. He also stresses that this competition is not only confined among national economies but also among geographical regions. According to him, S&T manpower is a representative example of a creative class. This means that creative manpower is essential in attaining firms', regional and national competitiveness.

South Korea's transformation into high-tech industries

The South Korean economy has developed remarkably over the last six decades (see Table 9.1). South Korea, which was a very poor country at the beginning

Table 9.1 Major indicators on South Korea

	1960	1970	1980	1990	2000	2010
Population (1000)	25,012	32,241	38,124	42,869	45,985	48,580
GDP (US$, billion)	2	8	62	253	512	1,014
Growth rate of GDP (%)	2.2	17.2	21.8	20.6	8.5	6.2
GDP per capita (US$)	80	248	1,632	5,900	11,134	20,759
Trade balance (US$, million)	−65	−597	−4,384	−2,004	11,787	41,172
Exports (US$, million)	32	660	17,214	63,124	172,268	466,384
Imports (US$, million)	97	1,256	21,598	65,127	160,481	425,212
Total R&D investment (US$, billion)	0.1 mil (1963)	9 mil	0.2	3	11	40
Total R&D investment as a share of GDP (%)	0.24	0.38	0.54	1.68	2.3	3.74

Source: Statistics Korea (KOSTAT) (Each Year); NTIS (National S&T Information Service (NTIS) (Each Year)

of its industrialisation, has become a developed country and could have many diverse innovative industries. The GDP per capita increased from US$80 to US$20,759 in 2010. The GDP growth rates were in the double-digits from the beginning of the 1970s till the end of the 1990s. For example, the years 1980 and 1990 showed 21.8 percent and 20.6 percent respectively. From the beginning of its industrialization, the South Korean government has implemented export-oriented policies. However, in the 1960s, South Korea showed a trade deficit because a poor agricultural country with no natural resources had no products to export. During South Korea's process of industrialisation, the trade deficit grew. Until the middle of the 1980s, the South Korean industrial structure was composed of low-tech industries. However, since the middle of the 1990s, the trade balance has been very positive because South Korea can export high-tech products and services to world markets.

The economic miracle of South Korea resulted from its rapid accumulation of technological and innovation capabilities (Kim 1997; Chung 2003, 2016). The total R&D investment increased from US$0.1 million in 1963, to US$3 billion in 1990, and up to US$40 billion in 2010. This indicates a 400,000 time increase in six decades. During the last three decades the total of R&D investments has increased more than 13 times. As a result, the total R&D investment as a share of the GDP increased from 0.24 percent in 1963 through 0.54 percent in 1980 and 1.68 percent in 1990 to 3.74 percent in 2010. From this indicator as of 2012, South Korea is the most R&D investing country as it invested 4.36 percent of its GDP in R&D activities by investing about

US$55 billion in R&D activities. This implies that the South Korean economic performance is a result of the active accumulation of indigenous technological capabilities. In the process of this accumulation, the S&T manpower has played an essential role.

For the last six decades, the South Korean industrial structure has been transformed from simple light-tech industries into high-tech ones. Based on the accumulation of indigenous technological capabilities in various high-tech areas, South Korea could export many high-tech products, for example mobile phones, semiconductors, petrochemical products, ships, automobiles, and so on. South Korea has accumulated its S&T capabilities not only by increasing R&D investment but also by actively nurturing and developing S&T manpower.

Table 9.2 shows South Korea's top ten export products since the beginning of its industrialization. This shows well that South Korea has transformed into a high-tech country based on its technological capabilities. As of 1960, the major export products were iron and tungsten ores and raw silk. It is interesting that South Korea exported ores, even though it had no sufficient natural resources. At that time South Korea also exported live cuttlefish, fish, and rice.

In the 1960s, South Korea started to industrialise, especially based on light industries. In those years, it could not accumulate indigenous technological capabilities because there was no S&T infrastructure such as legal framework, institutions, and policy programs. In particular, there was no well-qualified S&T manpower which was indispensable to the development of South Korean technological and economic capabilities. Therefore, South Korea could only produce and export some light-industrial products. As of 1970, the main export products were textiles, plywood, wig and iron ores. It could also export simple electronics products, footwear, iron and steel products.

Around the end of the 1960s, the South Korean government recognised the importance of S&T capabilities for developing national economy. In fact, there were no natural resources capital, or manpower in South Korea. Because of this it established the first public research institute, Korea Institute of Science and Technology (KIST) in 1966 and set up the Ministry of Science and Technology (MOST) in order to develop S&T capabilities through the concerted efforts of the government. In addition, from the beginning of the 1970s, the South Korean government made a great effort to develop heavy and chemical industries. For this purpose, it followed the model of KIST, the South Korean government established public research institutes, which were called government-sponsored research institutes (GRIs) in major S&T areas, machinery, chemistry, shipbuilding, electronics, energy and atomic research. Those governmental research institutes created a demand for well-educated S&T manpower in the efficient development of S&T and innovation capabilities. This indicates the importance of building institutions and nurturing S&T manpower. Therefore, many of South Korean scientists and engineers, who studied abroad, came back to those institutes after finishing their PhDs. This strategy of repatriation would be well applicable to

Table 9.2 Changes in the top 10 export products in South Korea

Year	Natural Resources	Light Industries	Light industry + Heavy & Chemical industries	Heavy & Chemical Industries + High-tech Industries		High-tech Industries
	1960	1970	1980	1990	2000	2010
1	Iron Ore	Textiles	Textiles	Textiles	Semiconductor	Semiconductor
2	Tungsten Ore	Plywood	Electronics	Semiconductor	Computers	Ships
3	Raw Silk	Wig	Iron & Steel Products	Footwear	Automobile	Automobile
4	Anthracite	Iron Ore	Footwear	Ships	Petrochemical Products	Flat Panel Display
5	Cuttlefish	Electronics	Ships	TV/VTR	Ships	Petrochemical Products
6	Live Fish	Fruits & Vegetable	Synthetic Fibers	Iron & Steel Products	Wireless Telecommunication Equipment	Wireless Telecommunication Equipment
7	Natural Graphite	Footwear	Metal Products	Textile Fabrics	Iron & Steel Products	Automobile Parts
8	Plywood	Tobacco	Plywood	Computer	Textile Products	Plastics
9	Rice	Iron & Steel Products	Fish	Audio	Textile Fabrics	Iron & Steel Products
10	Bristles	Metal Prod.	Electrical Goods	Automobile	Home Appliances	Computers

Source: Korea International Trade Association (KITA) (Each Year)

other countries. Around the end of the 1970s, South Korea could export heavy and chemical products as well as light industrial products. As of 1980s the major export products were textiles, electronics, iron, and steel products. Ship, synthetic fibres, metal products, which were very high-tech products as a standpoint of South Korea at that time, became major export goods for South Korea. This indicates that the South Korean industrial structure has started to transform into high-tech one.

During the 1980s, South Korean industrial companies recognised the importance of technological innovations for their attaining competitive advantages in the world markets. Therefore, they established their own R&D institutes in order to attain high-tech capabilities and to produce high-tech products which would be attracted by world markets. Several companies entered into high-tech industries such as semiconductors and ICT. The South Korean government supported them to establish their own research institutes through diverse policy measures such as exemption of military services for R&D manpower who would work in private research institutes. Such efforts were very successful and major South Korean companies could accumulate their R&D and innovation capabilities in diverse high-tech areas. As a result, they could export high-tech products to world markets and the total volume of exports increased dramatically from US$17.2 billion in 1980 to US$63.1 billion in 1990 (see Table 9.1). As of 1990, the major export products were textiles, semiconductors, footwear, and ships. It is interesting that some high-tech products such as ships, TVs and VTRs, iron and steel products, computers, and automobiles became major exports products of South Korea (see Table 9.2).

In the 1990s, the South Korean industrial structure was accelerated to transform into a high-tech one. During this period, South Korean universities, which had been the weakest area in the South Korean national innovation system, extended their R&D and educational capabilities (Chung 2003, 2016). Several major universities nurtured and produced well-qualified S&T manpower based on the Excellent Research Centre(ERC) Program, which started in 1990 to develop and produce world-class S&T manpower. In 1990, the first year of the ERC program, 13 centres were established. R&D activities diffused in most South Korean industrial companies and the number of private research institutes increased from 824 institutes to 9,070 institutes in 2001 (KITA Each Year). South Korean industrial companies had not only a strong demand on S&T manpower but also trained them remarkably. Based on such activities, South Korean industrial companies accumulated a sufficient level of technological capabilities and produced and exported high-tech products such as semiconductors, ICT, automobiles and steel-making. As a result, as of 2000, the top export products of South Korea were semiconductors, computers, automobiles, petrochemical products, ships and so on.

In the 2000s, South Korea approached developing countries and it could implement a world-class competent national innovation system, which was composed of good universities, public research institutes and industrial companies. South Korean universities produced well-qualified S&T man-power and they played an essential role of producing high-tech products in diverse industries, which could be sold in world markets. Most South Korean universities tried to become research-oriented universities, and gradu-ate programs in science and engineering were activated. From the beginning of the 2000s, the South Korean government has initiated and implemented a series of long-term comprehensive S&T manpower-oriented policies. Based on the efforts of innovation actors in the South Korean national innovation system, as of 2010, the major export products of South Korean industrial com-panies were semiconductors, ships, automobiles, flat panel displays, petrochem-ical products and wireless telecommunication equipment (see Table 9.2). This implies that the South Korean industrial structure has been transformed into a really high-tech one in five or six decades. In this transformation process, S&T manpower has played an essential role. At the beginning of South Korea's industrialization government-sponsored research institutes generated a strong demand for S&T manpower and South Korean industrial compan-ies have also generated a large demand for S&T manpower since the begin-ning of the 1980s. South Korean universities and colleges have also been successful in nurturing and producing S&T manpower based on the active support of the government.

Based on the accumulation of indigenous technological capabilities discussed above, South Korea could produce remarkable national and S&T performance. According to the IMD, South Korea's competitiveness ranked 29th in 2000. However, its national competitiveness was improved around the end of the 2000s and from 2010 to 2013 South Korea was ranked 22th in the world (see Figure 9.2). South Korea's national competitiveness as a whole had been ranked much lower than its science and technological competitiveness. Looking at national competitiveness, it seems that South Korea has not caught up to developed countries even as of the 2010s.

However, South Korea's scientific competitiveness has improved very rapidly since the end of the 1990s. Its ranking has improved from 20th in 1997 through 13th in 2005 to 4th place in 2010. Since 2010, South Korea's science ranking has stayed around 5th place (see Table 9.3). This implies that South Korean scientific capabilities have almost reached those of advanced countries. According to IMD, the indicator of science competitiveness includes total national R&D expenditures, share of national R&D expenditures in GDP,

Table 9.3 Ranking of South Korea's national competitiveness in the world

National competitiveness	1997	2000	2005	2010	2011	2012	2013	2014
South Korea	30	29	27	23	22	22	22	26

Source: IMD World Competitiveness Yearbook (Each Year)

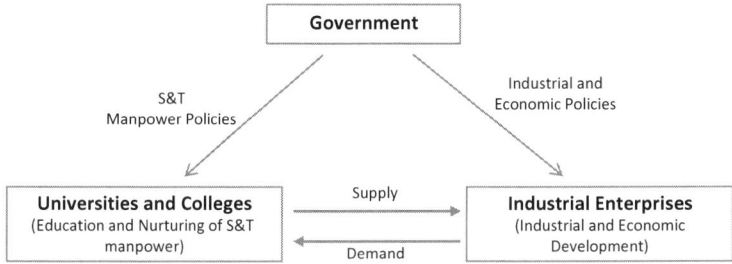

Figure 9.2 Role of the South Korean government in S&T manpower and industrial development

Table 9.4 Ranking of South Korea's science competitiveness

Science competitiveness	1997	2000	2005	2010	2011	2012	2013	2014
South Korea	20	20	13	4	5	5	7	6

Source: IMD World Competitiveness Yearbook (Each Year)

total R&D investment of domestic enterprises, total number of R&D manpower, total number of corporate R&D manpower and total number of patents grated and registered. Therefore, it represents how much one country could produce high-tech products in the near future.

Development of South Korean highly skilled labor forces

The economic success of South Korea has resulted from the rapid accumulation of technological and innovation capabilities of highly educated and skilled manpower. In the last five decades, South Korea increased its highly skilled S&T manpower dramatically. They played an essential role in the industrial development of South Korea (Cho *et al*, 2002). At the same time, as South Korean industries have developed and South Korean industrial structures have transformed into high-tech ones, there has been a strong demand in highly skilled S&T manpower. Here the governmental policies for education and S&T manpower development have played an important role. This is important for the countries which want to catch up in industries and technological innovations. We will discuss this further below.

Development of highly skilled S&T manpower

At the beginning of its industrialization South Korea had a severe shortage of skilled manpower, particularly S&T manpower (see Table 9.5). At that time

Table 9.5 Trend of the total number of R&D personnel in South Korea

	1963	1970	1980	1990	2000	2010	2012
R&D Personnel* (Researchers)	3,072 (2,962)	12,922 (5,628)	30,473 (18,434)	125,512 (70,503)	237,232 (159,973)	500,124 (345,912)	562,601 (401,724)
R&D Personnel (FTE)	-	-	-	-	138,077	335,228	395,990

* R&D Personnel includes researchers, technicians and other supporting staffs.
Source: Ministry of Science and Technology (Ministry of Science, ICT and Future Planning) and Korea Institute of S&T Evaluation and Planning (Each Year)

there were no innovation actors, i.e. industrial companies, public research institutes and R&D-oriented universities. In particular, there were no competitive industrial companies which demanded S&T manpower. In the year 1963, which was one year after the initiation of the *1st Five-Year Plan for National Economic Development*, there were only 3,000 R&D personnel in South Korea (MOST and KISTEP Each Year). At that time there were no S&T policy and S&T manpower policy.

In 1966, the South Korean government established the first government-sponsored research institute, *Korea Institute of Science and Technology* (KIST). However, there was no well-educated S&T manpower. Therefore, the South Korean government initiated a plan to repatriate South Korean S&T manpower who graduated from good universities in developed countries, especially in the US.

In 1973 the South Korean government established a S&T-specialised graduate school, Korea Advanced Institute of Science (KAIS), which was renamed as the Korea Advanced Institute of Science and Technology (KAIST) in December 31, 1980, in order to nurture and produce well-qualified scientists and engineers, who are needed in heavy and chemical industries which the government tried to develop in the 1970s with great ambition. There was also a strong demand on well-educated scientists and engineers by newly established government-sponsored research institutes (GRIs), which were established after the model of KIST. In the 1970s, the number of South Korean S&T manpower, i.e. R&D personnel, more than doubled by indicating 12,922 people in 1970 to 30,473 people in 1980. The number of well-qualified S&T manpower, i.e. researchers, were tripled by increasing 5,628 researchers in 1970 to 18,434 researchers in 1980 (see Table 9.5). Many of these researchers were employed by newly established government-sponsored research institutes (GRIs), which were set up according to major S&T areas.

In the 1980s, South Korean companies made a strong effort to develop their R&D and innovation potentials in order to produce high-tech products that could be exported in world markets. They created a strong demand on highly skilled S&T manpower and recruited lots of engineers from South Korean universities. South Korean universities, which had been heavily education-oriented, started to carry out R&D activities and could produce many skilled S&T man-power with good quality. In fact the number of students enrolled in South Korean universities and colleges increased dramatically from 554,178 people in 1980 to 1,364,991 people in 1990 and the number of graduate students from 33,939 people to 86,911 people in the same period (see Table 9.6). Therefore, the total number of R&D personnel increased from about 30,500 people to 125,500 people in 1990 (see Table 9.5).

In the 1990s, the number of R&D personnel increased from 125,512 people in 1990 to 237,232 people in 2000 (see Table 9.5). This represents nearly a double increase in ten years. In those years, South Korea could develop and implement the world-level national innovation system so that all innovation actor groups, i.e. industry, the public research sector and academia, could play a sufficient role in the national innovation system. From this time, South Korean universities expanded their R&D and education capabilities and produced lots of well-qualified S&T manpower. South Korean industrial companies, which started to produce many high-tech products, demanded and increased lots of S&T manpower. During the 1990s, the number of universities, colleges and graduate programs and the number of students increased dramatically: The number of universities increased from 107 universities in 1990 to 161 universities in 2000, the number of colleges from 117 colleges to 158 colleges, and the number of graduate programs from 298 programs in 1991 to 829 programs in 2000. As a result, the

Table 9.6 Development of the number of South Korean universities and colleges

			1980	1990	2000	2010
Universities and Colleges	Universities	Number of universities	85	107	161	179
		Number of students	402,979	1,040,166	1,665,398	2,028,841
	Colleges and Polytechnic colleges	Number of colleges	128	117	158	145
		Number of students	151,199	323,825	913,273	767,087
	Total	Number of universities and colleges	213	224	319	324
		Number of students	554,178	1,363,991	2,578,671	2,795,928
Graduate Schools		Number of Programs	121	298	829	1,138
		Number of Students	33,939	86,911	229,437	316,633

Source: Korea Education Development Institute (KEDI) (Each Year)

number of students enrolled in universities, colleges and graduate programs increased really dramatically: The number of students enrolled in universities increased from 1,040,166 people in 1990 to 1,665,398 people in 2000, the number of students in colleges from 323,825 people to 913,273 people and the number of graduate students from 86,911 people to 229,437 people in the same period (see Table 9.6). It is interesting that the number of graduate programs and students enrolled in those graduate programs increased much more strongly than those of universities and colleges.

It is also interesting that the number of R&D personnel decreased in 1998 for the first time in the history of South Korean industrialization, because of the economic recession in those years. The South Korean economy had to be under the jurisdiction of IMF and South Korean innovation actors had to lay off many R&D personnel because they were not directly related to main business functions. However, they soon realised the importance of technological innovations and R&D personnel in overcoming the economic recession so that from 1999, one year after the IMF jurisdiction, South Korean innovation actors, particularly industrial companies, increased the number of R&D personnel much more aggressively than before.

As discussed above, from the beginning of the 2000s the South Korean industrial structure has been transformed into a high-tech one. South Korean universities, which had strengthened their R&D and education capabilities by focusing on graduate education, could provide well-qualified R&D manpower to innovation actors. South Korean innovation actors increased the number of R&D personnel very aggressively. In particular, South Korean industrial companies increased R&D personnel much more aggressively in order to compete with world-class companies in advanced countries. Therefore, the total number of R&D personnel was more than doubled from 237,232 people in 2000 to 500,124 people in 2010 (see Table 9.5). From this time South Korea has been pouring great efforts to recruit creative and convergence-type manpower who can play an essential role in the knowledge-based society in the 21st century (Chung 2014). South Korean universities and colleges increased their potential to supply that well-qualified S&T manpower on a large scale. The number of graduate schools increased from 829 programs in 2000 to 1,138 programs in 2010 and the number of students enrolled in those graduate schools from 229,437 people to 316,633 people. It is also interesting that the number of colleges and students enrolled in those colleges decreased in this period, while the number of universities and students enrolled in those universities increased in the same period (see Table 9.6). This implies that South Korean universities could successfully provide highly qualified S&T manpower in this period.

Sectoral development of S&T manpower

South Korea has accumulated its technological and innovation capabilities very successfully, especially based on public research institutes, i.e. government-sponsored research institutes. As mentioned above, the South Korean S&T

development started with the establishment of public research institutes in the 1970s. Until the beginning of the 1970s, they were the biggest employers for well-qualified S&T manpower. As of 1970, a 43.7 percent of the total number of researchers in South Korea worked at public research institutes. At that time the South Korean industry employed only a 20.1 percent of the total researchers (MOST and KISTEP Each Year).

From the middle of the 1970s, the South Korean academia has been the biggest employers of well-qualified S&T manpower. In the 1970s, however, South Korean public research institutes were still important employers of South Korean researchers. As of 1980, about 25 percent of South Korean researchers worked in public research institutes, while the industry employed only about 28 percent of total researchers. South Korean industrial companies could not carry out serious R&D activities, because they did not recognise the importance of technological innovation and did not have S&T manpower to carry out R&D activities. It is noticeable that South Korean universities and colleges increased their researchers in the 1970s from 2,011 people in 1970 to 8,695 people in 1980 (see Table 9.7). Therefore, the South Korean academia was the biggest employer of researchers in 1980. However, most of the researchers in South Korean universities and colleges were professors who were heavily education-oriented. They played an important role in nurturing and educating well-qualified S&T manpower, who would make a great contribution to transform South Korean industrial structure into high-tech one.

In the 1980s, the South Korean industry increased researchers dramatically from 5,141 people in 1980 to 38,737 people in 1990 (see Table 9.7). This represents more than a 7.5 time increase in a decade. The heavy and chemical industrial companies, which had been actively supported by the government, established their research institutes and recruited researchers on a large scale. In those years, South Korean industrial companies, especially heavy and chemical industrial companies that had been nurtured by the government in the 1970s, established their own R&D institutes (Chung 2003, 2016). South Korean universities also increased lots of researchers as

Table 9.7 Trend of sectoral development of South Korean researchers

	1966	1970	1980	1990	2000	2010	2012
Public research sector	2,286	2,458	4,598	10,434	13,913	26,235	28,822
Academia	456	2,011	8,695	21,332	51,727	93,509	96,916
Industry	220	1,159	5,141	38,737	94,333	226,168	275,986
Total	2,962	5,628	18,434	70,503	159,973	345,912	401,724

Source: Ministry of Science and Technology (Ministry of Science, ICT and Future Planning) and Korea Institute of S&T Evaluation and Planning (Each Year)

they started to carry out serious R&D activities, which were necessary to nurture well-qualified scientists and engineers. South Korean public research institutes also increased researchers as their roles were still important in the South Korean national innovation system.

In the 1990s, South Korean industrial companies increased lots of researchers so that the total number was more than doubled. South Korean universities also increased their researchers very aggressively from 21,332 people in 1990 to 51,727 people in 2000 (see Table 9.7). In those years, many South Korean universities focused to become research-oriented universities, based on the governmental program called the Excellent Research Centre (ERC) Program. It is interesting to notice that the number of researchers of South Korean industrial companies decreased very sharply in 1997 due to economic recession, but they increased researchers very sharply since 1999. South Korean companies recognised the importance of R&D and innovation activities to overcome the economic recession and to compete in global markets and increased well-qualified researchers very aggressively thereafter.

In the 2000s the number of researchers in the South Korean industry increased from 94,333 people in 2000 to 226,168 people in 2010 (see Table 9.7). This is about 2.4 times increase and the share of industry in the total number of researchers was 65.4 percent in 2010. In this period, South Korean universities produced well-qualified S&T manpower, especially those having master's and doctoral degrees. In fact, as of 2010, there were 1,138 graduate programs and 316,633 graduate students in South Korea (see Table 9.6). Many of them were employed by South Korean industrial companies and they played an important role in producing high-tech products and services by South Korean industrial companies.

S&T manpower according to degree and female S&T manpower

As the South Korean economy has developed very rapidly, the demand for S&T manpower has also changed. At the beginning of its industrialisation, South Korea focused on nurturing and developing technicians, who were heavily needed in light and low-tech industries. However, since the beginning of the 1970s as South Korea has focused on developing heavy and chemical industries as well as high-tech ones, there was a strong and diverse demand for well-qualified S&T manpower in these industrial sectors. In particular, South Korea increased well-educated researchers since the middle of the 1990s. The number of researchers with PhD degree increased from 35,105 people to 81,442 people in 2010 (see Table 9.8). This number increased especially in the late half of the 2000s. This implies that South Korean universities could accumulate the capacity to produce that well-qualified S&T manpower. In addition, South Korean industrial companies also had a strong demand on PhDs, as they got into high-tech industries. The number of researchers with master's degree increased from 44,178 people in 1995 to 109,224 people in 2010. It increased especially in the first half of the 2000s. The number of researchers with bachelor's degree showed a bigger increase than other degrees. It increased from 44,991 people in 1995 to 138,285 people in 2010 (see Table 9.8). Most of them were employed by industrial companies, especially SMEs. All these indicate that South Korea has focused on nurturing and developing well-qualified S&T manpower since the beginning of the 2000s.

Female S&T manpower had played no significant role in South Korea due to the short history of industrial development. This could be confirmed that there had been no statistics in South Korea on female S&T manpower until 1996. However, the number of female researchers increased dramatically from 11,166 people in 1996 to 57,662 people in 2010. As of 1996, the portion of female researchers was only 8.5 percent. However, it increased through 12.9 percent in 2005 and 16.7 percent in 2010 to 17.7 percent in 2012 (see Table 9.9). It is interesting to see that the number of female researchers has been increased especially since the middle of the 2000s. One of the reasons for it is that South Korea has been focusing on developing biotechnology, medical, and pharmaceutical industries since the beginning of the 1990s, in which female S&T manpower could play an active role. In addition, as the role of female manpower in general has been improved in South Korean society, the portion and amount of female S&T personnel has

Table 9.8 Trend of researchers in South Korea according to degree

	1994	1995	2000	2005	2010	2011	2012
PhD	33,998	35,105	46,146	57,942	81,442	84,674	87,642
Master's	38,725	44,178	51,130	78,579	109,224	116,131	122,948
Bachelor's	40,893	44,991	54,026	87,829	138,285	154,733	169,162
Others	3,830	4,041	8,671	10,352	16,961	19,638	21,972
Total	117,446	128,315	159,973	234,702	345,912	375,176	401,724

Source: Ministry of Science and Technology (Ministry of Science, ICT and Future Planning) and Korea Institute of S&T Evaluation and Planning (Each Year)

Table 9.9 Trend of female researchers in South Korea

	1994	1996	2000	2005	2010	2011	2012
Male	0	120,857	143,588	204,528	288,250	310,109	330,727
Female	0	11,166	16,385	30,174	57,662	65,067	70,997
Total	117,446	132,023	159,973	234,702	345,912	375,176	401,724

Source: Ministry of Science and Technology (Ministry of Science, ICT and Future Planning) and Korea Institute of S&T Evaluation and Planning (Each Year)

also increased to a large scale. The South Korean government has implemented a series of policies to develop and increase female S&T personnel, for example a quota of female S&T personnel in public research institutes. As a result, South Korean female S&T personnel has begun to play an essential role in the South Korean national innovation system especially since the beginning of the 2000s. It is expected that their role will be increased to a large scale in the future.

South Korean policies for nurturing S&T manpower

South Korea has nurtured and developed lots of S&T manpower since the beginning of its industrialization. In this process the South Korean government has played an essential role and has implemented a series of important S&T manpower policies. The government recognised the importance of strong relationship between industrial development and the development of labour forces. As illustrated in Table 9.10, the South Korean government has implemented diverse S&T manpower policies according to South Korean industrial development. Like the South Korean S&T policies, we can classify the South Korean S&T manpower policies according to decades. The goals of the South Korean S&T manpower policies have been changed in full consideration of the national economic development: from technician development (in the 1960s) through well-qualified technician development (in the 1970s), S&T manpower development (in the 1980s), well-qualified S&T manpower development (in the 1990s) to creative S&T manpower development (in the 2000s and after). It also deserves mentioning that these S&T manpower policies have been closely related to the economic and S&T policies. We will discuss the development of South Korean S&T manpower policies since the beginning of its industrialisation.

1) In the 1960s

At the beginning of South Korea's industrialization there was a severe shortage of S&T manpower. At that time there were no innovation actors, i.e. industrial companies, public research institutes and R&D-oriented universities. In 1963, which was one year after the initiation of the 1st Five-Year Plan for National Economic Development, there were only 3,072 R&D personnel in South Korea (see Table 9.5). At that time, there was no S&T policy or S&T manpower policy. However, with the beginning of the Five-Year Plan, the South Korean government had started several initiatives for nurturing and training technicians who were needed in light manufacturing sectors. In addition, the government implemented programs for enlarging vocational high schools in order to improve both the quality and the quantity of skilled labour.

Table 9.10 Development of South Korean S&T manpower policies

Periods (Goals)	Major Economic and S&T Policies	S&T Manpower Policies
1960s (Technician development)	• Beginning of economic development • The 1st Five-Year Plan for Economic Development (1962) • Establishment of KIST (1966) • Establishment of MOST (1967)	• Nurturing technicians for developing light industries • Nurturing technical and vocational colleges • Increasing the number of universities and technical colleges • The *Five-Year Plan for Promoting S&T Education* (1966) • Beginning of repatriating Korean S&T manpower abroad
1970s (Well-qualified technician development)	• Nurturing heavy and chemical industries • Establishment of government-sponsored research institutes (GRIs)	• Expanding engineering schools within universities • Increasing the number of students for supporting heavy and chemical industries • Transforming vocational schools into technical colleges • Establishment of *Korea Advanced Institute of Science* (KAIS) (1971) • Active repatriation of Korean S&T manpower abroad
1980s (S&T manpower development)	• Expansion of industrial R&D and innovation activities • Transformation of Korean industrial structure into high-tech one	• Increase of R&D demand in major and high-tech industries • Increasing the number of well-qualified S&T manpower graduating universities • Establishment of S&T high schools in Korean regions • Establishment of Korea Institute of Technology (KIT) (1985) • Establishment of Pohang University of Science and Technology (POSTECH) (1986)
1990s (Well-qualified S&T manpower development)	• Expansion of academic R&D activities in Korean universities • Active development of high-technologies	• Nurturing well-qualified S&T manpower through strengthening academic education and R&D activities

Table 9.10 (Cont.)

Periods (Goals)	Major Economic and S&T Policies	S&T Manpower Policies
	• Increasing the efforts to secure generic technologies	• Nurturing researchers through strengthening R&D activities of graduate schools, for example by ERC program • Establishment of Gwangju Institute of Science and Technology (GIST) (1993) • Active supporting undergraduate and graduate engineering schools
2000s and after (Creative S&T manpower development)	• Implementing post catch-up S&T policies • Active promotion of basic sciences and researches • Promoting creative economy	• Implementing independent S&T manpower policies • Enacting the Special Law for Supporting Science and Engineering to Strengthen National Competitiveness • Implementing the Basic Plan for Nurturing and Supporting S&T Manpower (2006~2011) • Implementing the BK (Brain Korea) Program (1999~2012) and the BK21+ Program (2013~2019) • Establishment of Daegu Gyeongbook Institute of Science and Technology (DGIST) (2003) • Establishment of Ulsan National Institute of Science and Technology (UNIST) (2009)

In this period, the South Korean government increased the number of vocational and technical colleges in order to produce as many technicians as possible. In the process of implementing the 1st Five-Year Plan for National Economic Development, the South Korean government recognised very seriously the necessity of technicians which were needed for industrial development. However, there was no demand for well-qualified S&T manpower, because there was no public research institute and research-oriented university.

In 1966, the South Korean government established the first public research institute, Korea Institute of Science and Technology (KIST). However, there was no well-educated S&T manpower. Therefore, the South Korean government initiated a plan to repatriate South Korean S&T manpower who graduated from good universities in developed countries, especially in the US. The number of South Korean researchers repatriated was 29 people between 1968 and 1969. These promotions were implemented in earnest in the 1970s.

2)   In the 1970s

In the beginning of the 1970s, the South Korean government had implemented a series of economic policy for nurturing heavy and chemical industries. The government selected several cities along side of South Korean south coastal areas and built heavy and chemical plants such as petrochemical refineries (Ulsan), shipyards (Ulsan), and steel-making companies (Pohang). In order to support those heavy and chemical industries, the South Korean government established several government-sponsored research institutes according to major S&T areas following the KIST model. Therefore, in the 1970s, there was a strong increase in S&T manpower demand in these industries. As a result, the South Korean government aimed to produce as many well-qualified technicians as possible.

Therefore, the South Korean government implemented a S&T manpower policy to expand engineering schools within South Korean universities. In this period, new engineering departments such as ship building, chemical engineering, and mechanical engineering were established and expanded. As a result, the number of South Korean students in engineering increased dramatically. In order to supply well-qualified technicians, in 1977, diverse vocational training schools were transformed into two-year technical colleges and their curricula were also aligned to meet the demand of heavy and chemical industries. As of 1979, the number of technical colleges was 127 colleges and the total number of students was 78,455 people (KEDI 1979).

In 1973 the South Korean government established a graduate school, Korea Advanced Institute of Science (KAIS) in order to nurture and produce well-qualified scientists and engineers, who were needed in heavy and chemical industries. It was the first *S&T-specialised* university in South Korea, which has been under the Ministry of Science and Technology (MOST) and started with 7 departments (and about 200 graduate students): Industrial Engineering, Material Science, Machinery, Chemistry, Electrical Engineering, Bioscience and Basic Science. It has made a great contribution to the nurturing and producing well-qualified S&T manpower in South Korea. There was also an active repatriation of South Korean S&T manpower abroad in the 1970s. Between 1968 and 1980, there were 276 permanent repatriates and 277 temporary repatriates (MOST 1989). Many of those well-qualified repatriates, particularly temporary repatriates, were employed by newly established government-sponsored research institutes and South Korean universities.

3)   In the 1980s

In the 1980s, South Korean industrial companies made a strong effort to develop their R&D and innovation potentials in order to produce high-tech products that could be exported to world markets. They recruited lots of engineers from South Korean universities. South Korean universities, which had been heavily education-oriented, started to carry out R&D activities and educated and produced a lot of high-quality S&T manpower. The number of university students increased from 402,979 people in 1980 to 1,040,166 people in 1990 and the number of graduate students 33,939 people to 86,911 people in the same period (see Table 9.6). In particular, the South Korean government implemented a series of policy measures for establishing research institutes of industrial companies. For example, when a university graduate in science and engineering was employed by a research institute of industrial company and worked for 5 years, they could be exempt from military service which was mandatory and took about three years. This also activated a strong demand on well-qualified R&D manpower in South Korean industrial companies.

In the 1980s, South Korean universities improved their curricula in science and engineering and provided sufficient level of scientific and engineering knowledge to undergraduate students. In this period, most major universities recruited good professors who studied in excellent universities in USA and European countries. However, graduate schools in science and engineering in South Korean universities had not been activated as South Korean universities had focused heavily on education rather than R&D activities. In the 1980s, however, the support for university research activities began to increase. Although the existing major financial sources included academic research funding from the Ministry of Education (MOE) and research funding from the Korea Science and Engineering Foundation (KOSEF) which was under the Ministry of Science and Technology (MOST), the level was too low to stimulate sufficient level of R&D activities.

In 1982, the South Korean government initiated the Specific National R&D Program as the first national R&D program, in which basically the joint research projects between industrial companies, government-sponsored research institutes and universities were advised and preferred. This program focused on nine specific areas: semiconductor and computer, fine chemicals, machinery, energy and resources utilizations, system industries, biotechnology, materials, textiles and polymers and environment and construction including plant engineering. Under these areas, specific projects were divided into two types: government-initiated and company-initiated projects. The former type of projects attain much more support under this program than the latter ones. In 1982, the first year of the program, there were 40 government-initiated projects and 85 company-initiated projects, and the government invested 13.3 billion won (about US$13.3 million) and the industrial companies did 18.7 billion won (about US$18.7 million). In 1983, there were totally 180 projects with 22 billion Won (about US$22 million) and 122 billion won (about US$12.2 million) (MOST 1983). This program and followed national R&D programs played an essential role to strengthen industrial R&D activities and diffuse the importance of R&D activities in South Korean universities. In particular, these programs made a great contribution in activating a strong demand on well-qualified R&D manpower in South Korean industrial companies. In this period, some leading companies such as Samsung Electronics, LG Electronics, Hyundai Automobile, and several others recruited several important engineers who received doctoral degrees from world-best universities, especially in the US and they played a leading role in the development of South Korean high-tech industries. Since 1982, as part of the Specific National R&D Program, Ministry of Science and Technology (MOST) started to support basic research and it played an important role in activating full-fledged university research.

Since the middle of the 1980s, other ministries introduced diverse national R&D programs for their own purposes. In particular, in 1987, the Ministry of Commerce and Industry (MOCI) initiated the Program for Developing Industrial Base Technologies, based on the Act for Developing Industries, in order to effectively develop key technologies which were needed to develop diverse industries in South Korea. It was composed of three major areas, i.e. 1) bottleneck technologies common to SMEs, 2) key technologies needed to develop import-substitutable products, 3) process technologies for cost-saving. Between 1987 and 1990, about 257 billion won (US$257 million), in which the government invested 103 billion won and industrial companies did 154 billion won, was invested in 621 projects (Yoon 2006). This was a long-term program, even though the name of the program was changed several times and contributed to the development of skilled S&T manpower in South Korean industries.

In 1985, the South Korean government established the Korea Institute of Technology (KIT), which was an undergraduate S&T-specialised university to produce well-qualified S&T manpower. In 1989, it was merged into the Korea Advanced Institute of Science and Technology (KAIST), which was renamed after KAIS, established in 1973 as a graduate school. As a result, KAIST could provide undergraduate, master's, and PhD programs and produce very well-qualified S&T manpower in South Korea. KAIST was the first S&T-specialised university in South Korea and has attracted excellent professors and bright students because the professors have received higher salaries than other South Korean universities and students have received full scholarships and the exemption of mandatory military service. In addition, Pohang Iron & Steel Company (now POSCO), which was one of the world-leading steelmakers, established the Pohang University of Science and Technology (POSTECH) in 1986 as a private S&T-specialised university. POSTECH has grown into South Korea's representative science and engineering university by securing excellent professors, facilities and students within a short period of time. In this period, the South Korean government established S&T-specialised high schools in South Korean regions in order to nurture future well-qualified S&T manpower.

4)   In the 1990s

University research activities began to be strengthened in earnest around the early 1990s. The South Korean government declared the year 1989 as the

"First year of Basic Science and Technology Promotion," enacted the Basic Science and Research Promotion Act. This act prescribed various policy measures to promote basic science and research: expansion of investment to promote basic research; increase of support for research activities; promotion of basic research foundations; augmentation of industry-academia-research institute cooperation; and creation of a competitive research atmosphere.

The South Korean government implemented the Excellent Research Centre (ERC) Program to secure world-level university research capabilities of the major research-oriented universities. This program was composed of two sub-programs: SRCs (Science Research Centres) and ERCs (Engineering Research Centres). The main purpose of this program was to establish world-level research centres in universities, which had been heavily focused on education rather than R&D activities. Until the beginning of the 1990s, the major weakness of the South Korean national innovation system was the low level of R&D activities of South Korean universities (Chung 2003, 2016). This program was expected to solve this problem and to train well-qualified R&D manpower in the major South Korean research-oriented universities. Through this program the South Korean government supported a centre of about 1 billion Won (about US$1 million) per year for nine years to facilitate inter-disciplinary and academia-industry cooperative research and elevate the centres' research level to an international one by forming the groups of scientists leading specific S&T fields. The program started in 1990, when 13 SRCs and ERCs were established in the major research-oriented universities, and the number of excellent research centres increased to 38 centres in 1996. These centres focused on carrying out comprehensive inter-disciplinary, large-scale, long-term R&D activities and made a great contribution to the development of well-qualified R&D manpower in South Korea. As the majority of excellent research centres were heavily located in the capital city, Seoul, in 1995, the South Korean government introduced the Regional Research Centre (RRC) Program also for nine years to support universities located in South Korean regions. The regional research centres (RRCs) were expected to conduct basic and applied R&D activities in strategic industries in individual regions.

In order to promote balanced development and foster "brains" for cutting-edge industries, Gwangju Institute of Science and Technology (GIST) was established in the far south-west region, in Gwangju metropolitan city, in 1993. This was the second S&T-specialised university under the Ministry of Science and Technology (MOST), which was established according to the KAIST model. GIST had an ambition of becoming a world-class educational organisation and started with 584 students and 120 professors and five graduate programs: Information & Communication, New Materials, Mechatronics, Bioscience and Environmental Engineering. This institute has played an important role in the development of regional high-tech industries, for example, the photonic industry. Based GIST and its institutes, the Gwangju metropolitan city became the biggest cluster of photonic industry in South Korea (INNOPOLIS Foundation 2014; Chung 2015).

5)   In the 2000s and after

Since the beginning of the 2000s, South Korea could implement a competent national innovation system, which has a well balance among academia, public research sector and industry. In this period, the South Korean government has implemented a series of post catch-up S&T policies to get an access to one of developed countries by absolving a catch-up country. For this purpose, the South Korean government has implemented a comprehensive S&T manpower policy, the Brain Korea (BK) 21 Program, to nurture and provide creative well-qualified S&T manpower, especially who were trained in graduate programs. As the South Korean national innovation system has developed, there has been a strong demand on this well-qualified S&T manpower from industrial companies, public research institutes and universities and colleges.

The Brain Korea (BK) 21 Program started at the end of 1990s just after the IMF jurisdiction in order to nurture and produce creative and well-qualified S&T manpower. This program oriented to support graduate programs and provided substantial financial support for master, doctoral and post-doctoral researchers. It aimed to foster world-class research universities and produce top-notch human resources. This program was a long program which had two phases: 1) the first phase had US$1,300 million invested in it between 1999 and 2005 and 2) the second phase had US$2,030 million invested in it between 2006 and 2012 (MOE 2013). The BK 21 Program had pursued a significant international collaboration with world-class R&D organisations and graduate students was able to participate in practical R&D projects and take high-level education services. Also, this program had a strong effect on enhancing the South Korean national innovation system through improving the R&D and educational potential of South Korean research-oriented universities. The BK 21 program made a great contribution to strengthen R&D and the innovation potential of South Korea by providing lots of well-qualified S&T manpower. In this period, the South Korean government recognised again the importance of well-qualified S&T manpower in the development of nation. The S&T manpower policy, which hasd been treated as a part of S&T policy, was initiated and implemented as an independent and comprehensive policy for the first time (Hong 2012). The South Korean government enacted the Special Law for Supporting Scientists and Engineers to Strengthen National Competitiveness. Based on this law, the Basic Plan for Nurturing and Supporting S&T Manpower was implemented (MOSF and Other Ministries 2005). This basic plan, which was called the first basic plan, was targeted at five years from 2006 till 2010 and implemented five policy areas and 14 main tasks under the areas. The five policy areas were 1) institutional innovation for science and engineering education in universities, 2) nurturing core research manpower, 3) demand-oriented S&T manpower education, 4) welfare support for S&T manpower and 5) support of infrastructure for S&T manpower. It is interesting to recognise that the South Korean government started to nurture creative S&T manpower which was indispensable for getting access to one of developed countries.

In 2011, after finishing the first basic plan, the South Korean government initiated and implemented the 2nd Basic Plan for Nurturing and Supporting to Realise a Creative and Strong S&T Manpower Nation for the period from 2011 till 2016 (MOSF and Other Ministries 2011). The vision of the 2nd Basic Plan was to transform South Korea into a strong talent nation through nurturing and developing creative manpower. Special attention was paid to nurturing creative and convergence-type S&T manpower. This 2nd Basic Plan targeted five policy areas, mainly selected according to life cycle of S&T manpower and implemented 15 main tasks in these areas. The five policy areas were 1) education to increase understanding, interest and potential of elementary, middle and high school students, 2) specialisation and internalisation of education and strengthening global research capabilities for undergraduate and graduate education, 3) participation in education through using proprietary assets and development of research-intensive education for government-sponsored research institutes, 4) enhancing the demand-response capabilities of company R&D manpower and nurturing R&D-capable companies and 5) promotion of utilising potential S&T manpower and strengthening the base of S&T manpower policy. It is also interesting to recognise that this 2nd Basic Plan was comprehensive as it targeted nurturing manpower in the whole lifecycle of S&T manpower and in the all actor groups in the South Korean national innovation system.

In this period additional S&T-specialised universities were established in accordance with the policy directions of the government. The Daegu Gyeong book Institute of Science and Technology (DGIST) was established in 2003 and the Ulsan National Institute of Science and Technology (UNIST) in 2009 in order to develop creative and convergence-type S&T manpower. As these universities are located in south-eastern part of South Korea, they are expected to make a contribution to the development of south-eastern regional economies. As a result, South Korea maintains five S&T-specialised universities: KAIST, GIST, POSTEC, DGIST and UNIST.

Conclusions

The South Korean economy has been developing remarkably since the beginning of its industrialization. During the last five decades, South Korea has become one of the advanced countries. The South Korea's success has been due to its active accumulation of technological and innovation capabilities especially through well-educated manpower. At the beginning of its industrialization, in 1963, there were only about 3,000 R&D personnel and no S&T infrastructure. However, as of 2012, there are 562,601 R&D personnel in South Korea. This is about a 188 time increase in five decades. Even though it takes a long time to nurture and develop S&T manpower, South Korea has been successful in nurturing well-qualified S&T manpower in a relatively short period. The S&T manpower has played a pivotal role in innovation actor groups, i.e. universities and colleges, public research institutes, and industrial companies, in the South Korean national innovation system. Because of this S&T manpower South Korea have produced and developed diverse high-tech products in global markets.

It seems that South Korea has pursued rather different approaches to nurture and develop S&T manpower. This South Korean approach would be of interest for other countries. We can describe the South Korea-specific model as a good division of labour among the government, supplier and customer of well-qualified S&T manpower. In particular, the South Korean government has played an active role in the relationship between well-qualified S&T manpower and industrial and economic development (see Table 9.4). We will identify some characteristics of the South Korean approach to the development of S&T manpower.

First, it takes time to nurture and develop S&T manpower. Even though South Korea has been successful in developing S&T manpower, it took five decades to provide sufficient well-qualified S&T manpower. In order to effectively nurture S&T manpower, South Korea has had to establish new S&T-specialised universities, expand academic R&D capabilities and refine and maintain academic curricula. In addition, the demand on S&T manpower had to be created, especially by industrial companies.

Second, the South Korean government has played a pivotal role in nurturing and developing S&T manpower. It has prepared a series of legal frameworks, initiated relevant policy programs for nurturing S&T manpower, established S&T-specialised universities and set up government-sponsored research institutes which has created an initial demand on well-qualified S&T manpower. In addition, private research institutes of industrial companies, which were granted by the South Korean government, have created a lot of demand on S&T manpower.

Third, the S&T manpower policies of the South Korean government have been changes according to the economic development. The policy focus has been transformed from technicians (in the 1960s) through well-qualified technicians (in the 1970s) and S&T manpower (in the 1980s) to well-qualified S&T manpower (in the 1990s) and creative S&T manpower (in the 2000s and after). The changes in S&T manpower policies have made a great contribution to the development of the South Korean economy.

Fourth, as providers of S&T manpower, South Korean universities have played an important and successful role by employing good professors, providing relevant curricula and maintaining R&D facilities. Again here, the South Korean government has provided a series of policy programs according to the development of the South Korean economy. In particular, S&T-specialised universities such as KAIST, GIST and others, which received special favours from the Ministry of Science and Technology (MOST), have played an important role in developing and producing well-qualified S&T manpower. As they have been successful, the competitive environment has been created in South Korean universities, which has led to the enhancement of the education level of South Korean universities.

Fifth, industrial demand on S&T manpower is one of important success factors in South Korean experiences. The South Korean industry has been the biggest employer for well-qualified S&T manpower since the middle of the 1980s. For example, the South Korean industry's portion of researchers in the total number of researchers in the South Korean national innovation system increased 54.9 percent in 1990 through 59.0 percent in 2000 to 65.4 percent in 2010. The industrial portion of researchers has been still increasing since 2010. This industrial demand has created the supply of S&T manpower in South Korean universities and played a critical role in enhancing the education capabilities of South Korean universities.

Of course, there are many challenges to South Korea. Nowadays South Korea has the big ambition of transforming its national economy into a creative economy. However, South Korea has several difficulties, especially with regard to S&T manpower, in attaining this ambition. We could identify several issues as follows

First of all, South Korea should nurture and extend creative and convergence-type manpower who are indispensable for the knowledge-based economy. Even though the South Korean government has initiated a policy programs for it, South Korean universities are not well prepared for it as they are heavily discipline-oriented and no sufficient collaboration among disciplines. In these days South Korean industrial companies have been complaining that South Korean universities could not nurture and provide quality S&T manpower they need, and they have to re-train them.

South Korean female S&T manpower has not been sufficiently active in the South Korean national innovation system and they are not fully utilised. As of 2012, the share of female scientists and engineers are only 17.7 percent which are much below than that of advanced countries. The South Korean government should prepare for more aggressive policy programs to induce female students to science and engineering and to maintain them during their working life after finishing their degrees. It might also be important for female students to change their perception that male students will be more relevant to science and engineering. In advanced countries, there have been lots of female scientists and engineers in diverse sectors in the national innovation systems.

Another problem is that most of South Korean best S&T manpower is concentrated on universities. For example, as of 2012, a 62.5 percent of South Korean researchers with PhD degrees are working in South Korean universities. There has been a tendency for South Korean PhDs of predominantly prefer to work in universities than in industrial companies. These days, the major South Korean industrial companies such as Samsung, LG, have been very active in recruiting scientists and engineers with a PhD in prominent universities in the US and Europe. This kind of movement should be diffused in South Korean industrial companies.

Regarding the industrial S&T manpower, South Korean big enterprises have monopolised best S&T manpower. As of 2012, more than 25 percent of

South Korean industrial researchers are employed by 5 large enterprises. This indicates that South Korean SMEs have had big difficulties in recruiting well-educated S&T manpower, which have been the bottlenecks for South Korean SMEs' attaining a competitive advantage in global markets.

To summarise, S&T manpower plays an important role in accumulating indigenous technological capabilities and economic development, especially in developing countries. As Mazzoleni and Nelson (2007) emphasised, public research institutes and academic universities as social technologies or institutional base are essential for economic catch-up in developing countries. South Korea is one of the representative countries in succeeding the development of technological innovations through activating institutional innovations for nurturing and developing S&T manpower. This South Korean experience would be of much interest to other countries.

References

The Asian and Pacific Centre for Transfer of Technology (APCTT) (1986), *Technology Policies and Planning Republic of Korea*, Bangalore, India: APCTT.

Bell, R. M. N. 1985: *Technical Change in Infant Industries: A Review of Empirical Evidence.* New York, NY: World Bank. Working Paper.

Caillods, F. 1984: "Education, Organization of Work and Indigenous Technological Capacity", In: Fransman, M. and King, K. (Eds.): *Technological Capability in the Third World*. Houndmills and London: MacMillan Press, pp. 211–222.

Cho, H., Lee, E., Lee, C. and Kim S. 2002: *Review of S&T Human Resource Policies in Korea*. Seoul: Science and Technology Policy Institute (STEPI).

Chung, S. 2003: "Innovation in Korea", In: Shavina, L. V. (Ed.): *The International Handbook on Innovation*. Oxford: Pergamon, pp. 890–903.

Chung, S. 2012: "Technology and Developing Countries", In: Chung, S. (Ed.): *Technology and Management*. Seoul: Kyongmoonsa, Chapter 12, pp. 517–563.

Chung, S. 2014: *A Study on Improving Education System and Revising Curricula for Nurturing Convergence-Type Talent*. Seoul, Korea: Presidential Advisory Council on Science and Technology (PACST).

Chung, S. 2015: *A Policy Study on the Detailed Programs and Interaction among Universities, Public Research Institutes, and Universities in the INNOPOLIS Gwangju*. Daejon: INNOPOLIS Foundation.

Chung, S. 2016: "Korean Government and Science and Technology Development", In: Hilpert, U. (Ed.): *Routledge Handbook of Politics and Technology*. London and New York, NY: Routledge, pp. 222–235.

Clark, N. 1985: *The Political Economy of Science and Technology*. Oxford: Basil Blackwell.

Eom, M. and Park, J. 2007: "The Determinants of S&T Workforce Shortage in Korean Manufacturing Sectors", *Journal of Technology Innovation*, Vol. 15, No. 2, pp. 25–40.

Florida, R. 2002: *The Rise of the Creative Class. And How It's Transforming Work, Leisure and Everyday Life*. New York, NY: Basic Books.

Florida, R. 2005: *The Flight of the Creative Class: The New Global Competition for Talent.* New York, NY: HarperCollins.

Hong, S. 2012: "History and Future Direction of S&T Manpower Policy", *Science and Technology Policy*. Seoul: Science and Technology Policy Institute (STEPI), pp. 166–173.

INNOPOLIS Foundation. 2014: *Action Plan of INNOPOLIS Gwangju in 2014*. Daejon: INNOPOLIS Foundation.

International Institute for Management Development (IMD). Each Year: *The IMD World Competitiveness Yearbook*. Lausanne: IMD.

Jeong, K., Lee, J. and Lee, Y. 2010: "An Exploration of Compensation Satisfaction Determinants and Influence Analysis on Job Commitment for S&T Manpower", *Journal of Technology Innovation*, Vol. 18, No. 2, pp. 1–32.

Kim, L. 1997: *Imitation to Innovation: The Dynamics of Korea's Technological Learning*. Boston, MA: Harvard Business School Press.

King, K. 1984: "Science, Technology and Education in the Development of Indigenous Technological Capbility", In: Fransman, M. and King, K. (Eds.): *Technological Capability in the Third World*. Houndmills and London: MacMillan Press, pp. 31–64.

Korea Education Development Institute (KEDI). Each Year: *Korea Education Statistics*. Seoul: KEDI.

Korea Industrial Technology Association (KOITA). Each Year: *Annual Report of Industrial Science and Technology*. Seoul: KOITA.

Korea International Trade Association (KITA). Each Year: *Trade Statistics*. Seoul: KITA.

Mazzoleni, R. and Nelson, R. R. 2007: "Public Research Institutions and Economic Catch-Up", *Research Policy*, Vol. 36, pp. 1512–1528.

Min, C. 2012: "Analysis of the Compensation Level and Portfolio for Advanced S&T Manpower", *Journal of Technology Innovation*, Vol. 18, No. 1, pp. 219–245.

Ministry of Education (MOE) 2013: *Internal Documents*. Seoul: MOE.

Ministry of Science and Technology (MOST). 1983: *1983 Science and Technology Annual*. Seoul: MOST.

Ministry of Science and Technology (MOST). 1989: *1989 Science and Technology Annual*. Seoul: MOST.

Ministry of Science and Technology (MOST), Ministry of Science, ICT and Future Planning and Korea Institute of S&T Evaluation and Planning (KISTEP). Each Year: *Report on the Survey of Research and Development in Science and Technology*. Seoul: MOST.

Ministry of Strategy and Finance (MOSF) and Other Ministries. 2005: *Basic Plan for Nurturing and Supporting S&T Manpower to Realize a Creative and Strong Talent Nation*. Seoul: MOST.

Ministry of Strategy and Finance (MOSF) and Other Ministries. 2011: *The 2nd Basic Plan for Nurturing and Supporting to Realize a Creative and Strong S&T Manpower Nation*. Seoul: MOST.

National Academy of Sciences, National Academy of Engineering, and Institute of Medicine. 2005: *Rising Above the Gathering Storm: Energizing and Employing America for a Brighter Economic Future*, Washington, D.C.

National S&T Information Service (NTIS). Each Year: *S&T Statistics Services*. Seoul: NTIS.

Statistics Korea (KOSTAT). Each Year: *The Major Statistics of Korean Economy*. Seoul: KOSTAT.

Organisation for Economic Co-operation and Development (OECD). 1992a: "The Supply of Scientists and Engineers: Current Trends and Concerns", In: OECD

(Eds.): *Technology and the Economy: The Key Relationship*. Paris: OECD, Chapter 6, pp. 135–148.

Organisation for Economic Co-operation and Development (OECD). 1992b: "Human Resources and New Technologies in the Production System", In: OECD (Eds.): *Technology and the Economy: The Key Relationship*. Paris: OECD, Chapter 7, pp. 149–166.

Song, B. 1990: *The Rise of the Korean Economy*. Oxford and New York, NY: Oxford University Press.

Westphal, L. E., Rhee, Y. W. and Pursell, G. 1984: "Sources of Technological Capability in South Korea", In: Fransman, M. and King, K. (Eds.): *Technological Capability in the Third World*. Houndmills and London: MacMillan Press, pp. 279–300.

Yoon, J. H. 2006: *The Korean S&T Policy*. Seoul: Gyongmoonsa.

10 Diversified metropolitan innovation in China

Xiangdong Chen, Ruixi Li, Xin Niu, and Valerie Hunstock

Introduction

The role of geographically mediated knowledge externalities in regional innovation systems has become a hot topic in innovation and policy study journals, with research generally based on typical indicators such as patent records (refer to Acs et al. 2002). The geographical location of innovation and knowledge creation is often the topic of major discussion, which was originally organized in the 1980s in terms of spatial distribution or concentration, as represented by studies conducted by Malecki (1981) or Sweeney (1987), and the location of the high technology industry (e.g., Hall and Markusen 1985)—particularly the dynamics of regional innovative complexes (Stöhr 1986). These studies reflect the fact that innovation activities are not equally distributed in geographical space; rather, they occur in clusters—especially for high-tech content productions (e.g. as in the US's case by Varga 1999; or Europe's case by Caniëls 2000; Drüke 2003; Hickie 2003; Hilpert et al. 2003).

The uneven distribution of knowledge creation, and high-tech production with complex resources or influencing factors can be attributed to difficulties of technology transfer or knowledge sharing among different regions. These kinds of difficulties can be explained by the nature of human resources related to the transfer and knowledge spillover across regions (Baptista and Swann 1998; Bell 2005). This uncertain, non-codified, form of transfer seems to play a role, especially in knowledge intensive sectors; such transfers or spillovers generally cannot be fully explained by differences in hardware or equipment (in the case of developing countries), or via even well-established facilities in most emerging economies (Dosi 1988; Feldman 1994; Polanyi 1996). With regard to necessary facilities for better knowledge transfer or more evenly distributed innovation activities, extensive research was conducted to examine the efficiency of the policy-oriented efforts on the facilities in and at the regional level, or through so-called regional innovation systems (e.g. studies by Acs 2000; Braczyk et al. 1998; De la Mothe and Paquet 1998; Padmore and Gibson 1998; Padmore et al. 1998). Among all these studies, metropolitan-based innovation studies suggest that a new focus on precisely defined regional innovation frames (typically reflected in research by Fischer et al. 2001) would have merit.

These findings have not yet been fully explored in China-related studies of cases of *unevenly* distributed regional innovation, although studies have been conducted on related topics, such as innovation performance at the provincial level (Hao and Tang 2009; Liu 2005), and the innovation ranking of typical Chinese cities (Zhou 2010). Considering the rapid pace of industrialization in large regions of China, together with the rapid growth and penetration of overseas capital from the global market, it would be reasonable to extend the approach of city-based innovation studies to examine variation among cities in different geographical regions in China. Drawing on the variation observed in the previously noted cases, it appears that processes of innovation need to be equally divergent. Variation in metropolitan characteristics are apparent when compared both to non-metropolitan situations in China, as well as when Chinese metropolises are compared to each other. Research structures and industrial structures, as well as the agglomeration of highly skilled knowledge workers, equally reflect divergences.

This chapter contributes to the body of research exploring factors that potentially explain the facilitation of (or alternatively, variation in) innovation in different regions of China, particularly metropolitan locations. The remainder of the paper is organized as follows: the introduction presents fundamental research related to metropolitan innovation studies, followed by development of a research framework grounded in a city-based study of innovation, supported by relevant literature. Then, in the empirical investigation section, more detailed cities and metropolitan areas will be investigated through *Principle Factor Analysis* for diversified dimensions. Conclusions will be provided based on these examinations.

Literature on metropolitan innovation

The regional innovation system

Until the 1990s, regional innovation phenomena were not regarded as important for specifically focused study. Along with the faster pace of globalization and emerging knowledge economy, technology and related knowledge creation has proven important at the regional level—not just at the country level. The Regional Innovation System (RIS) framework has been an important policy and strategic concept since then, even outperforming the national innovation system (NIS) approach. Apparently, any technical innovation needs to be first in certain geographical regions, with unique social and cultural backgrounds. The RIS study seems more sophisticated than the NIS approach in that it incorporates diversified resources with multiple layers, being an important complementary part for overall study at the national, or the industrial level. Cooke's (1996) systematic research on RIS with fundamental theories and thorough empirical studies emphasized the importance of regional connections among production companies, research institutes, and higher educational organizations through internal linkages in the region. Nelson (1993) extended the research concept and the investigation framework. In China, related studies emerged on the contents, structure, and evaluation issues of RIS.

In recent years, a tremendous body of referential research on RIS regarding theoretical findings and methodologies has developed. For example, Buesa et al. (2010) study the determinants of regional innovation in Europe through a knowledge production function approach that combines factorial and regression analysis. The dependent variables are patents. While there are initially 21 explanatory variables, these are converted—by Principle Factor Analysis (PFA)—into five abstracted non-observable "hypothetical" variables reflecting five important aspects of the innovation systems: the national environment, the regional environment, innovating firms, universities, and R&D by public administration. These factors are all significant with respect to innovation activities. Fritsch and Slavtchev (2010) find through their research that regions dominated by large establishments tend to be less efficient than regions with a lower average establishment size. The more that innovation drives the modernization of industries and the more it attracts both innovative labor and specific enterprises to specific locations, the more it appears that neither *one* best practice, nor a *single* path of innovation can be identified: There are rich diversities of innovation opportunities.

Broekel (2012) presents an empirical investigation on this issue utilizing conditional efficiency analysis and patent co-application data for the electrical engineering and electronics industrial sector in 270 German labor market regions. The results show that the relationship between regions' innovation performance and the intensities of regional, as well as inter-regional, collaboration take the form of an inverted-U shape. Regions with average regional and inter-regional collaboration intensities are found to outperform those characterized by extremely low, high, or unbalanced collaboration behavior.

Based on these important references containing data on regional as well as metropolitan innovation studies, patent statistics appear useful to understand innovation output and for regional comparison. Similar methods are used for examining differences between clusters (Deyle and Grupp 2005). However, China-related metropolitan innovation studies are limited in detailed differences across typical cities. China has a wider range of geographical (e.g., eastern and coastal regions so close to overseas capital and active market operation, and other regions less accessible to the overseas market) and economic features (in terms of stronger policy generally in China's inner land and northern China, as opposed to stronger market response, generally in southern China) and it has a significantly more diversified business nature (in terms of industrial tradition and business culture), than is typical in other countries.

Cities as important elements to be studied in terms of regional innovation

The city as center of regional innovation system:

"City" can be conceptualized in many ways. For example, it might be used, alternately, in a sense as an "urban" entity, a "metropolis", a "megalopolis", an "urban region", and even a "metropolitan region" in order to focus on the characters by size. This implies that, on the one hand, "city" is considered a geographical concentration when used to explain regional change in economies and in social life, and on the other, the larger the territory of the city, the more significant is its impact or determinant function. US-based Metropolitan Region studies during 1930–1960 used to provide a standard measure on big cities and their surrounding regions (An 2006). In China, city-based studies are often conducted on a respective administrative city boundary as defined by government regulations. They focus on only geographically and economically important cities. Xie et al. define a so-called Urban Circle Innovation system (2007) and a related evaluation system; their subsequent work (2010) suggests that there are spatial structures in such city-based systems of innovation.

In terms of the character of regional innovation, there are several important issues explored in a number of pioneering studies, primarily of the networking relationship among cities. For example, Cooke and Morgan (1990) studied German high-tech industries in geographical areas, focusing on local networking effects. He proved, empirically, that intra-region interactions among different entities would positively function as an enabling factor on local high-tech industrial development. In fact, a number of important functioning network factors to be integrated into the characterization of city-based innovation, can include the quality of labor in the network and a labor market nearby, as well as network agglomeration of industrial enterprises and relevant universities, as suggested in Hilpert and Lawton Smith (2013). In China, during the comparatively early years of the implementation of the Opening-Up Policy, networking among smaller firms proved to be highly important. It remains one of the unique factors in regional economic development. Typical studies by geographical economy scholars such as Wang (1997) and Gai and Wang (1999) during that time emphasized more stable networking relationships in the region for better innovation output, often via the networking of local industrial firms, local governments with some local institutes, and local individuals. They were all considered important players in regional innovation at a city or even town level. And seen from a regional innovation research perspective, they could be considered an agglomeration of numbers of nearby towns.

The following factors may prove crucial in city-based regional innovation studies:

- **Knowledge clustering:**
  Cities may be a useful locus for examining knowledge-clustering phenomena. Jaffe (1989), by adopting patent information from respective industrial fields, showed that local patents in different states in the US were highly related to university R&D expenditures in the corresponding regions, which again implied a regional boundary of knowledge clustering.
- **Knowledge transfer distance and boundary of metropolitan areas:**
  Since it is clear that knowledge transfer is rather clustered in geographic regions, as it shows in numbers of international studies mentioned before,

it is reasonable to expect that city-based innovation is bounded in technologies and related engineering techniques (or tacit part of knowledge). Griliches (1992) suggested three kinds of distance in terms of knowledge spillover: market distance (in the sense of a value chain), technology distance (in the sense of distance between companies) and geographical distance, indicating that technology or knowledge spillover decreases along with geographical distance increases. Geographical closeness is always a key factor in knowledge clustering and transfer (Pavitt and Patel 1994; Verspagen 1993), and thus metropolitan areas may serve as a better research focus with respect to regional innovation activities.

China-related metropolitan innovation research:
Regarding China-related studies, Johnson and Liu (2011) empirically explore the connections among regional patenting behavior, technology markets and the number of technology firms across 30 regions of mainland China. The results suggest that markets for technologies are a useful linkage to connect paper-based patents and active technology-oriented business across regions. Such activities involve allocating patented technologies from the regions where they were created and transferring them to the region in which they are used. This is a time-driven dynamic movement, given the nascent understanding of technology markets in China and the country's drive towards promoting indigenous innovation, especially when the national industrial base is highly focused, as occurred during the 1950s (refer to Zhang et al. 2004)

Chen & Kenney (2007) explore the role of universities and research institutes (URIs) in the development of the Chinese economy through a comparison of the development of the Beijing and Shenzhen technology clusters. The two locations have exhibited completely different evolutionary trajectories. In the case of Beijing, the URIs have played an extremely important role in the development of the largest high technology cluster in China. In Shenzhen, by contrast, now the third most important cluster in China, policy makers have worked consciously over the last twenty years to establish and attract institutions of higher education. Li (2009) conducted a more thorough research, estimating a stochastic frontier model to explain an increasing disparity in innovation performance between Chinese regions. The estimated results show that (1) government support, (2) the constitution of the R&D performers, and (3) the regional industry-specific innovation environment are significant determinants of innovation efficiency. Due to the large difference in the firms' innovation performance across the regions, when regional innovation modes are transformed from research institute and university dominant to firm dominant, the overall innovation efficiency between regions is becoming more and more disparate. This shift underlies the widening gap in regional innovation performance. Consequently, situations are created which are characterized by highly differentiated opportunities. While government policies provide research opportunities in particular locations, they match already-existing enterprise and industry opportunities. However, it needs to be noted that policy strength is often stronger in three aspects in a comparative sense: namely, those that are basic and applied research related (with corresponding representative institutions/universities), state-owned enterprises (with corresponding heavily concentrated industries and metropolitan areas), and less market-oriented business operations (with corresponding geographical regions and industries). This provides the basis for the emerging diversities of innovation.

Also, a major aspect of regional studies in China are networked metropolises (composed of networking cities in certain geographical regions), influenced significantly by overseas capital (in coastal regions) or policies (in the northern Beijing area). These networking metropolises with embedded international players are highly diverse in different regions in China, and among the more popular research targets. This may be attributed to the fact that different regions (with different embedded resources) perform differently according to their economic and innovation resources. They are diversified and have non-linear levels of output. As such, they end up with only limited geographical regions attracting larger human capital as well as financial capitals. The biggest are areas in the Yangtze River Delta region, the Beijing-Tianjin area, and the Pearl River Delta region. This clearly indicates that there are important but diversified bases for regions, particularly cities, in which innovation manifests differently. The author's research team on this paper proposed an Urban Area Innovation System (refer to Song 2010; Song and Chen 2009) based on the function of cities nearby, with diversified players from regional industrial firms, universities, technical services, and local governments. Other studies, such as Han, Li et al. (2010) examined 21 cities in Guangdong Province, the province on the front line to Hong Kong and overseas markets. These suggest that cities with higher levels of innovation performance (usually represented by new product revenue and production value in high-tech fields and industries) tend to cluster in the Pearl River Delta region. Thus two layers of cities were formed as Sun-Affiliate pattern (meaning, one city is extremely large in economic and technology resource sense, other cities nearby are rather affiliated). Liu et al. (2010) did his research on cross-boundary cities, or in the Delta region, as Moon-Star pattern, emphasizing the role of the local government and many other active partners, including firms and universities in the city clustering. Such regional variations in interactions and function of different actors may create different opportunities for innovation, and a city's concentration will determine the metropolitan context. Such processes provide the basis for the geography of innovation divergences to be identified today.

Although interesting research findings are delivered by regional and city studies, there are still some un-addressed issues, especially such elements that support the hypothesis of diversities among regions in terms of innovation and related economic development. This chapter will discuss these issues further, in terms of Chinese cases.

Diversities of Innovation: Important Elements as Missing Factors

There are different elements worth noting when aiming to identify differences among regions in terms of innovation performance, including typical research bias, such as bias from subjective means, or theoretical hypothesis toward cities or regions. We would like to use more objective means or investigation angles in this study.

- **"Spatial" elements**

  In traditional regional studies, regions are separate and the geographical locations of certain regions are independent, with unique resources and factors that drive the local economies and social outputs in a culturally different way. However, modern geo-economic studies with econometric models tend to solve such rather geographically separate problems with a closed perspective in regional investigations in the fields of economic or technical innovation. On the other hand, industrial-based efficiency measures tend to be considered less frequently in studies that take into account separate regions or networking relationships among the regions. The key question is how to define "spatial" elements in different situations and under distinct research purposes: how to establish a scope large enough to include all networking cities in a typical metropolitan entity and small enough to focus on one tiny region that might be considered independent, so as to best reflect or to reveal real driving or influencing factors on innovation in the "city" or an idealistic *Metropolitan* with more meaningful boundary.

- **"Precise location" examination**

  Regional studies in China seem still less precise in the examination of different elements across regions. Traditionally, geographical terms such as Eastern, Middle, and Western China were used to classify large regions that is clusters of provinces; most regional studies tend to be conducted on a provincial level. However, along with rapid market development and the adoption of Information Communication Technologies (ICT) in many sectors, especially service sectors or mergers in manufacturing and services, regional economies tend to develop *across* provinces. But they may be more concentrated in certain cites, along an economic belt, or a block might be more precise for examining particular regional economic development.

- **"Remote" regions**

  "Remote" often indicates economically less-developed regions, where fewer research or geographical studies have been conducted, or on which studies are used simply as contrast to other, much more developed regions. It should be noted that those so-called remote regions or cities, may not be far away in distance from coastal or from larger cities, but they are regions with less capability to develop local economies, even though they are nearer to larger cities, therefore they are worth studying not only on their own terms but also worthy of study in light of their characteristic dynamic changes and efficiencies.

In response, this paper provides an integrated research framework in terms of a city-based examination of diversities of innovation in China. By investigating innovation contrasted with the economic development in the region, with various kinds of associated factors—including economic and social, growth and the nature of resource accumulation (more reflected in industrial traditions)—the research findings from this chapter provide notable city-based lessons for understanding diversities of innovation across different regions, particularly in terms of more spatial, contrasted, and business cultural elements.

Overall investigation on China's innovation in regions: which kind of factors are important?

In order to provide a picture of city-based innovation performance, related data of four typical indicators of innovation are collected, which include typical measures on innovation output (granted patents), economic development in the region (local production output), economic openness to market (Foreign Direct Investment, FDI), and social factors (population) across 106 cities in China.

It can be seen from Figures 10.1 (overall 106 cities) and 10.2 (only the 53 top-ranking cities for clearer picture) that innovation capacity (measured by granted patents), together with other two indicators, are correlated—to some extent—with economic output. They are differentiated in different regions, which can be better contrasted with Figure 10.2, where only the 53 leading sample cities are included. This may imply, on the one hand, that innovation movement is highly

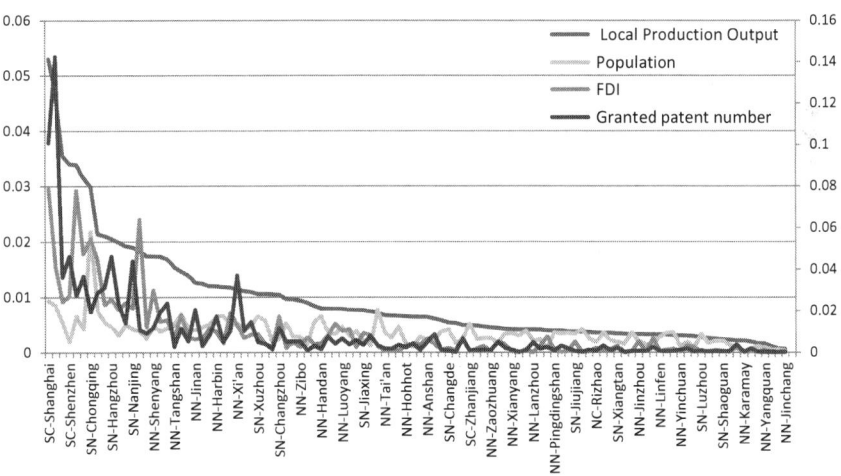

Figure 10.1 Sample cities (106 cities, 2014) in China, comparative examination on local production output (ranking indicator), foreign direct investment (FDI), granted patents, and population, (left scale: local production output, right scale: FDI, granted patents, and population)

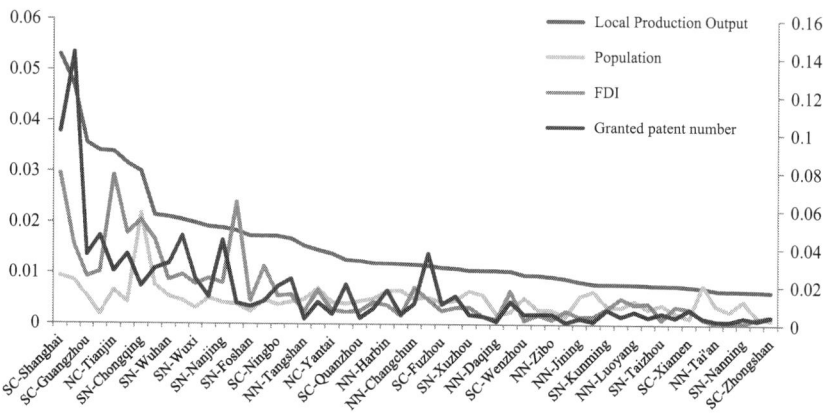

Figure 10.2 Sample cities (53 leading cities, 2014) in China, comparative examination on local production output (ranking indicator), foreign direct investment (FDI), granted patents, and population, (left scale: local production output, right scale, FDI, granted patents, and population)

correlated with economic development. But, on the other, it may merely imply that some social factors such as population or openness may also be relevant but differentiated factors to explain innovation output and economic performance in different regions. Besides, due to the nature of specific sectors (which vary in terms of demand in techno-scientific linkages and in closeness with other players for industrial development), large differences among cities or metropolises can exist depending on their industrial composition. Also, other multiple and diversified factors are noteworthy and ought to be studied in city-based regional innovation investigations. What is more important is that this also strongly suggests that the emergence of diversities is unavoidable in city-based innovation.

Based on these investigations, further research on diversified innovation over metropolitan areas is provided in the following.

Investigation framework on the metropolitan innovation system.

Although there are frequently used indicators on innovation such as patent count, or, if possible, newly developed product sales in the market, these are generally representations of what happened in the past. Measures of potentiality may be important for the future or for real innovation capacity. Knowledge generation potentiality can be input-based and procedure-based.

Given the previous literature discussion, together with what we did on Chinese regional studies, we would suggest an investigation that focuses on tracking the possible influencing factors over regional, and particularly metropolitan-based innovation movements. We categorize these along four dimensions based on an aggregation of associated factors.

Current economic and innovation—relative measures

This may generally involve input, output, and process measures on current production capacity supported by necessary innovation strength in the region. Input measures include not only financially relevant measures, such as R&D or S&T expenditures and investment volume to reflect quality expectations on economic progress in the region, but also density of industrial firms, since such concentration of business firms and investment can be active indicators for local regions. Additionally, overseas investments are included as an indicator of both market expectation and market openness at the same time. Since there can be larger variance among different metropolitan areas in China in terms of economic and innovation performance, relative measures (either relative to local indicators or to the overall total among all investigated areas) are more reasonable to compare in terms of efficiency or capacity of economic innovation. We also include patent records to indicate local innovation performance in relevant metropolitan areas in this study. However, we believe there are some differences between patenting volume and granted patent quantities. The relatively higher volume of former data may indicate active innovation attitude, or a higher level of enthusiastic movement for patents in the region, while the relatively higher volume of the latter cases may indicate innovation quality or capacity. All in all, it indicates a relationship between recent processes of innovation and divergences among metropolitan situations during the early stages of development. The divergences of innovation to be noted today are also based on such differences, which in turn have existed for a long time themselves.

Potential economic development impact of human resource and knowledge creation capacity

This study, by finding possible indicators on knowledge creation and human-resource-based indicators, compares potential resources among sample metropolitan areas. It should be noted that besides accumulated human resources in certain regions, dynamic movement of human resources may prove to be much more important indicators to contrast human flows (as temporary immigrants) and also knowledge flows among particular cities (for this refer to Hilpert and Lawton Smith 2013, in biotechnology-related analysis on the function of the human resource movement).

Altogether, these stable, accumulated and dynamic natures of local human resource and related knowledge creation may be reflected by following typical measures:

- Population-related measures to reflect size of potential human resource.
- Knowledge-based human resources, such as the R&D or engineering workforce, or more knowledge-creating human resources as educational institutions.

- Volume or density of communications by population, which can indicate demand degree or frequency of information exchange by the population in the region.
- Networking linkages among individuals involved, or between institutions. This can be reflected in formal collaboration deals or frequent linkages among a population or organizations in the region, however, in more solid collaboration sense, usually with targeted missions.
- Information exchange via communication channels, usually including random and more free sense communication (in comparison of networking linkages, in which collaboration is already formed), as such activities can often be a better vehicle to transfer information and knowledge, and possibly generate new ideas. Indicators implying cross-city information exchange or networking can always be considered important variables to city-based innovation movement.

Efficiency and other enabling factors

Efficiency measures are also considered in this study. Unit production of innovation output, such as patents, can be used to compare productive innovation among sample regions and to imply procedures of innovation, as efficiency is always the result of process innovation or management-based organizational innovation. Indicators of efficiency levels and of changes to these levels should be qualified for explaining, to a certain extent, regional innovation. Similarly, density of input, or unit input (in relative sense) measures can also be used to compare sample regions on their input strength during the process.

However, if considering differences between investment on tangibles and intangibles, there should be two kinds of efficiency measures, namely tangible-related and intangible-related efficiency measures, typically:

For tangibles:

- Efficiency on equipment or hardware-based output;
- Efficiency on production organization (for example, per enterprise-related measures) based output.

And for intangibles:

- Efficiency on R&D output measures;
- Efficiency on research output per science and technology/R&D personnel;
- Efficiency on unit human resource output, etc.

These efficiency-based indicators may also imply differences among regions in features of local production, and possibly in the nature of local innovation.

Influence of industrial culture

Cultural contents in the region or city are commonly considered important influencing factors on innovation. How to capture a cultural essence in innovation research, however, is highly challenging. We would consider that in industrial development, language, historical-industrial heritage or tradition, and geographically based characteristics of local people, business styles, etc., might be better suited to address the local cultural measures. In fact, industrial traditions (engineering and operation culture) and policies (governance culture) in China can be important factors to explain evolution in the development of heavy industries in different regions during the early 1950s and 1960s (refer to Zhang's study), and development of ICT-related industries in diversified regions since 1990s.[1] It is obvious that industrial traditions and business culture, together with dynamic changes in available resources and markets, can surely make an important impact on diversities, driving local industries and innovation movement more diverse. Therefore, dimensions of the past, including the industrial tradition and business routines alike, can be used for cultural-based study. Such situations indicate that processes of innovation are influenced by many different factors, and that effective innovation may arise from precisely these diverse opportunities. Traditions, cultures and businesses may constitute such divergent situations, and may contribute towards individual developments.

More precisely, this study compares some traditional features of sample cities, as these features of industries may provide important bases for further development of various industrial sectors in the region. For example, heavy industry (usually capital-intensive, upper-stream sectors, such as iron & steel, petrochemical, and heavy-textile sectors) based regions may need more novel resources and market opportunity to transfer into other different industries. Light industrial cities (such as traditional home appliance), on the other hand, can easily integrate other modern industries. In any case, traditional routines, embedded in their manufacturing manner, can be one of the important factors to represent local industrial cultural, along with those purely economic indicators.

Research framework

By considering the factors described above and their influence on each other, the following research framework, composed of the four elements in this study, is proposed to cover a broader range of interacting factors than merely economic and innovation performance. The most important feature of this framework is that human resource capacity and knowledge potential (e.g., human resource input for science and technology research, the value of temporary immigrants for knowledge sharing, and information/communication density) are included. The potential power of local human resources can also be reflected in higher level of value creation per unit fixed asset measure. There should also be elements to compare what occurs now with what might occur in the future (i.e., to mark innovation potential). Therefore, the four

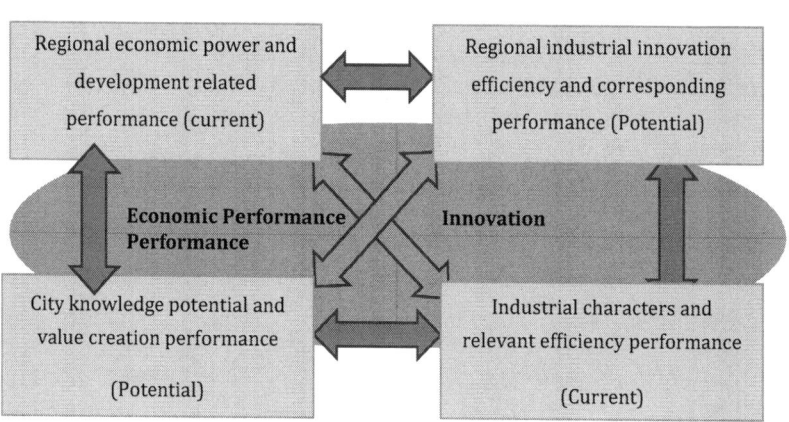

Figure 10.3 Investigation framework on metropolitan-based innovation movement regional economic and industrial performance (current linkage) vs. city human resource & knowledge and industrial innovation performance (potential linkage)

elements here are marked "current" and "potential". Moreover, efficiency-related measures are also included in order to catch characteristic features of local industries, which again may be connected to particular local industrial culture (history) and current practices.

In the above chart (Figure 10.3), four kinds of factors are clustered with different representative groups of available indicators to show the state of current economic development in the region and state of potential capacity for the future (indicated by industrial innovation and human resources (HR) as well as related knowledge creation and information transfer, given the fact that human capital and knowledge assets are key resources for innovation and for related industries in the near future). The following empirical studies will be conducted according to this framework over typical sample cities in China.

Empirical investigation: current economic performance vs. innovation potential

Based on the *China City Statistical Yearbook (2013, 2014, and 2015)*, we collect necessary indicators on those four dimensions.

The necessary innovation data are also selected from another resource, such as patent data from SIPO website in China. One-hundred and six sample cities are selected for this study. Principle Factor Analysis technique is applied, in order to keep the original information from all 14 indicators, while at the same time tremendously decrease the number of measures. In fact, in this study, only four factors are extracted from PFA procedure, representing

83.45% of original information from those indicators (refer to Table 10.2). In the following table, (Table 10.1) the detailed indicators selected are listed and grouped according to their kind of information, which correspond with the designed four-dimension investigation framework. Table 10.2 provides more precise information on correlations between each of the practical indicators and their corresponding extracted factors. It can be seen that, although there are also overlaps in the numbers of the indicators for their belonging factors, basically such extracted factors can still be highly relevant in terms of their own definitions, which summarize or extract most or part of the information from those relevant indicators.

From the results of the analysis, it can be seen that the value of Factor 1 (simplified as F1) clearly represents the current economic and innovation level of performance (such as the granted patent ratio to all sample cities) in the corresponding cities, while values of Factor 2 and Factor 3 (simplified as

Table 10.1 Grouped indicators

RFD	Ratio of FDI volume in the region (% of all sample cities)	Factor 1 (Current performance) Metropolitan economic power and innovation output related performance (simplified as MEIO)
RPG	Granted patent volume (ratio to average all sample cities)	
FDF	Overseas investment—ratio to local fixed asset investment (%)	
RGA	Green land ratio of the sample city (% of all sample cities)	
RIQ	Numbers of industrial firms (ratio to average of all sample cities)	
PSA	Patenting volume per science and technology personnel	Factor 2 (Potential capacity) Metropolitan industrial innovation capacity and corresponding performance (simplified as MIIC)
PSG	Granted patents per S&T personnel	
HSE	Science and technology expenditure per 100 S&T personnel	
HPC	Transporting passengers per 100 local residents	Factor 3 (Potential capacity) Metropolitan human resource and dynamic exchange capacity and relevant performance (simplified as MHRD)
HIE	Internet connection number per 100 population	
HEE	Educational expenditure per 100 population	
UFG	Regional production value per unit fixed assets	
PEP	Electrical energy (KW hour electricity) cost per enterprise in the city	Factor 4 (Current performance) Metropolitan industrial nature and efficiency performance (MINE)
UWI	Water supply cost per production output in relevant city	

Table 10.2 Extracted factors reflecting current vs. potential performance on metropolitan innovation (extracted using principle factor analysis)

Correlations of each indicator on the Principle Factor

Indicators	Principle Factors (% of information from all original indicators)			
	Factor 1 24.19%	Factor 2 23.03%	Factor 3 23.00%	Factor 4 13.23%
RFD	**0.926**	0.176	0.051	-0.052
RPG	**0.813**	0.002	0.287	-0.047
FDF	**0.746**	0.269	0.332	-0.081
RGA	**0.746**	0.269	0.332	-0.081
RIQ	**0.654**	0.562	0.236	-0.220
PSA	0.053	**0.958**	0.093	-0.071
HSE	0.094	**0.940**	0.153	-0.041
PSG	0.153	**0.943**	0.146	-0.079
HPC	0.058	0.101	**0.888**	-0.087
HEE	0.414	0.143	**0.797**	0.155
UFG	0.257	0.149	**0.779**	0.007
HIE	0.290	0.169	**0.808**	0.021
PEP	-0.094	-0.117	0.049	**0.939**
UWI	-0.062	-0.060	-0.016	**0.930**

Extracted method: PFA
Rotation: Kaiser standardized orthogonal method
Convergent after 6 times of rotation

F2 and F3, respectively) can be used as potential performance, since F2 is more industrial innovation efficiency related (e.g., patenting quantity per R&D person), and F3 is clearly a more dynamic human resource movement and information intensive relevant measure. Value of Factor 4 (simplified as F4) indicates more of an industrial nature of the investigated cities, however, the indicator relevant to this factor is type of energy intensive, thus, cities with higher value on this factor should be considered as more heavy industry related or more traditional industry related, and less effective under the current industrial output pattern.

Regarding the real position of the sample cities on those F1 through F4 dimensions, a further classification among all sample cities is conducted according to their economic power (industrial production value), economic openness or market mechanisms (measured by overseas capital ratio), and industrial tradition (measured by energy cost). The following table is provided to clarify differences of those grouped sample cities, with detailed description of those sample cities in each of the groups. In fact, this table provides a picture of the *Diversities of Economies* among the sample cities, in order to provide a better understanding of *Diversities of Innovation* across different regions with different economic development characters.

Three kinds of indicators from the yearly statistical book on cities are used to group sample cities in this study, namely Production Value (Indicator for Economic Power), Overseas Capital Ratio (Indicator for Market Openness), and Electricity Cost Per Firm (indicator for traditional nature of production, usually in heavy industries alike). Detailed rules for the classification and related groups with their marks are shown in following table (Table 10.3).

Special names in this table are used to classify different city groups Sample cities in Group NE1 (New Economic Region 1) are significant in both economic performance and energy efficiency, which implies that those cities are running in a newly developed manner of economic progress, either high-tech based or service industry oriented. In any case, we can call those samples in the group Newly Emerging. Similarly, sample cities in NE2 (New Economic Region 2) might be considered also significant in energy efficiency, but with less economic power compared with samples in NE1. On the contrary, sample

Table 10.3 Classification of the sample cities in this study to indicate diversities of economies

Economic Nature No. of Samples Industrial tradition	ID: Lower energy cost per firm (Bottom 30) S vs.N**	ID: Mid-level energy cost per firm (Other) S vs.N**	ID: Higher energy cost per firm (Top 21) S vs.N**
ID: Top Production Value /Top economic power (Eco Tp15 & OpenTp 12)	NE1 (Emerging economies & significant open cities) S: 4; N: 3	TE1 (Top economic & significant open cities) S: 4; N: 1	TE2*** (Top economic developed areas) S: 2; N: 1
Mid-level econo. power (with less openness) (EcoTp 60 & OpenTp 60)*	NE2 (Emerging economies local power) S: 10; N: 3	M (Medium) S: 10; N: 13	TR2 (Significant traditional economies) S: 0; N: 9
Lower economic power (Ebttm 46 & Openbttm 46)	RM1 (Remote areas with less developed economies) S: 6; N: 4	RM2 (Remote areas with more traditional economies) S: 14; N: 10	TR1 (Highly strong traditional economies) S: 1; N: 11

* Notice: EcoTp 60/Open Tp 60 or other figures indicate those samples at positions lower than 15 but higher and include 60 or related number.
** S: stands for sample cities in southern China, while N stands for sample cities in northern China. In this case, numbers of sample cities are listed and contrasted between south and north in each of the groups for further reference.
*** Notice, since there is no sample city in both the Top 21 group in terms of energy cost and Top 15 in terms of economic power, the energy cost rank is extended to the Top 50 in the TE2.

cities in TR1 (Traditional Economic Region 1) can be considered of a lower economic capacity but with much higher energy cost, which implies traditional industrial regions. Similarly, samples in TR2 (Traditional Economic Region 2) can be considered to be more capable in production but require higher levels of energy use. It should be noted that samples in TE2 (Top Economic Regions 2) are both highly capable in economic production and significant openness, and also have a higher level of energy cost, which indicates that those relevant sample cities may be in key positions in different manufacturing sectors, or *Top Economies*. Meanwhile, samples in TE1 (Top Economic Regions 1) can be economically capable of production value and less energy cost at the same time, which implies a new type of production or a technology-intensive nature. Finally, remote regions can be defined here as sample cities that are in lower economic positions and have lower energy cost. Samples in RM2 (Remote Economic Regions 2) are classified due to their higher energy input but still lower production output.

In this way, more diversified characters of those sample cities can be grouped and contrasted in terms of newly emerging industrial cities with higher efficient in energy cost (NEs), key industrial cities with top economic power and energy cost (TEs), traditional industrial cities with comparatively lower economic output and highest energy cost (TRs), more "remote" cities with comparatively lower energy cost but also lower economic output (RMs), and cities with a medium level of both economic output and energy cost (Ms, Medium Economic Regions). Consequently, among these divergences of innovation, the context of a particular process may make a significant difference.

Moreover, considering larger differences in terms of economic performance and innovation between inner land cities and coastal cities in China and differences in business culture between south and north in China, geographical differences are specially clarified among all sample cities in this study in order to look into diversities of innovation along these two dimensions. It is obvious that in Table 10.3, that while sample southern cities in NE2 and TE1 more significantly outperform in the **number** of cities than northern cities, northern samples in TR1 and TR2 are much larger in the **number** of cities than southern samples. This implies a meaningful classification for their production nature, especially in terms of industrial culture. When such divergent variables meet in a particular situation, they not only need to generate important diversity, but also aim at creating innovative solutions.

According to the above-defined rules, 106 sample cities are grouped in 9 divisions in Table 10.3. The respective numbers of sample cities are also given in order to provide a general picture of the economic sides of diversities among those sample cities in relevant locations. The following charts are then provided according to the results of PFA (refer to Tables 10.1 and 10.2) to contrast sample cities firstly with current economic and innovation capacity (F1) and potentiality with industrial innovation performance (F2) in Figure 10.5, as well as potentiality with human resource and knowledge creation performance (F3) in Figure 10.6. Since geographical locations are especially salient for this study (and which we also believe very much relevant to study diversities of innovation in China, particularly in terms differences between inner land and coastal, and between Southern and Northern China), over distributions of those 9 groups of samples, these respective figures (Figures 10.4, 10.5, and 10.6) are designed to contrast sample cities along with these dimensions and divisions.

It is apparent from Figure 10.4 that coastal cities appear to be more significant along the dimension of industrial innovation capacity (F2), while samples in a similar group are much more diversified in the dimension of market development and have an absolute advantage in patent volume (F1). In fact, typical big cities, such as the big three cities (Beijing, Shanghai, Tianjin, all marked with TE1 and TE2), are usually ranked top in F1 (the current economic and innovation output). While Shanghai (marked with TE1) is ranked top in F1, Suzhou (near Shanghai, marked with NE1) is the highest on F2. However, there are other NE1's and NE2's, as well as TE1's and TE2's scattered along dimension of F1. However, it should be noted that typical sample cities around Shanghai, or in Yangtze Delta region, are in the top cluster along the dimension of F2, or industrial innovation capacity measures.

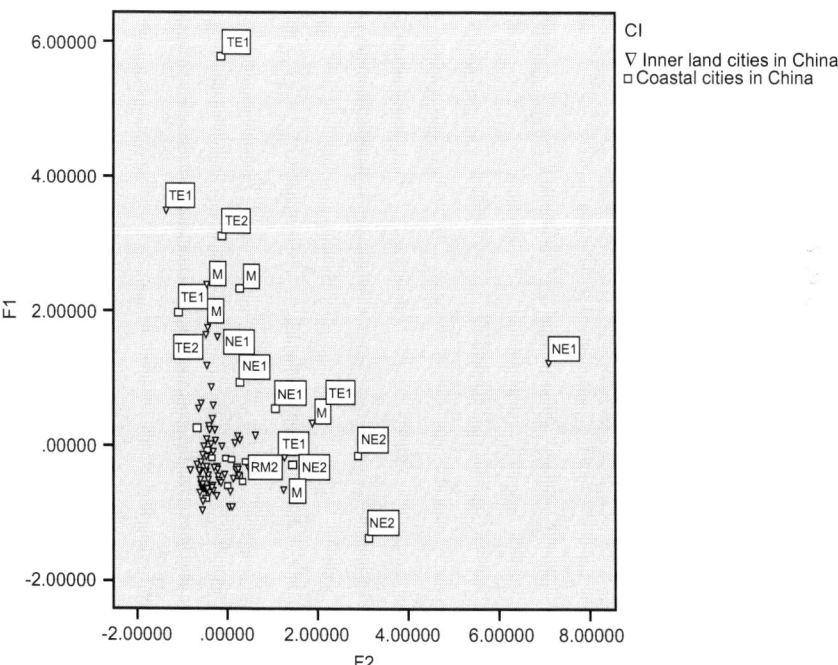

Figure 10.4 Regional economic power and performance (F1) vs. regional industrial innovation performance (F2): inner land cities vs. coastal cities (CI contrast)

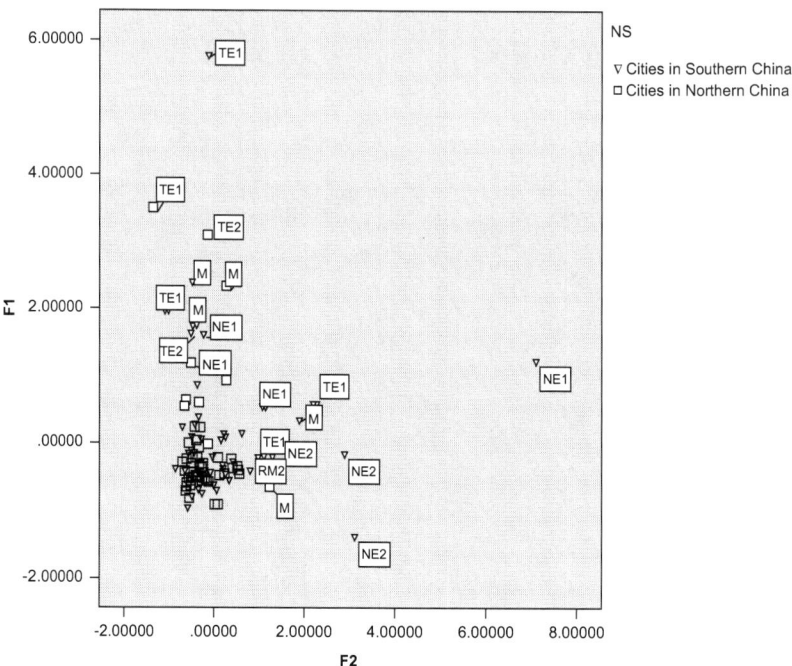

Figure 10.5 Regional current economic and innovation power (F1) vs. regional economic power and performance (F1) vs. regional industrial innovation performance (F2): southern vs. northern cities (NS contrast)

From Figure 10.6, it is also obvious that southern cities in China are more capable in terms of human resource movement and knowledge creation (F3). The city of Shenzhen, marked with TE2, is especially a shining star city with extraordinary speed of economic development, benefiting greatly from the Opening-Up Policy and more market mechanism- oriented policy, is on the very top in the dimension of F3. Other cities are similar in the second cluster on F3, however, most of them are actually in the Pearl River Delta region in China, although they are marked differently as TE1, NE2, and M.

F4 is the fourth dimension on energy efficiency considerations, which indicates the nature of industries in corresponding sample cities. Since the dimension is designed in the direction positively related to the energy (electricity and water supplies) intensive side, the dimension is correlated with strong traditional ways of production. From Figure 10.7, it is apparent that sample cities with lower market development position (F1) lie mostly northern in China and are among the top clusters in F4. Usually such metropolitan areas are characterized by heavy industries such as iron & steel, coal mines, and others, almost all marked TR1 or TR2. Traditions, competences, and industrial cultures which have emerged in

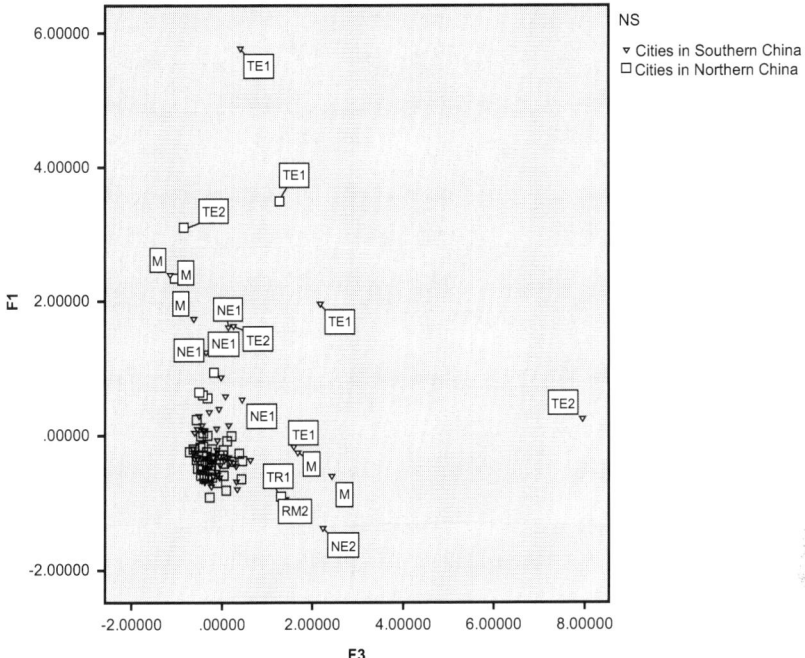

Figure 10.6 Regional economic power and performance (F1) vs. potentiality on human resource movement and knowledge creation (F3): southern vs. northern cities (NS contrast)

regions and cities may call for divergent applications, and they may equally create divergent innovative approaches.

Based on these distributions of the sample cities, Figure 10.8 is provided for more significant contrast between F2 (potentiality with industrial innovation capacity) and F4 (traditional nature of production), so that there is a clear and more interesting picture to show in this chart:

• Although typical sample cities in the TE1 and TE2 (e.g., Shanghai, Beijing, and Tianjin, the top three on F1) group may lead group F1, or in current economic and innovation performances, sample cities in NE1 group (typically Suzhou, the top one on F2), stand out as more important metropolitan locations in terms of potential capacity (refer to Table 10.3)

• On the other hand, along the axis of both F1 and F2, sample regions in TR1 or TR2, or in traditional manner of production, are always in low position, in terms of current and potential innovation capacity.

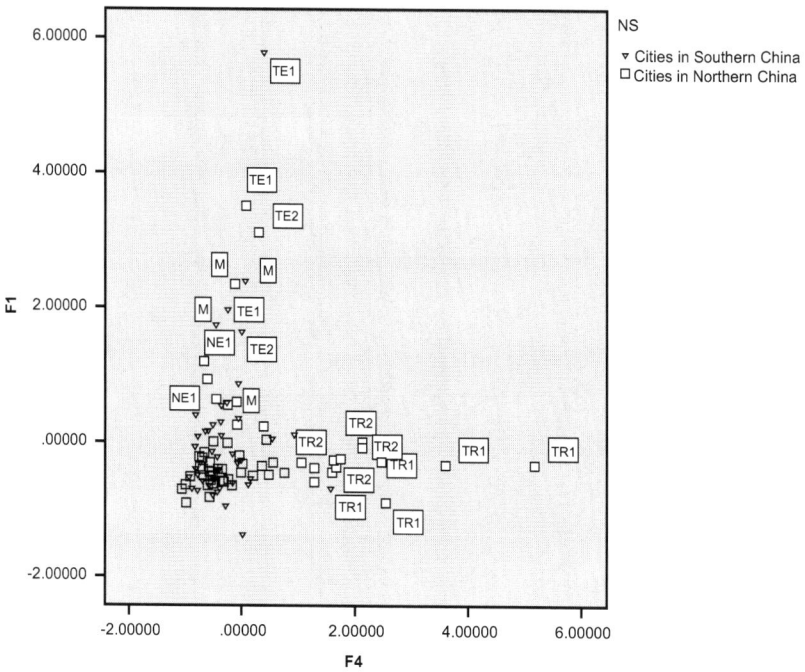

Figure 10.7 Regional current economic power and innovation (F1) vs. regional current industrial nature (F4): southern vs. northern cities (NS contrast)

- In any case, there are large diversities among TE1 and TE2, as well as NE1 and NE2, cities in the same group can be highly different along the two dimensions, F1 and F2.

In order to show the significant locations of those sample cities in the front lines in terms of F1 (Current performance on economic and innovation output), F2 (Potential capacity in industrial innovation), F3 (Potential capacity in human resources and dynamic exchange), and F4 (Current performance in more traditional industrial nature, or more energy intensive production), the following map (Figure 10.9) is provided with 31 sample cities, including the 10 top cities on F1 axis, and the top 7 cities for each of the rest three dimensions. Apparently, along the F4, all the top 7 cities are TRs (Top four TR1 cities and three TR2 cities) on the map, while the top cities along F1 are TEs, and most of the top cities along F2 are NEs. The top 7 cities on F3 are a mixture of TEs and NEs, as well as M cities.

(Please notice that areas of cities are defined according to the municipal governance. There are also black-framed samples that are cities in both top group on F2 and F3)

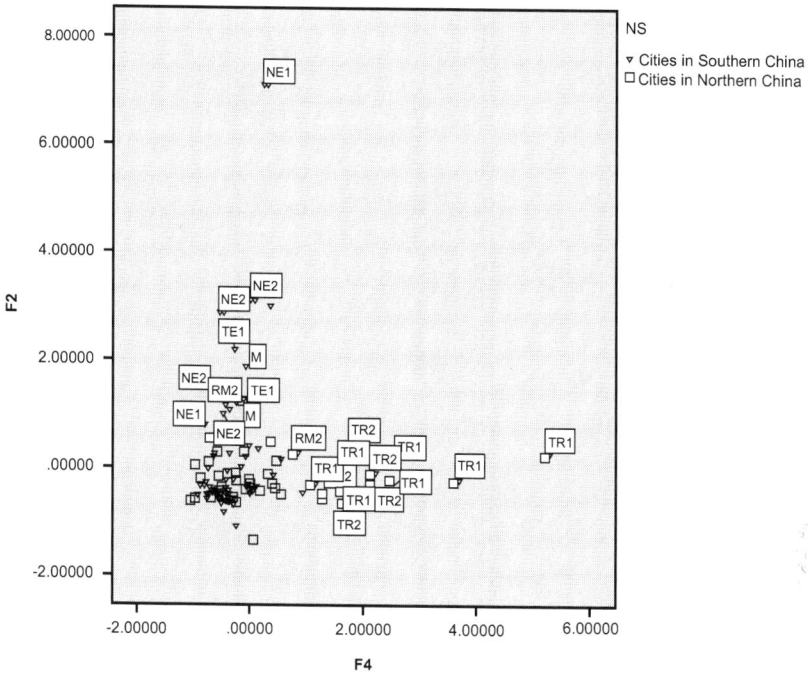

Figure 10.8 Regional potential industrial innovation capacity (F2) vs. regional current industrial nature (F4): southern cities vs. northern cities (NS contrast)

Also, from this research, it is very interesting that sample cities are clustered
in metropolitan belts rather than in typical economic and innovation indica-
tor-oriented groups. For example, Shanghai (marked with TE1) and Suzhou
(NE1), the two cities are geographically very close in Yangtze River Delta,
are ranked top in Figures 10.8 and 10.9 respectively. There are other similar
cases in Pearl River Delta region where Guangzhou, Shenzhen, and Zhong-
shan, as well as others are closer in their position along F1, F2, or F3. Of
course, there are individual cities that are separated in geographical terms, but
may have similar positions on these charts. This indicates that grouping
sample cities according to production value and market openness cannot fully
explain innovation capacity in those cities or diversities of innovation in geographical sense. However, the energy intensive factor can explain—to
a certain extent—the negative direction of regional innovation in this study.
Another kind of factor, location in the north or south of China, which can
reflect market development traditions, can be used to explain diversities of
innovation in sample cities.

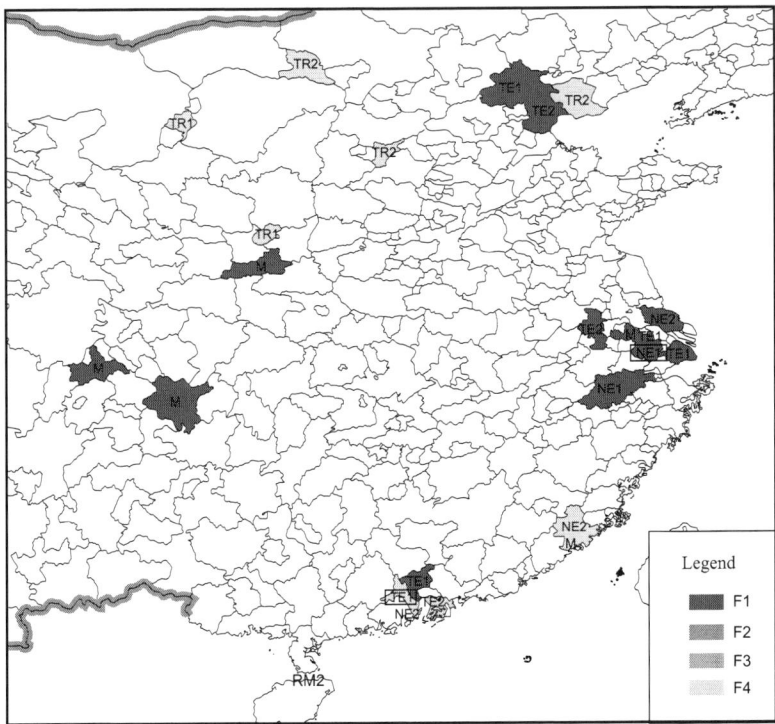

Figure 10.9 31 sample top cities along F1, F2, F3, and F4 in this study.

Conclusion

This research, applies a four-dimension model for metropolitan-based diver-sities of innovation studies, and provides a multiple factor-based framework for regional innovation studies. The research integrates current economic and innovation performance measures with potential measures of human resource movement and knowledge creation, together with usual industrial innovation capacity measures in general. Empirical investigation over 106 sample cities in China shows that the actual position on current and potential dimensions of sample cities in China can reflect the nature of metropolitan-area-based diversities of innovation and of possible correl-ated factors or elements.

Typical findings can be summarized as follows:

- Both economic strength in production value and market openness can explain sample cities' higher level of innovation capacity, in current and in potential measure, but only limited to numbers of extra-large cities, such as Beijing, Shanghai, Tianjin, and some others. Larger numbers of sample cities in the same group in terms of production value and economically openness measures are actually scattered and diversified along the typical three—especially the two dimensions integrated from this study, namely, current and potential innovation capacity (represented by F1 and F2, respectfully). These results also reveal that market openness, primarily indicated by overseas capital operations, is usually correlated with production volume in both quantity and in quality, however, with a larger concentration effect. Most cities still vary between economic production volume and innovation assets.

- In this study, F3 emphasizes the importance of human capital and information flows, defined as the potentiality of innovation through knowledge creation. However, the rankings of sample cities along this dimension can also vary by different sample groups. Most likely, those sample cities in NE or TE groups could be in the top rank.

- Industrial and business culture is especially considered in this study, through a classification of geographical locations in south vs. north in China, or coastal vs. inner land. From this study, southern vs. northern cities have proven to be the more important dimension for detailed investigation on diversified innovation in China. Overall, it can be concluded that southern cities are more innovative and have higher potentiality than cities in the northern regions of China. This indicates that southern cities, typically with more open markets, and dynamic characters in market culture, are more active to improve local production via innovation. Meanwhile, if industrial nature or tradition is included in the investigation, it is obvious that those typical cities with heavy industrial traditions appear less innovative, and also less economically competitive.

- In order to conduct more detailed studies, 9 groups are classified here according to production value, market openness, and energy cost per firm, or, put differently, economic and industrial tradition measures, for all the sample cities. The results based on this classification show that while sample cities in NEs and TEs groups are indeed typical in F1, F2, and F3, there are still diversified cases of sample cities, which implies that while innovation can occur for a number of other reasons, economic volume is still necessary.

- The belt phenomena stand out in this study, as numbers of high-ranked sample cities are clustered either in the Yangtze River Delta region or in the Pearl River Delta region, two very important economic areas in China, with close ties to business. Such research findings are significant in terms of diversities of innovation. While Shanghai stands out among the top cities in terms of economic and innovation power, Suzhou, not far from Shanghai, as well as Shenzhen, nearer to Hong Kong and Guangzhou in southern China, are two extraordinary cities with innovation potentiality. This also suggests a need for further study on the contrasting case of isolated cities with higher levels of industrial innovation.

• Industrial nature reflected by energy intensive character (either as larger and key manufacturing cities, usually with also higher economic power, or as highly traditional heavy industries, usually with lower economic power), is a meaningful dimension (defined by F4), which strongly corresponds with performance of those cities in TR groups according to the 9 divisions. It is a comprehensive finding from this study that highly traditional industrial-based regions (cities) are less capable of innovation, both in current and in potential terms.

City-based geography study on diversified innovation is an interesting research topic, there is no doubt that multiple and various factors or elements function jointly on local economic and innovation output. This Chinese-city based research may provide a useful framework and an investigation window for further study on metropolitan-area-based diversified innovation studies.

Note

1 There are many more studies on various regions in specific industrial development, for example, which refer to Wu, Qianpo, Ning, Yuemin, "Analysis on City Networking in China—from the perspective of electronic and information companies"<Geographical Studies> (in Chinese), Vol 31, No. 2, (2012).

References

Acs, Z., 2000: *Regional Innovation, Knowledge, and Global Change;* [M]. New York, NY, USA: Frances Pinter.

An, Z., 2006: *Regulation reformation and organizational change on harmonizing development of metropolitan regi2005ons (in Chinese)* [M]. Beijing, China: Economic Science Press.

Bell, G.G., 2005: Clusters, Networks and Firm Innovativeness. *Strateg. Manag. J., 26,* 287–295.

Braczyk, H.J., and Cooke, P.N. and Heidenreich, M., 1998: *Regional Innovation Systems: The Role of Governances in a Globalized World;* [M]. London, UK: Psychology Press.

Broekel, T., 2012: Collaboration intensity and regional innovation efficiency in Germany—A conditional efficiency approach. In: *Industry and Innovation 19* (2), 155–179.

Buesa, M., Heijs, J. and Baumert, T., 2010: The determinants of regional innovation in Europe: A combined factorial and regression knowledge production function approach. In: *Research Policy 39* (6), 722–735.

Caniëls, M.C., 2000: *Knowledge Spillovers and Economic Growth: Regional Growth Differentials across Europe;* [M]. Cheltenham, UK: Edward Elgar Publishing

Chen, K. and Kenney, M., 2007: Universities/research institutes and regional innovation systems: The cases of Beijing and Shenzhen. In: *World Development 35* (6), 1056–1074.

China City Statistical Yearbook, 2013, 2014, *and 2015:* edited by City Social and Economic Investigation Department, National Statistical Bureau, Published by China Statistic Press, Beijing, China.

Cooke, P., 1996: The new wave of regional innovation networks: Analysis, characteristics and strategy[J] *Small Bus. Econ*, *8*, 159–171.

Cooke, P. and Morgan, K., 1990: *Learning through networking: Regional innovation and the lessons of Baden-Wurttemberg [M]*. Regional Industrial Research Report no. 5. Cardiff: University of Wales.

De la Mothe, J. and Paquet, G., 1998: Local and regional systems of innovation as learning socio-economies. *Econ. Sci. Technol. Innov.*, *14*, 1–18.

Deyle, H. G. and Grupp, H., 2005: Commuters and the regional assignment of innovative activities: A methodological patent study of German districts. In: *Research Policy 34* (2), 221–234.

Dosi, G., 1988: Sources, procedures, and microeconomic effects of innovation. *J. Econ. Lit.*, *26*, 1120–1171.

Drüke, H., 2003: Selective performance admit government failure: the complexities of the Italian regionalism in innovation, in: Hilpert, U. (Ed.), *Regionalisation of Globalised Innovation: Locations for advanced industrial development and disparities in participation*. Routledge Ltd., London and New York, 73–93.

Feldman, M. P., 1994: Knowledge complementarity and innovation. In: *Small Business Economics 6* (5), 363–372.

Fischer, M. M., Diez, J. R., and Snickars, F., 2001: *Metropolitan innovation systems: Theory and evidence from three metropolitan regions in Europe* [M]. Berlin: Springer.

Fritsch, M. and Slavtchev, V., 2010: How does industry specialization affect the efficiency of regional innovation systems? In: *The Annals of Regional Science 45* (1), 87–108.

Fischer, M., Diez, J.R., and Snickars, F., 2002: Metropolitan Innovation Systems: Theory and Evidence from Three Metropolitan Regions in Europe. *Eur. Plan. Stud.*, *10*, 275–279.

Gai, W.q. and Wang, J., 1999: Function of regional networking on small high tech companies in China. In: *China Soft Science 9* (in Chinese), 102–106.

Griliches Z., 1992: The search for R&D spillovers. In: *The Scandinavian Journal of Economics 94* (Supplement), 29–47.

Hall, P. and Markusen, A., 1985: High technology and regional-urban policy. In: *Silicon Landscapes*. Crows Nest, Australia: Allen and Unwin, 144–151.

Han, L., Lachang L., Lezhang W., and Yuan R., 2010: Innovation space in metropolitan areas in Guangdong Province in China. In: *Economic Geography 12* (in Chinese), 1978–1984.

Hao, Y. and Tang, J., 2009: Regional innovation capacity and its constrain factors, province based panel data investigation between 1997 and 2007. In: *Management Journal 6* (9) (in Chinese), 1182–1187.

Hickie, D., Islands of Innovation in the UK economy: high-technology, networking and public policy, in: Hilpert, U. (Ed.), *Regionalisation of Globalised Innovation: Locations for advanced industrial development and disparities in participation*. Routledge Ltd., London and New York, 53–72.

Hilpert, U., Globalisation and selective localisation of industry and innovation: the role of government in regionalising socio-economic development, in: Hilpert, U. (Ed.), *Regionalisation of Globalised Innovation: Locations for advanced industrial development and disparities in participation*. Routledge Ltd., London and New York, 3–28.

Hilpert, U. and Lawton Smith, H. (Eds.), 2013: Networking of regionalised innovative labourmarket. Abingdon-on-Thames, UK: Routledge.

Jaffe, A. B., 1989: Real effects of academic research [J]. In: *American Economic Review 79*, 957–970.

Johnson, W. H. A. and Liu, Q., 2011: Patenting and the role of technology markets in regional innovation in China: An empirical analysis. In: *Journal of High Technology Management Research 22*, 14–25.

Liu, C., Li, Z., Xu, J. and Ye, J., 2010: Spatial analysis on restructuring of "Metropolitan Region" in Pearl River Delta in China—Example of facility construction cross-administrative boundary [J]. In: *International City Planning 25* (2) (in Chinese), 31–38.

Liu, X., 2005: Analysis and report on regional innovation capacity in China: 2004–2005, [J]. In: *Study of Science and Technologies 12* (in Chinese), 5–14.

Malecki, E. J., 1981: Science, technology, and regional economic development: Review and prospects. In: *Research Policy 10* (4), 312–334.

Nelson, R., 1993: *National innovation systems—A comparative analysis* [M]. Oxford, UK: Oxford University Press.

Padmore, T. and Gibson, H., 1998: Modelling systems of innovation: II. A framework for industrial cluster analysis in regions. In: *Research Policy 26* (6), 625–641.

Padmore, T., Schuetze, H. and Gibson, H., 1998: Modeling systems of innovation: An enterprise-centered view. In: *Research Policy 26* (6), 605–624.

Pavitt, K. and Patel, P., 1994: Uneven (and divergent) technological accumulation among advanced countries. In: *Industrial and Corporate Change 3*, 759–787.

Polanyi, M., 1996: *The tacit dimension*. London: Routledge & Kegan Paul.

Song, L., 2010: *Polarized development of metropolitan innovation system: Situations and evaluations* [D], (in Chinese). PhD thesis at Beihang University.

Song, L. and Chen, X., 2009: Comparison of innovation space among major four larger metropolitan areas in China. In *China Soft Science 10* (in chinese), 100–108.

Stöhr, W. B., 1986: Regional innovation complexes. In: *Regional Science 59* (1), 29–44.

Sweeney, G. P., 1987: *Innovation, entrepreneurs regional development*. London: Frances Pinter, ISBN 0-86187-647-4.

Varga, A., 1999: Time-space patterns of US innovation: Stability or change? In: Manfred M. Fischer, Luis Suarez-Villa, and Michael Steiner (Ed.), *Innovation, networks and localities*. Berlin/Heidelberg: Springer, 215–234.

Verspagen, B., 1993: Uneven growth between rivals: Informal know-how trading. In *Research Policy 16*, 291–302.

Wang, J., 1997: Networking environment: The new change of industrial organization, (in Chinese). In: *Strategies and Management Journal 3* (in Chinese), 109–144.

Wu, Q. and Ning, Y., 2012: Analysis on City Networking in China—From perspective of electronic and information companies (in Chinese).[J]. In: *Geographical Studies 31* (2) 201-219.

Li, X., 2009: China's regional innovation capacity in transition: An empirical approach [J]. In: *Research Policy 38*, 338–357.

Xie, F.J. and Xiaoyu, Y. and Zihui, G., 2010: The bottleneck problems and policy recommendations of the development of Shanghai patent technology industry [J]. In: *Technology and Economy 29* (8), 13–16.

Xie, F.J. and Xu, H.M., 2007: Study on the modes of metropolitan innovation system (in Chinese) [J]. *China Econ. Rev., 3*, 1–7.

Zhang, B., Yao, F. and Zhang, J., 2004: *Technology Transfer from Formal Soviet Union to China, 1949–1966* (in Chinese). Shandong, China: Shandong Press.

Zhou, T., 2010: *China city innovation report blue book*, (in Chinese). Beijing, China: Hong Qi Press.

Part V

Science-based and technology-based opportunities

11 New manufacturing trends in developed regions

Three delineations of new industrial policies – 'Phoenix Industry', 'Industry 4.0', and 'Smart Specialisation'

Alberto Bramanti

Introduction

In the aftermath of the financial crisis, a resurgence of interest in the manufacturing sector and industrial policy has spread throughout Europe (Dhéret et al. 2014; EC 2014; Bailey et al. 2015). The recent success of the BRIC countries, and the less recent but still prominent policies of Japan, South Korea, Germany, and the US suggest that a pro-active state can play a positive role in facilitating economic growth (Pisano and Shih 2009, 2012; Mazzucato 2013).

There are good reasons for this revival and for the rising interest within the European Union in maintaining a strong industrial base and a competitive position at the international level. The most striking figures in this regard are related to exports. EU exports consist mainly of manufactured products, which represent more than 80% of all EU exports. Small and medium-sized enterprises (SMEs) are the backbone of the manufacturing industry in the EU, as they provide around 45% of the industry's total value added and 51% of manufacturing employment. In this respect, they make a significant contribution to retaining jobs in European regions instead of offshoring them to distant, low-cost locations, a trend common among multinationals. Another key reason to look at this industry as a powerful engine of contemporary development is related to R&D investments and innovation processes. In the mechanical engineering sector, for instance, R&D expenditures totalled around EUR 8.3 billion in the EU-10 just before the 2008 crisis. Notably, this covers just one of the core sectors of European industry. A major consequence is that, in the long term, regions lacking the infrastructure necessary for advances in processes, engineering, and manufacturing will lose their ability to innovate. This is because firms without process-engineering capabilities find it increasingly difficult to conduct advanced research on next-generation process technologies. Finally, a strong and innovative manufacturing sector is able to address major societal challenges, such as climate change, energy and food security, and health and the aging population (Aghion et al. 2011; EC 2014).

This chapter addresses the evolving paths of advanced manufacturing industries[1] in strong regions that are passing through a turbulent phase characterised not only by significant uncertainties but also by meaningful opportunities and great challenges. One of the main changes affecting advanced manufacturing industries is related to a shift in their positioning within global value chains (GVCs). Moreover, the metric of GVCs is changing owing to stronger competition on three main dimensions (WEF-UNIDO 2014): competition over concepts (i.e., creating new products),[2] competition over processes (i.e., manufacturing new products) and competition over markets (i.e., delivering new products).

The real challenge for strong manufacturing regions is the need to upgrade their value chains by enhancing their capabilities (Timmer et al. 2010) and emphasising the new systems nature of manufacturing (O'Sullivan and Mitchell 2013). Core manufacturing regions are well positioned to face this challenge, as they nearly always share some common winning features (Bramanti 2016), including:

- A close relationship between leading-edge research and applications in more mature industries (e.g., mechanical engineering, precision engineering, medical instruments, apparatus building);
- A well-trained (blue collar) labour force as well as a university-educated labour force, with high average incomes; and
- Embeddedness in international networks.

In addition, most of these regions are relatively well positioned on the governance side (Hilpert 2016). They are endowed with capable sub-national governments, which can help them along their development paths. Moreover, they are highly responsive to change. Also, they tend to look to their traditional industrial apparatus for opportunities for innovation-oriented restructuring.

The goals for a new industrial policy are quite clear – to keep advanced regions on a sustainable development path while ensuring international competitiveness and local well-being without major imbalances related to social or environmental issues. However, the possible solutions are widely diversified, and they are deeply marked by the (sometimes divergent) national and regional frames, and rooted in innovative processes that are by no means the 'one-best-way' of the Fordist paradigm.

The chapter is structured in the following way. It starts by focusing on the new role of manufacturing in European developed regions (§ 1). Many territories are at a low point in their historical industrial cycles. However, they are showing reliable prospects for a resurgence in manufacturing sectors in terms of offering a positive contribution to their regions through value-added, investments, high-quality job creation, environmental sustainability and enhanced quality of life.

This positive role is largely the result of the dramatic changes that manufacturing sectors have undergone over the years (§ 2). The future of manufacturing will be very different from its history, and it is probably best captured by the label 'Industry 4.0', which refers to the fourth technological, industrial and societal revolution, which is slowly but steadily spreading across the globe. The trigger of, and the engine behind this fourth revolution is innovation. Moreover, the linkages between industry and open innovation (Chesbrough and Appleyard 2007) are now stronger, more powerful and more pervasive than in the past (Cooke 2012; Bailey et al. 2015).

The core of the chapter is developed in the next section (§ 3), where three national/regional answers to the same meta-goals are discussed. First, the UK case is captured in terms of the emerging need for 'related variety' (Frenken et al. 2007). This concept refers to the path towards smart diversification, which has emerged partly in response to the tyrannical predominance of the financial services economy. The urgency of the issue is even greater given the UK's vote in favour of exiting the European Union (Bailey et al. 2015) (§ 3.1). Second, the German case is depicted in relation to the developing trend of 'Industry 4.0', which characterises the major and deep transformation of the 'joyful war machine' that is the German manufacturing industry (Deloitte 2014; Heng 2014) (§ 3.2). Third, the Italian case is viewed through the lens of the new European policy of 'smart specialisation' (Foray and Goenaga 2013; Foray 2015). The reasons for this choice are twofold. First, the new model of open innovation is gaining momentum (at least in the country's northern regions). Second, Italy has to recover from its poor productivity growth from 1999 to 2013, which requires new alliances between public institutions and private actors (Bramanti and Lazzeri 2016) (§ 3.3).

The conclusion of this section is that the three paths – the renewal of manufacturing sectors through related variety diversification, the strengthening of competitiveness by moving towards Industry 4.0 and the regaining of productivity through smart specialisation – are unified by the role of innovation and by their attention to human capital. These are the two major, intertwined challenges developed regions face in their attempts to reach their planned future (§ 3.4). Different innovation processes are at work in each of the regions, each of which represents a special combination of a specific Regional Innovation System (RIS), a particular industrial mix, a distinct skilled workforce, and a precise form of governance. The outcomes of these combinations of multiple alternatives determine the level of innovativeness found in each territory. At times, this level of innovativeness is imitable (i.e., we can learn from best practices) but it can never be duplicated, as attested to by the numerous abortive attempts to replicate Silicon Valley around the world.

The next section (§ 4) highlights some policy implications arising from the strategies pursued in the three cases. The analysed implications are the place-based character of new industrial policies (§ 4.1), and the impact on job markets and the workforce (§ 4.2).

The final section (§ 5) offers a summary of the main findings on the centrality of innovation that underlie the spatial concentration of innovative efforts, which frequently takes the form of clusterisation. The emerging diversities that are a positive feature of core developed regions in Europe are determined by the quality of institutional endowments and human capital.

This suggests that governance structures are vital for the future competitiveness of any region. This is an area that is open to future research.

The role of manufacturing[3]

The manufacturing sector has one of the highest multiplier effects on the economy, as it is a major driver of knowledge building and job creation (Farshchi et al. 2009). Even though the share of manufacturing activities as a percentage of GDP continues to fall globally, manufacturing still plays a central role in forging capabilities and disseminating knowledge across GVCs (EC 2014).

Notably, de-industrialization is no longer perceived as a natural process of economic development. After decades of delocalisation, a change is underway in the European industrial panorama. The assumption that developed regions should (mainly) focus on knowledge-intensive services has been questioned in the light of the Great Recession (2008–2009). The evidence that developed regions have become too unbalanced and heavily dependent on a small number of business and financial services are widespread (Christopherson et al. 2014). Some are wondering if a new trend of onshoring could soon replace the offshoring trend, thereby reinforcing domestic employment, even if this move may be extremely difficult to achieve (Pisano and Shih 2012; Bailey and de Propis 2014). The trend of moving a significant portion of domestic production abroad has been taken to a dangerous extreme. The persistent trend of exacerbating outsourcing decisions within large firms has caused lasting damage not only to the firms' own capabilities but also to the entire domestic value chain, which encompasses suppliers of materials, tools, production equipment, and components. All of these collective capabilities are referred to as the 'industrial commons' (Pisano and Shih 2009).

In recent decades, many European regions have moved beyond the comparative advantage phase, which centred on factor endowments and cheap costs, into the 'competitiveness phase', which is focused on such elements as standards, infrastructure, education and finance (WEF-UNIDO 2014). However, the shift from competitiveness to global competition is shifting the focus toward a new capabilities phase in which firms attempt to maintain and improve competitiveness in light of declining comparative advantages (Dettori et al. 2013). As this stage tends to be innovation-driven, 'talent' and creative skills are what most matters. It is precisely the role played by innovative workers that changes the economy of cities and regions and enables them to attract other skilled workers up to the point at which these cities and regions leap into the knowledge-based world and become 'winners' (Moretti 2012).

Given these factors, manufacturing is of exceptional importance in this era of globalisation. Today's technological innovations will lead to a massive increase in manufacturing productivity on both the micro and macro scales. Manufacturing is still the second largest of the NACE sections within the EU-28 non-financial business economy in terms of its contribution to employment (30 million employees in 2012, or 22.4% of the total) and the largest contributor to value added by the non-financial business economy (EUR 1,620 billion in 2012, 26.2% of the total). If we look closely at the industrial sector, we find that the EU is the world's largest producer of mechanical engineering equipment, surpassing the US and Japan by far. Total exports of machinery from the EU represent 42% of total mechanical engineering production within the Union, and this share has increased in the last three years.

In addition, the European manufacturing sector is highly active in R&D and innovation. In 2011, the share of gross domestic expenditure on R&D (GERD) relative to GDP was 2.03%. The R&D intensity of mechanical engineering is as high as 3.6% of GDP, having passed well beyond the EU's target of 3% by 2020, and having achieved higher importance for overall technological performance than in the US and Japan (EC 2013).

Even though the EU sometimes struggles to maintain a strong industrial base and a competitive position on the international level, a need to renew coordinated policies at the European level has emerged, it is the need for the implementation of genuine multi-level governance[4] (Hooghe and Marks 2001; Kaiser and Prange 2004; Faludi 2012). 'Multi-level governance' has been used as a simplified notion of pluralistic and highly dispersed policy-making activities in which multiple actors (individuals and institutions) participate at different political levels as if the use of this buzzword will help simplify a rather intricate and difficult-to-manage reality. The focus is on co-ordination and partnership at various stages of the policy-making process.

Manufacturing is changing

A key feature of recent international analyses of the future of manufacturing is the emphasis on the systems nature of the industry. Modern manufacturing systems are constructed around supply chains, which may interact in highly complex ways. A number of major changes are underway: the blurring of traditional sector boundaries; the emergence of complex interdependencies between manufacturing systems and national innovation systems; and a shift towards highly complex products, which are the final point in a range of industries.

Research, development, design, and production are closely intertwined, with complex interdependencies emerging among system elements. In particular, the US Institute for Defence Analysis (IDA 2012) points to a set of converging trends associated with the transition from labour-intensive production to high-value production based on advanced technologies. Among these trends, certain factors are particularly relevant: i) the ubiquitous role of IT, ii) the increasing reliance on modelling and simulation in the manufacturing process and iii) the acceleration of innovation in global supply-chain management, which implies that separating R&D, design and production is impossible.

Over the past decade, a number of analyses have stressed the main features of manufacturing in advanced countries (e.g., O'Sullivan and Mitchell 2013;

Dhéret et al. 2014; Dolphin 2015). Some common elements emerging from those surveys include sustainable manufacturing; production technologies and bio-manufacturing; simulation and modelling; additive manufacturing; and responsive production networks. Moreover, in almost all core regions in advanced economies, producers are seeking out ways to achieve greater product flexibility and to manufacture them at a cost level close to that associated with mass production. This effort calls for a system-thinking approach (Fujimoto 2011), which requires sophisticated levels of coordination in terms of production engineering, design, and technology.

In addition to technological improvements and the ability to answer new, emerging needs, manufacturing systems are on the front line in terms of capturing significant value for the territories in which they are rooted. This entails translating innovations into new products and services and then scaling them up in a way that creates jobs and opportunities for the entire population. A twin area of attention places emphasis on addressing 'demand-pull' social and economic challenges, with specific attention paid to green innovation and life innovation.

In light of the changes mentioned above, a key question arises in the debate on new industrial policies: How do manufacturing systems need to be configured to support economic value creation and value capture? Policy makers, mainly at the regional level, pay significant amounts of attention to the potential to retain and create jobs, and the potential to retain and attract investments. There is a growing awareness that a knowledge economy that fails to interact with its production base may lose the ability to innovate next-generation technologies and, as such, compromise its potential to participate in important emerging industries. This is exactly what has happened to the US manufacturing system, which is threatened by the loss of a great part of the assets – skilled labour and specialised suppliers – required to manufacture many of the cutting-edge products it invented (Pisano and Shih 2009). Therefore, major efforts in national/regional industrial policies are understandably devoted to guiding regional manufacturing systems towards a new path of renewal and innovation.

The uniqueness of innovation – regional paths within a converging frame

This section, which is at the heart of this chapter, is related to three territorial approaches to innovation. It focuses on new industrial policies that are emerging in the UK (West Midlands), Germany (Baden-Württemberg) and Italy (the Lombardy region). Despite significant differences in the macro-frameworks of the three countries, the challenges that European core regions face seem quite similar (Tomaney 2009).

Of the different composite indicators covering innovation activities, the Ambrosetti Innosystem Index has two notable merits (Ambrosetti 2016): it looks at integrated innovation ecosystems in which the results of innovation are determined by interactions among key players (e.g., academia, government, and business), and it is up to date, as the 2016 edition has just been released. The leaders in this ranking are Switzerland (6.80 in the range of 0–10) and South Korea (6.47). Germany ranks fifth, with a rating of 5.67. The UK ranks seventh (5.16), while Italy is next-to-last with a rating of 3.36. A comparison of country innovative performance to performance on the regional level highlights the tremendous differences in the performance of local ecosystems. If we examine the 89 Nuts-2 regions of EU-15, the ratings of our regions are as follows (on a 100-point scale): Baden-Württemberg ranks first with a rating of 85.2, Lombardy is 18th with a rating of 44.3, while East Midlands is 31st (35.5) and West Midlands is 44th (28.0).

Even though a great deal of distance remains among the regions in terms of quantitative indicators of innovativeness, many of them have struggled to maintain their economic dynamism, which sometimes seems to be locked into sectoral profiles reflecting a long-standing over-reliance on existing path dependencies (Bailey et al. 2015). In all of these territories, new industrial-strategy policies are focusing on activity-based, technology-intensive sectors able to produce tradable and exportable goods and services with the potential to enhance national/regional competitiveness. These policies relate to the different needs and capabilities of the various regions, and they affect how and why the individual areas might win or lose (Boschma 2008; Bramanti 2016; Hilpert 2016).

The common denominator in the different strategies pursued by core regions is a shared vision on the future of industry in which manufacturing is (IDA 2012; EC 2013):

- An 'ecosystem' in which a variety of components, materials, production systems and sub-systems, and producer services work together;
- A productive field that prioritises emerging technologies and new research domains;
- A preferential field in which public-private partnerships are developed in areas ranging from pre-competitive consortia to public procurement policy, and in which the role of technical standards in supporting future manufacturing competitiveness emerges and needs to be managed;
- A powerful instrument useful for addressing societal challenges and an instrument that can benefit from a demand-side approach to the market in terms of learning to detect and master the new needs of an increasingly urbanised population.

Cities and metropolitan areas within core regions are increasingly recognised as potential environments for creativity (Hilpert 2016) and as possible drivers of economic growth (Moretti 2012). In fact, cities represent emerging markets for a number of new needs that require prompt answers. When manufacturing sectors learn to serve these new needs (Cappellin 2016), they can exploit the specific, idiosyncratic 'territorial capital' (OECD 2001) present within the cities (and the regions). This capital encompasses a wide set of skills, knowledge, and competences. This is the prerequisite for the development of diversity and technological heterogeneity, which offer uniqueness and distinction within global markets (Boschma 2008). Clearly, region-specific characteristics have a strong influence on innovative output and give rise to different RISs (Braczyk et al. 1998; de la Mothe and Paquet 1998; Niosi 2010; Isaksen and Trippl 2014). These RISs are determined by the innovative environment and research institutions; by the specific industry mix, as characterised by related and unrelated variety (which, in turn, depends on the competences accumulated at the local level); and the workforce and labour-market dynamics, which influence the degree of technological relatedness among different activities (Quatraro 2016).

We look at some successful strategies that are deeply rooted in innovation based on its broader definition,[5] and that target some of the main challenges that the English, German and Italian regions are facing.

The emergence of a 'Phoenix industry' in the Midlands

In the UK's case, it is widely accepted that manufacturing could serve as a rebalancing force that could help the region move from an over-reliance upon consumerism and the financial sector towards more sustainable production activities (Christopherson et al. 2014; Bailey et al. 2015). Even in the heartland of Anglo-American orthodoxy, there is a growing recognition of the need to rebalance economies that are overly focused on service employment and unregulated financial markets. We refer to this trend as the exploitation of 'related variety' (Frenken et al. 2007; Boschma 2008). The idea is simple but effective. Neither regional diversity nor regional specialisation per se may have a significant impact on innovation and change. Rather, regional-related variety is more likely to generate effective interactive learning and innovation. This is linked to diversification which, in turn, is rooted in the existing regional knowledge base. As such, related variety encompasses the two complementary dimensions of external knowledge flows – 'cognitive proximity' (which matters most in this discussion; Boschma 2005; Torre and Rallet 2005) and local 'absorptive capacity' (Cohen and Levinthal 1990; Caragliu and Nijkamp 2008), which is necessary for understanding external knowledge and transforming it into economic growth.

The challenge for industrial strategy in relation to older cities lies in widening their economic diversity, possibly by unlocking their existing expertise, competencies and knowledge bases, and combining them with new, complementary ideas and technologies in adjacent, related sectors (Moretti 2012). If industries downsize or disappear completely, their resources (including their skilled employees) are released. Intra-industry networks play an important role in enabling job seekers to find a job in the same or a related industry. Therefore, the competencies accumulated at the local level are important for shaping the process of industrial diversification – a change in the allocation of employees across sectors is influenced by the degree of technological related-ness among the involved activities (Cooke 2012; Morkuté et al. 2016).

Another benefit of labour pooling is that fluctuations in a firm's labour demand can be more easily accommodated. Consequently, all else equal, the unemployment rate in this situation will be lower than the rate achieved in any other way.

The problem in this regard is the need to increase exports of cutting-edge, high-quality manufactured products (Dolphin 2014). Frequently, old indus-trial cities seem to be locked into old ways of doing things. Moreover, although they have some key assets that can support process and product innovations, those assets may be difficult to move. This phenomenon has been described as the emergence of 'Phoenix industries'[6] (Christophenson 2009; Tomaney 2009), which are clusters of SMEs that are born of the ashes of pre-existing large firms and share similar technologies. They benefit from the firms' sunken investments, including the accumulation of technical know-ledge and workforce skills over the years. They add new R&D and, as a result, are able to produce sophisticated components for different industries. As such, they take on the role of 'enabling industries' (Amison and Bailey 2014).

In the UK, just as in the US,[7] several Phoenix industries have developed in the last decade. Sheffield (UK), for instance, has moved from production of routine steel products to the production of high-quality products for spe-cialised markets, such as surgical instruments (Christophenson 2009). The implementation of this kind of industrial rejuvenation requires working closely with SMEs, which are frequently the main actor in the downstream processes associated with new products.

One success story has emerged in the West Midlands,[8] where small, niche firms have developed an important presence in automotive design and engin-eering out of the disappearance of UK vehicle producers. Significant invest-ments were made in the automotive sector over an extended period, allowing for the accumulation of territorial capital (OECD 2001) and the creation of 'industrial commons' (Pisano and Shih 2012), which are innovation-prone environments in which knowledge and skills related to old technologies and emerging ones are combined.

According to the literature (Christophenson 2009; Amison and Bailey 2013, 2014), the necessary (but not necessarily sufficient) conditions for the birth of Phoenix industries are the following: i) the presence of relevant skills in the workforce and among potential suppliers, ii) technical skills and expert-ise in nearby universities and research facilities, iii) personal networks and market knowledge related to the focal industries, iv) reputational factors, and v) capital for investments. Apart from capital availability,[9] all of these condi-tions are present in the Midlands case. The skills necessary to manufacture innovative products or components are embedded within local firms' work-forces, even though some of these skills may be lost as the workforce ages. Expertise and specialisations are retained within local universities (e.g.,

Coventry, Warwick, Oxford, Birmingham). If we take SMEs and local academia together, we have an impressive pool of automotive- and engineering-related expertise. Furthermore, the area has been able to attract suppliers of vehicle-design and engineering services despite the loss of major big car manufacturers (e.g., the closure of MG Rover in 2005).

In the Midlands, SMEs play a central role in providing the more radical innovation needed for systemic change in the automotive sectors. In addition, and even more interestingly, many SMEs are serving industries beyond the automotive sector. Their innovation efforts are oriented towards aerospace, defence, and motorsports, as well as renewable energy and medical technology.

Given the reasoning developed in this chapter, a question emerges: Did industrial policy play a proactive role in triggering and/or sustaining this structural change? The answer is, at least to some degree, affirmative. For instance, the extent of collaboration among firms, and between firms and research institutions has been strongly supported by public programmes and R&D funds. Besides, regional policies have to play a positive role. They should address industry partnerships in terms of enhancing productivity and making room for innovation; bringing SMEs together and enabling them to act as more powerful networks; and directing public investments in a way that strengthens the linkages among the university system, local development agents and manufacturing firms (as in the case of the Marine Design Centre established in Newcastle to create a new industry from the old shipbuilding manufacturers).

In summary, new industrial policies aimed at promoting diversification through related variety must support industrial clusters. These clusters exert many positive impacts in the field of innovation, lead to productivity gains that enhance entrepreneurialism, and support economic diversification. In developed regions around the world, clusters represent proven areas of competitive advantage that also support high wages and high-skill levels (Dolphin 2014).

Two policy interventions are probably essential for the Midlands clusters. First, some form of support is needed to move from the prototype stage to the production stage, as the process of scaling up production of a new product to the point of full commercialisation is often difficult for SMEs to carry out on their own. One way to achieve this goal may be to create projects, such as joint procurement bids, that can support regional/national demand (we will see a similar challenge in the Lombardy case).

The second area of intervention is in the Vocational Education and Training (VET) system. The aims in this regard should be to provide the skills needed by firms, to address the skill gaps in the science, technology, engineering and math (STEM) subjects and to address the need for people with vocational skills (i.e., a number of firms in the area note that the younger generation of workers does not have the same practical skills as the older generation). The market for skilled labour is rapidly growing, as a significant number of global players have located their research facilities in the West

Midlands (e.g., Jaguar-Land Rover, Tata Motors, MIRA, Ricardo UK). Their investment choices have opened the local labour market up to a more national and global dimension. Many firms have declared that they have exhausted the local supply of required specialised skills and are therefore recruiting internationally.

On these grounds, employers within clusters need to work together to iden-tify future skills needs, and to coordinate, plan and purchase skills training. They need to develop transversal competencies within their workforces – such as problem-solving, critical thinking, initiative, risk-taking and collaboration. This implies that VET curricula should be transformed. This change will be better planned at the cluster level, working together with training suppliers.

The German 'Industry 4.0' approach in Baden-Württemberg

Baden-Württemberg is one of the leading regions for research, not only in Germany but also in Europe. This German Länd has the highest share of GDP spent on R&D as well as the highest number of patent applications per million inhabitants.

In 2013, the proportion of R&D expenditure in relation to GDP in Baden-Württemberg was 4.8% (the corresponding figure for all of Germany: 2.8%). Baden-Württemberg is, therefore, one of the leading regions in an international comparison, as the region's research intensity rate of 4.8% is the highest in the European Union. It is clearly in the lead when compared to other top-spending countries, such as Finland and Sweden (both at 3.3%). The predom-inant investor in R&D in Baden-Württemberg is the industrial sector, which has numerous in-house research facilities. In 2013, the industrial sector alone contributed almost 81% of the total R&D investments in the Länd, while the university sector was responsible for 8.7% and the public sector for 8.7%. With more than 100 R&D institutions, the public sector offers a broad spectrum of non-university research institutions. 13 of the 83 Max Planck institutes and 15 of the 67 Fraunhofer institutes, as well as 25% of the Helmholtz Association of German Research Centres' research facilities, are based in this region. In add-ition, more than 70 universities are located in Baden-Württemberg, including three of Germany's eleven elite universities. In addition to this strong and rich RIS, other key points are the cooperative industrial relations, and the close, long-term relations between banks and firms.

This region is therefore extremely well positioned to meet the potential of the new 'Industry 4.0' trend.[10] The German government is wholeheartedly sponsoring Industry 4.0, a multi-year strategic initiative that brings together leaders from the public sector, the private sectors and academia to create a comprehensive vision and action plan for applying digital technologies to the industrial sector.

In essence, Industry 4.0 involves deep and useful exchanges among actors operating in the fields of electronics, electrical engineering, mechanical engin-eering and IT. Such networks are particularly well developed and functional in the southern Länd of Baden-Württemberg, which can also count on such elements as a good educational system, established development partnerships between suppliers and users, market leadership in plant and mechanical engineering, strong and dynamic SMEs, and a position as the leading innovator in automatic methods (Heng 2014).

The role that Germany can play in Europe and that Baden-Württemberg can play in Germany is to lead the fourth industrial revolution, thereby enhancing EU competitiveness and offering an answer to some grand societal challenges (e.g., renewable resources, quality of life, active aging). Without overemphasising the role of interregional innovation spillovers, the southern Länd is well positioned to ensure widespread innovation throughout Europe.

It has a strong, well-established research network with many external linkages. To name but a few, this network includes the Heidelberg Academy of Sciences and Humanities, two Helmholtz Centres, six institutes of the German Aeronautics and Space Research Centre DLR, 12 institutes of the Baden-Württemberg Innovation Alliance, the Centre for European Economic Research (ZEW), the Max Rubner Institute, and the Federal Waterways Engineering and Research Institute.[11]

It is endowed with a number of large, multinational enterprises that weave a network of direct and indirect relationships. 2,000 companies have 250 employees or more. Of these, the 10 biggest companies include four automotive multinationals (Dailmler AG, Robert Bosch GmbH, ZF Friedrichshafen AG and Porsche AG), two wholesale pharma companies (Phoenix Group and Celesio AG), and companies belonging to the following industries: retail (Schwartz-Gruppe), energy (EnBW AG), software (SAP AG) and construction material (Heidelberg Cement AG).

It operates as the leading partner in articulated value chains, which gives rise to trust and a shared identity. This, in turn, facilitates collaboration with both firms and suppliers, as well as among personnel employed in partnered firms. According to the 'Competence Atlas' (Ministry of Finance and Economic Affairs B-W 2014) there are around 400 actors with Industry 4.0 competencies, with specialisation in niche markets with the presence of global leaders in their particular fields. They include Trumpf in laser technology, Festo in automatisation technology, Alfred Karcher in cleaning systems, ebm-papst in ventilation and drive engineering, Homag in woodworking machinery and Fischerwerke in fastening products.

One of the most interesting lessons from the Industry 4.0 process in Baden-Württemberg is that regional capabilities[12] are more than just competences. In regional development, the combination and creative interaction of existing assets are key. Within this region, a production system, a set of actors, a system of representation and an industrial culture have given rise to a dynamic, localised process of collective learning, which serves to reduce uncertainty in innovative processes (Ratti et al. 1997).

Many regions around Europe compete on some single component of the complex puzzle. However, to enable the discontinuity leap that will lead to the breakthrough of the fourth industrial revolution, a fully integrated, intelligent environment is needed, an environment in which the boundaries between industry and services, and among the different sectors become increasingly blurred. The impact on the economy should be highly pervasive, allowing for greater efficiency, increased flexibility, lower costs, reduced time requirements, and easier adaptations to customer requirements.

Obviously, this complex and ambitious outcome cannot occur without specific effort. In fact, it will entail addressing technical, economic, organisational and legal challenges, which is exactly where the 'German system' can make a difference (Industry-Science Research Alliance 2013; PwC, Strategy 2014) by enabling the numerous actors along the value chain to work together; coordinating public and private investments, and properly subsidising the latter; offering legal protection and addressing those risks arising from the imperfect appropriability of knowledge; providing suitable financing for the investments required; and ensuring job training and re-training for all workers affected by the radical changes occurring within organisations and on the job market.

Regions that have activated the positive cycle of innovation-productivity-growth are those that seem best positioned in terms of long-term systemic competitiveness. They also experienced greater resilience in the current crisis (Sedita et al. 2015; Fratesi and Rodríguez-Pose 2016). The uniqueness of the RIS functioning in the Länd under analysis consists of the idiosyncratic elements and relationships that interact in the production, accumulation, diffusion, and exchange of new, economically useful knowledge. The Länd is endowed with an economic community with robust system characteristics of mutual understanding, trust, and reciprocity. This community, in turn, can channel flows of information to its members. The region has its own social filter in which innovative and conservative components are combined. This social filter is highly influenced and shaped by local innovation institutions (Ratti et al. 1997).

However, the vision sometimes precedes reality. Due to the radical changes involved in the building of the new market scenario, a variety of opposing forces are at work (Heng 2014). They are mainly related to the marked changes in value chains and in generated margins; the wide-ranging fears about losing jobs or having one's responsibilities curtailed; uncertainties linked to the lack of generally applicable standards; and bottlenecks that may arise in communication networks in relation to availability and speed.

The economy of Baden-Württemberg appears well positioned to drive this complex upgrading process, as it is strong enough concerning technologies and competences, and inclusive enough in the labour market and in terms of societal-participation processes. Nevertheless, the region needs to further strengthen industrial co-operation (i.e., ensure a true coalescence) among the fields of electrical engineering, mechanical engineering, electronics and IT. In other words, it must work toward fully integrating the regional innovation system with the production system while applying even greater efforts concerning the VET and education systems.

The likely rewards of such an effort are significant. The impact of Industry 4.0 on the Germany economy is expected to be strongly positive and sizable in three different respects over a time horizon of only five years (Heng 2014; PwC, Strategy 2014):

- Productivity should increase via diminishing costs, and better management of both horizontal and vertical value chains. Companies directly involved in the process expect productivity to rise by more than 18% over the next five years.
- Average revenue growth related to the Internet of things and services is estimated at 2–3% per year.
- Investments in Industry 4.0 solutions should account for more than 50% of planned capital investment for the next five years, reaching the threshold of EUR 200 billion by 2020.

A relevant issue is related to the impact of the fourth industrial revolution on the labour market, as the revolution will entail a radical reshuffling within the workforce. The technological progress will deeply change the workforce from both a quantitative and qualitative point of view. In the coming decades, 45% to well over 60% of workers from EU-28 countries could see themselves displaced due to computerisation. At the same time, digital literacy will become critically important:

> Jobs that are not at risk of computerisation have something in common: they require and understanding of human heuristics or involve the creation of a novel idea – that is, they require social or creative skills. Many jobs in management, education or healthcare that involve social interaction, therefore, are unlikely to be automated. Similarly, science or engineering jobs that require creative skills will probably not see substantial job losses due to technological advances in the near future.
>
> (Dolphin 2015: 77)

However, there are also reasons to be optimistic about the future demand for employees. The loss of manufacturing jobs in the EU appears to have stopped. At the same time, a skill shortage exists and will probably increase in the medium term. According to Cedefop (2013), in a baseline scenario, EU-27 employment should return to its pre-crisis level between 2017 and 2018, after which it should steadily increase. Job opportunities will be associated with responding to expansion demand and replacement demand. As the replacement component is almost the same in various scenarios, the differences in terms of forecasting mainly relate to how well the economy generates new jobs (around 114 million job opportunities in Europe between 2012 and 2025). Most newly created jobs will require a higher skills level (e.g., technicians and associate professionals).

The competition will increasingly focus on the quality of products and services that only people with the right skills can deliver. According to Cedefop (2013) forecasts, jobs at all skill levels will become less routine and more demanding. Therefore, even the high-quality, above-average workforce of the southern Länder needs to focus on upgrading its digital skills and on continuous lifelong learning, as the digital skills of today are likely to become obsolete sooner than we may think.

In conclusion, we agree that Germany is well positioned to act as the factory outfitter of the world. It has a strong VET and educational system, which may provide the right skills in the labour market of the future. It has an imposing tradition of managing technical standards, as well as the political power and technical credibility needed to enforce those standards at the European level. It also has the core asset needed to co-ordinate a complex and difficult process – a governance structure that is up to taking on the role as well as the challenge.

The 'smart specialisation' strategy in Lombardy

The Lombardy region has used the smart specialisation strategy (S3) to escape the conventional top-down approach in which a policy is defined ex-ante, implemented mechanically and controlled ex-post. The new strategy blends the selection of some macro areas (called 'competence systems') with a bottom-up entrepreneurial process of discovery (Foray and Goenaga 2013; Foray 2015) that encompasses firms, higher education institutions, independent inventors and research centres. In short, all the stakeholders of the RIS are involved in S3 (Morgan 2013).

Lombardy and other regions in northern Italy have used the European S3 approach to match the presence of rich 'territorial capital' (OECD 2001) with a strong RIS. In so doing, Lombardy has adopted an open-innovation approach[13] (Chesbrough and Appleyard 2007), which is matched with strong regional manufacturing clusters.

To what extent does S3 differ from the strategies in the Phoenix industries and Industry 4.0 cases? At first glance, the Phoenix and Industry 4.0 cases may appear to be variations of S3 relevant for the UK and Germany. However, upon careful scrutiny, several differences emerge that enable us to consider the Lombardy case as a specific, distinct version of new industrial policies.

The pre-existence of major assemblers and the fact that the industry is limited to only one value chain (i.e., automotive) are two main features that distinguish the phoenix industries in the English case from a more generic S3 strategy. In the Lombardy experience, the focal competence systems are related to the nine pre-existing clusters, but no one sector is dominant. In the German case, Industry 4.0 is an all-encompassing strategy that goes far beyond a pure S3 strategy. That case involves numerous ingredients. An S3 strategy is by no means all-encompassing or as highly demanding as the design underlying Industry 4.0, which asks for perfect synchronisation among the different components of the new industrial system, as well as full integration of technologies, organisations, and people.

Moreover, there is a contingent situation that makes the Lombardy case unique: the political context in which citizens, for the first time, voted for the Council of the newly established 'Milan metropolitan area' (the election took place on June 19, 2016). Regarding governance, a new public actor will soon be at work. The S3 strategy relates to the entire region, but the metropolitan area of Milan will play a key role, as its weight, in economic terms equals approximately 50% of the entire region.

Finally, the availability of the site of Expo 2015 (the international exposition that closed its gates at the end of September 2015) is notable. This location, which has excellent infrastructure and is connected with the city of Milan, can be utilised as an industrial park devoted to innovative production and tertiary-level vocational training.

As mentioned above, the region can rely on a number of existing clusters. In fact, nine clusters have been officially recognised by the Italian Ministry of Industry: aerospace, agrifood, green chemistry, energy and the environment, smart plant, mobility, life sciences, living environments, and smart communities. The region can also utilise the new open-innovation platform[14] as an experimental lab (Bramanti 2015a) to mobilise SMEs and researchers. Entrepreneurial discoveries arising within the clusters may result in new value-chain strategies aimed at responding to citizens' new needs.

In the Lombardy region, a central role is played by medium-tech sectors, which combine well-made products with the trend towards incremental innovation and the recombination of different types of knowledge (Cappellin and Wink 2009). This is a type of ongoing innovation with a strong market-pull orientation, which horizontally involves all of the different functions in the firm – managers, technicians and blue-collar workers – in a circular, ongoing accumulation of know-how that nurtures a system capability and produces industrial commons (Confindustria Lombarda 2016).

The European S3 approach is well suited in this territorial context, as it allows for the concentration of resources in a few industrial domains. This has the valuable result of generating size and critical mass effects. In addition, regional firms have the opportunity to tackle society's problems through a new stream of broad collaboration among business, academia and the government. This process is pulled by market demand, which is closely linked to new urban needs and grand societal challenges, such as housing; mobility and logistics; energy and the environment; new urban industrial supply chains; health, welfare and education; and culture, tourism, leisure, sports, the media and the Internet (Cappellin 2016). Moreover, the presence of established clusters supports the development of collective actors with the view to discovering, exploring and experimenting with new opportunities. All of these preconditions enable Lombardy to restore the capabilities of its enterprises in developing and manufacturing new products, thereby reversing the decline in productivity and competitiveness that has occurred over the past decade.

In addition, the Lombardy region is taking part in the international Vanguard Initiative [www.s3vanguardinitiative.eu/], a European network born in November 2013 with the aim of coordinating the efforts of 30 EU regions to better align their regional specialisation strategies. The Initiative is committed to the creation of a platform[15] designed to generate bottom-up ideas, and to support synergies and alignment on an inter-regional level. It is focused on advanced manufacturing, and it develops pilot activities to foster interregional cooperation, the exchange of good practices, and the alignment of roadmaps to achieve complementarities. A specific Lombardy pilot node, which is connected to the electromechanical sector, includes the opening of a laboratory as well as the installation and integration of a reconfigurable and intelligent semi-automatic line designed to assembly different products that gather the several features on an electromechanical product. For this pilot node, which is expected to be in place by the end of 2016, the potential market – including end users, technology providers and machine providers – was clearly identified. In terms of funding opportunities, potential EU 'Horizon 2020' calls have been selected.

On a final note, the issue of the technical formation of human capital must be mentioned. Lombardy has a VET system that is better than the Italian average, but the implementation of the S3 strategy is a perfect occasion to rethink the VET curricula and training. A new, regional VET system that helps people innovate is needed. This basically implies the development of transversal competences and soft skills, such as problem-solving, critical thinking, creativity, initiative, learning to learn and to take risks, reflection, and collaboration. A new frontier for regional VET will be to validate non-formal and informal learning with the aim of increasing effectiveness and bringing out the on-the-job experiences of the workforce. In the Lombardy context, VET may become an innovation driver. An easy way to reach this goal is to involve a large number of firms in the process, thereby enhancing what has been called the 'educational firm' (Bramanti 2015b).

Unifying trends towards new industrial policies

The unifying trends in these different approaches are clear and can be summarised in three main points: the existence of a well-structured RIS, which enjoys the presence of leading firms and top-rated research institutions; the ongoing switch from product/services systems to services through products (a solution-oriented approach); and the strength of regional relations (horizontal as well as vertical) together with a high degree of international connections, all of which enable the productive systems to master the state-of-the-art of their core technologies.

Some features of the three territorial experiences examined here are highlighted in Table 11.1. The shared characteristics are the high level of

Table 11.1 Three delineations of new industrial policies

Areas	England (West Midlands)	Germany (Baden-Württemberg)	Italy (Lombardy region)
New industrial policies: main strategies	Related variety Rise of 'Phoenix industries'	'Industry 4.0'	'Smart Specialisation Strategy' (S3)
Main actors involved	SMEs Research institutions Labour market	RIS Firms (value chains) Government	Territorial clusters Research institutions Regional government
Multi-level governance		European Commission	
	Central UK government Local authorities	Federal German government Länder	Central Italian government Regions
Territorial capital and industrial commons	Industrial commons Sunken investments Skilled jobs Networks of suppliers	Strong networks between research institutions and firms Vocational training	Skilled jobs Network of suppliers Medium-sized firms leading the value chain Research institutions
Critical points	Integration of industrial research and production (scaling up) Availability of financial resources	Financing of new system's investments Tight coordination	Public-private co-ordination Risk sharing Vocational training Quality of government

Source: Author's own elaboration.

territorial capital and the strong RISs present in the different regions. Similarities also emerge from a comparison of Phoenix industries and smart specialisation, as the concept of diversifying through related variety is shared by these two strategies. The strengths of the cases are:

- A well-educated, technically skilled workforce, and good relations between firms and research institutions in the Midlands region;
- The power of the RIS in Baden-Württemberg together with a well-performing governance structure; and
- The presence of well-established clusters with good relations between leading medium-sized firms and a diffused network of suppliers in the Lombardy region.

We must also consider the alliance networks shared by a large number of firms within each region. The extent to which a firm is indirectly connected to other firms enhances its innovativeness, while the diversity of knowledge distributed across clusters provides the variety that strengthens regional resilience (Sedita et al. 2015; Fratesi and Rodríguez-Pose 2016). In addition, the three regions share some characteristics that help retain the positive effects of knowledge creation in the region: cognitive proximity among the different actors in the RISs, strong relational capital and careful management of collective goods.

Among the critical points that may eventually evolve into weaknesses are:

- The problem of 'scaling up' good prototype solutions in the English experience;
- The need for a tight co-ordination process in the German case together with the search for adequate financial resources given the huge amount of investments needed by the innovation system; and
- The difficulties associated with developing effective public-private partnerships in the Italian case together with the continued inadequacy of the regional VET system.

A common implication for labour markets and the workforce can be derived from the structural changes underway within the regions. New industries and new specialisations will generate new types of jobs requiring greater analytical abilities and skills in the use of digital technology; creative problem-solving; complex forms of communication; and collaboration and the ability to adapt to unfamiliar situations (i.e., dynamic flexibility). Therefore, current producers have to enhance their workforce's competencies, identify key areas for improvement and offer the right incentives. In many sectors – even those not directly connected with new manufacturing – firms may have to adapt roles, recruitment, and vocational training to provide their workforce with the additional IT skills that will be required.

When technological change is skill-based, and the labour supply fails to keep up with the demand for skilled jobs, inequality tends to increase (Dolphin 2015). On the larger scale of the European labour market, this trend is clearly emerging. A new pattern of job polarisation is evident in almost every country with an increase in low-level jobs in the social (caring) services and in personal services (more evident in the UK than in many other European countries); a declining proportion of mid-ranked jobs in such areas as administration and production; and a steady increase in highly skilled jobs resulting from task-based technological change.

Since the first study demonstrating the hollowing out of the UK labour market (Goos and Manning 2007), a number of studies have been carried out in the UK. Similar studies have been undertaken in the US (over the period 1980–2005) (Autor and Dorn 2009), Germany (1979–1999 and 1985–2008, including the Hartz reforms) (Kampelmann and Rycx 2011) and Sweden (1975–2005) (Andermon and Gustavsson 2011). Additional studies followed, using data at the European level and covering 16 countries (Goos et al. 2009). The results are the same across the board – an increase in the number of jobs in the highest quantile (or decile) and a corresponding increase in the lowest-quantile jobs, regardless of differences in the degree of protection and variations among labour-market institutions. This serves as strong evidence of a 'declining middle' in each country (McIntosh 2013).

These trends ask for renewed attention to be paid to the demand side of both the economy and the labour market in order to anticipate new societal needs related to personal services, environmental protection and quality of life. At the same time, policy is needed to provide the supply side of the labour market with answers, an effort that will involve the educational sector, the adaptation of school curricula, changes to training and tertiary education programmes, the strengthening of entrepreneurial approaches to increase IT-related skills and innovation abilities, and the expansion and upgrading of regional VET systems in order to produce a new technician class endowed with more systemic competences and soft skills.

Some policy implications

EU industrial policy is still far from a full-fledged and integrated strategy (EC 2014). After decades in which industrial policy has been held in low regard, it is time for it to once again take centre stage (Bianchi and Laboury 2016).

Governments are increasingly making innovation a key issue, recognising its potential to promote economic growth, and its ability to address societal and environmental challenges. This is true in all advanced regions, even where diverse innovation processes have emerged. This demonstrates that geographical context matters, and that this context is understood as including social, cultural and institutional characteristics (Ratti et al. 1997). We also need to consider the fact that processes of technological learning are cumulative and take time. Differences in geographical locations plus differences in the learning process require diverse policies. Therefore, it is not surprising that each region has taken its own route.

In the West Midlands (UK), the resurgence of a part of the automotive value chain has been pulled by highly specialised SMEs in niche segments of automotive design and engineering, while it has been pushed by a pool of relevant skills – technical and market knowledge – in the local workforce and among supplier firms. This creates conditions under which open innovation can be successful (Amison and Bailey 2014; Bailey and de Propis 2014). With the goal of strengthening the automotive cluster, the UK government has developed in 2014 a GBP 245 million "Advanced Manufacturing Supply Chain Initiative" [16] This fund can be used for capital expenditures, skills and training, and R&D projects. The implementation of the Initiative has been supported by the Automotive Council and by the Society of Motor

Manufactures and Traders, which has brought assemblers and suppliers together to determine whether more components can be sourced locally.

It is impossible to offer a full evaluation of the initiative, especially as the overall progress is fairly limited and considerable progress is required before the programme achieves its output targets. However, the response among beneficiaries (in terms of the number of requests versus the available budget) has been positive. The projects that have been launched to date are generating a positive impact by strengthening the supply chain in manufacturing activities (BIS 2015).

In the Southern Länd of Baden-Württemberg, the entire manufacturing system benefits from a strong, globally competitive position. However, the region needs to think about its future. In the automotive industry – one of the leading sectors in the German economy with revenue of EUR 357 billion in 2012 – future challenges are likely to relate to increasing the value of cars from the customer's point of view. Concerning the products, alternative drive systems are a first answer. These alternatives must match emerging needs in terms of safety, comfort, and efficiency.[17] Beyond product innovation, more far-reaching changes will relate to the mobility concept and related services. By 2020, about one-fifth of the global market for mobility is expected to relate to services that exclude private car ownership (Bormann et al. 2015). The idea of supplying global services as the most powerful way to increase the value of products is exactly what Industry 4.0 is prepared to deliver. 'Sharing' seems to be becoming the new philosophy of consumption, not only in the automotive sector. However, such sharing is only possible with a strict alliance between car producers and a number of other service providers, all of which must be gathered together within the framework of Industry 4.0.

Baden-Württemberg aims to become the leader in Industry 4.0 and has launched the 'Alliance Industry 4.0 Baden-Württemberg'. The region has an excellent starting position, as it is the centre of German mechanical and systems engineering, as well as home to premium enterprises active in the automotive industry and their suppliers. This, together with a leading information and communication technology cluster, means that the region covers a full range of technologies for the production of the future, and it aims to confirm itself as a leading industrial-equipment provider.

The Alliance, which is guided by a steering group of 23 high-level representatives of companies, associations, research institutions and trade unions, has been structured in different working groups (WG). For instance, the Technology and Products WG provides support for research projects that are to be implemented by research institutions in cooperation with businesses. The Transfer and Implementation in SMEs working group provides SMEs with an orientation that helps them find their own way to Industry 4.0. The Work and Organisation WG devotes itself to the support of employees and the design of specific training projects. The fulfillment of these goals requires an excellent educational system for engineers, specialist technicians and scientists, and places requirements on the organisation and structure of regional clusters of leading firms.

In the Lombardy case (IT), the S3 strategy leverages on the existence of different clusters with good governance mechanisms. It allows for large firms to be put together with SMEs, technology providers, universities and research institutions to work towards strengthening the demand-side attention paid to the market in terms of new societal needs. Two clusters deserve specific attention in this regard. The first is the aerospace cluster, which is well widespread in the region and highly competitive, especially in the helicopters segment. Large system integrators are present in the region, as are equipment suppliers, engineering services and high-level design services. The productive partners match established university departments. The regional government is working to enforce research on, and production of, the next aeronautic platform as well as innovative electro-avionics systems, with a specific focus on the involvement of innovative SMEs in the cluster. The second cluster is related to advanced manufacturing with the aim of developing new production systems suitable for horizontal use in a number of different end-user industries (see § 3.3).

A new law ('Lombardy is research'), which is under consideration and undergoing a process of public consultation, aims to strengthen regional intervention in these fields. The law points to:

- Strengthening the governance of the RIS with a steering committee, and defining a strategic programme for search and innovation.
- Developing the operational instruments needed to implement the regional strategy. These instruments include partnership agreements, pre-commercial public tenders and contracts, co-funding schemes, and investments in digital infrastructure.
- Setting up a regional agency for the Research, Innovation and Technological Transfer (ARRITT) as an operative arm on the political level.
- Supporting and fostering a Ph.D. programme in innovation, a higher-education programme involving firms as well as universities in the field of technology and applied sciences.

A key impact of these new industrial policies devoted to innovation is found in the job market. A new industry calls for a new workforce. However, at the same time, only the right skills can be conducive to the structural modification of manufacturing (Beaven et al. 2014; Dolphin 2015).

Policy implications from the newly emerging industrial paradigm are therefore far-reaching and deeply challenging. In this section, we specifically address just two of them, both of which are widely horizontal and relatively general. As such, they are adaptable to all three territorial cases. The first policy implication is the place-based character that new industrial policies should have if they wish to contribute to regional growth through knowledge accumulation and production diversification (Barca 2009; Garcilazo et al.

2010; Bramanti and Lazzeri 2016). The second is related to the fundamental shift in the types of jobs that will be available for workers and the skills demanded by employers across Europe (Hilpert and Lawton Smith 2012; Beaven et al. 2014).

The place-based dimensions of new industrial policies

The foundations for new place-based approaches are rooted in the necessity of distributing policy design and implementation among different policy levels in order to tailor policy measures to local conditions. If local growth is not truly place-based, then what is the alternative? We are not interested in entering the ill-fated debate on the place-based approach considered as 'old regional policies in new bottle' (Gill 2009) nor in simplifying it by setting up false dichotomies between place-based and people-centred approaches:

> It is obvious that good economic policies should be 'people-centred', in the sense that they should maximise welfare (…). We argue that in order to maximise aggregate growth and welfare, economic policies may in some instances have to take the spatial or territorial dimensions into account.
>
> (Garcilazo et al. 2010)

A place-based approach is characterised by the production of bundles of integrated, place-tailored public goods and services, which are designed and implemented by eliciting and aggregating local preferences and knowledge through the participation of political institutions (Barca 2009). A place-based approach looks at what Garry Pisano (Pisano and Shih 2012) calls the 'industrial commons', which is related to the networks of jobs and knowledge, and to the pool of innovative suppliers and potential partners. Many experiences from around the world suggest that a cumulative virtuous cycle is at work in locations where industrial commons are strong. For instance, the Swiss pharmaceutical giant Novartis chose to move its research headquarters from Basel, Switzerland to Cambridge, Massachusetts to be close to universities and research institutions that are global leaders in the biosciences, and to the hundreds of biotech firms already in that area (Pisano and Shih 2009).

All three cases described here include investments in a specific industrial commons with the support of appropriate system policies. This is exactly why the governance of the entire process is of extraordinary importance (Hooghe and Marks 2001; Faludi 2012; Stephenson 2013) – a typical multi-level, multi-actor system represents the core of the process of defining objectives, setting priorities, and designing and implementing specific investments. As a consequence, policy coordination is essential for overcoming the old top-down scheme of linear innovation policies or national-champion industrial policies.

The new industrial policies exemplified here – phoenix industries, Industry 4.0, and smart specialisation – are all rooted in a mix of top-down and bottom-up approaches that typically belong to multi-level governance schemes. In this regard, it is important to note that vertical policy co-ordination tends to be very complicated because actors share decision-making competencies at different territorial levels.

Even within the framework of overall policy objectives on the European level, there is room for tailored interventions at the regional level. In both Germany and Italy, priorities are to be decided in negotiations between the federal/national level and the Länder/regional level. Multi-level governance creates a problem of coordination and challenges the efficiency of the different administrations given the clearly defined distinctions of responsibilities.

Germany has a long tradition of co-operation between the different territorial levels, and Länder are involved in joint policy co-ordination processes at the federal level. However, the Länder have also fostered regional innovation policies which, in turn, have:

> Gained importance as an instrument of competition and differentiation among the states, while the federal level has focused its activities either on cross-cutting infrastructural programmes or specialized priority programmes funding technologies at a pre-competitive stage.
>
> (Kaiser and Prange 2004: 255)

Italy has experienced some difficulties in the co-ordination phase. These difficulties led to the recent revision of the Constitution (Article 5), which reduced the power and competences of regions relative to the national level. In contrast to other European contexts, the regional resources for new industrial policies in Italy come almost entirely from the European structural funds. As such, staying within the operational programmes (ERDF) is compulsory, as is adjusting the regional priorities to fit the European guidelines, even though policy makers try to preserve some degree of flexibility (Bramanti 2015a).

In conclusion, place-based approaches require adaptation of the governance structures in a way that allows for the formulation and implementation of regional policies. Moreover, the quality of government institutions has become a determinant factor in the improvement of regional innovative performance (Rodríguez-Pose et al. 2014). As such, good institutions seem to be a significant pre-condition for the development of innovative regional potential and for ensuring that S3 works properly.

Labour market changes and new job skills

In terms of the second policy implication, we must recognise that Europe will lose many low-skilled manufacturing jobs over the next ten years (with the risk that mid-skill jobs will also be affected), while demand for workers with high-level skills able to complement the new technologies is likely to rise (McIntosh 2013; Beaven et al. 2014). In particular, technological innovation will have a significant impact on labour markets over the next decade. Up to 45% of jobs in the US and a similar percentage in Europe are at risk from digitalisation (Dolphin 2015). The demand for technical talent is likely to drive a shift in job creation within the manufacturing industry toward a situation requiring more qualified personnel on the shop floor.

Productivity gains from technological innovations will increasingly accrue to the owners of technology and the relatively few workers required to operate it, while a vast majority of the workforce may face stagnant real wages at best and unemployment at worst. New jobs will require people with entrepreneurial, scientific, creative and emotional skills. Therefore, new jobs will result in demand for workers trained in cross-functional areas, and with the capabilities needed to manage new processes and information systems. Thus far, these requirements are not very well developed, and some skills deficits will be a major problem over the next ten years. A new approach to skills policy will, therefore, be imperative, not only for the enhancement of competencies within the existing workforce but also for helping local job markets enhance employees' skills levels to match those demanded by employers.

A new industrial policy also needs to encourage higher levels of innovation among firms. It must also help a sizeable number of firms that are not currently engaged in innovation to become so. What skills do such firms need if they are to become more innovative? What changes in training policy and institutions might help develop those skills?

To preserve a high level of regional innovation, we need numerous jobs at the top level of the workforce distribution. In fact, a recent study prepared by the OECD (2015) shows evidence of a positive association between firms' involvement in innovation and proxy measures of skills as workforce qualifications. Many of the key mechanisms through which skills influence innovative performance are connected with new technologies. In addition, skills are an essential ingredient of firms' absorptive capacity (Caragliu and Nijkamp 2008).

New manufacturing will imply an increasing level of inter-organisational cooperation and communication, making networking and interconnectedness a focal component of Industry 4.0. As a consequence, the learning curve within production networks should steepen. At the same time, the number of external partners involved in collaborations will rise.

All of the observed regions are endowed with a relatively high-skilled workforce and can count on top-rate university systems. The main issues to be addressed are therefore related to the new competences needed by already trained employees and the need to increase the average qualitative level of technical workers.

The qualifications and skills required will therefore change. We can place required skills into two broad categories: technical skills and personal qualifications. The first group includes, for instance, skills related to IT, information and data processing, organisational and process understanding, and the working and interacting with modern interfaces. Within the personal-skills group, soft skills are the most relevant, such as social and communication skills, teamwork skills, and self-management abilities.

These elements require not only a skilled workforce but also some major changes within the educational and vocational systems. As such, the transition from school to work (Bramanti 2015b) and continuous vocational training will become more central.

Changes are also needed on the demand side of the labour market. Individuals should take personal responsibility for acquiring and constantly updating their skills in order to ensure progression. The boundaries of specialised knowledge will become blurred as technologies and disciplines converge in the constant search for innovation. Individuals should be willing to develop a blend of technical training and softer collaborative skills, while regional governments will need to help effectively align public and private investment around these new needs.

Conclusions and a look ahead

There is widespread agreement in Europe that innovation (in its broader meaning) is key for achieving sustainable long-term economic development and a better quality of life. Beyond public finance control and monetary stability, sustainable growth is mainly expected from increasing productivity, which involves, first and foremost, better use of inputs thanks to the strong support offered by the process and organisational innovations, and by more intense use of immaterial resources, mainly brain ware and creativity (Cooke 2012).

Despite the impressive progress in information and communications technologies and related areas, knowledge is not a free and costless commodity. On the contrary, knowledge is subject to path dependency. In other words, economic agents try to search close to the knowledge that they already have, which implies significant territorial variance in the capability to extract value from knowledge. As a consequence, the final result of the entire process – innovation – is spatially concentrated and strongly supported by a specific, idiosyncratic, systemic context, which scholars often call RIS (Braczyk et al. 1998; de la Mothe and Paquet 1998; Niosi 2010). Therefore, it is not surprising that regions are becoming increasingly important nodes of the economic and technological organisation in the new age of global, knowledge-intensive capitalism (Rutten and Boekema 2007).

Innovation is the outcome of an interactive process, as the three case studies show, and it appears to be a largely clustered phenomenon (Bramanti 2016) with important regional and city poles; a clearly-defined net-like structure and fundamental feedback loops; and lock-ins governing all growth, fluctuations and decay processes. Regional clusters are therefore regarded as a tool that can be used to improve regional growth, to prevent the delocalisation of production and even to ensure the re-localisation of some previously delocalised activities (Pisano and Shih 2009; Bailey and de Propis 2014; Christopherson et al. 2014).

Governance and leadership are very important for fostering successful world-class clusters and transnational collaboration. In fact, organisations and institutions play a growing and decisive role in framing regional systems of innovation in which collective agents matter and make a difference, not only because innovation is shaped by a variety of institutional routines and social conventions, but also because these agents take on the fundamental role of gateways (Braczyk et al. 1998; Niosi 2010). They help put the RIS in contact with the global economy, and serve as a key channel for renovating and augmenting the local knowledge base, and for mitigating the potential risks of lock-ins. For instance, in the analysed cases, universities and research systems play a fundamental role in enforcing firms' regional networks.

Europe is a unique world of diversities in terms of rules, routines, habits, institutions, sectoral specialisation and innovation. However, due to the presence of more general, common elements – linked to a widespread manufacturing culture, a specialised labour market, the thickness of industrial clusters, and strong relations between machinery suppliers and end-users – different regions are able to develop strong collaborative relations, to exchange good practices and to learn from each other, as the Vanguard Initiative demonstrates. Heterogeneity is an important factor in local development and regional growth. Networks of firms and regions may gain an advantage by recombining processes. Diversity among the different European RISs (even if we only look at advanced regions) creates greater variety in the knowledge base and, thereby, serves as a greater source of cross-subsector knowledge spillovers and opportunities for new activities. Distributed networks within regional systems and among different regions transcend industries and sectors, and they sustain and enhance firms' absorptive, explorative and exploitative capacities (Asheim et al. 2011). Multinational corporations have rapidly learned to leverage on national, regional and even local differences.

A great deal of research supports the idea that institutional endowments can explain differences in economic performance and specialisation across regions. Such endowments include rules, routines, habits, and traditions. Appropriate institutions are of great importance (Storz and Schäfer 2011), as they can: i) affect and stimulate knowledge production (via R&D and via 'soft' investments); ii) facilitate the patenting process; iii) disseminate ideas and promote cooperation among researchers; iv) speed up the diffusion of scientific knowledge; and v) reduce uncertainties related to new projects. Therefore, although institutions matter, they are the result of a long, interdependent path of accumulation that is historically embedded. Consequently, cross-country differences remain relatively stable over time, giving differences a non-temporary nature.

Even though RISs are rooted in different combinations of institutions, organisations and policies, their 'raw material' is always human capital. Human capital strengthens innovation process in numerous ways. Moreover, human capital lies at the origin of rising productivity, fosters absorptive capacity (i.e., the way in which firms take advantage of external knowledge inputs) and speeds up the adoption of innovation.

The true function of RISs, which make existing firms competitive and contributes to attracting new ones, springs from achieving the right balance between internal robustness and external openness (Bramanti and Fratesi 2009). Territory matters, as it offers at least four core assets in the process of generating and implementing advances in technology and innovation. Territories are here viewed as:

- 'The birthplace of technology and innovation – i.e., the progress from given resource allocation processes to a collective build-up of specific resources';
- 'A place for co-ordinating industrial activities, a link between external territorial economies and organisational and inter-organisational firm trajectories';
- 'A political decision-making unit governing localisation, able to create and redistribute resources, and expressing specific governance structures in the relations between actors'; and
- 'A place in which untraded inter-dependencies (means through which the actors growth technologically and organisationally, and co-ordinate themselves) form, express themselves, and evolve.' (Bramanti and Fratesi 2009: 60).

Moreover, while training and higher education can enhance labour productivity, and tend to increase individuals' income and life satisfaction, tertiary education is neither the only, nor an automatic, source of highly skilled workers and competitiveness. Skill upgrades and learning can play a significant role, especially when linked to labour market needs. This is particularly evident in medium-technology sectors where the regional character of the cognitive processes of interactive learning and knowledge creation is strongly developed (Cappellin and Wink 2009).

In conclusion, there is clear evidence of the incredible resilience of RISs, which are heavily rooted in a productive manufacturing environment. Several strong, self-reinforcing mechanisms are at work in an endless spiral that brings together information, knowledge, competence, and creativity, which in turn contribute to the production process, and the accumulation and exchange of knowledge and know-how (Bramanti and Fratesi 2009).

From a European policy perspective, the awareness of this unique and differentiated process that leads to innovative outcomes has pushed in favour of a European S3, which is convenient for different territorial contexts due to its main characteristic – flexibility. It allows for full exploitation of existing differences in territorial capital, enables regions to root their economic activities in the local institutional fabric, and fosters the generation, acquisition, and exchange of knowledge. For these reasons, the S3 approach has been diffused as a blueprint of the Commission's industrial policies, and it represents a provocative and somewhat new articulation of a place-based approach to regional development policy (Koschatzky and Stahlecker 2010). In addition, it has been used to emphasise the need to exploit-related variety (Frenken et al. 2007; Boschma 2008), to enable strategic diversification and to build regional embeddedness. New industrial policies represent a specific way of promoting innovation and of modifying existing manufacturing systems from the inside.

While the geographical centre of global manufacturing production will shift to Asia, European core regions can – and must – preserve a rich manufacturing base that is higher on the global value chain. The focus must be on deriving more systemic and articulated answers to new needs in the home market – a wealthy market encompassing around 500 million ageing consumers (Cappellin 2016).

As this chapter has testified, manufacturing remains vital for at least four reasons: trade and global competition; productivity growth; demand for skilled employees and creativity; and quality of life and environmental sustainability. The device that will enable us to reach our goals is innovation. Moreover, spillovers between neighbouring regions make a positive contribution to regional innovation in the EU. Innovative output depends on more than just R&D. It mainly relates to region-specific characteristics, such as the industry mix, market opportunities, the innovative environment, and social capital. Knowledge spillovers are also captured in social and cooperative network relationships (Guastella and van Oort 2015).

Europe needs to ensure a future that includes new manufacturing. Consequently, it needs workable policies to support that future. However, the future will not be deterministic. Uncertainties will arise related to the market and technological environments as well as political changes and social development, which are constantly evolving (Brexit and migration flows are two major concerns in the short term). To a great extent, the future of manufacturing systems can and will be co-determined by policy packages, which will affect the business climate and the socio-economic environment in which industrial production takes place in Europe (Brandes et al. 2007; Dhéret et al. 2014). Even if politicians seem frightened by diversity and this feeling results in backward-oriented behaviour and nation-states with well-guarded borders, enterprises still need skilled labour and diversity, which makes them more forward oriented. They need to move, to interact, to exchange and to build together on the basis of diversity (Sedita et al. 2015).

All of this will be possible if Europe delivers systemic answers that are all-encompassing and inclusive. European policy has to use the complementary levers of regulation, finance, techno-infrastructures, and grand societal challenges to guide and boost enterprises and private actors in their efforts to align themselves with the main drivers of the future of European manufacturing (Brandes et al. 2007; EC 2013; Dolphin 2015). These drivers are globalisation and international competition, technological progress, socio-demographic change, energy and resource scarcity, and climate change and the environment. Europe needs a set of policies that address skills improvement, reduce the administrative burden and enhance energy efficiency. Together, these policies may provide a favourable industrial environment and lead to important results.

The most pressing questions are related to the governance issue (Kaiser and Prange 2004; Stephenson 2013). We cannot deny that multi-level governance represents opportunities for some and risks (of the loss of power and influence) for others, which could lead to conflicts. Due to the systemic nature of innovation, and the coordination challenges of working with different public and private actors, regions have to take on the role of 'flexible gatekeeper' within the rise of flexible 'type 2' arrangements.[18] The need to determine the best ways of governing the process, and of aligning the different, sometimes contrasting, objectives, functions, and incentives is an issue that European Commission, as well as regional governments, will face for years to come.

Notes

1 The Global Agenda Council on the *Future of Manufacturing* (WEF–UNIDO 2014: 7) states:

> Advanced manufacturing is defined as the technological, organisational, social and environmental strategies that improve manufacturing so that it can meet the goals of enterprises, society and governments, and adapt to change. This definition reflects the growing level of integration across the value chains of the functions of production, distribution and consumption.

2 Products are not necessarily physical objects. Increasingly, they are platforms for new services and complex systems that address new needs and/or offer new answers to old ones. For example, in the case of the UK manufacturer Rolls-Royce:

> Over 50% of its revenues are now accounted for by their servicing of aircraft engines, while engines themselves are sold at near cost, to create lock-in and quasi-captive service recipients-customers. Important in such cases is that servicing requires manufacturing skills, knowledge, and capabilities to start with – this renders the two inseparable in a fundamental, even definitional, manner, hence the emergence of terms such as 'manuservices'.
>
> (Pitelis 2015: 26)

3 According to Eurostat classifications, manufacturing includes all activities in section C of the NACE (rev 2). This section encompasses industries involving the physical or chemical transformation of materials, substances or components into new products.
4 Multi-level governance requires a system of continuous negotiations among nested governments at different territorial tiers as a result of the broad process of institutional creation and decisional reallocation that had affected some previously centralised functions of the state (Marks 1993).
5 Here, the 'broader definition' refers to all that exceeds technological progress. Cultural, societal and aesthetic innovations – sometimes referred as 'soft innovation' (Stoneman 2010) – are key for shaping the developing paths of advanced regions.
6 In Greek mythology, a phoenix is a long-living bird that is cyclically regenerated or reborn. A phoenix rises to life from the ashes of its predecessor. A 'phoenix industry' is a new productive activity born from the ashes of a previous producer (frequently a large firm) that maintains some elements of its predecessor and adds new lifeblood.

7 The story of photonics in Rochester (NY) is particularly instructive. Photonics – the science of using light in processes from advanced manufacturing to data transmission – has a strong footprint in Rochester. It emerged from the old photographic equipment and supply industry (Kodak's sector), and resulted in a hub focused on the design, manufacturing and packaging of circuits that combine photonic and electronic components. Integrated photonics have the potential to revolutionise the carrying capacity of Internet networks, improve performance in biological research, and they have applications in such areas as cyber defence, banking, investing, video conferencing and weather modelling. This sector accounts for an estimated 17,000 jobs in the region. In 2014, Rochester was chosen as the headquarters of the American Institute for Manufacturing Integrated Photonics (AIM Photonics), a first-class national institution. This is likely to boost the visibility and the attractiveness of the region.

8 Much of this case on the automotive industry in the West Midlands is based on Amison and Bailey (2014). Further information on the case is available in a detailed research report by the same authors (Amison and Bailey 2013).

9 *'In the Midlands case, rather than being a supporting factor, lack of access to capital has been a drag on the sector (…). Domestic finance for investment in manufacturing has been a problem for British industry, stretching as far back as to late XIX Century. Several interviews expressed the belief that "there is no finance available in the UK for manufacturing"'* (Amison and Bailey 2014: 403–404).

10 *'In essence, Industry 4.0 will involve the technical integration of Cyber-Physical Systems (CPS) into manufacturing and logistics, and the use of the Internet of things and services in industrial processes. This will have implication for value creation, business models, downstream services and work organisation'* (Industrie-Science Research Alliance 2013: 14).

11 All of the information reported here is extracted from the rich and up-to-date 'Regional Innovation Monitor' developed by Technopolis in partnership with the Fraunhofer Institute for Systems and Innovation Research ISI on behalf of the European Commission (Zenker and Schnabl 2016).

12 Different labels are used in the literature to indicate the pool of idiosyncratic regional assets enabling innovation processes and enhancing development paths. They include 'territorial capital' (OECD 2001), 'industrial commons' (Pisano and Shih 2012) and 'innovative milieu' (Ratti et al. 1997).

13 In an open-innovation model, firms use external ideas and internal ideas, as well as internal and external paths to market. Firms utilise open innovation to address two growth objectives: growth in the current business (incremental change) and growth in new business areas (step change).

14 Lombardy has promoted an open-innovation platform to serve as a new tool for sharing and exchanging knowledge, and for defining networking activities among innovative firms. The platform aims to be a two-way communicational channel with the view to co-defining regional innovation policy and the operative tools needed to support it.
   See www.openinnovation.regione.lombardia.it/.

15 The platform should have a strong service orientation, and focus on developing and delivering concrete services (e.g., advisory services, data and analysis services). At the same time, it should act as a vehicle to encourage and support collaboration among firms, clusters and regions.

16 This funding scheme is designed to improve the global competition of the UK's advanced manufacturing supply chain, and to help create or safeguard 5,000 jobs over the next five years (2015–2020).

17 For example, 4,750 units of the model S Tesla were sold in the US in the first quarter of 2013, which was more than conventionally powered premium cars in the EUR 70,000–90,000 price range produced by Audi, BMW, Lexus and Mercedes, each of which had sales of 1,500 to 3,000 cars in the same period.

18 A 'type 2' arrangement is an alternative vision of multi-level governance. In this vision, the number of jurisdictions is vast rather than limited; jurisdictions are not aligned on just a few levels, but operate on diverse territorial scales; jurisdictions are functionally specific rather than multi-task; and jurisdictions are intended to be flexible rather than fixed (Hooghe and Marks 2001).

References

Aghion, P., Boulanger, J., Cohen, E. 2011: *Rethinking Industrial Policy*. Brussels: Bruegel Policy Brief Issue 2011/04, June.

Ambrosetti. 2016: *The Environment for Innovation: Drivers for the Growth of Italian Company and Italy*. Milan: The European House.

Amison, P., Bailey, D. 2013: *Industrial Diversity and Innovation Spillovers: Dynamic Innovation and Adoption*. Working Paper No 45. WWW for Europe, Welfare Wealth Work, Coventry University, November.

Amison, P., Bailey, D. 2014: Phoenix Industries and Open Innovation? The Midlands Advanced Automotive Manufacturing and Engineering Industry. In: *Cambridge Journal of Regions, Economy and Society* 7 (3), 397–411.

Andermon, A., Gustavsson, M. 2011: *Job Polarization and Task-Biased Technological Change: Sweden 1975–2005*. Working Paper No. 15, Department of Economics. Uppala: Uppala University.

Asheim, B., Boschma, R., Cooke, P. 2011: Constructing Regional Advantage: Platform Policies Based on Related Variety and Differentiated Knowledge Bases. In: *Regional Studies* 47 (7), 893–904.

Autor, D., Dorn, D. 2009: *The Growth of Low Skill Service Jobs and the Polarization of the US Labour Market*. Working Paper, No. 15150. Washington, DC: NBER.

Bailey, C., de Propis, L. 2014: Manufacturing Reshoring and Its Limits: The UK Automotive Case. In: *Cambridge Journal of Regional Economy and Society* 7, 379–395.

Bailey, D., Cowling, K., Tomlinson, P.R. (Eds.). 2015: *New Perspectives on Industrial Policy for a Modern Britain*. Oxford: Oxford University Press.

Barca, F. 2009: *An Agenda for a Reformed Cohesion Policy. A Placed-Based Approach to Meeting European Union Challenges and Expectation*. Independent Report prepared at the request of Danuta Hüber, Commissioner for Regional Policy, April.

Beaven, R., May-Gillings, M., Hay, G., Steve, J., Wilson, R. 2014: *Working Futures 2012–2022*. Evidence Report No 83, March. London: UK Commission for Employment and Skills.

Bianchi, P., Laboury, S. 2016: *Towards a New Industrial Policy*. Milan: McGraw Hill Education.

BIS. 2013: *Hollowing Out and the Future of the Labour Market*. BIS Research Paper, No 134. London: Department for Business Innovation & Skills.

BIS. 2015: *Advanced Manufacturing Supply Chain Initiative: Process Evaluation Study*. BIS Research Paper, No 223. London: Department for Business Innovation & Skills.

Bormann, R., Fink, P., Iwer, F., Schade, W. 2015: *Like a Phoenix from the Ashes? On the Future of the Automotive Industry in Germany*. WISO Diskurs, No. 19. Bonn: Friedrich Ebert Stiftung.

Boschma, R. 2005: Proximity and Innovation: A Critical Assessment. In: *Regional Studies* 39 (1), 61–74.

Boschma, R. 2008: *Constructing Regional Advantage: Related Variety and Regional Innovation Policy*. Report for the Dutch Scientific Council for Government Policy. Utrecht: University of Utrecht.

Braczyk, H.-J., Cooke, P., Heidenreich, M. (Eds.). 1998: *Regional Innovation Systems*. London: UCL Press.

Bramanti, A. 2015a: *Policy Paper sulle politiche di rilancio e sostegno all'economia lombarda*. Rapporto Finale, ECO 15014. Milano: Éupolis Lombardia.

Bramanti, A. 2015b: Nuove alleanze nel percorso scuola–lavoro. In: *Scuola Democratica* 3, 617–641.

Bramanti, A. 2016: Clusters, Unlike Diamonds, Are not Forever. The European Way to Global Competition. In: Hilpert, U. (Ed.), *Routledge Handbook of Politics and Technology*. Abingdon, Oxon: Routledge, 354–366.

Bramanti, A., Fratesi, U. 2009: The Dynamics of an 'Innovation Driven' Territorial System. In Senn, L., Fratesi, U. (Eds.), *Growth in Interconnected Territories: Innovation Dynamics, Local Factors and Agents*. Berlin: Springer Verlag, 59–91.

Bramanti, A., Lazzeri, G. 2016: Smart Specialisation and Policy-Mix: Economic and Political Challenges within the Italian Experience. In: *RSA Annual Conference, Building Bridges: Cities and Regions in a Transnational World*, 4–6 April, Graz.

Brandes, F., Lejour, A., Verweij, G., van der Zee, F. 2007: *The Future of Manufacturing in Europe*. The Hague: CPB, Netherlands Bureau for Economic Policy Analysis.

Cappellin, R. 2016: Investments, Balance of Payment Equilibrium and a New Industrial Policy in Europe. In: *RSA Annual Conference, Building Bridges: Cities and Regions in a Transnational World*, 4–6 April, Graz.

Cappellin, R., Wink, R. 2009: *International Knowledge and Innovation Network. Knowledge Creation and Innovation in Medium-Technology Clusters*. Cheltenham: Edward Elgar.

Caragliu, A., Nijkamp, P. 2008: *The Impact of Regional Absorptive Capacity on Spatial Knowledge Spillovers*. Discussion Paper, No. 119. Amsterdam: Timberger Institute.

CEDEFOP. 2013: Roads to Recovery: Three Skill and Labour Market Scenarios for 2025. In: *Briefing Note* June 2013.

Chesbrough, H.W., Appleyard, M.M. 2007: Open Innovation and Strategy. In: *California Management Review* 50 (1), 57–75.

Christophenson, S. 2009: Building 'Phoenix Industries' in Our Old Industrial Cities. In: Tomaney, J. (Ed.), *The Future of Regional Policy*. London: The Smith Institute, 77–86.

Christopherson, S., Martin, R., Sunley, P., Tyler, P. 2014: Reindustrialising Regions: Rebuilding the Manufacturing Economy? In: *Cambridge Journal of Regional Economy and Society* 7, 351–358.

Cohen, W.M., Levinthal, A. 1990: Absorptive Capacity: A New Perspective on Learning and Innovation. In: *Administrative Science Quarterly* 35 (1), 128–152.

Confindustria Lombarda. 2016: *Lombardia 2030. Piano Strategico*. Milano: LIUC Università Cattaneo, Fondazione Edison.

Cooke, P. 2012: *Complex Adaptive Innovation Systems. Relatedness and Transversality in the Evolving Region*. Regions and Cities. London: Routledge.

de la Mothe, J., Paquet, G. (Eds.). 1998: *Local and Regional Systems of Innovation*. Boston, MA: Kluwer Academic Publishers.

Deloitte. 2014: *Industry 4.0 – Challenges and Solutions for the Digital Transformation and Use of Exponential Technologies*. Zurich: Deloitte Switzerland.

Dettori, B., Marrocu, E., Paci, R. 2013: Total Factor Productivity, Intangible Assets and Spatial Dependence in the European Regions. In: *Regional Studies* 46 (10), 1401–1416.

Dhéret, C., Morosi, M., Frontini, A., Hedberg, A., Pardo, R. 2014: *Towards a New Industrial Policy for Europe*. ECP Issue Paper No 78, November.

Dolphin, T. 2014: *Gathering Strength. Backing Clusters to Boost Britain's Exports*. London: IPPR.

Dolphin, T. (Ed.). 2015: *Technology, Globalisation and the Future of Work in Europe. Essays on Employment in a Digitised Economy*. London: IPPR.

European Commission. 2013: *Factories of the Future*. Luxembourg: Publications Office of the European Union.

European Commission. 2014: *For a European Industrial Renaissance*. COM (2014) 14/2, Luxembourg: Publications Office of the European Union.

Faludi, A. 2012: Multi-level (Territorial) Governance: Three Criticisms. In: *Planning Theory & Practice* 13 (2), 197–211.

Farshchi, M.A., Janne, O.E.M., McCann, P. (Eds.). 2009: *Technological Change and Mature Industrial Regions*. Cheltenham: Edward Elgar.

Foray, D. 2015: *Smart Specialisation: Opportunities and Challenges for Regional Innovation Policies*. Abingdon, Oxon: Routledge.

Foray, D., Goenaga, X. 2013: *The Goals of Smart Specialisation*. S3 Policy Brief Series, No 01/2013. Sivilla: JRC Scientific and Policy Reports.

Fratesi, U., Rodríguez-Pose, A. 2016: The Crisis and Regional Employment in Europe: What Role for Sheltered Economies? In: *Cambridge Journal of Regions, Economy and Society* 9 (1), 33–57.

Frenken, K., Van Oort, F., Verburg, T. 2007: Related Variety, Unrelated Variety and Regional Economic Growth. In: *Regional Studies* 41 (5), 685–697.

Fujimoto, T. 2011: The Japanese Manufacturing Industries: Its Capabilities and Challenges. *21st International Conference on Flexible Automation and Intelligent Manufacturing*.

Garcilazo, J.E., Martins, J.O., Tompson, W. 2010: *Why Policies May Need to be Place-Based to be People-Centred*. VOX, CEPR's Policy Portal. www.voxeu.org

Gill, I. 2009: *Regional Development Policies: Place-based or People-Centred?* VOX, CEPR's Policy Portal. www.voxeu.org

Goos, M., Manning, A. 2007: Lousy and Lovely Jobs. The Rising Polarization of Work in Britain. In: *The Review of Economics and Statistics* 89 (1), 118–133.

Goos, M., Manning, A., Salomons, A. 2009: Job Polarization in Europe. In: *American Economic Review. Papers and Proceedings* 99 (2), 58–63.

Guastella, G., van Oort, F.G. 2015: Regional Heterogeneity and Interregional Research Spillovers in European Innovation: Modelling and Policy Implications. In: *Regional Studies* 49 (11), 1772–1787.

Heng, S. 2014: *Industry 4.0 – Upgrading of Germany's Industrial Capabilities on the Horizon*. Current Issues, Sector Research. Frankfurt am Main: Deutsche Bank.

Hilpert, U. 2016: The Culture–Technology Nexus. Innovation Policy and the Successful Metropolis. In: Hilpert U. (Ed.), *Routledge Handbook of Politics and Technology*. Abingdon, Oxon: Routledge, 149–161.

Hilpert, U., Lawton Smith, H. (Eds.). 2012: *Networking Regionalised Innovative Labour Markets*. London & New York, NY: Routledge.

Hooghe, L., Marks, G. 2001: Types of Multi-Level Governance. In: *European Integration online Papers (EIoP)* 5 (11), 1–32.

IDA. 2012: *Emerging Global Trends in Advanced Manufacturing*. IDA Paper No 4603. Alexandria: Institute for Defense Analysis.

Industry-Science Research Alliance. 2013: *Recommendations for Implementing the Strategic Initiative INDUSTRIE 4.0*. Frankfurt am Main: Final Report of the INDUSTRIE 4.0 Working Group.

Isaksen, A., Trippl, M. 2014: Regional Industrial Path Development in Different Regional Innovation Systems: A Conceptual Analysis. In *Paper in Innovation Studies*. No 17, CIRCLE. Lund: Lund University Press.

Kaiser, R., Prange, H. 2004: Managing Diversity in a System of Multi-Level Governance: The Open Method of Co-ordination in Innovation Policy. In: *Journal of European Public Policy* 11 (2), 249–266.

Kampelmann, S., Rycx, F. 2011: *Task-Biased Changes of Employment and Remuneration: The Case of Occupations*. Discussion Paper, No. 5470. Berlin: IZA.

Koschatzky, K., Stahlecker, T. 2010: *Cohesion Policy in the Light of Place-Based Innovation Support. New Approaches in Multi-Actors, Decentralised Regional Settings with Bottom-Up Strategies?* WP Firms and Regions, No R1/2010. Karlsruhe: Fraunhofer ISI.

Marks, G. 1993: Structural Policy and Multilevel Governance in the EC. In: Cafruny, A.W., Rosenthal, G.G. (Eds.): *The State of the European Community*, Vol 2, *The Maastricht Debates and Beyond*. Boulder, CO: Harlow Longman, 391–410.

Mazzucato, M. 2013: *The Entrepreneurial State. Debunking Public vs. Private Sector Myths*. UK and USA: Anthem Press.

McIntosh, S. 2013: *Hollowing out and the Future of the Labour Market*. Research Paper No 134, October. London: Department for Business Innovation & Skills.

Moretti, E. 2012: *The New Geography of Jobs*. Boston, MA: Houghton Mifflin Harcourt.

Morgan, K. 2013: The Regional State in the Era of Smart Specialisation. In: *Ekonomiaz* 83 (2), 102–125.

Morkuté, G., Koster, S., Van Dijk, J. 2016: Employment Growth and Inter-Industry Job Reallocation: Spatial Patterns and Relatedness. In: *Regional Studies* Online article (DOI: 10.1080/00343404.2016.1153800).

Niosi, J. 2010: *Building National and Regional Innovation Systems*. Cheltenham: Edward Elgar.

O'Sullivan, E., Mitchell, N. 2013: *International Approaches to Understanding the Future of Manufacturing*. Future of Manufacturing Project: Evidence Paper, No 26. London: Government Office for Science.

OECD. 2001: *OECD Territorial Outlook*. Paris: OECD Publishing.

OECD. 2015: *Education Indicators in Focus*. April. Paris: OECD Publishing.

Pisano, G.P., Shih, W.C. 2009: Restoring American Competitiveness. In: *Harvard Business Review* 87 (7–8).

Pisano, G.P., Shih, W.C. 2012: Does America Really Need Manufacturing. In: *Harvard Business Review* 90 (3).

Pitelis, C. 2015: DIP-ly Speaking: Debunking Ten Myths, and Business Strategy-Informed Development Industrial Policy. In: Bailey, D., Cowling, K., Tomlinson, P. R. (Eds.), *New Perspectives on Industrial Policy for a Modern Britain*. Oxford: Oxford University Press, 17–40.

PwC, Strategy 2014: *Industry 4.0. Opportunities and Challenges of the Industrial Internet*. Munich: PricewaterhouseCoopers Aktiengesellschaft Wirtschaftsprüfungsgesellschaft.

Quatraro, F. 2016: Co-evolutionary Patterns in Regional Knowledge Bases and Economic Structure: Evidence from European Regions. In: *Regional Studies* 50 (3), 513–539.

Ratti, R., Bramanti, A., Gordon, R. (Eds.) 1997: *The Dynamics of Innovative Regions. The GREMI Approach.* Aldershot: Ashgate.

Rodríguez-Pose, A., di Cataldo, M., Rainoldi, A. 2014: *The Role of Government Institutions for Smart Specialisation and Regional Development.* JRS Technical Report, No. 4. Brussels: European Commission.

Rutten, R., Boekema, F. (Eds.). 2007: *The Learning Regions. Foundations, State of the Art, Future.* Cheltenham: Edward Elgar.

Sedita, S.R., de Noni, I., Pilotti, L. 2015: How Do Related Variety and Differentiated Knowledge Bases Influence the Resilience of Local Production System? In *Paper in Innovation Studies.* No 20, CIRCLE. Lund: Lund University.

Stephenson, P. 2013: Twenty Years of Multi-Level Governance: 'Where Does it Come From? What is it? Where is it Going?'. In: *Journal of European Public Policy* 20 (6), 817–837.

Stoneman, P. 2010: *Soft Innovation. Economics, Product Aesthetics, and the Creative Industries.* Oxford: Oxford University Press.

Storz, C., Schäfer, S. 2011: *Institutional Diversity and Innovation.* London: Routledge Studies in Global Competition, Routledge.

Timmer, M.P., Inklaar, R., O'Mahony, M., van Ark, B. 2010: *Economic Growth in Europe.* Cambridge: Cambridge University Press.

Tomaney, J. (Ed.). 2009: *The Future of Regional Policy.* London: The Smith Institute.

Torre, A., Rallet, A. 2005: Proximity and Localization. In: *Regional Studies* 39 (1), 47–59.

WEF-UNIDO. 2014: *The Future of Manufacturing: Driving Capabilities, Enabling Investments.* Geneva: World Economic Forum.

Zenker, A., Schnabl, E. 2016: *Regional Innovation Monitor-Plus 2016.* Brussels: Regional Innovation Report, Baden-Württemberg (Industry 4.0 and Smart Systems).

12 Globalization, competitiveness and the supply of highly skilled labour in civil aerospace

Desmond Hickie, Neil Jones and Florian Schloderer

Introduction: islands of innovation in the civil aerospace industry

This chapter sets out to elucidate the critical role of highly skilled labour as a basis for the innovation and competitiveness of islands of innovation in high technology industries using the example of the civil aerospace industry. It does so by: briefly describing the structure of the industry's supply chain and the firm-level competences required at different tiers of the supply chain; analysing the different types of highly skilled labour required by the industry; explaining the impacts of on-going market and technological changes on the structure of the supply chain; and, analysing in depth the varying impacts of these structural changes on the skills and labour supply needs of well established, and more recent entrants into the aerospace supply chain. Finally, the chapter concludes with a discussion: summarizing the critical impact of labour supply issues upon the aerospace supply chain; distinguishing the different challenges posed for both established firms and regions, and for new entrant firms and regions; and identifying two key enablers necessary to address these challenges effectively.

To provide a conceptual framework for this chapter, we define islands of innovation (Hilpert 2016) in the aerospace industry as a specific type of regional aerospace ecosystem (Adner 2017), which has acquired the capacity to innovate, i.e. it has the capability to produce new scientific research findings, to develop new products, or new manufacturing processes, or some combination of the three. Thus, the presence of an aerospace ecosystem is a necessary, but not a sufficient condition for an aerospace region to become an island of innovation. As the supply chain of the aerospace industry is globally distributed, so too are aerospace regions and islands of innovation. However, islands of innovation, which have developed the capacity to innovate, have a critical competitive advantage over regions without this capacity. Examples of major, established islands of innovation in the aerospace industry are Toulouse, the Hamburg Metropolitan Region, or Washington State (Hickie 2006). Each is not only a cluster of multiple aerospace firms and other institutions, but also a hub within a complex network of geographically distributed but interconnected aerospace islands of innovation.

To provide data for this research we have combined multiple data sources, such as industry reports, research papers, media coverage and insights from industry experts.

Like any industry, the global civil aerospace industry has its own specific characteristics. These specificities with regard to industry structure, technology, product and market structure entail that innovation in aerospace has its own particularities and distinctiveness. Aerospace is an old, well-established, high technology, producer goods industry in which innovation is driven both by endogenous engineering advances and by the application of technological advances from other sectors (e.g. new materials, digitisation). In this complex manufacturing context successful innovation can depend upon contributions from employees with very different educational qualifications, skills and competences – in particular engineers, manufacturing workers and managers. The industry's products are both large and complex (e.g. a Boeing 787 has 2.3 million parts). They are the result of lengthy development processes (e.g. engineering development on the Airbus A380 began in 1994 and it entered service in 2007) and, if commercially successful, they have very long product life cycles (e.g. the Boeing 747 first flew commercially in 1970).

The industry is increasingly a global one, and was estimated to be the 8th most globalized by Price Waterhouse Coopers (PwC 2010). Given the size and complexity of its products and the global market for them, it experiences enormous economies of scale and high sunk costs, and hence the large airliner market is concentrated and dominated by the Boeing/Airbus duopoly. The intensity of these duopolists' competition acts as a constant spur to innovation. Partly as a consequence, aerospace can lay claim to the highest quality standards of any manufacturing sector (Vertesy and Szirmai 2010), however, its supply chains are increasingly dispersed and globalized. In this globalizing context, the maintenance of quality standards and continuous innovation necessitate managerial and organizational innovation, in order to effectively integrate large numbers of geographically dispersed suppliers with very varied levels of experience and competence.

Supply chains and the diversity of firms' competences: the tiered structure in civil aerospace

The design, development and manufacturing of aircraft requires a diverse range of firms participating in a highly integrated production system (ICF International 2012). The industry is organized into tiers, broadly according to the functions and responsibilities of the companies involved. At the top are Primes or OEMs (i.e. Original Equipment Manufacturers) responsible for the aircraft concept, its systems architecture, the design and manufacture of some critical systems, final assembly and sales. At Tier 1 are suppliers of major aircraft systems (e.g. landing gear, avionics). These are usually (and increasingly) large transnational enterprises, which design, partly manufacture and assemble whole aircraft systems and which manage their own supply chains. At Tier 2 are assemblers of aircraft subsystems (i.e. principal components within aircraft systems, such as the batteries within an aircraft's electronic systems), which will have design as well as manufacturing and assembly roles. Again, Tier 2 companies are often major, transnational, manufacturing businesses. At Tier 3 are Build-to-Print (or Make-to-Print) suppliers of smaller components. However, these can be smaller businesses and do not need a significant design capability. They do need a capacity to understand and interpret the engineering plans prepared by their customers. Finally, at Tier 4, are companies which supply raw materials and carry out specialist manufacturing processes.

Within the totality of the supply chain, different firms perform very diverse roles and have different opportunities to innovate depending upon their precise role (or roles) within the supply chain. For example, a Tier 1 supplier will have opportunities to innovate in terms of product design, materials, manufacturing processes and supply chain management, whereas a Tier 3 Build-to-Print supplier may be restricted to process innovations and perhaps limited supply chain management developments. Hence, each firm requires a particular set technological and managerial competences to perform its role in the supply chain. These can vary greatly in their nature, variety and complexity, depending for example on the tier(s) at which the firm operates, its products, its technologies, its suppliers and the regional ecosystem(s) within which it operates. However, like a jigsaw puzzle, each firm's role and competences must be integrated into the supply chain as a whole, if it is to play an effective part in the design and manufacture of high quality, cost-efficient and safe aircrafts.

This tiered model of the aerospace supply chain is, inevitably, a simplification, which requires additional qualification. Firstly, a single company may operate simultaneously at more than one tier. Secondly, the hierarchy of tiers does not necessarily directly reflect levels of competitiveness or technological competence; hence, for example, some firms in Tier 4 may possess highly advanced, rare and economically valuable technological competences. Thirdly, a Prime will not just deal directly with its Tier 1 suppliers but may purchase subassemblies, components and materials directly from firms in Tiers 2, 3 or 4.

The variety and specificity of highly skilled labour in the global supply chain of a high technology industry: the case of civil aerospace

The aerospace industry requires a wide variety of highly skilled and qualified labour to function. This reflects the particular characteristics of the industry and its innovation system. Each firm's particular skills needs depend upon its particular role in the supply chain and the capabilities it can draw upon from its regional ecosystem. Very broadly, the different kinds of aerospace worker can be categorized as follows: manufacturing workers, who make the aircraft; engineering workers, who design aircraft, systems and manufacturing processes; and managers, who run the companies' key business functions. In an advanced and complex manufacturing industry, like aerospace, each of these categories of worker, can play a critical part in innovation processes. Each of these categories is explained briefly below. Clearly, however, even within these broad categories, workers perform a wide variety of roles in the design and manufacture of aircraft: manufacturing involves process workers, tool makers, maintenance technicians, operations managers, production engineers, ICT support workers and so on; design involves design engineers, CAD specialists, stress engineers and so on; R and D involves aerodynamicists, materials scientists, environmental scientists and so on; and managing the broader business involves marketers, supply chain managers, HRM managers, public affairs specialists and more.

The role of manufacturing labour in innovation and competitiveness in a high technology industry

In aerospace manufacturing workers are responsible for more than repetitive manual processes to produce simple components or products, or even just for the operation of complex machinery to make high value components or products to very high industry standards. It is difficult to over-estimate the importance of an advanced manufacturing company's shop floor labour (or "touch labour"), its supervisors and operatives, to its competitiveness and its capacity for process improvement. This labour needs to be well trained, qualified and certified to aerospace industry standards. Furthermore such workers are likely to need on-going training throughout their careers to add to their existing skills base, in particular to meet the requirements of new product and process technologies. Critically, they also acquire tacit knowledge and practical experience as they spend their careers working in the industry. Manual workers, who enter the industry straight from high school *via* apprenticeship schemes, often rise to play a key role in managing production lines, even managing production for the whole business in some small Build-to-Print suppliers (especially in more traditional subsectors of the industry). Experienced production workers are the group from which mentors and front-line supervisors (foremen, shop leads, etc.) are usually drawn. Their knowledge, skills and experience are critical to solving everyday production problems, as well as developing the knowledge and skills of manufacturing employees for the future, and hence for on-going competitiveness. They have a vital role to play in passing on the culture and values of the business and of the wider aerospace industry. Currently, the industry is experiencing buoyant demand and is seeking rapidly to ramp up production, hence these experienced manufacturing workers have a key role to play in the development of new employees, who lack prior aerospace experience. The industry needs to develop these new workers if it is to fulfil its growing order books. Whilst the need for highly skilled manufacturing labour is common in the industry, different firms will require their own particular mix of manufacturing skills, depending upon the niche they occupy within the supply chain, and also upon the manufacturing competences they can draw upon from elsewhere, notably in their regional ecosystems.

The pervasive and wide-ranging demand for engineering labour

Engineering labour, with a wide variety of different types of expertise and education, is required throughout the supply chain and, as with manufacturing labour, a firm's precise requirement for engineers depends on its particular niche within the supply chain. Even relatively small Build-to-Print aerospace businesses require graduate, and even postgraduate, engineers with a range of closely related engineering specialities (e.g. production engineering, manufacturing engineering, process engineering). Even at Tier 3 of the supply chain, a business has to take a product blueprint and be able to design and implement an efficient manufacturing process in order to make it. This can be particularly challenging in some subsectors where there may not be a fully standardized manufacturing process (e.g. manufacturing composite aero-structures). Such activities require a wide range of critical engineering and related activities, such as process design, tooling and tool design, ergonomics, lean manufacturing, production planning, materials management and quality management. Manufacturing system innovations can cut costs, improve quality, increase delivery speeds and improve reliability, so creating significant competitive advantage.

It is not sufficient to employ graduate engineers straight from university. They need to be given specialist training in order to equip them with the knowledge and skills required of them in the aerospace industry (Confederation of Indian Industry 2010). Just as with manufacturing workers, it is vital that engineering and other professionals have practical experience – in aerospace design and manufacturing environments – as well as academic qualifications. Where professionals have formal qualifications, but lack sufficient practical experience, this impacts on the company's performance and its capacity for process improvement. In addition, it is essential to complement well-trained engineers with experienced operatives and supervisors (as discussed above) and with well-trained technicians who may, for example, be educated to two-year degree or certificate level in a local technical or community college within a regional aerospace ecosystem.

At Tiers 1 and 2, firms unable to innovate effectively are likely to lose their place in the supply chain. Primes and Tier 1 suppliers are imposing a requirement to co-innovate upon their suppliers so that financial and technological risks are shared. Co-innovation requires close collaboration between a Prime's design engineers and its suppliers' design, process and production engineers, so that the former can appreciate and accommodate both the design potential and constraints identified by key suppliers. Obviously, this applies especially strongly to Design and Build suppliers and creates strong ecosystem interdependencies between them and their customers.

The growth in demand for managerial labour in a globalizing supply chain

Aerospace suppliers at all levels are having broader management responsibilities placed upon them by Primes, as the Primes restructure and globalize their supply chains. These responsibilities become more onerous, and therefore more managerially demanding, as the supplier moves up the tiers of supply chain. In particular, suppliers are expected to manage their own suppliers in what may be a global supply chain; to manage risk within their supply chain; and to be familiar with the management of international trade processes, such as importing, exporting, managing overseas operations and dealing in foreign currencies. The demands made of a global Tier 1 supplier are greater in number and complexity than those made on a small Build-to-Print supplier operating lower down the supply chain. However, challenges in Build-to-Print suppliers may be considerable, given the smaller size, resources and management experience likely to be available in an engineering SME. Even at Tier 3, a Build-to-Print supplier must have expertise and experience in pricing and tendering, in risk management, often in international supply chain management, in aerospace quality and certification management and probably have a portfolio of customers in order to manage its work-flows, its plant utilization and to maintain competitiveness. If it is ambitious, and wishes to move up the supply chain to become a Tier 2 systems integrator, it will need both to upgrade its existing managerial competences and to build a formidable range of additional ones (e.g. global market intelligence, intellectual property protection and experience of establishing and managing new plants overseas). A globalizing supply chain requires more managers, with a broader range of skills, to integrate a more diverse range of companies, skills and innovative capacities.

The evolution of specific combinations of innovative competences within the global supply chain: the impacts of increasing global demand, globalization of the supply chain and technological advances

The supply chain in the aerospace industry is distributed across many regions, mainly islands of innovation. These islands of innovation are functionally diverse (each with its unique collection of firms, aerospace organizations and competences), play their own particular roles in the supply chain and are geographically dispersed in an increasingly globalized, but highly integrated, manufacturing system. The skilled labour requirements of any particular island of innovation will be contingent on the choices made by the firms and governments, and sometimes also by other actors, such as universities and private research institutes, located in that island. It may also be influenced by the choices made by new firms, which may choose to locate in that island. In order to derive the skills requirements of different types of aerospace islands of innovation, this section analyses the key features of today's aerospace industry that create pressures on the supply chain, in particular: *the worldwide growth in demand for commercial aircraft, and major developments in R and D.* These features have created opportunities for established and new firms in the aerospace supply chain, and have been critical in shaping both the industry's tiered structure and its geographical distribution. In general terms, each tier of the supply chain has defined sets of capability requirements. To be globally competitive, islands of innovation must be able to meet the skills needs of the supply chain tiers located within their ecosystem – either locally or by drawing on external resources.

Globalization is partly the consequence of a steady *worldwide growth in demand for commercial aircraft*, reflecting both growing passenger numbers and fleet replacement, as airlines purchase new planes which are cheaper to operate. Boeing estimates that by 2036 there will be 46,950 commercial aircraft in service, compared to 23,480 in 2016 and that 41,030 new aircraft will have to be manufactured to meet this demand (Boeing 2017). The Airbus demand forecast for this period is a little more conservative, at 34,900 new aircraft (Airbus 2017), but either estimate represents a period of continuous growth in demand unprecedented in the industry's history. This growth is not projected to be evenly distributed across all global markets, but anticipates continuing rapid growth in newer markets. For example Boeing projects demand for 16,050 new aircraft in Asia and 3,350 in the Middle East by 2036. If these projections are accurate, combined demand in these two newer markets will exceed that of the industry's two most established markets, Europe (7,530 aircraft) and North America (8,640 aircraft).

This rapid and continuing rise in demand has created opportunities for established and new suppliers in the collaborative network that is the aerospace supply chain. Moreover, the globalization in demand has encouraged the development of more geographically dispersed supply chains by both Boeing and Airbus. For example, key elements of the Boeing 787 Dreamliner's wing structure are made in 5 countries – the US, Canada, Australia, Japan and Korea (Ro 2013). Competition between these duopolists, in combination with customer policies, has resulted in offset agreements under which an airline buys aircraft and in return Boeing, Airbus, or one of their established suppliers, buys aircraft structures, equipment or components in the purchasing airline's home country. Given the rising demand for aircraft in markets which previously lacked an indigenous commercial aerospace sector, this has provided the opportunity for new suppliers and new regions to enter the supply chain. Where these new suppliers and regions have sufficient competences, they can move beyond being build-to-print suppliers to become new islands of innovation. By bringing their own product and process innovations to the global supply chain, they contribute both to the diversity within the global aerospace supply chain and to its collaborative interdependence.

The intensity of Boeing-Airbus competition has spurred a downward pressure on costs in their supply chains. This has encouraged both companies, and their Tier 1 and 2 suppliers, to expand their supply chains in new regions (e.g. Mexico, China, Morocco, Singapore) where costs, notably labour costs, are lower than in the established islands of Europe and North America. Furthermore, the growth in global demand for commercial aircraft has encouraged new manufacturers of whole jet airliners into the market. Currently, these new entrants (or re-entrants) are marginal players (e.g. COMAC, Bombardier, Irkut), but Embraer of Brazil has clearly established itself as major player in the market for smaller, regional airliners over the past three decades. Finally, the growth of air travel, with new routes and airlines, has helped globalize the Maintenance, Repair and Overhaul (MRO) sector of the industry (e.g. in Singapore, in Dubai) to provide aftercare for aircraft already in service.

R and D has also played a key role in the restructuring of the aerospace supply chain. As a mature industry with well-defined product markets, most technology development is: incremental, building on existing technologies; engineering-based; and takes place primarily in firms or in specialist research institutes (e.g. ONERA in France). Most R and D "… is normally planned and carried out in a way correlating with the introduction of a specific new aircraft model" (IATA 2013: 59), although the EU has developed a longer term strategic framework for more generic, applied aerospace R and D (European Union 2011). R&D in aerospace is critical in making aircraft safer, more economical to fly and less polluting – and hence plays a vital role in product differentiation, competitiveness and meeting increasingly exacting regulatory requirements. Currently, the industry's key R and D foci are on: advanced materials (e.g. carbon fibre composites), advanced manufacturing techniques (e.g. robotics, 3D printing) and digitization – perhaps most notably fly-by-wire (PwC 2011). This R and D trajectory involves increasing risk, technological complexity, uncertainty and rising costs, because these new technologies are expensive to develop and their commercial success is not guaranteed. It has had two particular impacts upon the structure of the aerospace supply chain. Firstly, the high levels of specialist expertise and the vast investment costs, associated with developing these new technologies, has led to specialization and industrial concentration (even oligopoly) among the leading global suppliers. They alone have the skills (often built up over decades) and the financial muscle to invest in leading edge technological advances. This specialization and concentration has been encouraged by the Primes: partly as a means of sharing costs and risks; partly to create a simpler, easier to manage, supply chain; but also because they recognize the greater expertise of their suppliers in some technologies. Secondly, however, these new technologies have sometimes created the opportunity for new suppliers and new regions to enter the supply chain where they have the necessary expertise (e.g. Aernnova built a new composites aero-structures business in the Spanish Basque Country, which had little prior engagement in aerospace).

The impacts of structural and technological change upon the industry's labour skills needs

Increased global aerospace demand, globalization of the aerospace supply chain and technological advance are raising skills and labour supply issues for the aerospace industry. For example, increased production volumes may require factories to staff second or third work shifts, or set up new production lines; new technologies may require new skills (e.g. new composite manufacturing technologies); suppliers may need new skills simply to manage their participation in global supply chains; or, a completely new skilled and certificated aerospace workforce may need to be established *ab initio* in countries or regions wishing to enter the industry for the first time, thus making major demands on the local educational and training infrastructure. Hence, both established and emerging aerospace islands of innovation must demonstrate the necessary labour competences to participate in the aerospace supply chain. Different islands will require their own particular sets of competences, depending on the precise role they play within this diverse system of firms and regional ecosystems.

Thus, this evolution of the industry structure is driving significant quantitative increases and qualitative changes in the skilled labour requirements of new regions in the aerospace industry. Even established islands of innovation need continuously to upgrade their skilled labour to compete successfully in the future. Therefore, this section will start with a discussion of the enhanced labour skill requirements for established islands of innovation. The prospect of quantitative and qualitative labour skills gaps in established islands of innovation potentially create windows of opportunity for new regions to break into parts of the aerospace supply chain, especially where they can supply aerospace accredited labour at lower cost than more established islands. The evidence of recent decades suggests that the most successful of these new aerospace regions (e.g. Singapore, Tianjin, the Basque Country) are capable of building a regional infrastructure of sufficient sophistication and innovation capacity to emerge as new aerospace islands of innovation. This section will, therefore, conclude with a consideration of the labour supply and skills issues faced by recently emerged aerospace islands of innovation and of regions which have recently entered the aerospace supply chain, some of which may have the potential to develop sufficient innovation capability to become fully fledged islands.

Labour skill requirements in existing islands of innovation

Issues related to highly skilled labour supply, education, training and experience, have broader implications for regional, national and continental competitiveness in the global aerospace market. Established aerospace islands of innovation (e.g. Toulouse, Seattle, North West England, San Jose dos Santos) possess a degree of competitive advantage, potentially enabling them to retain (even enhance) their particular position in the aerospace supply chain, because they already possess a skilled aerospace labour force that has enabled them to build their particular regional niche within the diversity of the supply chain. Furthermore, that labour force may have taken decades to develop. However, it is vital that they continue to educate their own manufacturing, engineering and managerial labour and imbue it with the tacit knowledge and industrial culture that have been essential in creating the region's global competitiveness. Furthermore, such islands must identify, educate and train the workers it will need to develop the new technologies (e.g. composite materials, avionics, 3D printing) that are driving innovation in the industry, if they are to retain and enhance their global competitive advantage. The following discussion will focus on four key labour challenges that existing islands of innovation in the aerospace industry can face: *skilled labour shortages, technological challenges, management challenges and longer-term strategic capability challenges.*

Aerospace is a mature manufacturing industry, where competitiveness, innovation and technological advance are heavily dependent upon engineering and manufacturing skills. Price Waterhouse Coopers' study, *A and D Insights. Accelerating Global Growth* (PwC 2010), found *skilled labour shortages*, due to increased production volumes and demographic changes, to be a global issue in the aerospace industry. These shortages can cover postgraduate and graduate engineers, technicians, supervisors and "touch workers" (Azouzi 2014; Walker 2014; Washington State 2015). This is critical because the skill base is key to innovation, and hence to product differentiation and competitiveness. Of course, this labour shortage plays out differently in different regions, depending on factors such as: whether they are established islands or newcomer regions; the particular subsectors of the industry in which they seek to compete (e.g. aero-structures, avionics); the strengths and weaknesses of their education and training infrastructures; the extent and competence of the regional supply chain; the industrial culture of the region; competition with other industries; and so forth.

Skilled labour shortages can be a key barrier to rapid increases in production in both Europe and the US. For example, in the US, there is evidence of a significant demographic problem, as skilled and supervisory workers in established aerospace regions are approaching retirement age in the foreseeable future. In 2013, the average age of US aerospace and defence workers was 45 years and rising. By 2014, 18.6% of the workforce in these US businesses was already eligible to retire (Walker 2014). This issue even applies to the owners of some long established supplier businesses, who are looking to sell up and retire, taking decades of expertise and cultural understanding with them. In the UK, 8,000 experienced aerospace workers are expected to have retired by 2020, and the national strategy for aerospace identified the need to employ 7,000 more scientists and technologists between 2012 and 2017 to meet projected demand (Aerospace Growth Partnership 2012). Such retirees represent a major loss of knowledge and skills to the industry. Still, shortages are not necessarily problematical for all firms. There is some evidence that Primes and global Tier 1 suppliers can offer attractive salaries and career opportunities, enabling them to fill skill vacancies, but it may be that this is at the expense of less favoured firms within the supply chain. Equally, some established regions (e.g. Hamburg,

Washington State) are clearly making strenuous efforts to train the workers needed to maintain and enhance their competitiveness.

The *technological challenges* underpinning product improvement in aerospace make additional and distinctive demands upon the supply of qualified labour. In such fields it is already time-consuming, but not sufficient, to formally qualify and accredit workers, because such workers will still lack the experience and tacit knowledge to work effectively (e.g. in the hand laying up of composites), especially if the processes are new to their firm. In such firms, it is also likely that the operations managers and shop leads who must pass on tacit knowledge to their newly-trained subordinates are both few in number, and may themselves be relatively inexperienced. In the immediate future these skilled labour shortages are likely to be most acute in manufacturing, as suppliers try to ramp up production in order to meet the needs of their Prime customers servicing full order books.

Aerospace design activities do not appear as likely to experience similar shortages, as labour intensive design and pre-production activities come to a close on major projects at Airbus and Boeing, and these new aircraft go into production. A foretaste of this was seen in April 2013, when Boeing announced it was reducing its engineering jobs by up to 700 in Washington State as design and pre-production work on existing design projects came to an end, but the new 777X and 787–10 were not yet authorized (*Seattle Times* 18 April 2013). Neither Airbus nor Boeing has a wholly new airliner in design for service by the mid-2020s.

For Primes and Tier 1s, the globalizing of the supply chain raises major *supply chain management challenges*, such as stretched logistics, loss of direct control and risk management, relationships management, data sharing and communications. They have taken some strategic steps to manage these issues (e.g. the Airbus Extended Enterprise, and Boeing's Partnering for Success). However, the creation of a dispersed and globalized supply chain also raises issues for suppliers, especially those setting up plants in locations remote from the Primes and Tier 1s, where there may be little history of aerospace manufacturing. Primes no longer simply demand technological and manufacturing excellence from their suppliers. They also demand that they demonstrate a much broader range of business competences. As the h&z and Key and Partners' joint report *Internationalization and Competitiveness of Aerospace Suppliers. A Joint Analysis of Germany and France* (2013) clearly illustrates, many of these requirements are ones that demonstrate a capability to function effectively in a global supply chain.

These emerging supply chains must be managed differently to their predecessors (where a highly integrated Prime could control its much smaller, often regionally-based suppliers). The increasing globalization of supply chains requires a capacity to coordinate design and manufacturing activities over long distances and across time zones. This necessitates the development of complex ICT/data handling systems, concurrent engineering capabilities, novel logistical solutions (e.g. the Boeing 747 Dreamlifter) and an ability to manage relationships across cultures. The delays experienced with the A380 and 787 suggest the Primes' difficulties in managing complex supply chains, and the extent of the organizational learning that has to take place.

Suppliers, too, have to undertake tasks new to them, which pose their own management and attitudinal challenges. Suppliers need to develop a demonstrable mastery of their design, supply chain and manufacturing processes to cope with increased rates of production, whilst maintaining a downward pressure on costs and enhancing quality. They have to manage and control risk for those immediately below them in the supply chain. Internationally, they must manage issues such as importing, exporting, controlling overseas operations and dealing in foreign currencies. Clearly the managerial demands made of a global Tier 1 supplier are greater in number and intensity than those made on a small, Build-to-Print supplier operating lower down the supply chain. However, they are not necessarily more challenging, given the smaller size, resources and management experience likely to be available in a small Build-to-Print business (Maisonneuve et al. 2013).

Well-placed external observers have suggested that many established suppliers, often located in well-established islands, are not strongly placed to meet these new challenges. Price Waterhouse Coopers has suggested that "… [m]any American and European suppliers are at risk of losing their [market] leadership positions." (PwC 2012: 1). Recent supply chain studies, by Price Waterhouse Coopers (2012) and by the consultancies h&z Unternehmensberatung AG and Kea & Partners (Santo and Schmid 2012; Maisonneuve et al. 2013), have both found that many established suppliers were not ready to make the investments needed to grow or win orders globally. In part these deficiencies can be financial (i.e. lacking the capital to invest), but they are also critically due to skills deficits and, as a consequence, to organizational and managerial deficiencies. Price Waterhouse Coopers found that only 26 of 139 suppliers surveyed were currently ready to invest abroad to take advantage of lower costs overseas, while h&z and Kea & Partners found that only 17 of 135 European SME suppliers were wholly ready to win orders globally.

Arguably, even more concerning for Primes in the longer term than the ability of their supply chains to meet the increasing pressures being placed on them, is that the wider technology development, design and manufacturing responsibilities being given to Tier 1 suppliers may mean that Primes are foregoing incremental developments in their own organizational and team-based knowledge and skills. This, in turn, would pose potential *longer-term strategic capability challenges*, creating a negative path dependency, in which the Tier 1s develop critical knowledge and skills, which the Primes do not have and would find it very difficult and expensive to recoup. It could be very difficult to rebuild design and manufacturing teams, and close gaps in organizational knowledge that have been delegated to suppliers. It is interesting in this context, that Boeing decided to develop the wing for the 777X in-house, rather than place it with Mitsubishi Heavy Industries, which was responsible for the original 777 wing (Wilhelm 2014).

Labour skill requirements in new, emerging and potential islands of innovation

For new entrant firms and regions, they have to educate and train, or attract from elsewhere, their own highly skilled labour force: capable of achieving individual and company aerospace certification; and, which has sufficiently internalized the industry's culture and values to manufacture products on-time and to the highest industry quality standards once pro- duction starts. Achieving industry cost levels and profitability are likely to take more time to achieve. This is a daunting task for aspiring new entrants, which may well lack a regional or in-company education and training infrastructure equipped readily to deliver the labour force the industry needs.

Of course, new entrant firms and regions are impacted upon by the same supply chain pressures affecting their more experienced competitors. Positively, some new and recent entrants to the aerospace supply chain have major business opportunities, because parts of the existing supply chain seem unable to grow fast enough to keep pace with demand. During the last decade or so, cost cutting by aerospace Primes and Tier 1 suppliers has led to the outsourcing of the manufacture (and even aspects of the development) of more significant components and subsystems overseas to new aerospace loca- tions (e.g. Malaysia, Singapore, Mexico, Morocco). However, it is clear that it is usually far less demanding, both in skills development and capital invest- ment, for a new entrant to become a Build to Print supplier at Tier 3, than a Design and Build supplier at Tiers 1 or 2. More negatively, new entrants face similar technological costs and uncertainties, global shortages of highly skilled labour and relentless downward pressures on costs, to their more experienced competitors.

This section explores the labour supply challenges that globalization poses both: for new Primes entering the large airliner industry, either for the first time or after a significant gap (e.g. COMAC, Mitsubishi, Bombardier); and for geographically dispersed new or recent entrants at Tiers 1 to 4 of the supply chain. New or recent entrants need to be embedded in an aerospace ecosystem preferably with an education and training infrastructure able to supply them with well-trained technicians and shop-floor/"touch" labour, and with postgraduates and graduates in a variety of engineering and other disciplines. These graduates will provide much of the management within the business and its key engineering expertise. These core skills requirements are easier to meet if the regional ecosystem is larger, with more aerospace or related businesses likely to call on these services when provided regionally. Equally, the labour supply needs of individual firms vary according to their place in the supply chain, so that Primes and Design and Build suppliers generally will make much greater specialist skills demands, in the variety, edu- cational level and quantity of workers needed from the local labour force, than would Tier 3 or 4 suppliers. Below, we will focus the discussion on four key labour supply challenges that new or recent entrants are likely to face: *lack of shop-floor industrial skills and experience; lack of managerial and technological skills and experience; deficits in industry culture and values; and regional ecosystem weaknesses.*

New regional entrants into the aerospace industry, perhaps the beneficiaries of offset agreements, will find it more difficult to meet aerospace suppliers' needs for factory labour if there is a *lack of shop-floor industrial skills and experience* in the local labour force. Indeed, a key driver of globalization has been the search by established aerospace companies for competent, or potentially competent, low cost suppliers in developing economies. However, it is essential that these factory workers have a strong basic education (e.g. in mathematics) if they are to be able to take advantage of the specialist training the company will need to give them. It is even advantageous if they have a basic knowledge of English. Rolls Royce's successful experience in Singapore illustrates the benefits that can accrue to companies in a new aerospace ecosystem where the labour force is generally well educated (de Meyer et al. 2014). However, not all new entrants are as advantaged, in which case a key requirement is to improve the quality of school education, so that there is an adequate supply of workers who are able to work in an advanced manufacturing environment and can undertake the necessary training programmes to give themselves job specific knowledge and skills.

A newly trained factory worker, even one with good secondary education, in a newly established factory is likely to be unproductive in comparison with more experienced workers in established factories elsewhere. This reflects the vital importance of tacit knowledge and of an appropriate industrial culture. The favourable experience of the Basque Country, which in the past 25 years, has successfully built an aerospace region specializing at Tier 1 in aero-structures, is instructive. The region already contained well-established engineering businesses and skilled workers, whose prior experience and acquired skills and industry culture, facilitated their adaptation to aerospace skills and industry culture. It has been suggested that ideally, in regions without an existing engineering culture and skills in advanced manufacturing, such inexperienced workers could be sent abroad to gain practical experience, perhaps in a customer's factory. However, such training is costly (not least in terms of output lost) and has other risks (e.g. the workers may not return). Another partial solution to such inexperience is to employ experienced supervisors from overseas, or have them seconded from a customer company, to help with training and demonstrate the skills needed at the new plant. However, even for a Build-to-Print manufacturer, the problem of an inexperienced labour force is likely to take years to overcome fully, even when strenuous steps are taken to address it. If a new entrant seeks to build a Design and Print business *ab initio,* it is likely to take a decade or more to get fully up to speed, even if it has the support of an experienced external partner.

The shortage of engineering labour in the established aerospace islands presents a particular opportunity for emerging economies which have strong supplies of well qualified and relatively cheap engineering labour (notably

India and China), but conversely other aspiring entrants could face significant entry problems if they have a *lack of managerial and technological skills and experience*. The availability of such highly qualified and experienced labour is critical if an island is to be able to participate effectively in the global supply chain. For example, the ready supply of well-educated engineers is a key factor in attracting aerospace foreign direct investment to favoured regions, like India's Bangalore aerospace cluster. However, it is not sufficient for a developing economy or region to produce graduate engineers. Firstly, these newly qualified engineers need to be given specialist training and to gain practical experience in order to equip them with the knowledge and skills required of them in the aerospace industry (Confederation of Indian Industry 2010). Experience, in particular, is likely to be measured in years. Secondly, *suppliers need experienced managers and other professionals (e.g. in finance, in supply chain management) to provide the commercial and organizational context in which they will work*. The higher up the supply chain a company wishes to proceed, the greater will be the range of advanced skills it will require to become competitive.

Although a typical Build-to-Print supplier would probably only need to employ or develop engineering and managerial staff to engage in a limited range of functions – incremental process design, plant-based production planning, manufacturing and simpler assemblies, these professionals need a consistent focus upon hitting quality standards and driving out costs. For inexperienced Build-to-Print suppliers, this process improvement is critical, as the firm, its managers and workers, seek to understand its manufacturing processes better (e.g. managing the firm's tools and its maintenance processes) and find ways to implement and enhance them more effectively (e.g. moving from hand-laying up to advanced fibre placement technologies in composites manufacturing).

Because process improvement is such a wide-ranging activity, it makes demands on many parts of a business, its staff and processes and significant process improvement is unlikely to be accomplished very quickly as a result of the long learning curve to be mastered. The Build-to Print supplier's engineers and managers need to be able to draw on the process experience of factory workers and supervisors. They are key "fact-holders" who need an intimate, hands-on experience of the company's manufacturing processes. Experienced "touch workers" on the factory floor are important to competitiveness, because they can both effectively implement new plans and processes proposed by managers, and identify and solve practical production and maintenance problems as they arise. This, of course, is problematical for new entrants in the supply chain, because their factory workers are likely to lack this experience. Even if these workers are well trained, educated and formally accredited, it is likely to take them years to achieve this level of tacit knowledge and experience. Yet it is the enhanced competitiveness resulting from such experience that is likely to earn new suppliers and islands a secure, long-term place in the supply chain.

For a Design and Build supplier all the above labour requirements apply, but to a greater degree in both the quality and quantity. However, they are not by themselves sufficient. The activities of a Design and Build supplier are, by their nature, both technologically and managerially more complex. In particular, such a supplier would need to develop and maintain its own independent design team, which would place significant demands on its company finances and, more widely, on its regional ecosystem. In the short run it may be possible to send trainee design engineers abroad, especially for their postgraduate education, but this is expensive and risky, as a newly qualified engineer may not choose to return home. Longer-term competitiveness is likely to require that a local university develops teaching and supporting research capabilities in these disciplines. It is likely to take years before significant numbers of qualified engineers are graduating. A new Design and Build supplier would also need rapidly to develop its in-house managerial capabilities, for example the capacity to manage a large, international supply chain and to support and develop the capabilities of its supplier companies lower down the supply chain. As with engineers and technologists, the regional ecosystem may lack a ready supply of experienced, well-qualified managers to support a company's ambition to achieve Design and Build status.

Of course, it is possible to make up a shortfall in suitably experienced engineers and professionals in the region with engineers and professionals from abroad. However, employing expatriates raises its own issues. They are often expensive and time consuming to hire, costly to employ and potentially footloose. In addition, given that there are global shortages of skilled aerospace labour, it may become more expensive to attract foreigners, especially of the right quality. Such an approach also undermines the local employment objectives of many new aerospace regions.

These shortfalls in the supply of industrially experienced graduate and postgraduate labour are expensive and time consuming to overcome. Nevertheless, some new entrants in new regional aerospace ecosystems appear to have overcome them with significant success. The Price Waterhouse Coopers study also noted that 20 of 26 companies best prepared to expand in the new growth markets (e.g. in Asia) were in fact indigenous to those markets, and were "... a new class of emerging aerospace suppliers." (PwC 2012: 5).

The building of a reputation for quality, reliability and cost consciousness with the Primes is vital to the success of any new supplier. In the last resort, Primes are responsible for their aircraft and must be totally confident that the supplier can deliver. Achieving formal accreditation of the quality management system according to AS9100 is a necessary, but not a sufficient, condition for becoming a competitive supplier. These quality standards are underpinned by norms and behaviours to which suppliers must conform, if they are to be accepted as competent participants in the supply chain. Hence, regional *deficits in industry culture and values* can be a major barrier to achieving competitiveness in the aerospace supply chain. In very well established regional ecosystems (e.g. Seattle, Toulouse, Hamburg), aerospace norms and behaviours are an ingrained aspect of a regional industrial culture that often pass inter-generationally between senior and junior colleagues within a business. New entrants to the aerospace industry, outside well established regional ecosystems and outside established islands of innovation, are unlikely to have fully adopted the industry culture and values initially, but they need to adopt it quite quickly in order to grow and succeed – as has been done, for example, with some success in Mexico.

A supplier's ability to compete successfully in the aerospace supply chain does not depend solely upon its own capabilities, but also upon resources received from its regional ecosystem (see the discussion of education and training above). Consequently, *regional ecosystem weaknesses* will inhibit the development of local aerospace supplier companies. Even relatively straightforward, Tier 3 Build-to-Print manufacturing makes significant demands on the local supply chain and infrastructure. A Build-to-Print manufacturer will usually be more competitive if it has access to local suppliers of inputs such as raw materials and of the downstream manufacturing processes it needs to finish its products for assembly (e.g. a supplier able to coat composite components and sub-assemblies). For example, efficient manufacturing requires different kinds of engineering support, such as a production engineering consultancy to troubleshoot and resolve equipment problems, or local engineering businesses capable of maintaining and repairing manufacturing equipment. It can purchase necessary parts, equipment and services abroad, but this is likely both to add to its costs and make it less reliable and flexible in responding to customer requirements. A single Build-to-Print business is unlikely to be large enough to support a local infrastructure of supplier companies to support it, or to justify local colleges and universities setting up specialist aerospace educational programmes. Hence, it is highly beneficial if there are a number of aerospace companies and companies from related industries within a regional ecosystem, to broaden the demand for these services and so gain beneficial agglomeration effects. When the local aerospace industry has reached a critical mass, it can lead to the creation of a locally based research and education facility (e.g. the University of Sheffield's Advanced Manufacturing Centre has a facility in Malaysia).

The strength and diversity of a region's aerospace ecosystem (its customer and supplier companies, the subsectors they are in, the capabilities of its technical colleges and universities, etc.) impacts critically upon the labour supply available to new aerospace businesses located there. Hence, it influences how new firms should choose to enter the industry (e.g. in MRO, in avionics, in aero-engines; as a Build-to-Print supplier or as a Design and Build supplier). The more developed the regional ecosystem, the better it is able to support the development of an economically and technologically ambitious new supplier.

Discussion and conclusions: managing innovation, supply chain diversity and the development of highly skilled labour

This closing section begins by briefly summarizing the critical role of labour skills in determining the competitiveness of both established and of new, emerging and potential aerospace islands of innovation, which has been analyzed more fully above. Based on this analysis, we draw important policy implications for stakeholders who wish to maintain or enhance the competitive advantage of islands of innovation in the evolving global aerospace supply chain, which is a challenging task. We close by proposing that industry and government policy makers focus on two key enablers, which underpin the infrastructure for the supply of the highly skilled labour: promoting effective collaboration between private and public sector actors within islands of innovation; and, the provision of long-term government policy support.

The aerospace industry case is clearly one where labour skills are a critical success factor in global competitiveness, both for established and for new, potential and emerging, islands of innovation. The nature and specificities of aerospace (as a long-established manufacturer of large, technologically advanced and complex products in a global, highly competitive market) are critical in determining the characteristics of its innovation system (e.g. that continuous technological advance is critical to firms' competitiveness; such advance is largely product focused, engineering-based and very expensive; and it widely applies new technologies from other sectors). These innovation characteristics in turn directly impact upon the precise labour supply needs of the industry (e.g. the need for: a wide range of highly educated and industry-trained engineers; very highly skilled manufacturing workers capable of process innovation; managers able to manage a globally distributed and highly diversified supply chain and internal complexity within their firms).

However, while labour skills are a necessary component of a regional aerospace ecosystem, it is important to note that they are not a sufficient condition for competitive advantage. To be globally competitive, islands of innovation require an infrastructure and resources far greater and more complex than simply the labour skills in their regional ecosystems. For example, they need capital equipment and specialist suppliers of materials, components and services. However, these broader requirements for the regional aerospace ecosystem are not the focus of this chapter.

Different regional aerospace ecosystems face different labour supply issues. Each has its own particular specialisms (e.g. Hamburg in aircraft interiors and MRO; Singapore in aero-engines and MRO). These are reflected in its labour force, which has particular skills, cultural norms and educational paths. Each is impacted upon by its geographical location (e.g. its proximity to firms with complementary skills; its attractiveness to expatriate labour). The aerospace supply chain as a whole, therefore, is made up by diverse and interconnected regional ecosystems, where the labour force both reflects and reinforces the region's technological specialization and innovation capabilities. Thus, these diverse and interconnected regional ecosystems constitute the diversity of the global supply chain.

Despite this regional diversity, some broader patterns have been identified above in the labour supply challenges faced by different types of regional aerospace ecosystem. Established islands of innovation already have a highly skilled labour force that has successfully been integrated within the aerospace supply chain. This acts as a powerful attractant both in retaining existing firms and potentially in attracting new ones. For them, the challenge is not simply to rely on the infrastructure that has successfully generated competitive labour skills in the past; instead, their future global competitiveness necessitates that they adapt this existing labour supply infrastructure to meet the new labour skill requirements required by the evolving industry structure, which is changing significantly due to increasing global aerospace demand, globalization of the aerospace supply chain and technological advance. As for newer, emerging and potential islands (e.g. in Mexico, in China), their challenges are in some senses even more demanding, especially if they wish to become more than Tier 3 Build-to-Print suppliers. The need is to develop a supply of highly skilled and experienced shop-floor, engineering and managerial labour. This often has to be done from a relatively low skills base with an inadequate educational infrastructure – both to secure their current competitiveness and to be able to respond to uncertain future changes of the global supply chain. Lower labour costs may be an important attractant to both local and outside firms contemplating the creation of aerospace plants in a new or emerging aerospace ecosystem, but they cannot be sufficient by themselves. The existence of shop-floor industrial as well as managerial and technological skills and experience base (as in the Spanish Basque Country), or the potential rapidly to develop one capable of achieving aerospace manufacturing standards, is necessary for the creation of a sustainable aerospace industry.

Those islands of innovation which are most effective in adapting their supply of skilled labour to meet these challenging industry conditions will be best placed to ensure their long-term competitiveness in this rapidly growing global aerospace industry. This adaptation requires a systemic response from within and beyond an island of innovation, involving locally based firms, national and regional governments, international agencies (e.g. the EU), universities, technical colleges and national and regional industry and cluster representative organizations (e.g. the Royal Aeronautical Society in the UK; HEGAN in the Basque Country). Hence, resolving these important skills and labour supply issues for islands of innovation to ensure long-term competitiveness necessitates a high degree of effective, long-term collaboration between private and public sector actors within, and sometimes beyond, the regional aerospace ecosystem.

Finally, a word is required about the broader role of governments in supporting the aerospace industry. Governments have exercised their influence over the industry in many ways, for example through facilitating international alliances, subsidizing R and D and manufacturing, requiring offset agreements and through conducting research and providing education and training. Aerospace is a business whose competitiveness is focused on the very long run, and hence regional and national ecosystems require consistency in government policy and support, not least in education, skills development and the supply of highly skilled labour. For example, the success of Embraer in the regional jet market is the result of decades of government support beginning in the 1940s. More recently, the rapid development of Chinese civil aerospace clearly indicates the existence of a coherent, long-term policy to develop a national aerospace ecosystem capable of competing in global markets (Cliff, Ohlandt and Yang 2011).

References

Adner, R. 2017: "Ecosystem as Structure: An Actionable Construct for Strategy". In: *Journal of Management*, vol. 43, no. 1, 39–58.

Aerospace Growth Partnership. 2012: *Aerospace Growth Partnership, Reach for the Skies. A Strategic Vision for the UK Aerospace Industry*, UK Government, London, UK.

Airbus. 2017: *Global Market Forecast. Growing Horizons, 2017–2036*, Airbus, Toulouse.

Azouzi, R. 2014: "Training the Next Generation". In: *Aerospace*, vol. 41, no. 10, 36–37.

Boeing. 2017: *Current Market Outlook 2017–2036*, Boeing Commercial Airplanes, Seattle, WA.

Cliff, R., Ohlandt, C. & Yang, D. 2011: *Ready for Takeoff. China's Advancing Aerospace Industry*, RAND Corporation, Washington, DC.

Confederation of Indian Industry. 2010: *Changing Dynamics. India's Aerospace Industry*, Confederation of Indian Industry/Price Waterhouse Coopers, New Delhi.

de Meyer, A., Williamson, P., Joshi, H. & Dula, C. 2014: *Rolls-Royce in Singapore: Harnessing the Power of the Ecosystem to Drive Growth*, Singapore Management University, Singapore.

European Union. 2011: *Flightpath 2050. Europe's Vision for Aviation*, European Union, Brussels.

Hickie, D. 2006: "Knowledge and Competitiveness in the Aerospace Industry: The Cases of Toulouse, Seattle and North-west England". In: *European Planning Studies*, vol. 14, no. 5, 697–716.

Hilpert, U. 2016: "Metropolitan Locations in International High-tech Networks: Collaboration and Exchange of Creative Labour as a Basis for Advanced Socio-economic Development". In: *The Routledge Handbook of Politics and Technology*, ed. U. Hilpert, Routledge, Abingdon, UK, 281–298.

IATA. 2013: *IATA Technology Roadmap*, 4th edn, June. Available: www.iata.org/what wedo/environment/Documents/technology-roadmap-2013.pdf.

ICF International. 2012: *Global Aerospace Sector. M&A update*. Available: www. catalystcf.co.uk/56-global-aerospace-industry-sector-note-summer-2012.pdf.

Maisonneuve, F., Santo, M., Ménard, H. & Schmid, J. 2013: *Internationalization and Competitiveness of Aerospace Suppliers, a Joint Analysis of Germany and France. h and z Unternehemensberatung AG, Munich and Kea and Partners*. Available: www.keapartners. co.uk/sites/default/files/keapartners/hz_keapartners_aerospace_0.pdf.

PwC 2010: *A and D Insights. Accelerating Global Growth*, Price Waterhouse Coopers, London.

PwC 2011: *A and D Insights. Gaining Technological Advantage*, Price Waterhouse Coopers, London.

PwC. 2012: *Gaining Altitude. Globalization. Aerospace Suppliers Need a Flight Plan to Sustain Growth*, Price Waterhouse Coopers, London.

Ro, S. 2013: *Boeing's 787 Dreamliner Is Made of Parts from All Over the World*, Business Insider UK. Available: www.uk.businessinsider.com/boeing-787-dreamliner-structure-suppliers-2013-10?r=US&IR=T.

Santo, M. & Schmid, J. 2012: *Internationalization and Competitiveness of Aerospace Suppliers*, h and z Unternehemensberatung AG, Munich.

Seattle Times. 2013: *Up to 700 Engineers at Boeing Losing Jobs*. Available: www.seattletimes.com/business/up-to-700-engineers-at-boeing-losing-jobs/.

Vertesy, D. & Szirmai, A. 2010: *Interrupted Innovation: Innovation System Dynamics in Latecomer Aerospace Industries*, United Nations University, Maastricht.

Walker, C. 2014: "Mind the Skills Gap". In: *Aerospace*, vol. 41, no. 4, 18–21.

Washington State. 2015: *Workforce Training and Education Coordinating Board. Aerospace Manufacturing Skills. Supply, Demand and Outcomes for Washington's Aerospace Training Programs*, Washington State, Olympia, WA.

Wilhelm, S. 2014: "Boeing Takes 737 and 787 Lessons to Better Build the 777X Wing", In: *Puget Sound Business Journal*, Available: www.bizjournals.com/seattle/news/2014/10/23/boeing-taps-737-and-787-lessons-to-better-build.html.

13 Contextualisation of innovation

The absorptive capacity of society and the innovation process

Bill O'Gorman and Willie Donnelly

Innovation takes many forms and has many different meanings. Innovation is as much influenced by society, societal needs, levels of educational attainment of society, societal values, and the absorptive capacity of society as it is influenced by the advancement of technology itself. It is well documented that innovation is closely connected to economic growth. Therefore, for decades, policy makers and policy implementers have been chasing the 'holy grail' of 'best-in-class' and trying to emulate leading innovation regions, such as Silicon Valley, within their own regional domains. However, based on previous studies, it is very clear that there exists no one 'best-in-class' model fitting all regions nor is there an ideal pathway for regions to design and implement a 'best-in-class' regional innovation system (see for example Welter, Kolb, O'Gorman, Bugge, Hill, Peck and Roncevic 2008; Bugge, O'Gorman, Hill and Welter 2010). Just as Dicken (2003) stated

> so when we talk about globalisation we must always remember that it is a set of *tendencies* and not some kind of final condition. These tendencies are both geographically and organisationally uneven. There is neither a single predetermined trajectory nor fixed endpoint.
>
> (p. 1)

So too the authors of this chapter contend that *innovation* is not a singular concept and neither geographically nor organisationally bound. Rather we contend that innovation is fuzzy and evolutionary and is probably more dependent on societal constructs than merely on technology alone. No matter how advanced technology becomes, its use will be limited by the absorptive capacity and capability of the society in which the technology is being implemented. This may explain why there is such diversity in innovation across countries and across regions within countries. Hence, the title of this chapter is the *Contextualisation of Innovation*.

In this chapter the authors explore innovation in broad terms and to some extent determine what innovation may mean in different societal contexts. The chapter starts by setting the scene as to how innovation has impacted society since the first industrial revolution. The chapter then examines different meanings of innovation. Next the chapter presents a case study as to how one society (Ireland) adapted to benefit from the evolution of innovation. Finally, the chapter concludes with some further thoughts about the diversification of innovation, innovation pathways and trajectories.

Introduction

From the middle of the 18th century the industrial revolution across Europe, Russia and the Americas introduced significant innovations and brought about huge societal changes. Even though many innovations appeared to be for the *common good*, for example the harnessing of steam to power large machines to create mass production and jobs, or the harnessing of steam to mobilise society at a faster pace using steam-engine trains and steam-ships, or the harnessing of water to generate electricity. It appears that it is at this time the divergence between inventors (researchers and innovators), entrepreneurs (business owners and investors), and society at large (the productive work force, the producers) took shape.

Over the centuries it seems that, in some countries and regions, this divergence has grown larger and larger through the different phases of the industrial 'evolution', to the extent that it is now recognised and accepted as a major concern in most economies. The second industrial revolution, also known as the *technological revolution* from the mid-19th to early 20th century, saw increased levels of automation, greater degrees of mass production and a huge increase of uneducated, unskilled labour force. The third industrial revolution, a product of the late-20th century incorporating the Information Age, is notably categorised by 'manufacturing going digital', the convergence of technologies, the almost total disappearance of manual labour, and the emergence and growth of the 'highly educated, intelligent worker'.

Today, in the early decades of the 21st century, society and economies are embarking on the Fourth Industrial Revolution – Industry 4.0. The Fourth Industrial Revolution is the term used that embraces current levels of automation and the promise of higher degrees of efficiencies through greater degrees of automation by combining converging technologies, data exchange, and manufacturing technologies. It is a platform for integrating the 'Internet of Things' (IoT). According to the Schwab (2016), the Fourth Industrial Revolution presents unprecedented opportunities to accelerate progress in addressing economies' growth and development challenges. Unlike the previous industrial revolutions, this Fourth Industrial Revolution is embedded in intelligence rather than brute mechanical strength. The Fourth Industrial Revolution will see a paradigm shift in the innovation and commercialisation process. Heretofore, it was the preserve of the scientists, engineers, and industrialists to design and develop new products and services. The relationship between producer and consumer will become much more complex. In the first instance, the social and environmental impact of new products and services has led to the emergence of responsible innovation and social innovation. The emergence of the prosumer where the consumer becomes involved with designing or customizing products for their own need is changing the innovation process. What is currently referred as 'responsible research and innovation' (RRI) is where the ultimate consumer, the citizen, is integral to the innovation process. In this scenario, citizens are the producers (and consumers) of goods and services, as well as at the same time being the generators (and users) of knowledge, along with being at the heart of society where there is a free flow of knowledge shaping and reshaping innovations to address societal needs. However this is not, and will not be, a trans-world homogenous process; rather it will continue to be situational, educational, geographical, and societal-knowledge based. This is why the *diversification of innovation* is a constant, natural, phenomenon.

But to what extent will Industry 4.0 benefit the whole of society? To what extent is society involved in shaping (or indeed embracing) the Fourth Industrial Revolution? Or will it be a case of simply magnifying the divergence (or chasm) between the 'haves and have nots', between the propagation of innovation for pure profit and the propagation of innovation for cohesive societal needs? These are very difficult questions to answer especially as it is extremely difficult to argue against the espoused belief that innovation benefits all society. But it also creates a need for the diversification of innovation across all levels of society, and at the same time questions what we mean by 'society'. Or more to the point, it questions how local/regional societal needs can be addressed without embracing the diversification of innovation and the need to include dimensions of innovation beyond boundaries (territorial, institutional, and societal) of control. Also a question that needs to be considered is that, in a globalised world where information is more freely available than ever before, can there be acceptance that societies evolve at different paces, on different trajectories, and therefore what is a 'has been' innovation in one society is perfectly adaptable and innovative in a different society?

The meaning of innovation

According to O'Gorman and Donnelly (2016), 'it is not the innovation itself that is key but rather the process and location of innovation and the commercialisation and internationalisation of research outputs that matters' (p. 264). This is a modern observation of innovation compared to Schumpeter's view of innovation as a process of industrial mutation that continuously revolutionises economic structures from within, destroying the old one and creating a new one (Schumpeter 1934). In such a scenario, according to Schumpeter, the consumer plays a passive role in economic development (Schumpeter 2003). On the other hand, O'Gorman and Donnelly contend that innovation is a process of co-creation, co-design, and co-implementation of solutions to meet societal needs whereby society (including the consumer) must be an integral dimension of the innovation process.

In basic terms, innovation is often described as the translation of an idea/ concept into a good or service that creates value and satisfies an economic (or social) need. An innovation 'creates value' in the sense that customers are willing 'to pay'[1] for that value. Innovation is also considered to be the deliberate application of information, imagination and initiative to derive different values from different processes and/or resources. This is in essence the basis of the phenomenon of the diversification of innovation. From a technology perspective innovation is the generation and conversion of new ideas into new products and services. In a business sense, innovation is the application of new processes to increase productivity and profitability and satisfy customers' increasing needs and expectations. As regards the societal domain, innovation can be considered to be the adoption, and adaptation, of technologies and processes to improve the wealth and well-being of citizens.

One innovation that was the application of information, imagination and initiative, which has totally transformed industry, business, economies, society, communications, and the way we live, think, behave, work and interact with each other, is the World Wide Web. As Tim Berners-Lee wrote in 2000:

> The vision I have for the Web [www] is about anything being potentially connected with anything. It is a vision that provides us with new freedom, and allows us to grow faster than we ever could when we were fettered by the hierarchical classification systems into which we bound ourselves ...... it brings the workings of society closer to the workings of our minds.
>
> (Berners-Lee 2000, p. 1)

As stated earlier it is the combination of elements (concepts, materials, technologies, and so on) combined with location, societal need and the absorptive capacity of society that really makes innovation happen. Therefore, in the opinion of the authors of this chapter, innovation is not constant. It is malleable, it is fluid. Innovation is contextually and situationally dependent. These are reasons why there is such a diversification of innovation between countries and regions. But just as fluids can be 'defined unambiguously as a material that deforms continuously and permanently under the application of a shearing stress, no matter how small' (eFluids 2016) so too can innovation. However, in the case of innovation, the *shearing stress* can be considered the tensions between scientists, inventors, innovators, investors, profiteers, industry, educationalists, governments and society.

Innovation in its broadest context is an extremely difficult phenomenon to fully comprehend. Most studies about innovation are based on technology and on technological innovations as being the drivers of enterprise creation and growth, and as the source of regional and national economic development. It is only within the last two to three decades that the 'notion of social innovation' has emerged and been addressed more seriously by academic researchers and policy makers (Benneworth, Amanatidou,

Edwards Schachter and Gulbrandsen 2016). Therefore, it is important to explore the link between innovation and society through the ages.

Innovation and societal change

Innovation plays a major role in the economic and social development of most countries and is heralded as being one of the principal tools for developing regional competitiveness and coping with major global challenges. Innovation is considered as the main source of economic growth, productivity improvement, foundation of competitiveness, welfare progress, and therefore crucial for poverty alleviation (Ghazal and Zulkhibri 2015). In general, economic geographers, regional studies scientists, economists and researchers of the impacts of innovation agree that innovation in regions is very much dependant on a region's economy, governance, human capital, levels of education, infrastructure, levels of investment in R&D and innovation, and the cohesiveness of collaborative arrangements between the region's stakeholders. Hence, the seminal article by Oughton, Landabaso and Morgan (2002) about the 'regional innovation paradox'. According to Ghazal and Zulkhibri (2015), 'the state of innovation and research and development (R&D) in selected developing countries can be characterised by large disparities among different geographic regions in terms of knowledge, information, research, and scientific capacities' (p. 237); and '...... [the] poor outcome in innovation and R&D [in regions] is partly attributed to the low quality of higher education and curricula, lack of infrastructure, dependency on natural resources, lack of comprehensive R&D policy, and brain drainage' (p. 238). This also explains why there is such a diversity in innovation between countries and even between regions within countries, and/or between urban and rural areas within a given region or country.

However, the concepts of innovation that have been emphasised most by policy makers, researchers, economists and other commentators have been on the creation and diffusion of new technologies and knowledge mostly for the benefit of profit and economic gain via the commercialisation process with industry. Nevertheless, through such a process there are gains for society, for example through the creation of new jobs and increases in earning and spending power. Society also gains from the development and commercialisation of new technologies in that some of these technologies lead to advances in medicine, surgical procedures and healthcare in general. Equally, societies and the economies in which they learn, work, rest and play, gain from these technological advances in that citizens are more educated and information is more freely available at all levels of society. Advances in technologies related to logistics and transportation have enabled people to be more, physically and mentally, globally focused and have greater reach beyond where they were born, live and work. Consumerism is endemic which adds to a continuous evolutionary cycle of economic gain, re-investment in innovation, and the generation of new knowledge and technologies. The detail and information about innovations' benefits to society and its economy is endless. But with all these evolutionary, and revolutionary, gains chaos and complexity have also increased exponentially. Not alone does it appear to be the case that consumers play a passive role in economic development (Schumpeter 2003), but it also seems that society at large plays a passive role in the evolution of innovation and technological advances.

It is not possible to stem the tide of innovation and technological advancement, nor should we try to do so. Since the beginning of time inventions have benefitted society – eventually. Take for example fire, the wheel, the shield and the sword, and so on. But often it has been the limited few, be they scientists, alchemists, sorcerers, druids (medicine men), entrepreneurs, or investors, who have had the immediate to long-term gain from innovation. Many, if not most, inventions have emerged in isolation of the 'masses', in isolation of society, where society in general has played a passive role. One needs to question if this is the result of blind ambition, or the greed of a few, or is it the result of society's lack of understanding of advancement, or the fear of the unknown or is it society yielding to its collective imagination and allowing it to be more powerful than reality itself? Or is it just a disconnect between the inventor, innovator, entrepreneur and society?

It took many decades before electricity was generally accepted by the masses. In the second half of the 19th century, according to Simon (2004), 'although electricity generated excitement and electrical companies worked hard to gain a domestic market for the power, the use [of it] spread surprisingly slowly suggesting consumer resistance. However, the application of electricity as a medical therapy spread rapidly, embraced by physicians and patients', (p.3). This apparent contradiction of the value of inventions to society permeated throughout the 19th and 20th centuries. For example, the light bulb invented by Edison in 1879, Edison went bankrupt several times mostly because the general public was afraid to use electricity in their homes; nowadays electricity is like the air we breathe, we cannot live without it. Another example is the telephone, it took many decades for the telephone to take over from the telegraph and be popularised as a necessary utility in developed economies. In the closing decades of the 19th century, the telephone 'providing an opportunity for two people to interact when they were apart physically in the same way they would in the same space, failed to capture the public's imagination. In fact, some people believed that the telephone would be used just as a telegraph, with operators forwarding voice messages, receiving them back and relaying them to the customer. Certainly few saw a market for telephones in the home, except perhaps as a kind of intercom to summon servants', (Simon 2004, p. 64).

The personal computer (PC) had a similar take-off rate as the telephone. One of today's major PC manufacturers, Apple Computers, was founded in 1976, but it was not until the mid-1980s that the use of PCs in homes became prolific. In the 1980s, many leading industrialists at the time questioned the public value of PCs. Most notably, Ken Olsen, CEO and founder of Digital Equipment Corporation (DEC) asked publicly who'd want to own a PC and especially who'd want to have a PC in their home? Many other inventions such as microwave ovens and mobile phones were also very slow to be accepted by the general public, mostly because of the publicity at the time of release to market suggesting that such devices were dangerous to one's health. Today, even the most underdeveloped of economies have embraced these devices; in particular these societies have highly developed mobile technologies and access to such devices.

Two other innovations that have had a major impact on society are EDI (electronic data interchange) and the www (World Wide Web). As regards EDI, in the early 1980s computer companies such as Digital Equipment Corporation (DEC), IBM, Olivetti, Xerox, and many others had the capability to manage certain aspects of their businesses (for example placing orders with and 'call off' of orders from suppliers, proof or receipt and delivery of goods and payment of goods) using EDI. But because of, mostly, legal reasons and the legal profession's interpretation of what was (and was not) a binding contract using electronic means; and also because of fear on behalf of users; fear that orders, notifications of delivery/receipts of goods, or the transfer of money would get lost in the electronic (ethereal) transfer process, EDI between firms did not gain traction until the late 1980s/early 1990s. But as the Information Age (the third industrial revolution) matured with the development of mobile phones, mobile technologies, internet, and the www, society has 'gained' substantially in that most personal transactions in the mid-2010s as regards payment for goods/services, ordering holidays and other goods/services is performed electronically (performed through what was once called EDI).

The second innovation that, eventually, had a major impact on society was the World Wide Web (www). The www was invented by Tim Berners-Lee and developed in CERN[2] in 1989. In the 1980s, CERN worked with many scientists and engineers from all over the world investigating the fundamental properties of matter. The research was intense and with so many scientists and engineers working on the same (or similar) research from diverse and geographically spaced locations, there was an urgent need to exchange and share data among these researchers. This exchange and sharing of knowledge between researchers led to the World Wide Web (www); to what Berners-Lee (2000) coined the bringing together of 'the workings of society closer to the workings of our minds' (p. 1). As a result, the www has had a far-reaching impact on, and in, society in the first, second and third worlds. One of the most profound and significant societal impacts has been its use as a conduit for electronic social media platforms which facilitated the Arab Spring[3] that changed so many people's lives.

In summary, throughout the ages innovations have happened. These innovations have had a major impact on society in general from the creation of wealth to the improvement of health and education. Even though society at all levels has been affected by these innovations, to what extent has society being playing the role of passive consumer in economic development (Schumpeter 2003); and to what extent has society, at large, struggled with the 'intellectual and emotional revolution that occurred as ordinary men and women, eagerly and anxiously, grappled with the greatest new idea of their time' (Simon 2004, p. 23)?

The divergence of technology and society

During the first industrial revolution in the mid-to-late 18th century, Adam Smith (1991) published his seminal work, *Wealth of Nations*, in 1776. The basic premise of his thesis is that economic development and prosperity, and therefore the *'wealth of nations'* could only be achieved as a result of the 'division of labour'. Smith provides many examples of why there was a need to divide work into smaller tasks. Basically he contends that by providing people (farm labourers, workers in factories, and people in service) training and skills, and giving them part of a job (a task) to perform, as opposed to the whole job, they will become more efficient and productive at their task, and collectively, will be much more productive than a similar number of people each doing the entire job of work. Smith also advocated that if government abstained from interfering with free competition, the invisible hand of capitalism would emerge from the competing claims of individual self-interest; industrial problems would be resolved, and maximum efficiency would be reached (Smith 1991).

The first and second industrial revolutions greatly facilitated these two concepts, and thus the process of disenfranchising labour and compartmentalising individuals into specialist roles took root. The 'division of labour' still exists today, even in the most advanced economies. One very explicit seminal work clearly depicting the disenfranchisement of labour is Robert Linhart's (1981) *L'etabli* (The Assembly Line) published in 1978. This book provides, among other social themes, a vivid portrait of the 'division of labour' (the working class) in a car manufacturing plant in France and states 'feudalism is a fine thing for [x company]' (Linhart 1981).

As automation and computerisation became more embedded in developed capitalist economies, the disenfranchising of blue-collar workers increased at a more rapid pace and as these economies progressed through the Information Age (the third industrial revolution) white-collar jobs were also at risk. Many commentators, for example Kitson and Michie (2014)[4] suggest that manufacturing in the UK has been in decline since the 1970s. However, they contend that manufacturing in Western Europe is in more serious decline since major multinational corporations began to transfer their low value-add, high labour-intensive work to the emerging economies of the former Eastern Bloc countries in the early 1990s. Whether this migration of work forced, or provided the opportunity for, developed economies to accelerate the Information Age through focusing more on innovation, high-value add jobs, and the knowledge economy, is a matter for debate.

But one thing is for sure, in the 1990s component miniaturisation, the advancement of computer technology and software development, the uptake of the world wide web (www), the focus on the 'knowledge economy' and 'knowledge workers', and the investment in innovation has changed the paradigm of work, research, education, leisure, and living irrevocably. The shape of industry has changed. For example, many so-called blue-collar workers are now white-collar workers working in call centres, or as software developers, or code writers, and the like. The advancement in technology, speed of data transfer and the availability of data is such that the philosophy and thinking in relation to technology and work is that 'today knowledge navigators are finding innovative ways to transfer information at dramatically lower prices' (Ogden 1993, p. xvii); and because of the upheaval Handy (1995) introduced us to the career portfolio and 'empty raincoat' paradigm. In the words of Handy:

> .... to me that empty raincoat is the symbol of our most pressing paradox. We are not destined to be empty raincoats, nameless numbers on a payroll, role occupants, the raw material of economics or sociology, statistics in some government report. If that is to be its price, then economic progress is an empty promise. There must be more to life than to be a cog in someone else's great machine.
>
> (p. 1, 2)

As we zoom into the fourth industrial revolution (Industry 4.0) where the focus is ever increasingly on new forms of technological innovation to increase the use, speed, manipulation, and management of information (through the Internet of Things) for citizens in general these words are probably even more apt today than in 1995.

The re-convergence of technology and society innovation

According to Hilpert (2016),

> technologies are related to everyday life, and to the future of socio-technology development, as well as to urgent or pressing problems. Electronics help to make life easier. Biotechnology or genetic engineering may help to overcome diseases. New energy technologies provide for the efficient use of resources and climate protection ...... many technologies or technological improvements also help to modernise industries and products and keep these industries innovative.
>
> (p. 1)

Even though Hilpert has expressed this sentiment in current terms, the words could equally have been expressed (and probably were) by commentators during the first, second and third industrial revolutions. There is no doubt that innovation and technology have improved economies from a wealth creation perspective. In the words, attributed to John F. Kennedy, President of the United States of America from 1961 until 1963, 'a rising tide lifts all boats', meaning that if a nation state improves and creates wealth within its economy, then all citizens will benefit from this gain. During the 1980s and 1990s, this mantra was often heard expressed by senior executives of major multinational corporations (MNCs) (mostly American) to motivate their employees and stroke their investors. The mantra was equally used by economists in the 1990s and 2000s, especially during recessionary times, to express that through government spending and reinvestment into the economy that the 'tide will rise and lift all boats'. But the question is, how global is the 'rising tide'? Does the 'rising tide' affect all of society equally or just a minority share of society?[5]

From the 1960s, countries including Hong Kong, Singapore, South Korea, and Taiwan followed similar economic trajectories and patterns of development. By the mid-1980s these economies had become known collectively as the Asian Tigers. Their success is attributed mostly to the investment into these economies by the United States of America government and American and Japanese multinational corporations (MNCs) setting up subsidiaries and sub-contracting companies in these countries. According to Poverty Education[6], when a foreign company (through foreign direct investment [FDI]) builds a factory or office building in a third world nation and employs the nation's poor citizens, they tend to make that country wealthier through creating jobs. In addition, the government of that country collects taxes from the company. The government can then (and often do) invest this tax money into healthcare (investing in hospitals which allow people to live longer and be more productive), education (building universities and research centres), physical infrastructure (for example building roads and ports needed to reduce transportation costs) and state-of-the-art technology (such as cell phones and internet) for their citizens. This increases the competitiveness of the country, which causes a further influx of FDI. In turn, the wealth generated by this additional FDI is used to further improve healthcare, education, infrastructure and technology, once again making the country more competitive in the global market generating more wealth and more educated, skilled and qualified citizens.[7]

Ireland followed a similar pattern as the Asian Tigers. In the early 1930s, Ireland was predominately an agrarian society. At that time its economy was very much based on low-tech industry and a policy of self-sufficiency and protectionism using high import tariffs in an attempt to make imported goods uncompetitive in the Irish market. It was only from the late 1950s that Ireland began to encourage FDI into the country. This, along with policies specifically related to enterprise and education, led to a gradual increase in wealth in the Irish economy and Ireland being dubbed the Celtic Tiger in 1999 (Walsh 1999). As a result, the economy continued to grow with significant advances in infrastructure in roads, communications, transport and education culminating in unemployment levels fell to below 4% in 2006. According to the EU (2012) Ireland's economic growth is attributable to two key factors: (i) favourable demographics gave rise to an increase in the number of workers entering the labour market, and (ii) an improvement in the educational level of the labour force meant that these new workers had higher education levels and productivity than their predecessors. In 2011, the Department of Finance (Ireland) published a report reviewing Ireland's economic growth over the previous 20 years, stating that the economy 'was transformed over the past two decades' (p. 2) with the GDP rising to a peak of almost 12% in 1997 (average for the period 1994 to 2001 was almost 10%). According to the Department of Finance (2011) report, data for 2009 show that the number of people aged between 20–24 in Ireland who are educated to at least an upper secondary level is the highest in the EU15 which was well above the Euro area average (source Eurostat in Department of Finance 2011); almost 45% of those in the 25–34 age cohort have at least third level education, above the OECD (38%) and Euro area (30%) averages (source National Competitiveness Council in Department of Finance 2011); Ireland produces the third highest number of maths, science and computer graduates per 1,000 of population (aged 20–29) in the Euro area (source National Competitiveness Council in Department of Finance 2011); the number of PhD students per 1,000 population is above the OECD-24 average (source National Competitiveness Council in Department of Finance 2011); and Ireland has achieved critical mass in a number of high-technology sectors. According to Eurostat (Department of Finance 2011), nearly one-third of Irish exports were classified as high tech (such as IT and chemicals) as business functions shift to higher value activities. This compares with an average of 17% in the EU-27. In the words of the Department of Finance (2011):

> the high concentration of our exports in high technology sectors is a key factor behind our relatively resilient export performance despite the very sharp global economic downturn. While Irish exports contracted by 4.1% in 2009, exports in the Euro area as a whole declined at a much more rapid pace, falling by 13.1%

(p. 43)[8]

Many economies in transition follow a trajectory from a policy of protectionism through to a focus on foreign direct investment (FDI) (O'Gorman and Cooney 2007) which, if managed well, leads to sustained economic development, greater levels of employment, increased salary levels, improved infrastructures as regards roads, transport, healthcare, and education leading to citizens that are more educated, professional, productive, healthier, and with greater levels of disposable income than their predecessors. Then again, national and regional policies must not be 'copy cats' of leading innovation regions, rather they should be adapted to the specific contexts of a region's or country's innovation trajectory and growth path (Carayannis, Campbell, Grigoroudis and De Oliveira Monteiro 2017).

In summary, the view of John F. Kennedy in 1963 that 'a rising tide lifts all boats' seems to hold true for advancing, advanced, and developing economies. But tides rise at different times to different levels, just as innovation trajectories occur at various paces, which is also why the diversification of innovation is a constant phenomenon. This is a pertinent observation, especially as '... modern nation states are expected to provide policies that allow for economic growth, prosperity, employment, and a sound environment, [and that] government policy makers are confronted with changing policy needs of increasing complexity' (Hilpert 2016, p. 1).

The absorptive capacity of society – the essence of diversification of innovation

As stated at the beginning of this chapter, innovation is as much influenced by society, societal needs, levels of educational attainment of society, societal values, and the absorptive capacity of society as it is influenced by the advancement of technology itself. Therefore the evolution and spread of innovation is not homogenous, it is situationally and contextually based. Therefore, even though leading edge 'world class' attainments in science, medicine, materials, physics, chemistry, technology, manufacturing, and processing are theoretically available to all societies, there are significant variances in innovation processes and activities between countries and indeed between regions within countries. Take, for example, the European classification of regions, the Regional Innovation Scoreboard (RIS). Annually the European Union (EU) reviews and publishes the *innovation performance* of EU regions. The RIS is a regional extension of the European Innovation Scoreboard, assessing the innovation performance of 214 European regions (across 22 EU countries) on a limited number of indicators. The report categorises regions into four distinct groups (i) Innovation Leaders (36 regions), (ii) Strong Innovators (65 regions), (iii) Moderate Innovators (83 regions) and (iv) Modest Innovators (30 regions). According to the RIS (2016) summary report the most innovative regions are located in the most innovative countries. However, this is within an EU context and it is certain that there are many regions around the world that would not attain even the 'modest innovator' classification.

How regions progress and develop their innovation capacities and capabilities is very much dependent on a country's or region's (if the region is autonomous from its State such as the Länder in Germany) enterprise and innovation policies, investment (from public and private funds) and the absorptive capacity of its citizens and regional/national institutions. However, as pointed out by Oughton, Landabaso and Morgan (2002), many regions/ countries are incapable of absorbing or capitalising on the public funds they receive to enhance the innovation process and practices in their regions/ countries. This 'innovation paradox' of societies not being able to absorb the investments (knowledge as well as monitory) they badly need to improve their innovation capacities and capabilities has been studied by many researchers and policy makers since 2002 (see for example De Bruijn and Lagendijk 2005). The conclusions from all this research are still mixed, complex, and paradoxical.

Therefore it is no wonder that many national and international fora are focusing a lot of resources (time and money) to develop National Systems of Innovation that will transform innovation lagging states into 'innovation leaders'. However, this is neither possible nor appropriate for many economies. For example, because innovation has become more global and dispersed than it used to be, the dynamics of innovation have changed dramatically over the last three decades. According to Dutta and Lanvin (2013), for real local and regional innovation progress to occur, critical region-specific dimensions need to be identified, explored and measured. Dimensions such as examining the strengths and weaknesses of local industries and knowledge institutions, access to finance and to markets within and outside national borders, and the knowledge pool and absorptive capacity of the region's/country's human capital. What always must be kept in mind is that 'firms, organisations, and institutions, as well their interactions, differ substantially across countries. This implies that policy responses to systemic imperfections will [always] be country specific' (OCDE 2011, p. 230).

As indicated by O'Gorman and Cooney (2007) many economies in transition follow a trajectory from a policy of protectionism through to a focus on foreign direct investment (FDI). However, to what extent host economies can benefit from the existence of multinational enterprises (MNEs) in their locale is very much dependent on the degree of autonomy the subsidiary in the host economy is permitted to have by its parent company. This level of autonomy will be very much influenced by the *subsidiary mandate* the MNE headquarters (HQ) permits the subsidiary to have and on the level of control of the MNE HQ over its subsidiaries (Zahra, Dharwadkar and George 2000; Holm, Malmberg and Solvell 2002; O'Gorman 2007). Based on his research into understanding to what extent MNE subsidiaries have a direct impact on the creation on high-tech enterprises in the regions in which they are located, O'Gorman (2007) established that one of the main reasons why MNEs locate into a particular region or country is based on that region's or country's low rates of technological absorptive capacity. This supports Kugler's (2002) assertions that

...... empirical studies have found that local producers fare badly in the aftermath of FDI in their own sector. The result is not surprising if we take into account that the MNE requires incipient monopoly power to recover its sunk investment and will, thus, avoid strong competition. In equilibrium, the sectoral pattern of FDI is likely to feature concentration in industries where local firms in the subsidiary's own industry have limited *absorptive capacity* to adopt advanced techniques that could be imitated given the proximity of the MNE operation. As FDI is targeted to sectors in which the domestic competitive fringe is restricted by the scarcity of specific human capital and by limited access to equipment and machinery embodying frontier technology, *intra*-industry spillovers to domestic producers are unlikely even if MNE affiliates deploy novel techniques.

(p. 3)

Contrary to this, there is evidence to suggest that MNEs do recognise the contribution their subsidiaries can provide through their cultural diversity, innovation, and knowledge of local market dynamics and therefore can have a significant positive impact on their (MNEs') global performance (Zahra, Dharwadkar and George 2000), which in turn leads to a richness and diversification of innovation in the host region/country.

Knowledge – a nutrient to enhance the absorptive capacity of innovation systems

As well as the role of inward investment, through FDI, education is also an essential dimension in enhancing the absorptive capacity of regions (and countries) resulting in greater levels of innovation capacity and capabilities of regions and countries. According to Donnelly and Weber (2017) it will become increasingly necessary for education systems to evolve and equip individuals with the skills and flexibility required to be employed or create employment in the digital economy. They continue, that it is not only machinery and labour that are important when investing in R&D; another significant, if not the most significant, factor of production [and innovation] is knowledge that was acquired in the past. A researcher makes use of knowledge that he or she created previously and combines it with other researchers' knowledge. Donnelly and Weber also suggest that different types of knowledge play different roles in the production and innovation process. For example, the more theory-driven knowledge from universities is traditionally generated with the specific purpose of making it freely available; and on the other hand, the more application-driven knowledge generated in a corporate [enterprise/industry] R&D department is often kept secret or commercially protected. The first of these knowledge domains takes the form of a quasi-public good whereas the knowledge generated by an enterprise can be more readily appropriated to generate new products or processes. However, the market is only capable of creating and applying part of the knowledge that society requires through privately financed R&D. Therefore, governments supplement private funding of R&D with public funding of R&D by subsidising higher education and by providing grants or tax facilities to stimulate private R&D.

Then again, according to Fallah and Ibrahim (2004), the generation of knowledge comes from two distinct sources: (i) formal, through educational institutions (primary, secondary, and tertiary), published research, government departments and their agencies, media, and (ii) informal, through the unintended transmission of knowledge, or knowledge spillover between the quadruple helix of partners in any given societal setting.

In depth comprehension of the actual process as to how knowledge spillover happens is illusive. But it is the contention of the authors of this chapter that, in order to increase the absorptive capacity of a given society, the learning by osmosis and seepage generated by the knowledge spillover process is as essential, probably even more essential, as the formal channels of knowledge generation and related enterprise, education, and innovation policies. Because, according to Donnelly and Weber (2017), existing knowledge makes the R&D process more effective and the way in which knowledge is shared across the economy influences the effectiveness of R&D investment. It is this interactive, diffusion of knowledge between a given region's (country's) quadruple helix of stakeholders that increases the absorptive capacities and capabilities of that region (country) which ensures the dissemination of innovation throughout an economy whereby its effect on GDP becomes more tangible, measurable and beneficial to that society.

From non-innovation to strong innovator: Ireland a case study

In the 2016 version of the European Union Innovation Scoreboard, Ireland is considered to be a Strong Innovator. The Innovation Scoreboard states

> Ireland's innovation performance increased until 2012. Performance declined strongly in 2013, after which it increased again in 2014–2015. Performance relative to the EU shows a similar trend, with a significant drop in 2013, and increased relative performance in 2014–2015. Ireland's relative strengths are in Innovators and Human resources. Ireland performs well above the EU average on License and Patent Revenues from abroad and International Scientific Co-publications. Other strong performing indicators are: Exports of Knowledge-intensive Services and Employment in Knowledge-intensive Activities.
>
> (p. 53)

A glowing report indeed, but Ireland was not always this advanced as regards innovation processes and practices.

According to O'Gorman (2007), since Ireland's independence from Great Britain in 1921, the first Government of the Irish Free State in 1922 took an interventionist approach to developing Ireland's economy. In 1922 Ireland was heavily reliant on agriculture, with over half of the total employment population concentrated in that sector. Also food and drink amounted to over 85% of total merchandise exports at that time (Kennedy 1995, p. 53). The first government operated a free trade policy and rejected industrialisation through import substitution and monetary experimentation and placed its main hopes on a dynamic agricultural sector specialising in livestock and dairying. However, the government elected in 1932 introduced a policy of protectionism. Protectionism as a policy remained in force, through a succession of Acts such as the Imposition of Tariffs (1932) and the Control of Manufacturers Act (1932), until this introduction of the Anglo-Irish Free Trade Agreement in 1965.

Initially protectionism and self-sufficiency had some merit, but overall, they had a devastating effect on the Irish economy. As Garvin (2004) pointed out, the government of the day 'had distorted the economy by wholesale subsidisation of economic activities, rather than letting entrepreneurial activity find the correct product for the correct market' (p. 33). These policies were more devastating for economic growth as not only did they limit competitiveness through high importation tariffs, they also limited businesses to trading internally within the state. Thus the development of export markets was restrained.

In 1949 however, even though the policy of protectionism was still in place, there was a change in thinking among a small number of politicians and public servants and, through an Act of government within industry policy, the Industrial Development Authority (IDA) came into existence in 1950. The sole focus of the IDA was to tackle the unemployment problem by attracting foreign-owned companies to set up manufacturing facilities in Ireland.

It was the success of the IDA, the changes in government policies, and the introduction of the Anglo-Irish Free Trade Agreement in 1965 that started Ireland on a trajectory of education, knowledge attainment and innovation. As Drudy (1995) summarised, 'the Republic of Ireland is an interesting example of a small open and peripheral economy which has whole-heartedly changed from inward-looking, "protectionist" policies to an "outward-looking" approach in the hope of resolving its various economic and social difficulties' (p. 71).

The role of education and knowledge in Ireland's innovation trajectory

Between the 1930 and 1970, mainly because of the lack of employment opportunities in Ireland, Ireland's greatest export during those decades was people. Some commentators suggest that it was government 'policy' to encourage emigration during those decades in order to reduce levels of unemployment in the State. However, the vast majority of those emigrating were poorly educated. Because between 1930 and 1970 basic education in Ireland was provided to the masses by a system of church-controlled state-supported National schools, the vast majority of which were one- or two-teacher schools. Secondary schools (also largely controlled by the churches) provided further fee-paying education for a privileged minority, while the state-supported Vocational sector provided a largely technical education. Many pupils did not complete their primary education, few went on to second level, and only a tiny proportion reached third level (CSO 2000). A significant proportion of young school goers would have left school before the age of 15 to gain employment (mostly in agriculture) or emigrate. Education was very much a 'privilege for the privileged' (Garvin 2004).

However, in the late 1960s, government began to reform its education policy starting with the introduction of 'free education' in 1967 and increasing the minimum age that a school-goer could stop going to school to 15 in 1972. Both of these reforms alone had a significant positive impact on increasing the numbers of school goers progressing from primary to secondary to tertiary education. Around the same time, largely to cater for the Vocational Education Sector and to provide progression to third level for school goers coming through the 'technical education' stream, government introduced new types of school, Comprehensive and Community schools (for second level) and the National Institutes of Higher Education (NIHE) and the Regional Technical Colleges (RTCs) (for third level). This resulted in a major expansion in the number of third-level-fulltime students in the technological sector (CSO 2000, p. 45). Which in turn was the starting point of Ireland becoming a knowledge-based economy.

In 1950, the number of fulltime students attending universities in Ireland was only 7,900. Since then, especially since 1970, because of the introduction of free education, changes in curriculum, and the introduction of the NIHEs and the RTCs, the number of fulltime students at third level (in 1970) was about 25,000. By 1998, the number of students had more than quadrupled to 112,200 (of which 61,300 were university students and 41,900 were students at the various Technological Colleges) (CSO, 2000). In 2015, this number increased to 173,200 (of which 95,100 were university students and 78,100 were students at the various Technological Colleges). Only 1,100 undergraduate degrees were awarded in 1950; in 2000 that number was more 14 times greater; and in 2015 the number of total graduates was 37,640.[9]

The increase in the number of postgraduate degrees is far more dramatic. There were only 116 such degrees awarded in 1950, in 2000 over 7,600 postgraduate degrees were awarded, and in 2015 this increased to 10,808.[10] Of the 10,808 postgraduate degrees awarded in 2015, 1,558 were PhDs; almost 50% (745) of which were in the science, engineering, technology, and information technology domains.

The Ireland Census of Population results show that, in 1971, a total of 22,000 people had scientific or technological qualifications. By 1996, this number had increased to 158,000 (CSO 2000). In 2011, the number of people in Ireland that had PhDs in science, mathematics and computing was 8,140.[11]

As a result of the changes in education policy in Ireland in the late 1960s early 1970s, Ireland began to produce well-educated, highly qualified people. Such a scenario, along with stability in government and relevant enterprise policies, made Ireland an attractive location for foreign direct investment (FDI). Much of the FDI coming into Ireland at that period of time was in the electronics industry sector, what was considered at the time 'high-tech jobs'. The foreign-owned multinational enterprises (MNEs) hired graduates and trained them to be highly qualified technicians and engineers. These

MNEs also trained operatives (what one time would have been considered low-skilled, blue-collared workers) into highly skilled and adaptive employees. In essence though, in today's terms, these jobs were low-tech and cost sensitive.

Ireland's changing trajectory

Ireland's reputation of producing young, well-educated, highly qualified people grew to the extent that in 1980s Ireland was 'exporting' graduates. One advertisement used by the IDA in 1980 featured a gradation class photo of 20 graduates. The by-line read 'The Irish: Hire them before they hire you'. The following detail was also provided in the advertisement,

> It is a fact that Ireland produces more science graduates per capita than the US, spends more (as a percentage of GDP) on education than Britain or Japan. So it is no surprise to find Irish managers among senior executives in top international companies. However the best way to get your share of Irish talent is to locate in Ireland. You'll be in good company. More than 300 manufacturing and service companies have already done so.

Unfortunately, because of the lack of a sufficient quantity of executive and/or technology jobs in Ireland at the time, 19 of these 20 graduates emigrated in their year of graduation[12]

In the late 1980s and early 1990s, globalisation placed significant pressure on MNEs to reduce costs, become more competitive, and maintain high profit margins. As a result, the cost per unit of production became a major focus for these companies. Because the jobs were repetitive and easily transferrable many MNEs began to close down their Irish subsidiaries and move their production to low-cost counties such as India, China, Asia and the former Eastern Bloc countries. Even though Ireland had performed an excellent job in educating its citizens, it had not done so to the degree of embedding foreign owned MNEs in the State (O'Gorman 2007). Unemployment increased significantly by the late 1980s. The Irish government needed to, once again, address and change its education, industry, and enterprise policies. The focus was to attract high-tech, high-value add, knowledge-based, non-cost-sensitive careers into Ireland.

The Irish government responded to this challenge by placing greater emphasis on STEM (science, technology, engineering and mathematics) subjects in second and third level education institutions. At the same time, the investment into R&D and entrepreneurship increased dramatically. The IDA began to attract pharmaceutical, medical devices, and information technology companies (mostly software related such as Microsoft) into Ireland. The result of this change in emphasis and focus culminated in Ireland's economy gradually improving from 1991 to eventually being dubbed the Celtic Tiger in 1995 (Walsh 1999) because of the extent to which its economy was outperforming all other European Union economies at that time. Even though Ireland's economy suffered greatly during the economic crisis of 2008 and subsequent years, Ireland's government, through its Programmes for Government 2011 and 2015, has continued to invest heavily in education, knowledge generation, technology, science, innovation, and R&D. Thus Ireland remains on a trajectory of innovation that enabled it to be considered a Strong Innovator by the 2016 version of the European Union Innovation Scoreboard.

The diversification of innovations – why regions differ

According to many authors including Dicken (2003), Scheerer (2016), and Ridley (2016) innovation happens in phases or what is often referred to as 'long-waves'. However, these phases or long-waves, on a country-by-country and region-by-region basis are not synchronised, they are out of phase. This is the basic reason why innovation is not uniform across the world, it is why innovation (or technology) happens in different forms at different rates in different countries and regions. According to Dicken (2003),

> technology is one of the most important processes underlying the global-isation of economic activity. But, in saying that, we must avoid adopting a technologically deterministic position. It is all too easy to be seduced by the notion that technology 'causes' a particular set of changes, makes particular structures and arrangements 'inevitable' or that the path of technological change is linear.
>
> (p. 85)

However, technology in itself is 'merely' an enabler. It is a facilitator of change, it provides people and institutions (industry, government, education) with the means to restructure organisations, communication patterns, combinations of commerce, economic activities, and geographic scope (as in span of communication and 'control').

Dicken (2003) also professes that 'technological change and knowledge creation [in other words *innovation*] also have a distinctive geography, one characterised by both concentration and dispersal' (p. 85). He continues, 'despite the transformative influences of … changes in communication technologies that facilitate the rapid and geographically extensive diffusion of innovations and knowledge, there continues to be a strong geographical localisation of innovative activity' (p. 85). As such, local and regional nuances have a major impact on innovation patterns, absorptive capacities and capabilities in any given region or state. Yet regions and states continue to emulate 'best in class' and/or good practice regions. National and regional governments attempt to plan their innovations; however, innovation is not deterministic it cannot be planned; rather it has 'to be taken advantage of'.

Innovation, a term that is often misused, is, by its very nature, unstructured therefore it cannot be planned. Yet governments and industry can provide monies to universities and research centres to research and invent things but not 'to innovate'. Innovation is needs and opportunity driven. Sometimes innovation is the recombination of existing technologies or processes and sometimes it is the incorporation of new ideas, technologies or processes into existing ones. It is an emergent, rather than a designed, phenomenon using dispersed knowledge as opposed to centralised controlled knowledge. As per Ridley (2016),

> just as the Industrial Revolution took the world by surprise because it emerged from thousands of individual fragments of partial knowledge, rather than as a plan [nobody planned it], so every innovation to this day is the result of thousands of people exchanging ideas. We can never predict innovation; we can only say that it will mysteriously emerge whenever people are free to exchange …… [innovation] will happen in well-organised efforts without direction, controls or plans.
>
> (p. 110)

This is, in essence, the diversification or innovation.

Regions taking advantage of the trajectory they are on

As presented in this chapter, innovation is very difficult to define. Innovation is a situational and contextual phenomenon. Some economists, such as Ridley (2016), suggest that states (and their regions) need to progress through different phases of industrialisation from agriculture to high-tech, high-value-add before they can be innovative. On the other hand, the authors of this chapter contend that states and their regions can 'piggy back' on current world technological advances in energy, sciences, health, and communications (to mention but a few) and 'leap frog' their innovation processes and procedures. Governments need to harness the potential of these technological advances with the abilities and capabilities of their societies.

In the current fourth industrial revolution where people are, in general, better educated, nation states and their regions have greater capacity and capability than ever before to 'leap frog' in terms of societal economic development. However, it must be clear that in using terms such as 'better educated' or 'highly educated intelligent worker', the authors do not mean education in the narrow sense of education attainment at primary, secondary, and tertiary levels. Rather the meaning is education in the broader sense of knowledge attainment, knowledge transfer, knowledge exchange and knowledge sharing. It is the degree to which the free-flow of knowledge is exchanged and shared between citizens, researchers, innovators, inventors, educators and policy makers that determines the absorptive capacity and capability of states and their respective regions. Increasing a society's absorptive capacity and capability will lead to an innovation process of co-creation, co-design, and co-implementation of solutions to meet societal needs whereby society (including the consumer) is an integral dimension of the innovation process; where the consumer no longer plays a passive role in economic development. But the rate of absorption differs and this is the essence why there is, and will continue to be, diversification in innovation.

In summary, governments (national or regional) should not seek to emulate so called leading innovation regions (such as Silicon Valley), rather they should leap frog their innovation processes and procedures based on what their societies are exposed to (www, mobile technology, medicine, and so on) and harness this potential. Therefore, even though a state or region is currently on a particular innovation trajectory, it does not mean it has to go through all the economic development steps that other countries have progressed through during their economic and social progression. For example, children born in Ireland in 2016 will never know what a telephone landline looks like, or what a wireless is, or what a slide rule is, nor indeed what a main frame computer looks like, unless they see them in museums or old photographs. Previous Irish generations have been exposed to such technologies, but countries that have not been exposed to such technologies, such as third world countries, do not need to be exposed to such technologies before they learn how to use a mobile phone.

But regions and states need to have visionary leaders who can and will bring relevant stakeholders together to define and develop their societal contexts (through education, learning, and trial and error) to create an environment where their citizens can take advantage of today's (and tomorrow's) technological advancements so they too are numbered among the 'thousands of people exchanging ideas' (Ridley 2016, p. 110) and generating innovations. The diversification of innovation phenomenon will continue.

Notes

1 The term 'to pay' should not be restricted to the concept of financial payment. Rather the concept of 'to pay' should be taken to mean many dimensions including acceptance, adoption, use, and propagation (to mention but a few aspects) of an innovation.
2 The name CERN is derived from the acronym for the French 'Conseil Européen pour la Recherche Nucléaire', or European Council for Nuclear Research, a provisional body founded in 1952 with the mandate of establishing a world-class fundamental physics research organisation in Europe. At that time, pure physics research concentrated on understanding the inside of the atom, hence the word 'nuclear'. Today, our understanding of matter goes much deeper than the nucleus, and CERN's main area of research is particle physics – the study of the fundamental constituents of matter and the forces acting between them. Because of this, the laboratory operated by CERN is often referred to as the European Laboratory for Particle Physics. (Available at www.cern.ch).
3 The Arab Spring was a swell of revolutionary activity that began in Tunisia on 18 December 2010 and spread throughout other Arab League countries.

4 The Deindustrial Revolution: The rise and fall of UK manufacturing, 1870–2010 Centre for Business Research, University of Cambridge Working Paper No. 459 by Michael Kitson Centre for Business Research and Judge Business School, University of Cambridge Email: mk24@cam.ac.uk and Jonathan Michie Kellogg College and Department for Continuing Education, University of Oxford Email: jonathan.michie@kellogg.ox.ac.uk June 2014.

5 www.jfklibrary.org/JFK/JFK-in-History/JFK-on-the-Economy-and-Taxes.aspx [accessed March 2016].

6 For more details see www.povertyeducation.org/the-rise-of-asia.html [Accessed February 2016].

7 Ibid

8 For more details about the demise of Ireland's economy see http://ec.europa.eu/ireland/economy/irelands_economic_crisis/index_en.htm.

9 For more insight information about education in Ireland, see www.hea.ie/node/1557 [Accessed January 2017].

10 Ibid

11 For more in-depth information see www.cso.ie/en/media/csoie/census/documents/census2011profile9/Profile_9_What_we_know_full_doc_for_web.pdf [Accessed January 2017].

12 This was an IDA (Industry Development Authority) Ireland advertisement in 1980 to attract increased levels of FDI into Ireland.

References

Benneworth, P., Amanatidou, E., Edwards Schachter, M., Gulbrandsen, M. 2016: *Social Innovation Futures: Beyond Policy Panacea and Conceptual Ambiguity.* Working Paper for the TIK Group Series. Norway: University of Oslo. (online) Available from: http://hdl.handle.net/10261/132837 (Accessed March 2016).

Berners-Lee, T. 2000: *Weaving the Web.* London, UK: Butler and Tanner.

Bugge, K.-E., O'Gorman, B., Hill, I., Welter, F. 2010: Regional sustainability, innovation and welfare through an adaptive process model. In: Sarkis, J., Cordeiro, J.J., Vazquez Brust, D. (Eds.): *Facilitating Sustainable Innovation through Collaboration: A Multi-Stakeholder Perspective.* Dordrecht, The Netherlands: Springer, 77–96.

Carayannis, E.G., Campbell, D.F.J., Grigoroudis, E.T., De Oliveira Monteiro, S. 2017: Introduction. Chap 1. In: De Oliveira Monteiro, S., Carayannis, E.G. (Eds.): *The Quadruple Innovation Helix Nexus.* New York, NY: Palgrave, 1–38.

Central Statistics Office (CSO). 2000: A Redmond (Ed.): *That Was then This Is Now: Change in Ireland, 1949–1999 A Publication to Mark the 50th Anniversary of the Central Statistics Office.* Dublin: CSO.

De Bruijn, P., Lagendijk, A. 2005: Regional innovation systems in the Lisbon strategy. *European Planning Studies* Vol. 13 No. 8, 1153–1172.

Department of Finance 2011: *The Irish Economy in Perspective.* Dublin: Government Publication Office.

Dicken, P. 2003: *Global Shift: Reshaping the Global Economic Map in the 21st Century.* New York, NY: The Guilford Press.

Donnelly, W., Weber, M. 2017: *The Creation and Impact of Open Innovation Ecosystems for the Digital Markets of the Future.* Research, Innovation and Science Policy Experts Open Knowledge Markets Report. Brussels: European Commission. (pending).

Drudy, P.J. 1995: From protectionism to enterprise: A review of Irish industrial policy. In: Burke, A.E. (Ed.): *Enterprise and The Irish Economy*. Dublin: Oak Tree Press, 30–48.

Dutta, S., Lanvin, B., (Eds.) 2013: *The Local Dynamics of Innovation*. (online) Available from: www.wipo.int/edocs/pubdocs/en/economics/gii/gii_2013.pdf (Accessed October 2016).

eFluids. 2016: *Characteristics of Fluids*. (online) Available from: www.princeton.edu/~asmits/Bicycle_web/fluids.html (Accessed November 2016). Princeton, NJ: Princeton University.

European Innovation Scoreboard (EIS). 2016: (online) Available from: http://ec.europa.eu/DocsRoom/documents/17842 p.53 (Accessed December 2016). Brussels: European Union.

European Union. 2012: *Ireland's Economic Crisis* (online) Available from: http://ec.europa.eu/ireland/economy/irelands_economic_crisis/index_en.htm (Accessed February 2016). Brussels: European Union.

Fallah, M.H., Ibrahim, S. 2004: Knowledge spillover and innovation in technological clusters. *Proceedings, IAMOT 2004 Conference*, Washington, DC, 1–16.

Garvin, T. 2004: *Preventing the Future – Why Was Ireland so Poor for so Long?* Dublin: Gill and Macmillan.

Ghazal, R., Zulkhibri, M. 2015: Determinants of innovation outputs in developing countries evidence from panel data negative binomial approach. *Journal of Economic Studies* Vol. 42 No. 2, 237–260.

Handy, C. 1995: *The Empty Raincoat*. London, UK: Arrow Books.

Hilpert, U. 2016: *Routledge Handbook of Politics and Technology*. Devon, UK: Routledge.

Holm, U., Malmberg, A., Solvell, O. 2002: *MNC Impact on Local Clusters: The Case of Foreign Owned Subsidiaries in Sweden*. Working Paper Series, Institute of International Business. Stockholm: School of Economics.

Kennedy, K.A. 1995: Irish enterprise in the 20th century. In: Burke, A.E. (Ed.): *Enterprise and The Irish Economy*. Dublin: Oak Tree Press, 39–56.

Kitson, M. and Michie, J. 2014: *The Deindustrial Revolution: The rise and fall of UK manufacturing, 1870–2010*, Working Paper No. 459, University of Cambridge; Centre for Business Research.

Kugler, M. 2002: Externalities from foreign direct investment: The sectoral pattern of spillovers and linkages. (online) Available from: http://elsa.berkeley.edu/users/bardhan/e271_f01/nov5.pdf (Accessed October 2003).

Linhart, R. 1981: *The Assembly Line*. Translated from the French, by M. Crosland. Amherst, MA: University of Massachusetts Press. (Original work published in 1978).

OCDE. 2011: *Economic Policy Reforms 2011: Going for Growth*. OECD Publishing. (online) Available from: http://dx.doi.org/10.1787/growth-2011-en (Accessed October 2016).

Ogden, F. 1993: *The Last Book You'll Ever Read*. Macfarlane and New York, NY: Walter and Ross.

O'Gorman, B. 2007: *MNEs and New Enterprise Creation: Do MNEs Have a Direct Impact on the Amount of New Indigenous High-Tech Strt-Ups in Ireland*. PhD Thesis. London, UK: Middlesex University.

O'Gorman, B., Cooney, T. 2007: An anthology of enterprise policy in Ireland. In: Cooney, T. (Ed.): *Special Edition of Irish Journal of Management*. Dublin: Blackhall Publishing, 1–27.

O'Gorman, B., Donnelly, W. 2016: Ecosystems of open innovation: Their applicability to the growth and development of economies within small countries and regions. In: Hilpert, U. (Ed.): *Routledge Handbook of Politics and Technology*. Devon, UK: Routledge, 262–278.

Oughton, C., Landabaso, M., Morgan, M. 2002: The regional innovation paradox: Innovation policy and industrial policy. *Journal of Technology Transfer* Vol. 27 No. 1, 97–110.

Regional Innovation Scoreboard (RIS). 2016: (online) Available from: https://ec.europa. eu/growth/industry/innovation/facts-figures/regional_en (Accessed November 2016). Brussels: European Union.

Ridley, M. 2016: *The Evolution of Everything: How Small Changes Transform Our Word*. London, Great Britain: 4th Estate.

Scheerer, W. 2016: Technology and scoio-economic development in the long run: A 'long-wave' perspective. In: Hilpert, U. (Ed.): *Routledge Handbook of Politics and Technology*. Devon, UK: Routledge, 50–64.

Schumpeter, J.A. 1934: *The Theory of Economic Development: An Inquiry into Profits, Capital, Credit, Interest and the Business Cycle*. Harvard Economic Studies Vol. 46. Cambridge, MA: Harvard College.

Schumpeter, J.A. 2003: *Capitalism, Socialism and Democracy*. Abington, UK: Taylor and Francis. (Original work published in 1943).

Schwab, K. 2016: *The Fourth Industrial Revolution*. New York, NY: World Economic Forum: Crown Business.

Simon, L. 2004: *Dark Light: Electricity and Anxiety from the Telegraph to the X-Ray*. Orlando, FL: Harcourt.

Smith, A. 1991: *Wealth of Nations*. New York, NY: Prometheus Books. (Original work published in 1776).

Walsh, B. 1999: What's in store for the celtic tiger? *Irish Banking Review*, Spring, Vol.1 No.1, 2–15.

Welter, F., Kolb, S., O'Gorman, B., Bugge, K.E., Hill, I., Peck, F., Roncevic, B. 2008: How to make regions (more) innovative. In: Fueglistaller, U., Volery, T., Weber, W. (Eds.): *Innovation, Competitiveness, Growth and Tradition in SMEs*. Papers presented to the Rencontres de St-Gall 2008, Beiträge zu den Rencontres de St-Gallen 2008, KMU-Verlag HSG ISBN 10: 3-906541-26-6 ISBN-13: 978-3-906541-26-6. St. Gallen: University of St. Gallen, 440–464.

Zahra, S.A., Dharwadkar, R., George, G. 2000: *Entrepreneurship in Multinational Subsidiaries: The Effects of Corporate and Local Environmental Contexts*. Working Paper No.99. Atlanta, GA: Georgia State University.

Part VI
Conclusions

14 Systematics and opportunities of diversities of innovation

Ulrich Hilpert

Thinking about innovation there is clearly a rich diversity of situations, conditions and opportunities. It is obvious that countries, regions, societies, cultures and histories are different and even within a country, region or metropolis-based industry may relate to divergent opportunities and histories. This may refer to the different technologies and different points in time when these opportunities emerged (e.g. modern information technology vs. the steam engine) or they may relate either to processes of manufacturing (e.g. automobile industries or mechanical engineering) or to the development of new materials or biotechnological opportunities. Similarly, industrial history provides for a continuation of areas of competences, which can be modernised and improved constantly and merged with other areas of expertise (e.g. application of biotechnology for new medical instruments or microelectronics in automobile industries). This already indicates that understanding innovative situations requires more than just one or a handful of particular indicators. It clearly asks for a possible relationship between opportunities for modernisation and change with the potential of the precise situation in question. Once such opportunities for application are identified and realised a process is introduced which finally leads to new situations. This relates to new requirements and changes the whole arrangement of variables.

Thus, new and traditional industries, competences and research are forming specific constellations, which are frequently unique and provide the basis for particular opportunities for change based on industries, competences and research. In addition, skills and levels of education may be divergent because of the labour markets, which attract particular personnel, the existing history of research and industry (which may inhibit competences and market orientation) and the orientation of societies towards well-skilled and educated labour, which is the basis for research and manufacturing on a higher level. Competences of labour and opportunities for innovation need to match, whether or not this is leading-edge technology or only the advancement of countries which are in the process of development based on low-labour costs and unskilled or semi-skilled workers. Climbing the ladder of innovation is widely influenced by the previous situation in at least two ways, because: (i) low levels of industrial development allow an innovative impact even for

Industry 2.0 or 3.0: and, (ii) appropriate skills and education provide for the exploitation or development of new technologies.

Since the arrangements and potentials of such situations are clearly highly diverse and opportunities in international markets are different, consequently, empirically there is a rich diversity of innovation. Although the processes individually are highly divergent and need to suit particular situations and opportunities, nevertheless, one can identify general dimensions which are decisive, for both the opportunities of innovation and the processes that are realised or can be approached. Thus, processes of innovation at other places or countries in different societies with different industrial histories help to understand both the divergences and how to take advantage of them for a development in question. Since innovation has become a collaborative process the partners and the capability to become a contributor have become important, whereas simultaneously the context of the individual country, region or metropolis is continued, and societies provide their own particular labour forces.

Global and continental embeddedness of processes

The different industrial structures also correspond to different competences of the labour forces. Consequently, despite differences of competences, or even because of such differences, complementary and matching situations can emerge and become exploited. Similarly, there are highly divergent competences in R&D and in strategies of research. Given the large number of research institutes and the wide range of opportunities for application and collaboration, there are rich sources available for combination and collaboration. Highly individual opportunities for innovation might be generated when merging techno-scientific competences, while taking advantage of such opportunities in reference industries and their labour forces, which are ready to apply them. The mutual complementarity helps to create synergy and to develop new ideas, to generate new findings and to introduce new technological products into the markets. It is important to understand the contributions from different locations, which clearly demand regional or metropolitan situations formed out of the relationship between institutions and enterprises and between industries and existing competences. Such situations include opportunities for products and markets and allow for the economic exploitation of new or improved products. The embeddedness in international or global networks provides a context which allows for merging competences and R&D-strategies despite long distances.

New areas of research or leading-edge research are characterised by the novelty of its profile and, consequently, by a limited number of potential partners in research and manufacturing, or a lack of personnel which is already educated or skilled in the new areas. When merging competences this can help to overcome such deficits and problems based on a division or labour in research and manufacturing. Even in complex research particular tasks can be divided and the results can be shared among the contributors despite large geographical distance. This can help concerning shared areas of research, or it can provide for synergy across different areas of competence in science and engineering, which can generate mutual benefit for the contributors. New and innovative products become available by such collaboration of appropriate partners. Beyond pure collaboration and additional synergy in innovative products, it contributes in providing for additional market access and to allow for culturally sound modifications, which may meet different customers' demands much more appropriately. The adjustment of technological products according to different industries, areas of manufacturing, cultural situations and societal structures generates a clear spin-off effect and adds advantages to collaborative networks of innovation. When it comes to marketable products, in the end, the process of innovation is more than just a matter of new knowledge and outstanding research, it clearly exhibits social and cultural elements, which need to be taken into consideration.

Such divergencies of innovation become particularly noticeable when new technologies are applied in more traditional products, or merge with traditional competences to generate new products. Existing competences, structures, clusters and regional collaborations provide for opportunities, as well as defining limitations concerning the wide range of possible applications. In addition, the existing labour force provides the basis for manufacturing advanced products or a large metropolitan labour market makes it possible to attract outstanding personnel while providing jobs for spouses and partners. It is important to identify the human capital and its areas of expertise, which is required to generate the socio-economic development, which is associated with innovation. This relates innovative ideas and breakthroughs with global markets on the one hand, and conditions of a location on the other hand. The embeddedness in global or continental networks provides for a context, which is decisive when such processes are expected to become successful and to generate advantageous socio-economic development. When existing competences are re-modernised in merging with new technologies and creating synergy, the context at a certain location is important but turns into socio-economic development only, when it matches with wider – often global – contexts and dependent on whether or not there are market opportunities which are accessible and can be exploited.

Although it is both the quality of the product and the level of innovative impact which matters a lot, markets, prices and production costs still remain important. Whether such markets are available and how these can be addressed is widely related with international or global agreements on trade and intellectual property. Terms of trade, taxes and transaction costs play an important role, whether an international or global embeddedness can be realised. The purchasing power of the growing middle classes may create a demand for products, which are manufactured on the basis of low production costs but can be improved by innovative opportunities, which are widely understood as Industry 2.0 or Industry 3.0; at the same time, particular services might be improved (e.g. health services, data processing, new integration into the global economy). Simultaneously, industrial development is associated with an increasing demand for advanced plant construction and specialised machinery. Socio-economic development creates an increasing demand for infrastructures and transportation technology. If such markets are available despite the origin of the supplier, consequently, societal, industrial and economic development can be related to competences elsewhere.

Thus, there is a correspondence between the context situations, which can be identified within particular countries, regions or metropolises and their relationship with the global context of this situation which make it possible to take advantage of the benefits from socio-economic processes elsewhere. The situation of the product suppliers and technology developers or researchers as well as the competences of industries and their labour forces are fundamental for the way these can participate in constantly advancing global economies and how they contribute and participate in international networks of innovation. Both areas of competences, in manufacturing and services as well as in the development of new technologies, mutually provide for situations, which are of benefit for those embedded.

Innovative labour and the challenge of contextualisation/to contextualise

In the light of highly diverse processes of innovation and different opportunities in relation to both with their local as well as global embeddedness, consequently, understanding such processes demands that mutual contributions from different locations, their institutions, enterprises, industrial opportunities and competences of the labour forces are considered. It is fundamental to understand that such constellations are highly diverse and how these build upon the synergy, which is created even among distant partners offering different levels of innovation. Even highly complex products contain simple parts, which can be produced at the levels of Industry 2.0 or 3.0, using personnel which have different skill and education levels. High-wage countries, of course, have to continue with leading-edge research and high value-added products based on knowledge societies, which allow for the development of new technologies and the manufacturing of outstandingly complex products. Processes of maturation in industry are faced by the competition of low cost countries, whereas highly individual competences in leading-edge research and technology still have to meet customers' demands, which, predominantly, are oriented towards quality and innovativeness. Maturation of products and industries and improving industrialisation and education in Newly Industrialised Countries (NICs) put pressure on the technologically and scientifically leading countries to continue both innovation and the arrangements which are fundamental to it.

Thus, there is not merely a race in innovation characterised by an ever-increasing competition in markets, but there is also the search for combinations among competences, which either help to collaborate on the realisation of research aims (while shortening the time to generate results), or to find new and marketable applications by merging innovative competences. This is indicated by both international networks of collaboration and the exchange of innovative personnel which create new ideas and synergy. Consequently, such locations, regions or metropolises will both contribute to, and participate in, such networks that arrange particularly suitable situations for research or for matching competences, which mutually contribute to such processes – based on the conditions which exist at such places. Where large and highly attractive local labour markets exist there are significantly higher potentials for a sustainable agglomeration of such personnel and such processes of cross-disciplinary or cross-industry collaboration providing new ideas and products. When the creation of new ideas and synergy in an existing situation is slowed down, attempts to exchange personnel aims at arranging new opportunities and a continuation of the firm and/or locality's position within collaborative networks. The demand for such new ideas and innovative technologies is clearly re-strengthening the existing participants in the networks. Such collaborative networks become systematically open for new contributions and locations with innovative contexts, which are recognised as attractive partners in development. In particular some Asian countries have indicated their strong capability to arrange for innovative contexts, which are increasingly included in collaboration in research and technology development (e.g. Seoul, Beijing, Shanghai, Hong Kong and Shenzhen, Singapore, Bangalore). New contributors to the innovative networks emerge and allow for both new technological products or solutions, and for meeting new market demands.

Such access to the global body of knowledge and the exchange of personnel can also be induced by appropriate government policies. Investment in education, skills and industrial innovation can provide for meeting future demand for skilled labour and university graduates, while investment in industrial modernisation helps to build modern industrial structures and research capabilities, which provide attractive jobs. Policies of developmental states can introduce changes of situation by constantly attempting to advance the labour force, modernising societal structures and providing future jobs in an economy of higher value added. It is interesting that some cultural situations and societies are less affected by outward migration of innovative personnel. East Asian countries indicate the strong tendency of university graduates to stay in their home countries, to return after a while, or to keep close contact although they may live abroad or have started a business abroad. Cultures of these societies clearly indicate a strong influence on innovative development by referring to an innovative labour force, which is developed in relation to appropriate policies. The change of a situation and a re-arrangement of the context through government policies provides for situations which offer jobs that help to generate innovative processes.

Human capital of all levels of skills and education becomes crucial for innovation and industrial modernisation while responding to their situations and their contexts. Whether a country, location or metropolis can participate and contribute to such networks or can benefit from global markets widely depends on the labour force available. Leading-edge innovation and high value-added manufacturing both demand labour, which suits their particular requirements. Consequently, innovation also needs to be understood in the light of its realisation through appropriately skilled labour. While this was, and still is, associated with the risk of an outward migration of knowledge workers and highly skilled labour, today there are new opportunities based on the internet. The increasing numbers of university graduates in low wage countries, and the fact that work can be 'taylorised', so that individual small contracts can be granted to freelancers in countries far away from the application of their work. Such labour has enjoyed education similar to that in Western countries and meets the requirements of those who give out the contracts. Because they can do the work a lot cheaper, the situation of people from industrialised countries is affected fundamentally when aiming to win such contracts.

Thus, a brain drain towards leading industrial countries or Islands of Innovation will not be identified as long as cheap, skilled or educated labour can be contracted for the work or contributions required at low cost places. In addition, new technologies and efficient transportation allows for manufacture of even highly individualised consumer products (e.g. textiles, clothing, shoes) in low cost countries by transferring the information and data (e.g. measurements, special demands) via the internet and allowing delivery of a highly customised product almost the next day. Consequently, certain competences, even at the level of university education and skilled labour, can continue to be available at locations in low cost countries, which are prepared to win contracts and to deliver either by internet or fast transportation (e.g. as is already the case with flowers from Kenya or fruits and vegetables from South America). The contextualisation in a global situation will allow for contributing tradable goods and services at a new level of skills and quality. Nevertheless, this will have little impact on the development of a societal situation ready to prepare for sustainable processes, which can take advantage of the diversities of innovation. Such processes associated with the GIG-economy and platform economy are not effective in changing the societies of low cost countries in a way that they can provide a specific and individual basis of innovative products, which are recognised internationally. Contracting out certain pieces of labour does not arrange for socio-economic situations, which can take advantage of global opportunities. Although skills and education may help individuals to win contracts – and to deliver to places with high labour costs – this hardly helps to arrange for improved development and the upgrading of competences in relation to industries of innovative potential and government policies. Such blue-collar skills and university graduates continue to be oriented towards contracts from abroad, rather than on building their own situation based on capabilities of their socio-economic or industrial situation, which can take advantage of opportunities in the richness of diversities of innovation in a global context. Such development demands pro-active government policies with a clear orientation to arrange a situation, which is suited to its context.

Culture and society matching the diversities of innovation

The relationship between innovation and societal situations allows for a better understanding of which opportunities among the diversities are appropriate. While this is often thought of from the points of view of entrepreneurs and gifted researchers, this is incomplete without taking into consideration the use of a technology for both the manufacturers and the location. The context may be particularly useful for certain technologies and innovations. While the development of new internet apps or biotechnological research is clearly focussed on individual competences, and often on highly advanced university education, in contrast, other technologies (e.g. environmental technologies) are based on existing industrial competences and skilled labour forces, and the improvement and manufacturing of products which help to find solutions for widespread problems concerning air, water and soil pollution. Social values with regard to the environment, and the need to face these situations by developing and employing such technologies, clearly build a relationship between a society's values and both the area of innovation and its effects on socio-economic development. In societies, which aim at widespread effects in employment and at attractive working-class incomes, governments will take different decisions on policies from those which are focussed on data concerning economic development and capital profits.

Thus, innovation can refer to the improvement of existing products based on established competences and, in addition, demand and employ new technologies or knowledge to complement and modernise existing manufacturing and products. Traditional competences and labour can continue their established innovative potential because, when merging with new opportunities, these provide the basis for new processes of socio-economic development. Such contexts can be arranged widely through government policies, which prepare for an embeddedness within the local networks. The more such situations at particular locations refer to international or global contexts, the more such activities will be linked to a global body of knowledge and how to apply them to meet opportunities of markets. A continuing modernisation of skills and education, clearly, provides a basis for such processes to be techno-industrially and economically successful; social attitudes, which are open towards modernisation and change help to cope with such constant changes. The agglomeration of particular industries and related labour forces and research institutes in particular regions or metropolises consequently indicate that these, predominantly, will be places for ideas about opportunities for innovation and change in particular technologies or industries. Such situations can also provide opportunities for entirely new or specialised industries or products and help to change economic situations by improving and modernising industries, skills and education.

This indicates that there is a mutual relationship between innovation and society. Innovative industries with strong economic development rely on an appropriate labour force, which is not just formally skilled and university educated but is also located in areas, where jobs exist and competences are demanded. Consequently, the diversities of societies provide the basis for different levels of innovation from Industry 1.0 to the cutting edge of Industry 4.0. There are also divergencies among industries concerning their potential for innovation. While in textiles and clothing industries, besides a change towards industrial textiles, there is limited potential and this refers predominantly to innovation by manufacturing or more advanced materials, there are areas like electronics, mechanical engineering, precision engineering or medical instruments, which allow for the advancement of their products because these are based on design and new findings. The relationship with knowledge and competences introduced through skills and education provides the basis for upgrading processes of innovation and economic development towards more modern products of higher value added. The more the final product is characterised by knowledge and research, the better are the opportunities to learn from a mode of manufacturing, which is prepared to advance processes and products – and finally to gain techno-scientific or industrial recognition which allows for both attractive contributions to, and participation in, collaborative networks of innovation. When considering this mutuality of innovation and society, clearly, the individual situation and context is important for identifying and understanding which industrial potentials, knowledge, competences and societies are empirically available.

Such processes of development and recognition based on competences take quite some time. Thus, it is not simply the structure that matters but whether the situation enables particular processes and how these correspond with appropriate activities. Opportunities for technologies, industrial modernisation and management form situations, which refer to different requirements. Although there are, in general, processes of innovation that will link up to particular countries, regions or metropolises only, when theses can be applied to inform our understanding of other contexts. A participation in research, manufacturing and modern development demands an appropriate composition of a labour force, which allows for the improvement of existing structures in industry and research. These refer to a relationship between research and development on the one hand and manufacturing and even management on the other hand. The more advanced such processes are, the more competences and knowledge are required. This is embodied in the capabilities of the personnel and can be realised only if such appropriate labour force is available. While Industry 1.0 asks for rather limited research but for the efficient organisation of manufacturing and appropriate management, this changes dramatically when it comes to Industry 4.0. Here, clearly, more highly skilled and university-educated personnel are required, which relates such processes with societal structures which are characterised by a greater proportion of university graduates, constantly modernised skills and highly educated and experienced freelancers providing industry-related services.

Long waves indicate such processes of innovation, which are closely related to social change. This provides the basis for socio-economic development. It is clearly important to consider time as a condition to realise such processes and to provide for the change necessary. The fact that innovation is increasingly inclusive, concerning different talents and competences at all levels, also indicates that an increasing share of the population needs to be prepared and supported in gaining education and skills to contribute their talents to processes of innovative development. Consequently, successful innovation-based socio-economic development is associated with strongly increasing shares of population, which have gained high skills and high levels of education. Government policies, which are effective creating a more complete societal inclusion into education and skills provide a critically important basis of innovation. The on-going and highly diverse processes of innovation clearly refer to a correspondence between contexts and appropriate public policies in social and techno-industrial change.

Time and social change in innovative situations

Processes of innovation inhibit a rich diversity, which indicates much more than differences in the national, regional or metropolitan phenomena that can be identified. Already, when paying attention to different industries and areas of research it is obvious that there are diversities, which indicate that the empirical situations differ a widely. There are highly diverse constellations formed because industries are different by product, processes of manufacturing, knowledge intensity and transfer of new findings from academia and research, context situations and global embeddedness. In addition, there are different levels of innovation according to the opportunities which exist at locations where such processes are to be identified. In such situations opportunities for change need to be both adopted and exploited to induce socio-economic development. Constantly growing shares of university-educated personnel and highly skilled blue-collar labour, as well as a knowledge-based improvement of industry-related services, are preparing for situations which are appropriate for processes of innovation that suit both these modernised structures and traditions of competences. Thus, change is not to be considered as a result of innovation but the permanency of social and industrial change is an important basis to realise innovative processes.

When it comes to the level of enterprises, of course, this is identified as a question of human capital. Whereas, a changing labour force and constantly changing societal structure, in fact, both highlight that the phenomena identified on national, regional or metropolitan levels are clearly related with social change; and even more, it indicates that the realisation of innovation requires societal resources of knowledge, labour and education. As such processes take time to be arranged and realised. The analysis of innovation at the point of identification of phenomena needs to be complemented by the dimension of time – while noticing that divergent processes of innovation refer to their own time horizon and the time passed during preparation for the empirically noticeable change. While the application of new technologies based on engineering may change products rather rapidly, on the other hand, scientific breakthroughs as a basis for new technologies clearly have a longer time horizon. Finally, the different technologies may also create divergent situations during their maturing and their opportunities for re-modernisation in changing contexts or by applying different technological opportunities or new materials – again associated with processes of societal and industrial change as a necessary context of innovation.

This helps to understand why some countries, regions or metropolises are participating at different periods of development. This can help identify why the engagement or participation in certain processes of innovation is earlier or later, and also why some continue their well-recognised outstanding competences whereas others manage to catch up significantly. The correspondence of an existing situation – formed out of societal potentials and industrial structures – at some point in time with emerging opportunities – new technologies and changing contexts of development – help to better understand both the innovation processes and why there are diversities of empirical phenomena. This also indicates that additional contributors to collaborative networks of innovation help to expand the body of knowledge and allow for more opportunities of application, as well as for more findings and breakthroughs in scientific research. While identified as new competitors in innovative products, they are also the partners for new products to supply existing needs better or to meet newly emerging demands and markets. Different views on problems to be solved or different ideas of application relate to individual experiences or social orientations in research, design, manufacturing and related services. When merging a growing number of views and competences of divergent origin, there is more potential for synergy and, finally, also for more opportunities of commercial products, jobs and satisfaction of needs.

Thus, the divergent social cultures of different societies provide for different views and opportunities in processes of innovation. Traditions in research, engineering, managing or organisation of social interests and groups have a deep influence on innovative processes and how these are realised. The understanding of innovation, of course, takes into consideration the industries and related services, academic research, engineering and design, and increasingly the organisation of work and styles of management. The divergencies of these processes become clear when the time horizon of societal and industrial change is taken into consideration of such development that is based on the situation at a place, which is embedded in a global environment. Processes of innovation need to be identified and analysed within the full situation – including long waves of development and different levels of context – to learn about suitable policies on development referring to the diversity of opportunities that is represented as innovation. Government policies play an important role in providing for long-term development in education, skills and research, as well as in planning short- and medium-term adaptation to, and adoption of, innovative opportunities. The more such public policies address change as necessary when building new and capable societal structures, competences and industries, which are ready for a knowledge-based future, the more these can contribute and mutually participate in the global diversities of innovation.

Index

For Product Safety Concerns and Information please contact our EU
representative GPSR@taylorandfrancis.com Taylor & Francis Verlag GmbH,
Kaufingerstraße 24, 80331 München, Germany

Printed and bound by CPI Group (UK) Ltd, Croydon, CR0 4YY
01/05/2025
01859210-0001